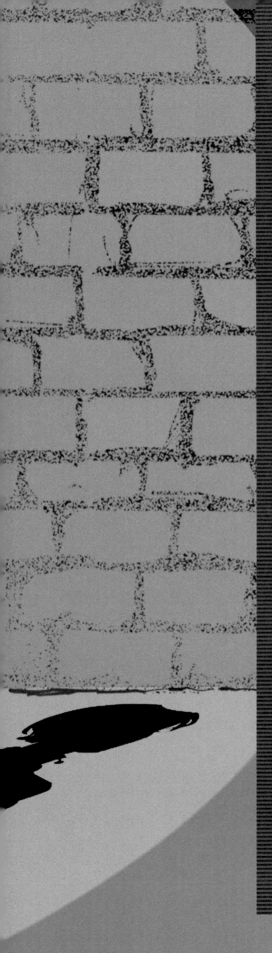

CATWOMAN
COPYCATS

writer
JOËLLE JONES

artists
JOËLLE JONES
FERNANDO BLANCO

colorists
LAURA ALLRED
JOHN KALISZ

letterer
JOSH REED

collection cover artists
JOËLLE JONES & LAURA ALLRED

VOL. **1**

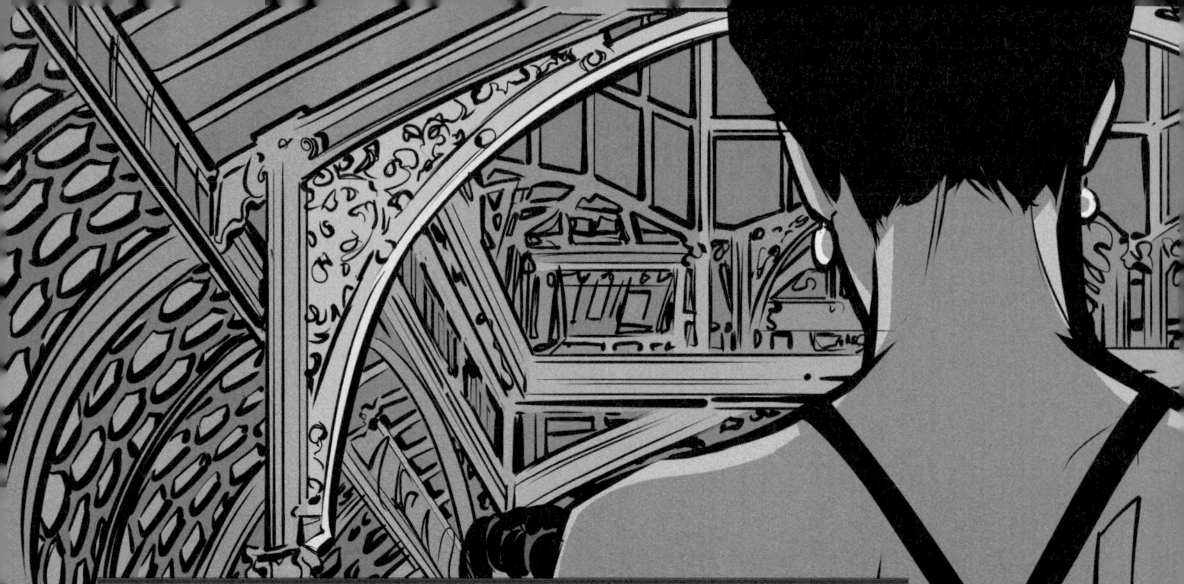

JAMIE S. RICH Editor – Original Series
BRITTANY HOLZHERR Associate Editor – Original Series
JEB WOODARD Group Editor – Collected Editions
ROBIN WILDMAN Editor – Collected Edition
STEVE COOK Design Director – Books
SHANNON STEWART Publication Design

BOB HARRAS Senior VP – Editor-in-Chief, DC Comics
PAT McCALLUM Executive Editor, DC Comics

DAN DiDIO Publisher
JIM LEE Publisher & Chief Creative Officer
AMIT DESAI Executive VP – Business & Marketing Strategy, Direct to Consumer & Global Franchise Management
BOBBIE CHASE VP & Executive Editor, Young Reader & Talent Development
MARK CHIARELLO Senior VP – Art, Design & Collected Editions
JOHN CUNNINGHAM Senior VP – Sales & Trade Marketing
BRIAR DARDEN VP – Business Affairs
ANNE DePIES Senior VP – Business Strategy, Finance & Administration
DON FALLETTI VP – Manufacturing Operations
LAWRENCE GANEM VP – Editorial Administration & Talent Relations
ALISON GILL Senior VP – Manufacturing & Operations
JASON GREENBERG VP – Business Strategy & Finance
HANK KANALZ Senior VP – Editorial Strategy & Administration
JAY KOGAN Senior VP – Legal Affairs
NICK J. NAPOLITANO VP – Manufacturing Administration
LISETTE OSTERLOH VP – Digital Marketing & Events
EDDIE SCANNELL VP – Consumer Marketing
COURTNEY SIMMONS Senior VP – Publicity & Communications
JIM (SKI) SOKOLOWSKI VP – Comic Book Specialty Sales & Trade Marketing
NANCY SPEARS VP – Mass, Book, Digital Sales & Trade Marketing
MICHELE R. WELLS VP – Content Strategy

CATWOMAN VOL. 1: COPYCATS

DC Comics, 2900 West Alameda Ave., Burbank, CA 91505
Printed by LSC Communications, Owensville, MO, USA. 3/8/19. First Printing.
ISBN: 978-1-4012-8889-1

Library of Congress Cataloging-in-Publication Data is available.

PEFC Certified
This product is from sustainably managed forests and controlled sources
www.pefc.org
PEFC™
PEFC/29-31-337

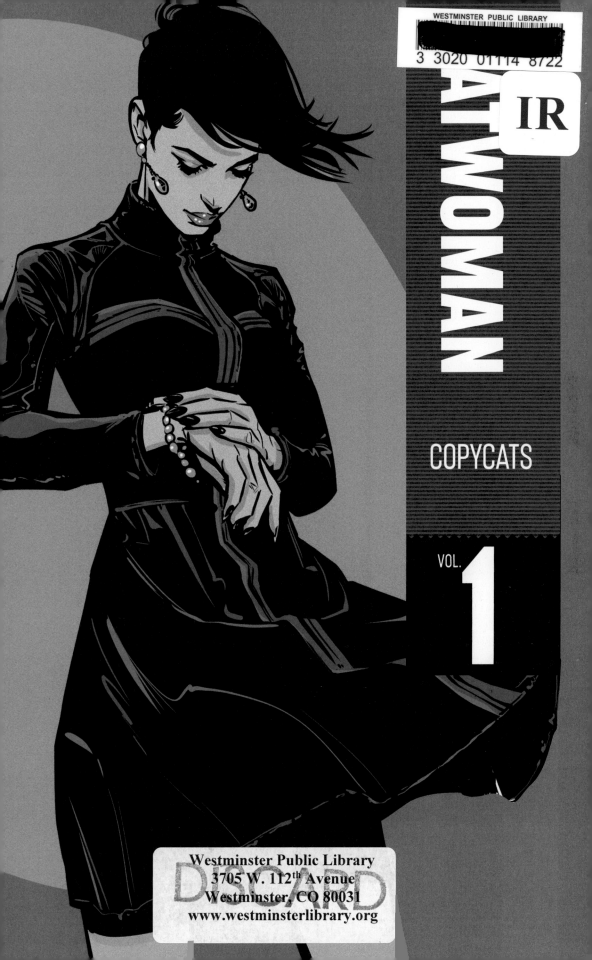

CATWOMAN

COPYCATS

VOL. 1

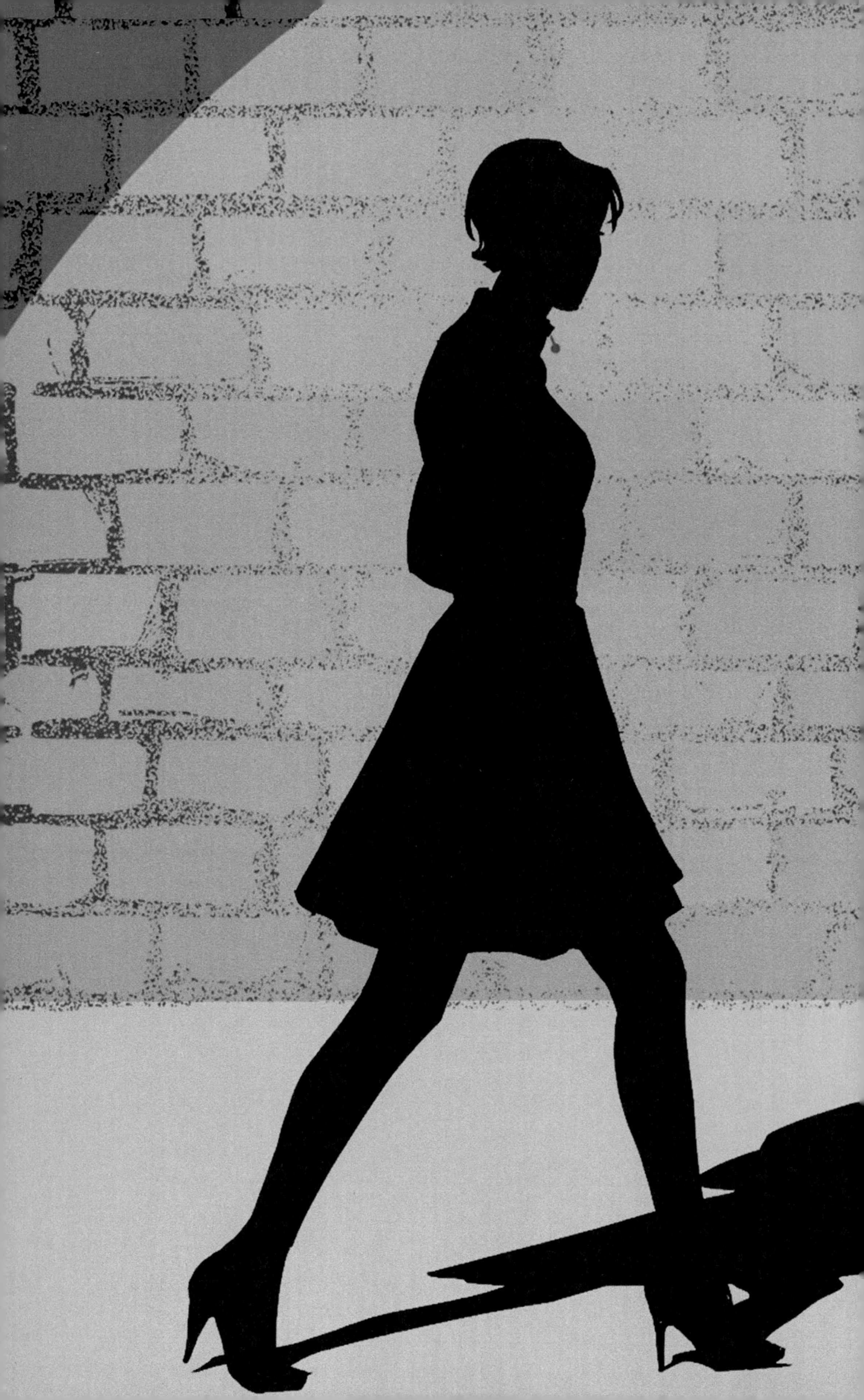

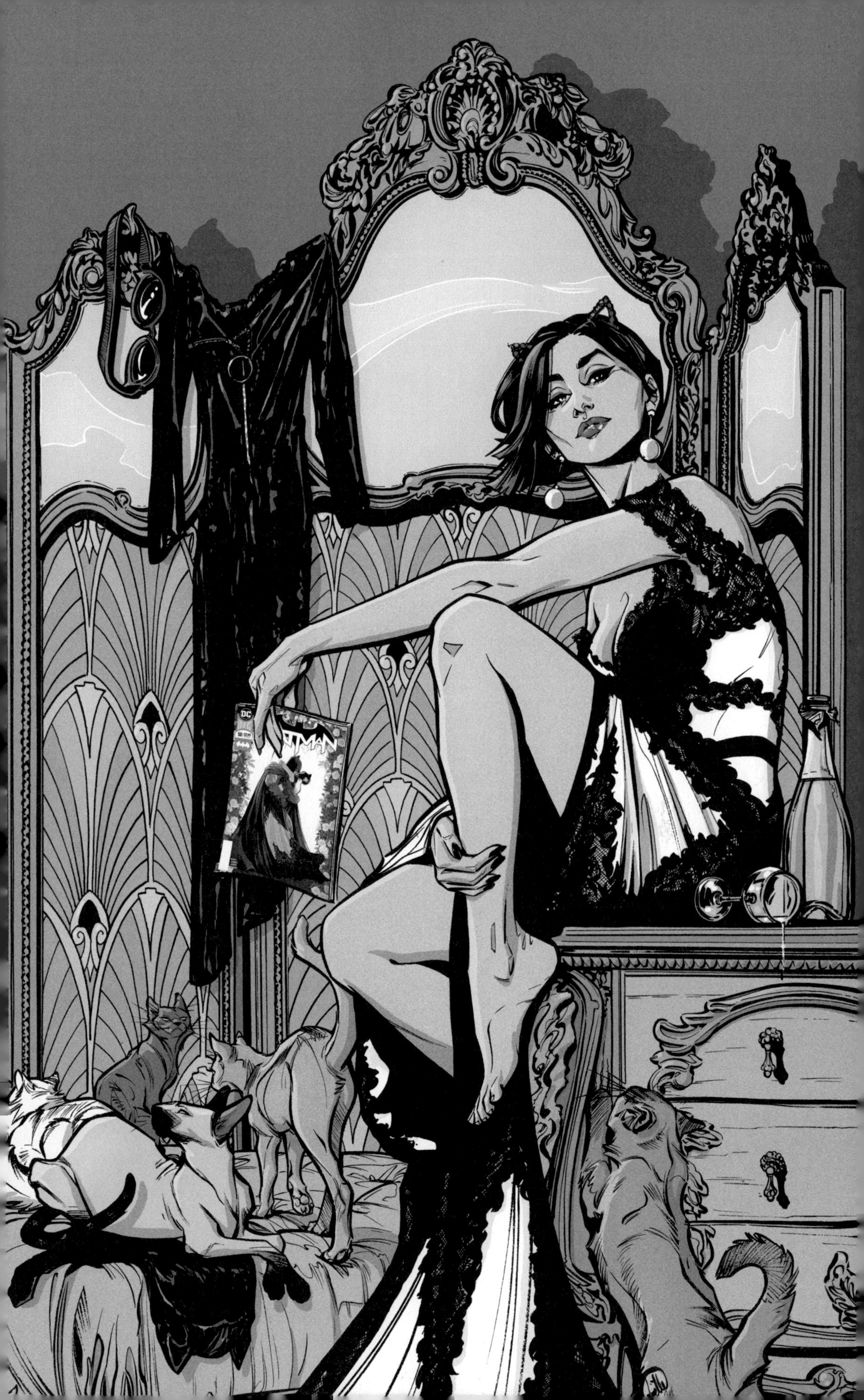

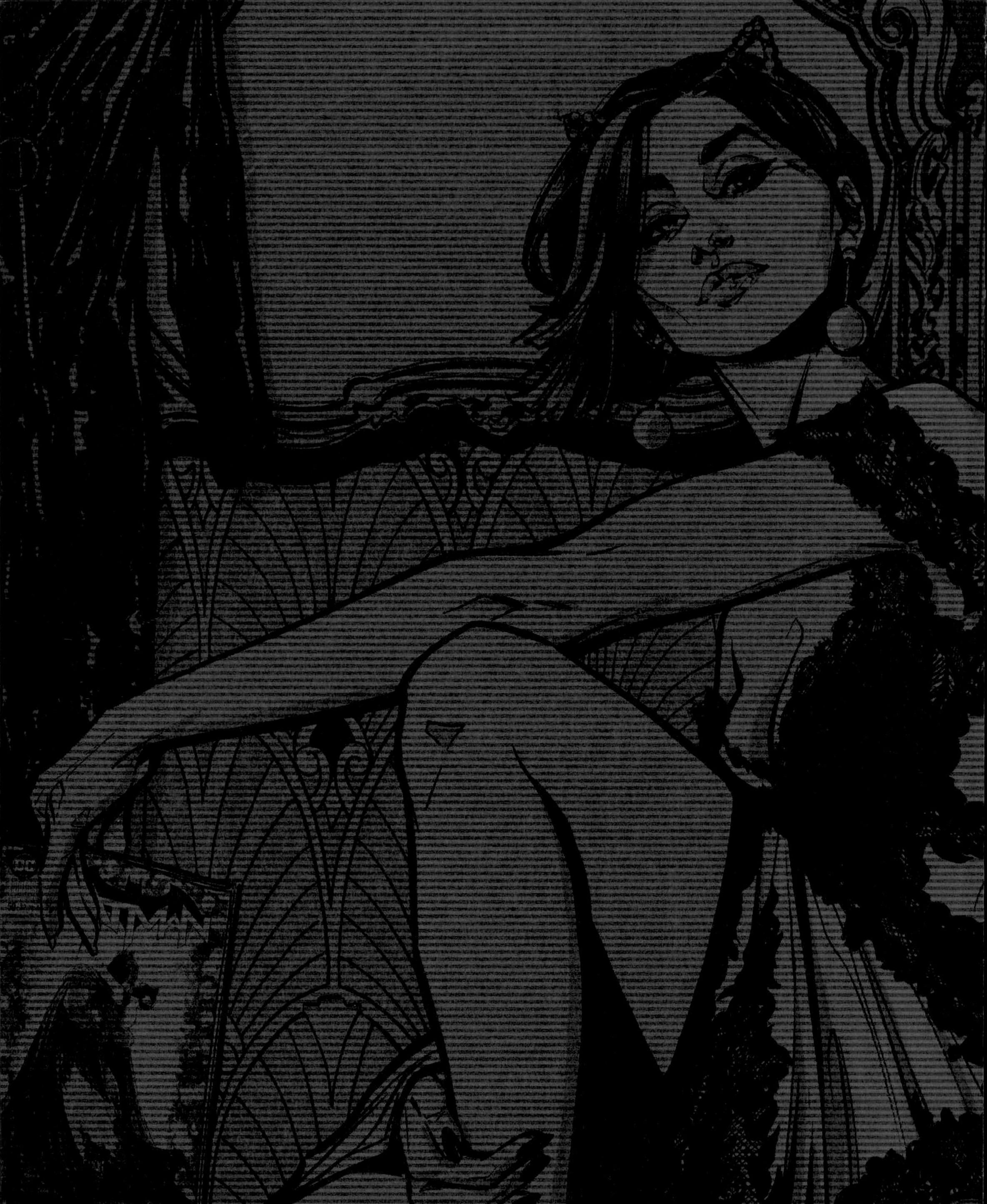

CATWOMAN
#1

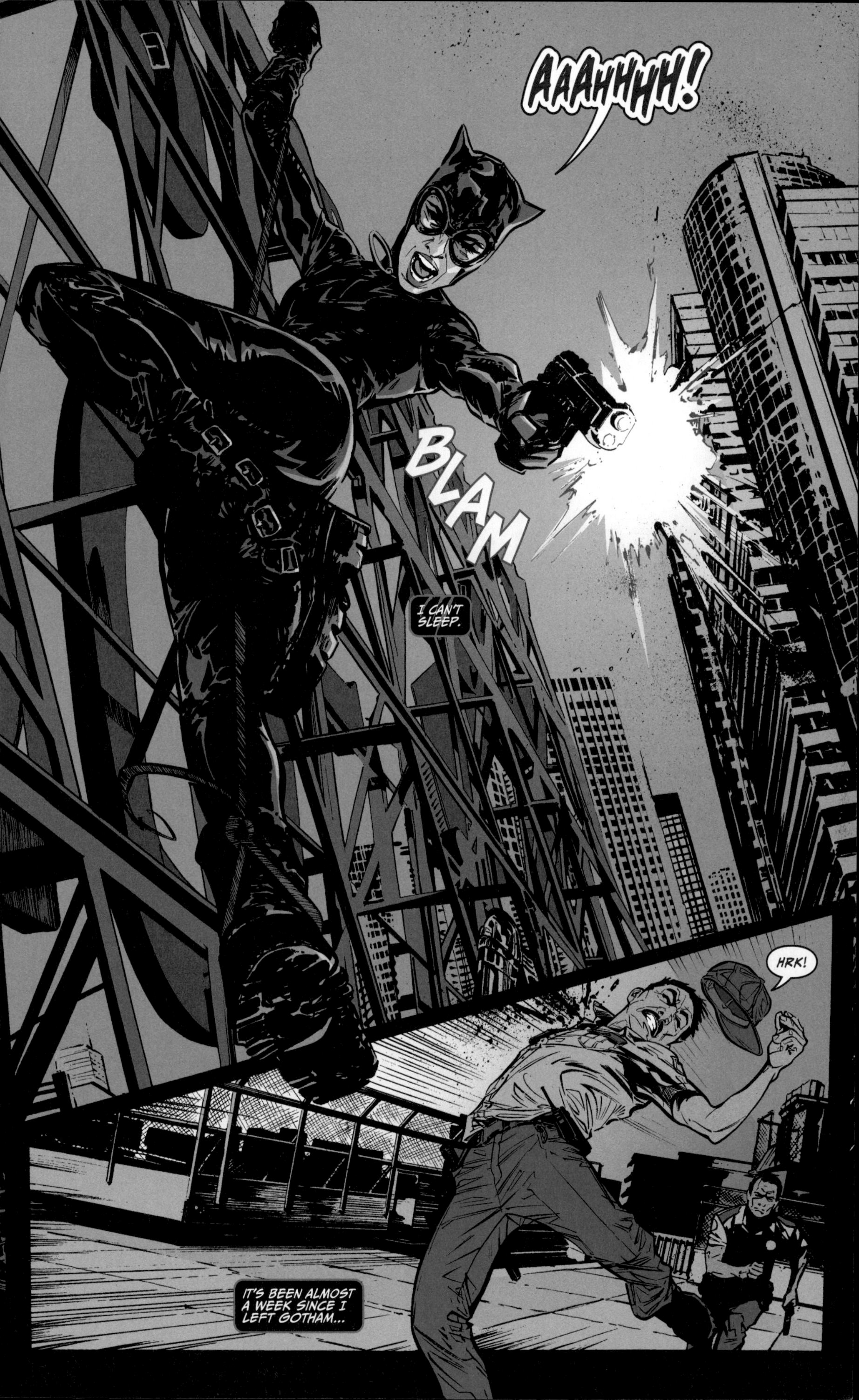
AAAHHHH!
BLAM
I CAN'T SLEEP.
HRK!
IT'S BEEN ALMOST A WEEK SINCE I LEFT GOTHAM...

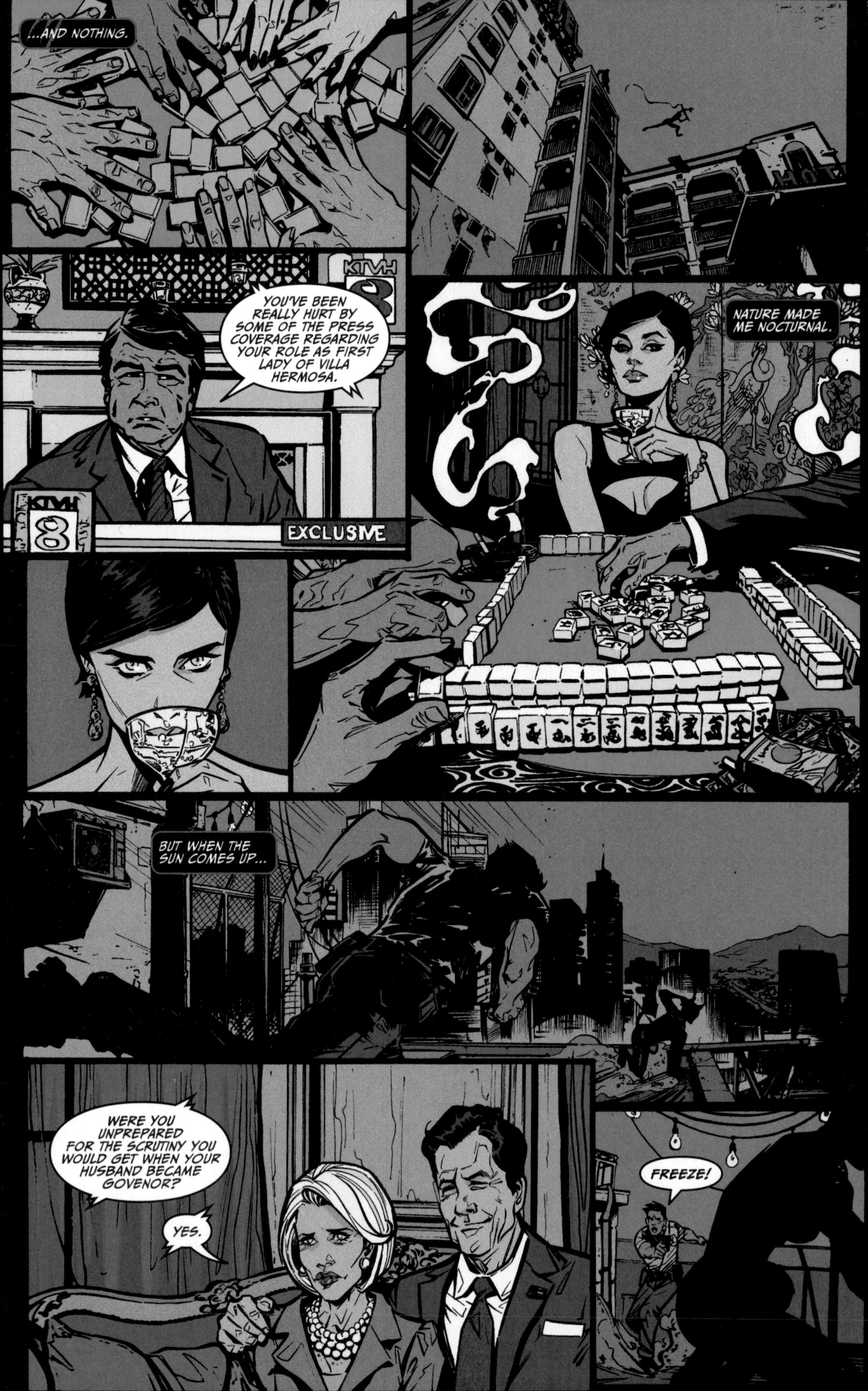
...AND NOTHING.
YOU'VE BEEN REALLY HURT BY SOME OF THE PRESS COVERAGE REGARDING YOUR ROLE AS FIRST LADY OF VILLA HERMOSA.
KTVH 8
KTVH 8
EXCLUSIVE
NATURE MADE ME NOCTURNAL.
BUT WHEN THE SUN COMES UP...
WERE YOU UNPREPARED FOR THE SCRUTINY YOU WOULD GET WHEN YOUR HUSBAND BECAME GOVENOR?
YES.
FREEZE!

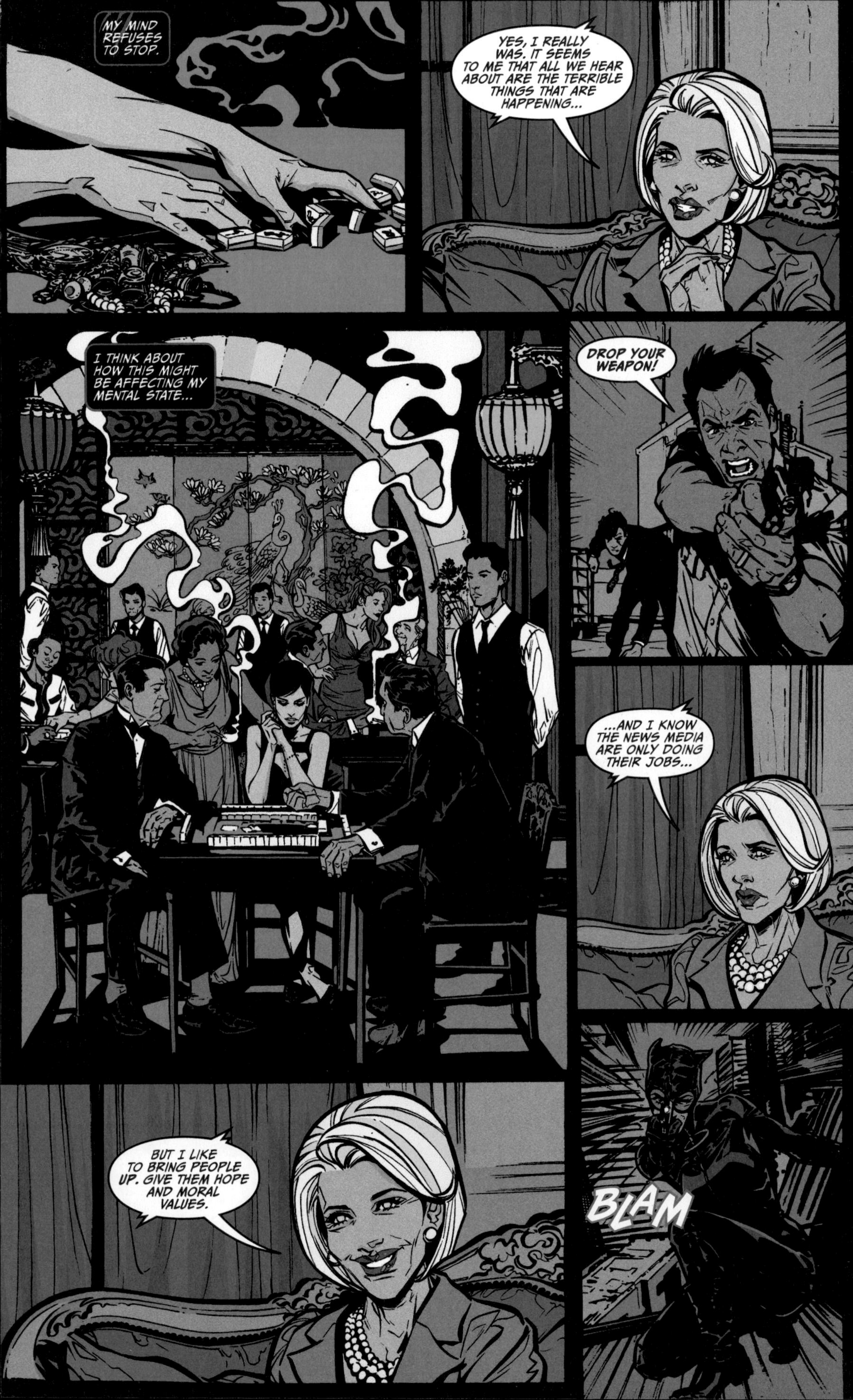
MY MIND REFUSES TO STOP.
YES, I REALLY WAS. IT SEEMS TO ME THAT ALL WE HEAR ABOUT ARE THE TERRIBLE THINGS THAT ARE HAPPENING...
I THINK ABOUT HOW THIS MIGHT BE AFFECTING MY MENTAL STATE...
DROP YOUR WEAPON!
...AND I KNOW THE NEWS MEDIA ARE ONLY DOING THEIR JOBS...
BUT I LIKE TO BRING PEOPLE UP. GIVE THEM HOPE AND MORAL VALUES.
BLAM

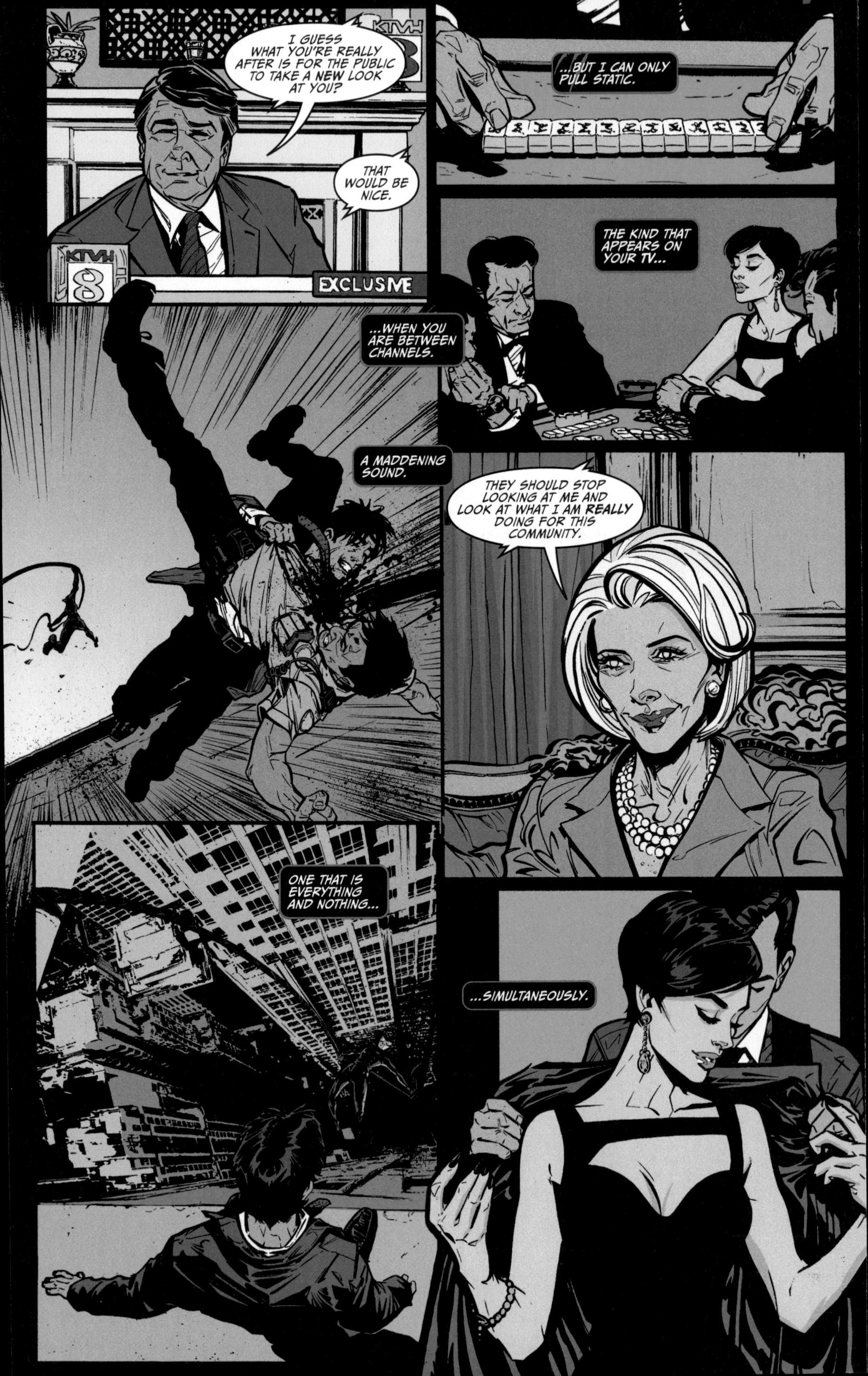
I GUESS WHAT YOU'RE REALLY AFTER IS FOR THE PUBLIC TO TAKE A NEW LOOK AT YOU?
KTVH 8
THAT WOULD BE NICE.
KTVH 8
EXCLUSIVE
...BUT I CAN ONLY PULL STATIC.
THE KIND THAT APPEARS ON YOUR TV...
...WHEN YOU ARE BETWEEN CHANNELS.
A MADDENING SOUND.
THEY SHOULD STOP LOOKING AT ME AND LOOK AT WHAT I AM REALLY DOING FOR THIS COMMUNITY.
ONE THAT IS EVERYTHING AND NOTHING...
...SIMULTANEOUSLY.

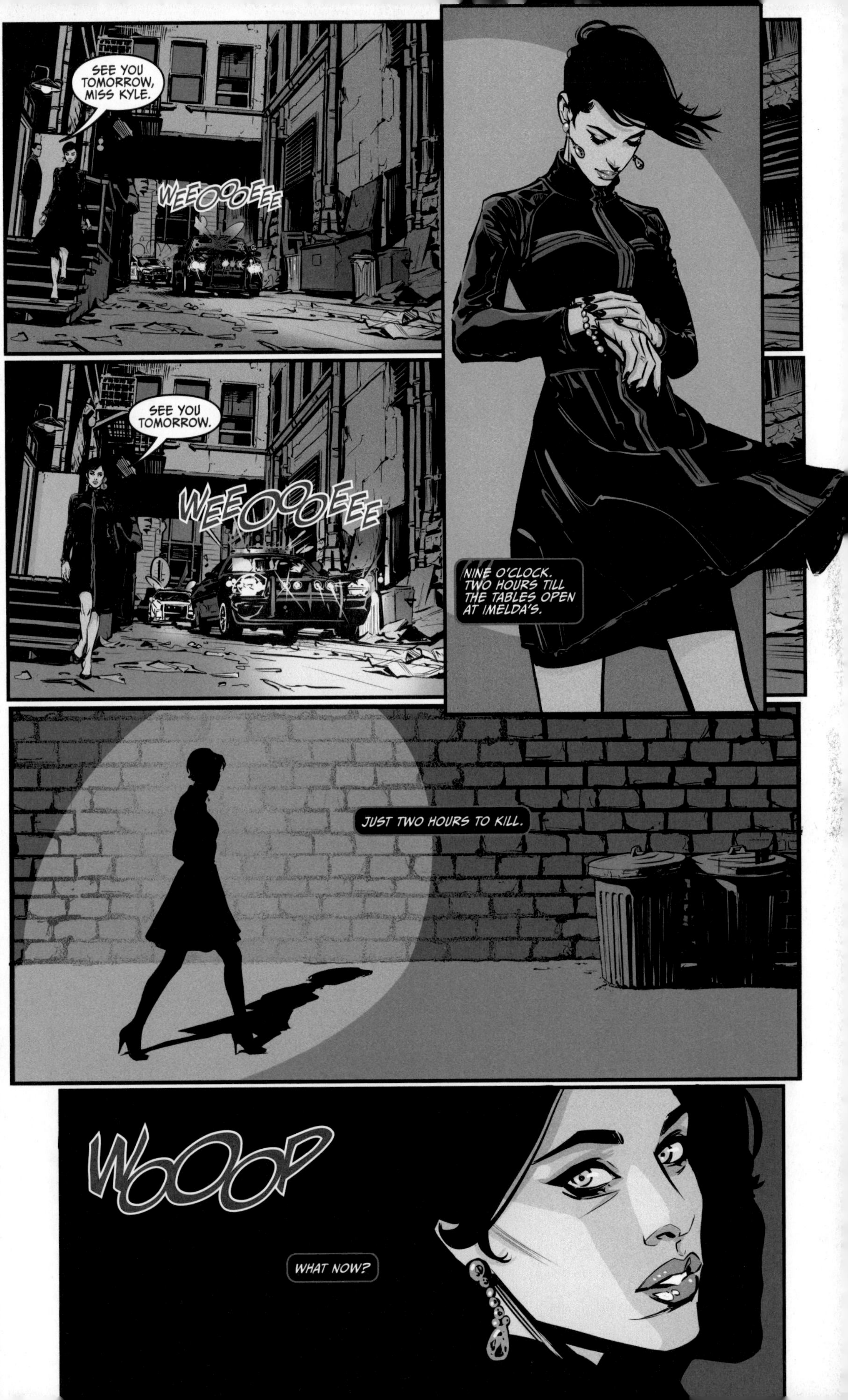
SEE YOU TOMORROW, MISS KYLE.
WEEOOOEEE
SEE YOU TOMORROW.
WEEOOOEEE
NINE O'CLOCK. TWO HOURS TILL THE TABLES OPEN AT IMELDA'S.
JUST TWO HOURS TO KILL.
WOOOP
WHAT NOW?

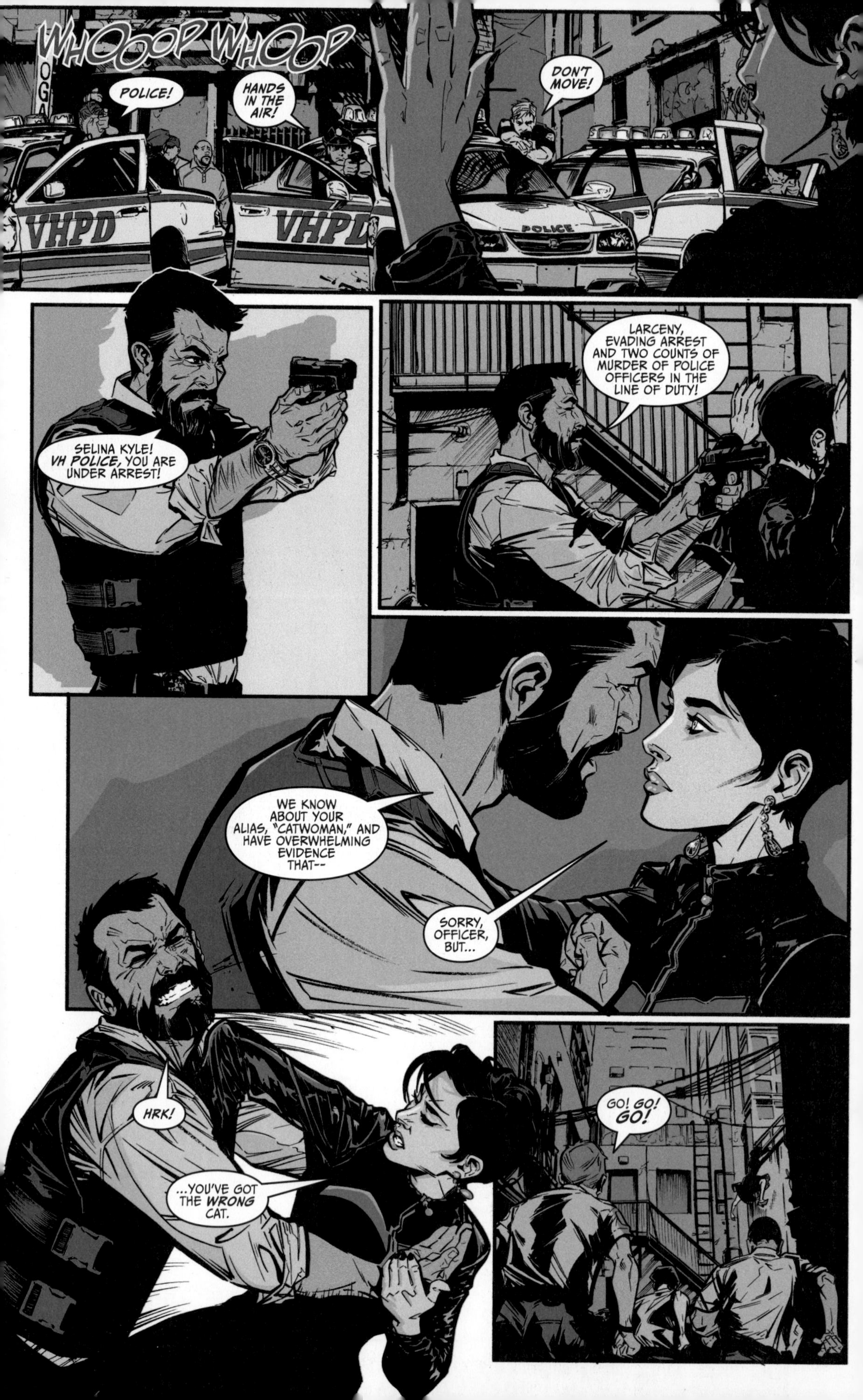
WHOOOOP WHOOP
POLICE!
HANDS IN THE AIR!
DON'T MOVE!
VHPD
VHPD
POLICE
SELINA KYLE! VH POLICE, YOU ARE UNDER ARREST!
LARCENY, EVADING ARREST AND TWO COUNTS OF MURDER OF POLICE OFFICERS IN THE LINE OF DUTY!
WE KNOW ABOUT YOUR ALIAS, "CATWOMAN," AND HAVE OVERWHELMING EVIDENCE THAT--
SORRY, OFFICER, BUT...
HRK!
...YOU'VE GOT THE WRONG CAT.
GO! GO! GO!

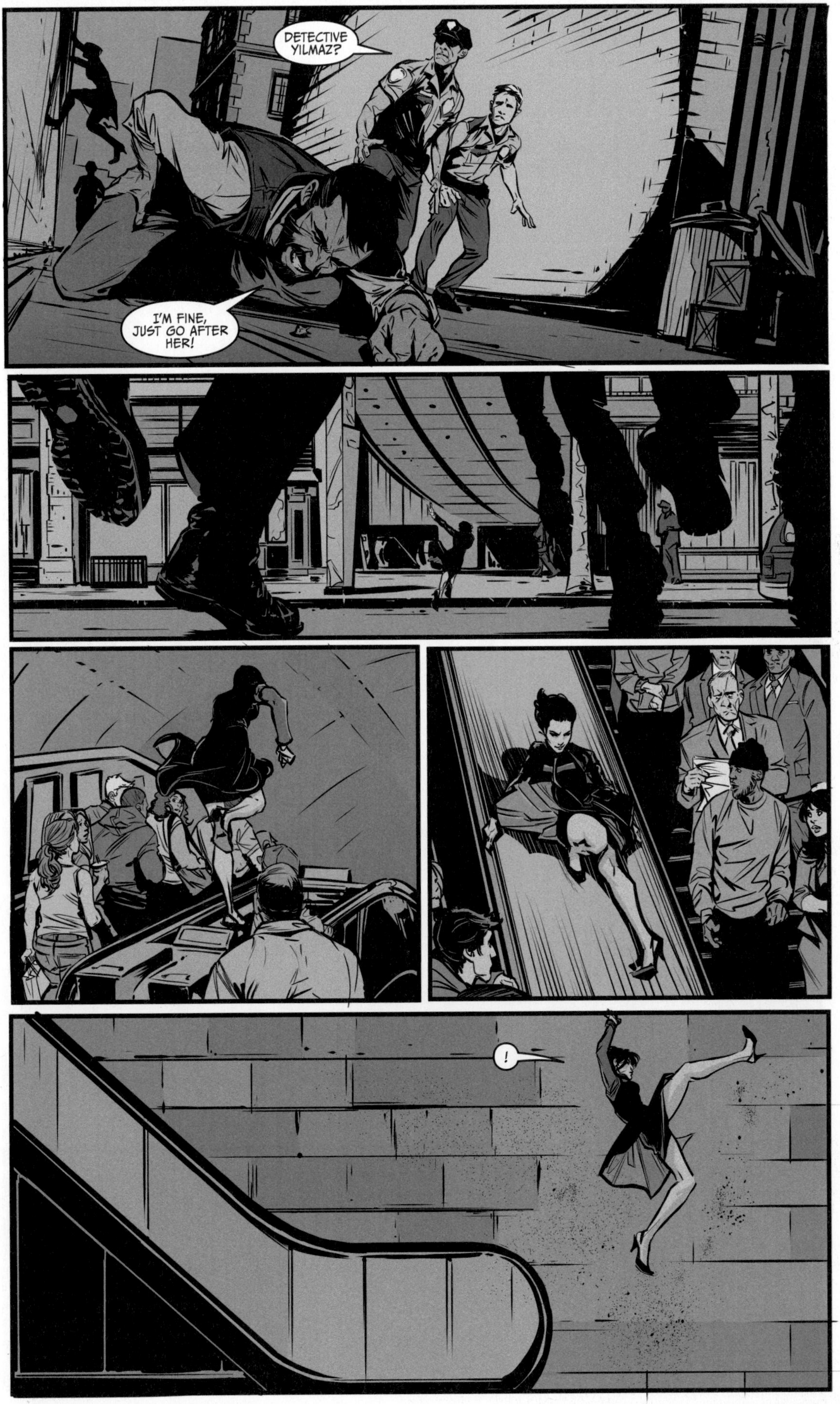
DETECTIVE YILMAZ?
I'M FINE, JUST GO AFTER HER!
!

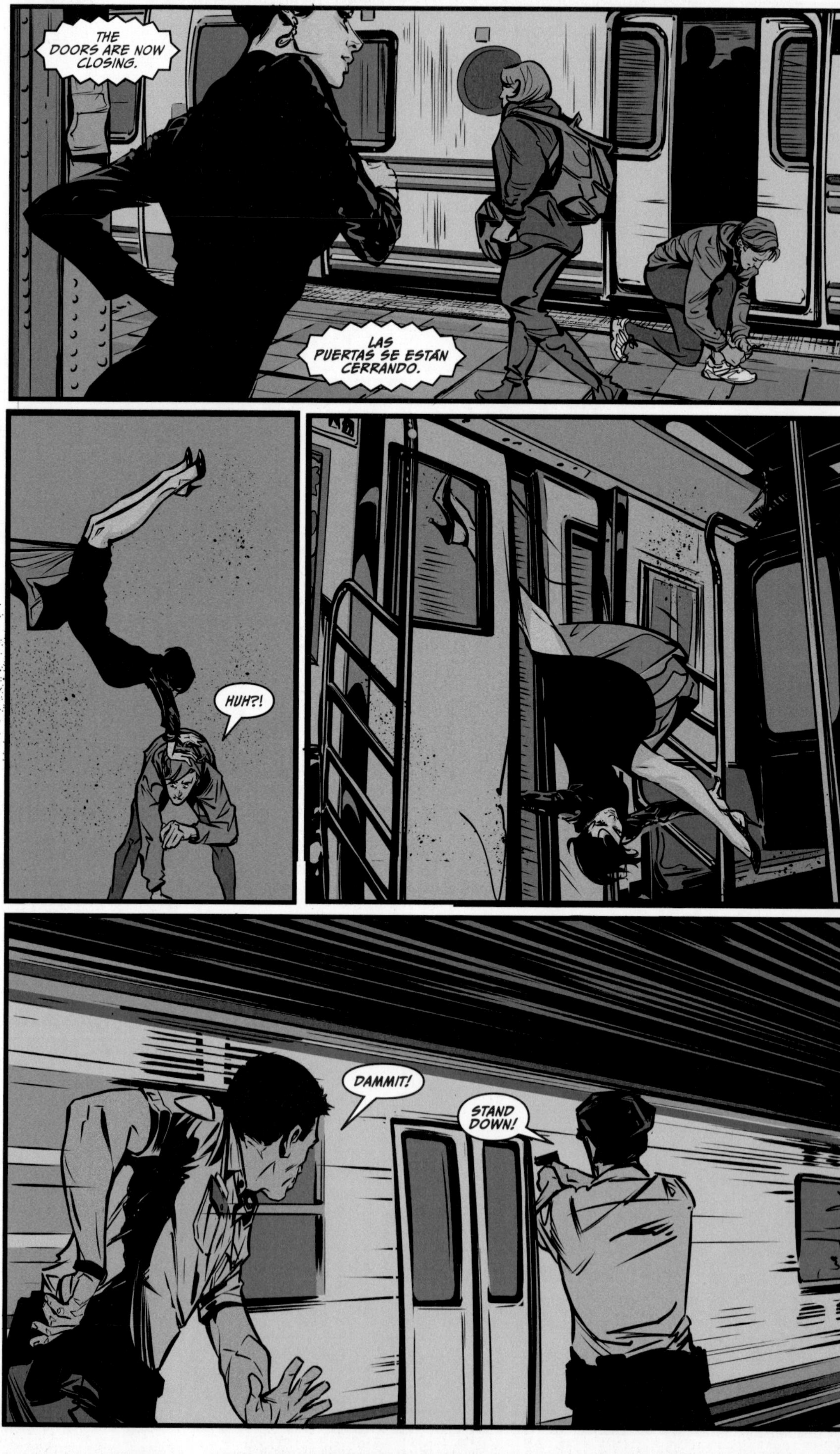
THE DOORS ARE NOW CLOSING.
LAS PUERTAS SE ESTÁN CERRANDO.
HUH?!
DAMMIT!
STAND DOWN!

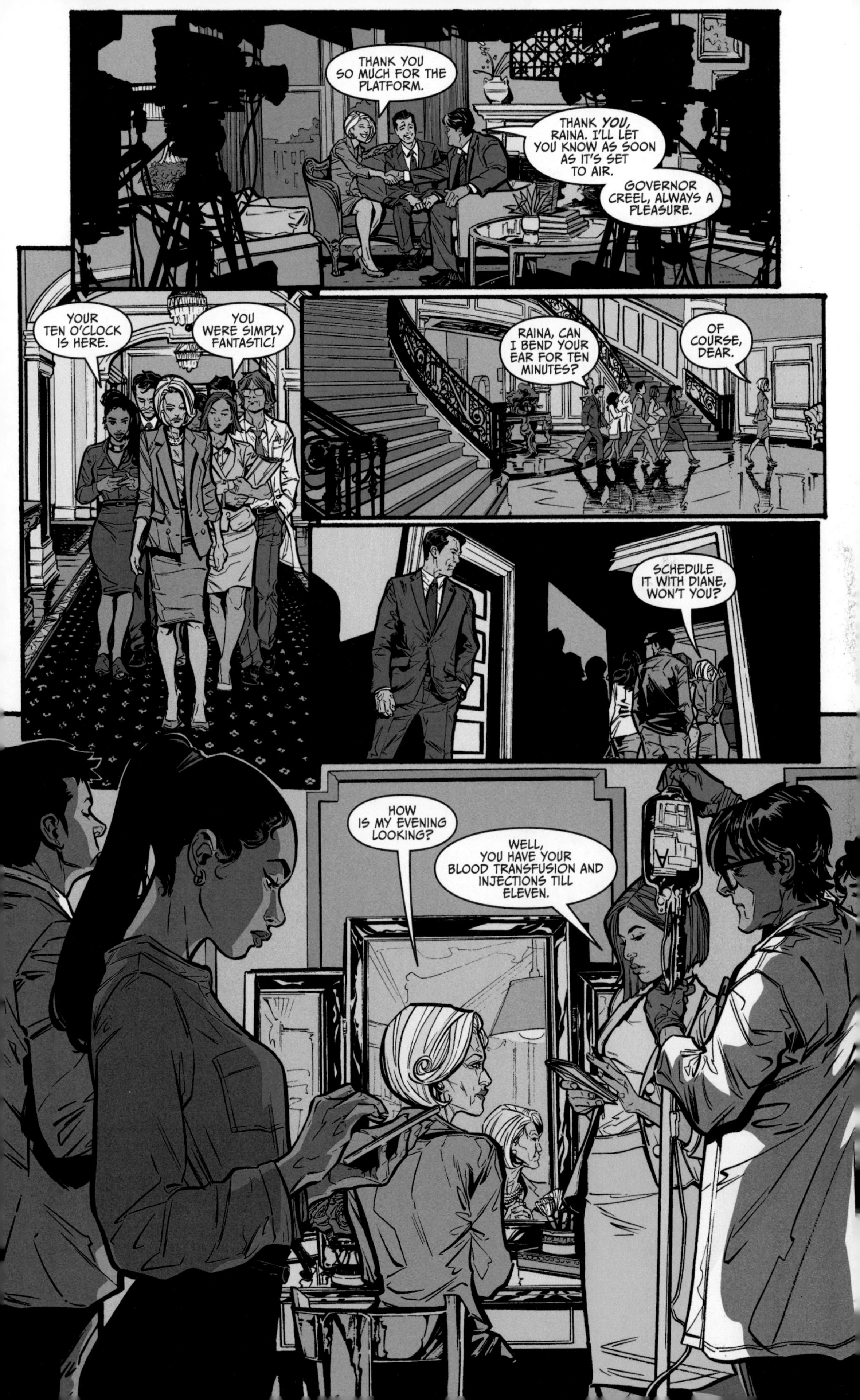
THANK YOU SO MUCH FOR THE PLATFORM.
THANK *YOU*, RAINA. I'LL LET YOU KNOW AS SOON AS IT'S SET TO AIR.
GOVERNOR CREEL, ALWAYS A PLEASURE.
YOUR TEN O'CLOCK IS HERE.
YOU WERE SIMPLY FANTASTIC!
RAINA, CAN I BEND YOUR EAR FOR TEN MINUTES?
OF COURSE, DEAR.
SCHEDULE IT WITH DIANE, WON'T YOU?
HOW IS MY EVENING LOOKING?
WELL, YOU HAVE YOUR BLOOD TRANSFUSION AND INJECTIONS TILL ELEVEN.

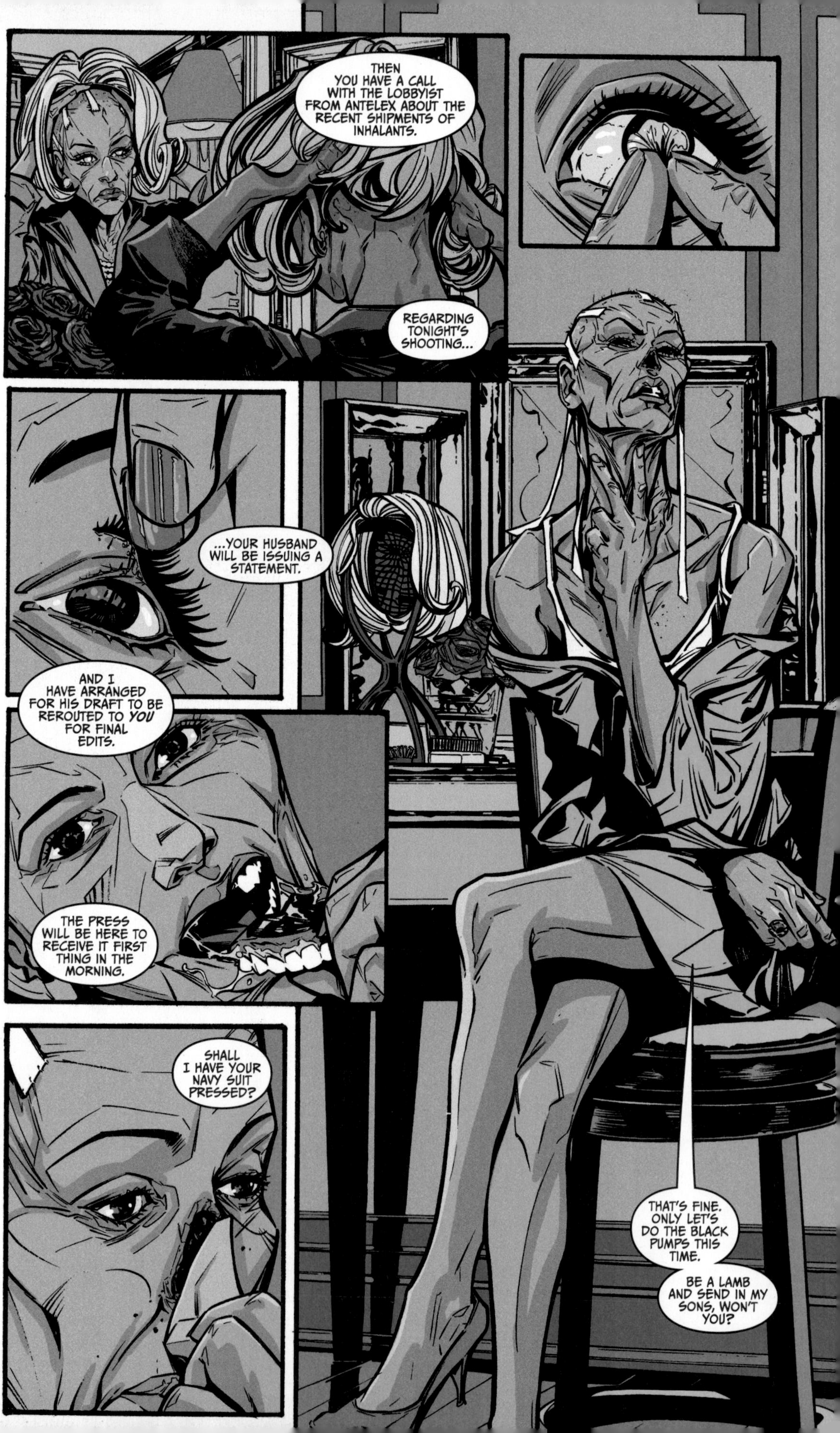
THEN YOU HAVE A CALL WITH THE LOBBYIST FROM ANTELEX ABOUT THE RECENT SHIPMENTS OF INHALANTS.
REGARDING TONIGHT'S SHOOTING...
...YOUR HUSBAND WILL BE ISSUING A STATEMENT.
AND I HAVE ARRANGED FOR HIS DRAFT TO BE REROUTED TO *YOU* FOR FINAL EDITS.
THE PRESS WILL BE HERE TO RECEIVE IT FIRST THING IN THE MORNING.
SHALL I HAVE YOUR NAVY SUIT PRESSED?
THAT'S FINE. ONLY LET'S DO THE BLACK PUMPS THIS TIME.
BE A LAMB AND SEND IN MY SONS, WON'T YOU?

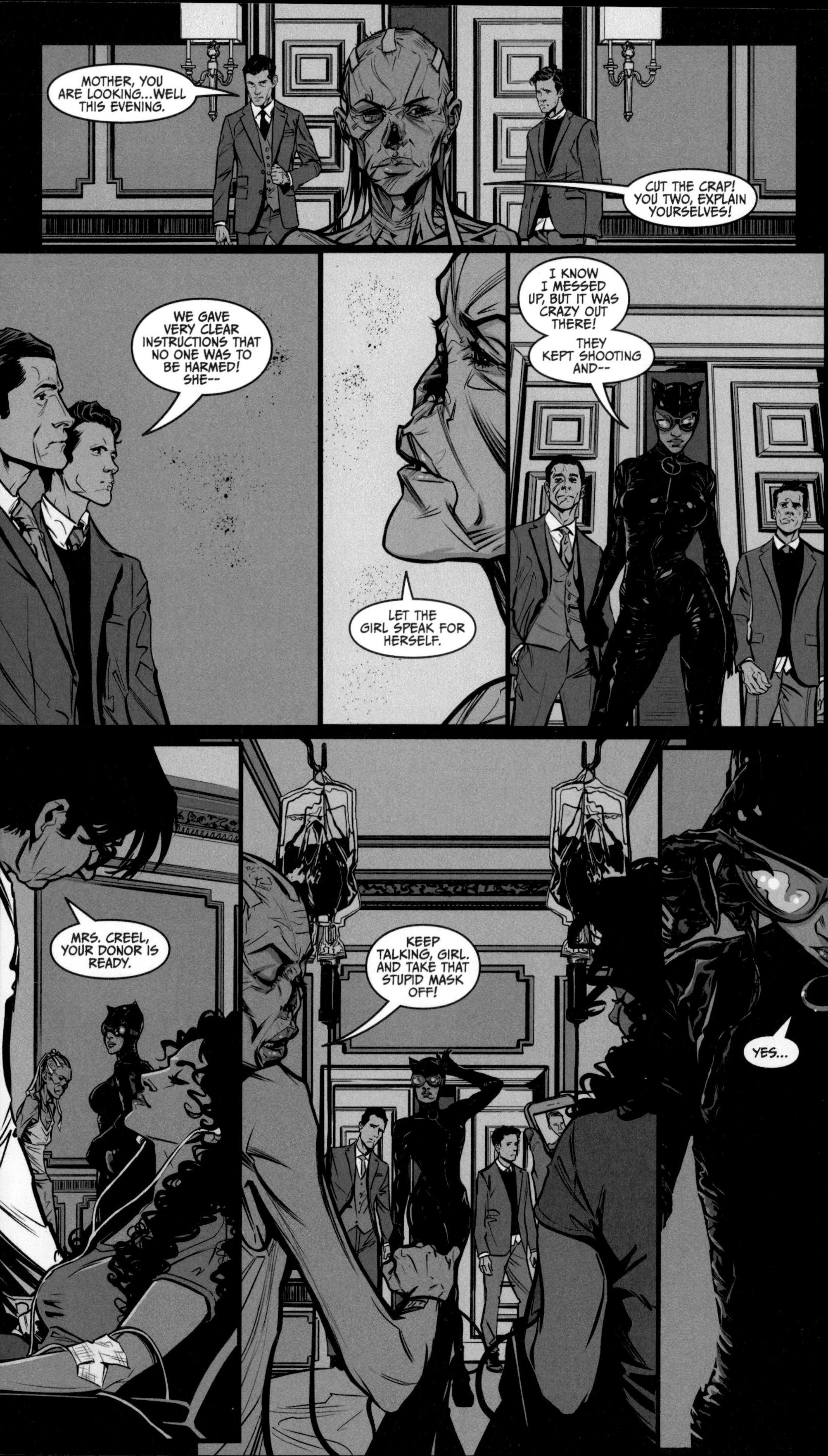
MOTHER, YOU ARE LOOKING...WELL THIS EVENING.
CUT THE CRAP! YOU TWO, EXPLAIN YOURSELVES!
WE GAVE VERY CLEAR INSTRUCTIONS THAT NO ONE WAS TO BE HARMED! SHE--
LET THE GIRL SPEAK FOR HERSELF.
I KNOW I MESSED UP, BUT IT WAS CRAZY OUT THERE!
THEY KEPT SHOOTING AND--
MRS. CREEL, YOUR DONOR IS READY.
KEEP TALKING, GIRL. AND TAKE THAT STUPID MASK OFF!
YES...

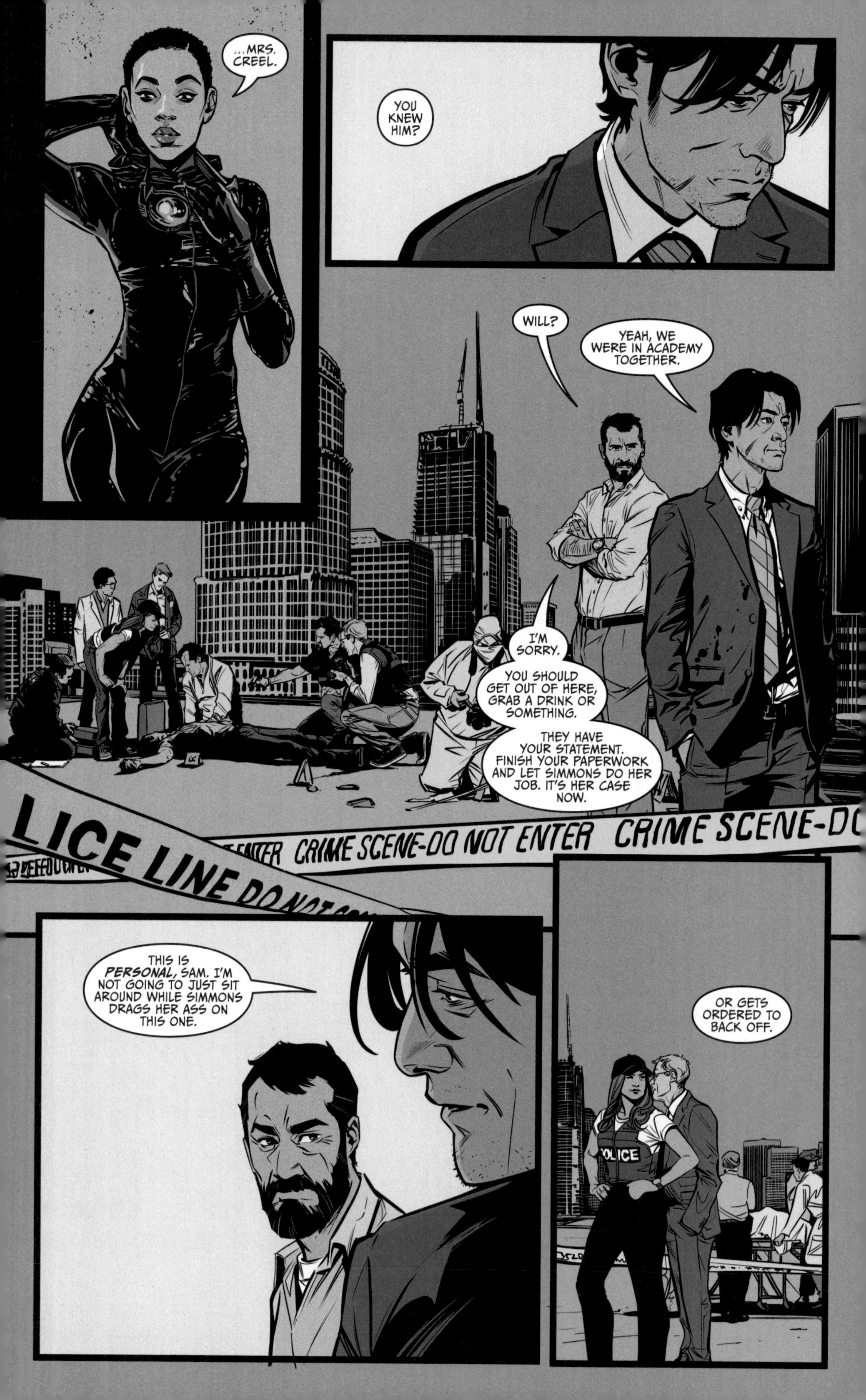

...MRS. CREEL.
YOU KNEW HIM?
WILL?
YEAH, WE WERE IN ACADEMY TOGETHER.
I'M SORRY.
YOU SHOULD GET OUT OF HERE, GRAB A DRINK OR SOMETHING.
THEY HAVE YOUR STATEMENT. FINISH YOUR PAPERWORK AND LET SIMMONS DO HER JOB. IT'S HER CASE NOW.
POLICE LINE DO NOT CROSS
CRIME SCENE-DO NOT ENTER
CRIME SCENE-DO
THIS IS PERSONAL, SAM. I'M NOT GOING TO JUST SIT AROUND WHILE SIMMONS DRAGS HER ASS ON THIS ONE.
OR GETS ORDERED TO BACK OFF.
POLICE

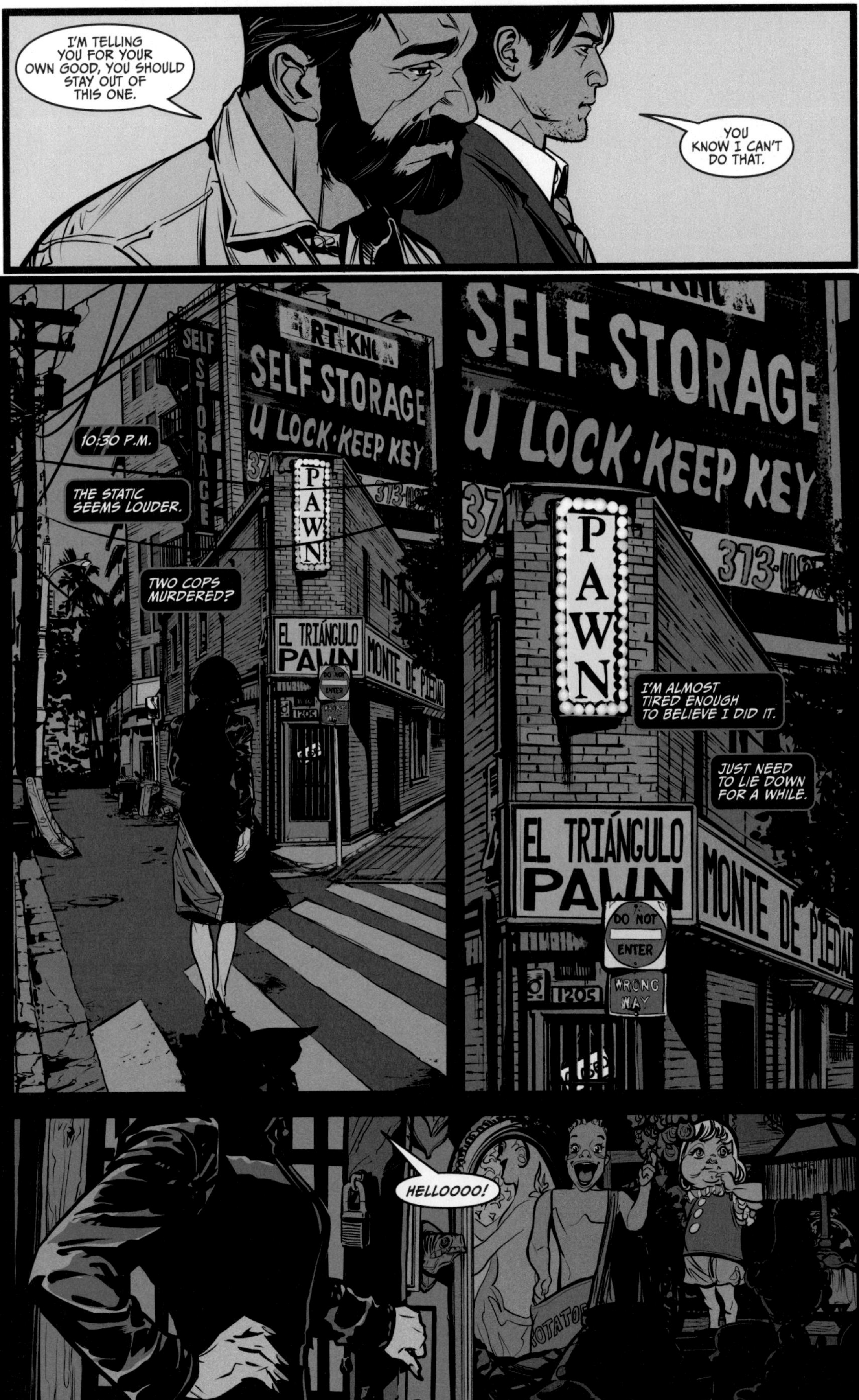
I'M TELLING YOU FOR YOUR OWN GOOD, YOU SHOULD STAY OUT OF THIS ONE.
YOU KNOW I CAN'T DO THAT.
SELF STORAGE
SELF STORAGE
U LOCK · KEEP KEY
PAWN
10:30 P.M.
THE STATIC SEEMS LOUDER.
TWO COPS MURDERED?
EL TRIÁNGULO PAWN
MONTE DE PIEDAD
DO NOT ENTER
WRONG WAY
1205
I'M ALMOST TIRED ENOUGH TO BELIEVE I DID IT.
JUST NEED TO LIE DOWN FOR A WHILE.
HELLOOOO!

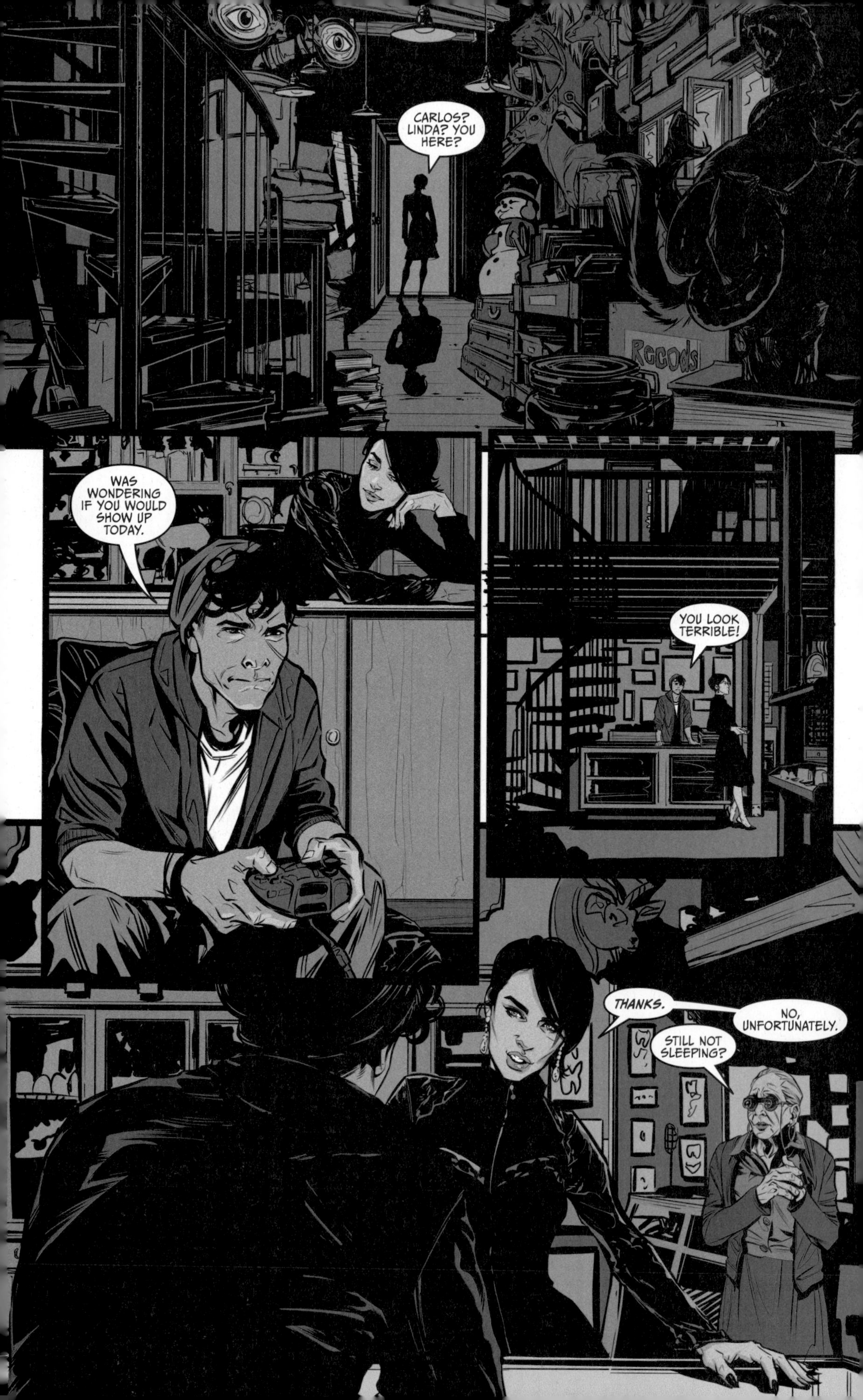
CARLOS? LINDA? YOU HERE?
WAS WONDERING IF YOU WOULD SHOW UP TODAY.
YOU LOOK TERRIBLE!
THANKS.
STILL NOT SLEEPING?
NO, UNFORTUNATELY.

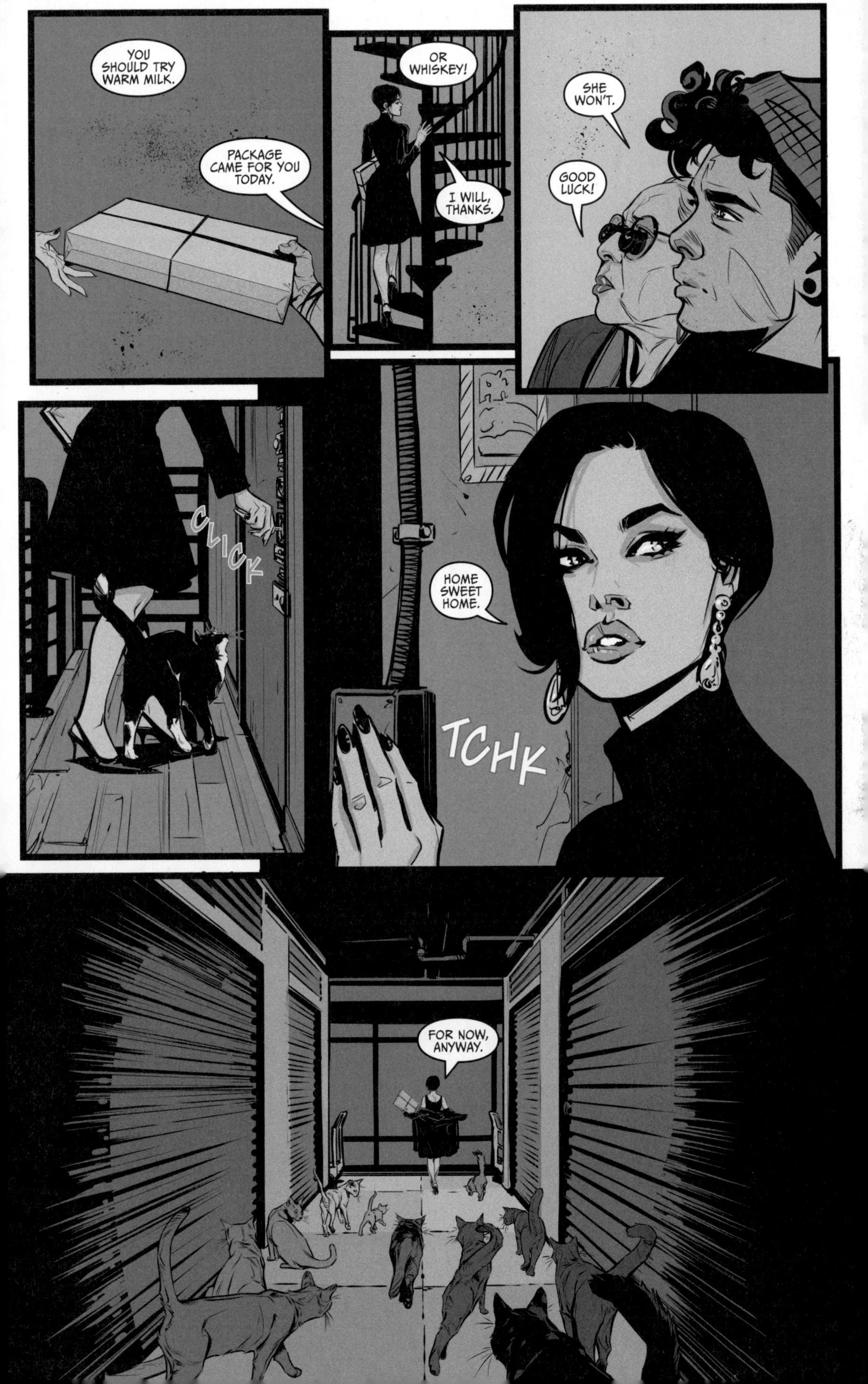
YOU SHOULD TRY WARM MILK.
PACKAGE CAME FOR YOU TODAY.
OR WHISKEY!
I WILL, THANKS.
SHE WON'T.
GOOD LUCK!
CLICK
HOME SWEET HOME.
TCHK
FOR NOW, ANYWAY.

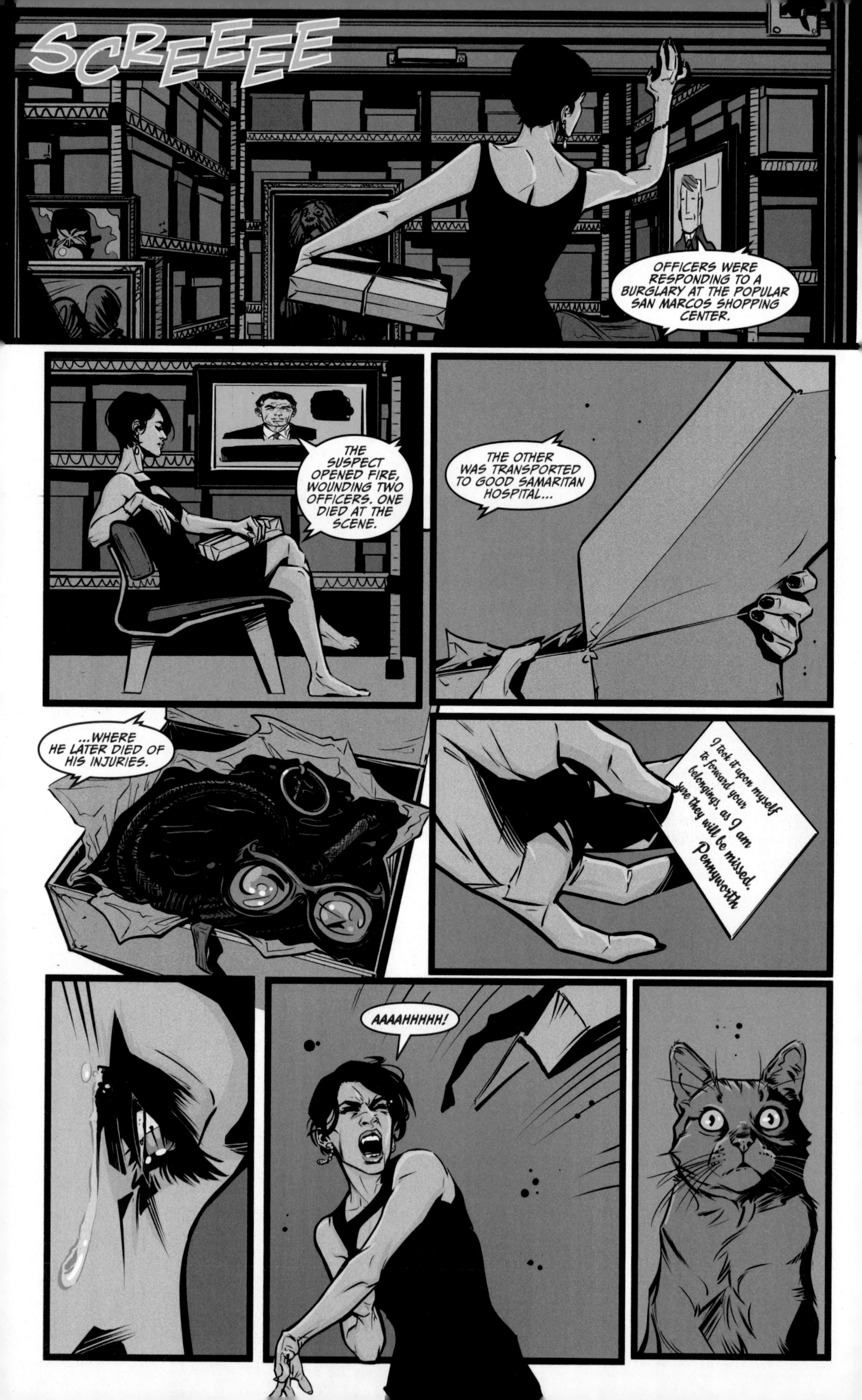
SCREEEEE
OFFICERS WERE RESPONDING TO A BURGLARY AT THE POPULAR SAN MARCOS SHOPPING CENTER.
THE SUSPECT OPENED FIRE, WOUNDING TWO OFFICERS. ONE DIED AT THE SCENE.
THE OTHER WAS TRANSPORTED TO GOOD SAMARITAN HOSPITAL...
...WHERE HE LATER DIED OF HIS INJURIES.
I took it upon myself to forward your belongings, as I am sure they will be missed.
Pennyworth
AAAAHHHHH!

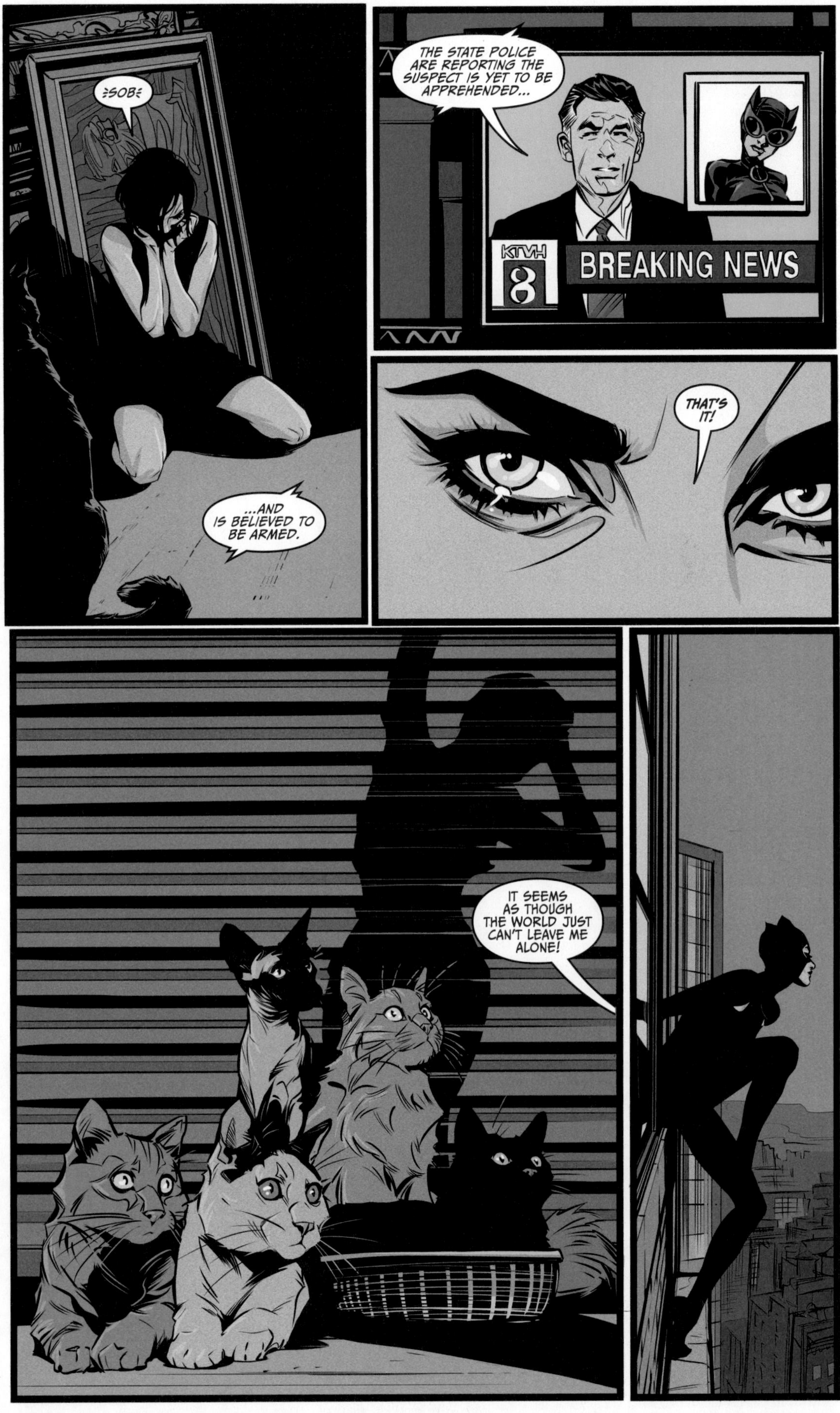
SOB
THE STATE POLICE ARE REPORTING THE SUSPECT IS YET TO BE APPREHENDED...
KTVH 8
BREAKING NEWS
...AND IS BELIEVED TO BE ARMED.
THAT'S IT!
IT SEEMS AS THOUGH THE WORLD JUST CAN'T LEAVE ME ALONE!

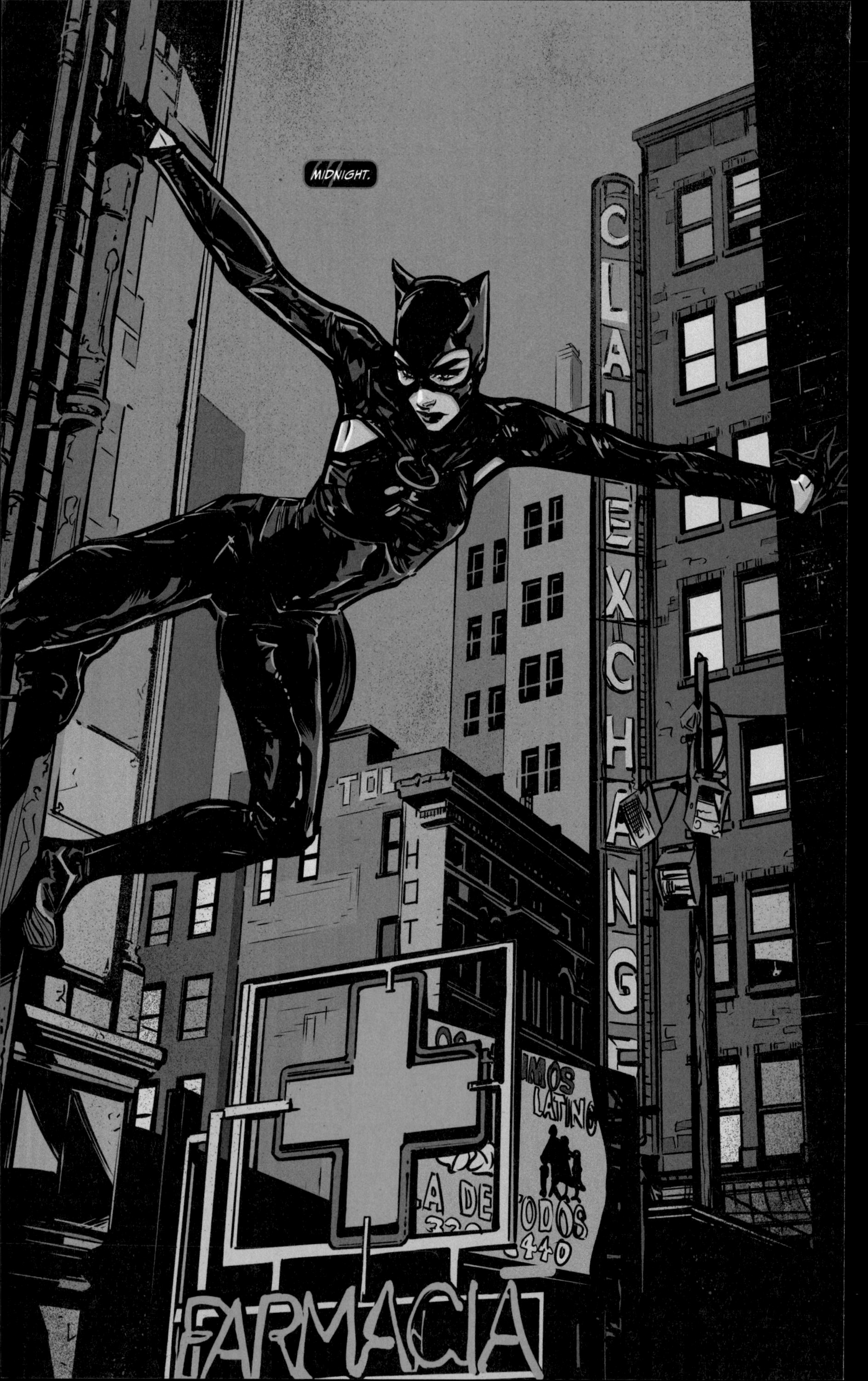
MIDNIGHT.
FARMACIA

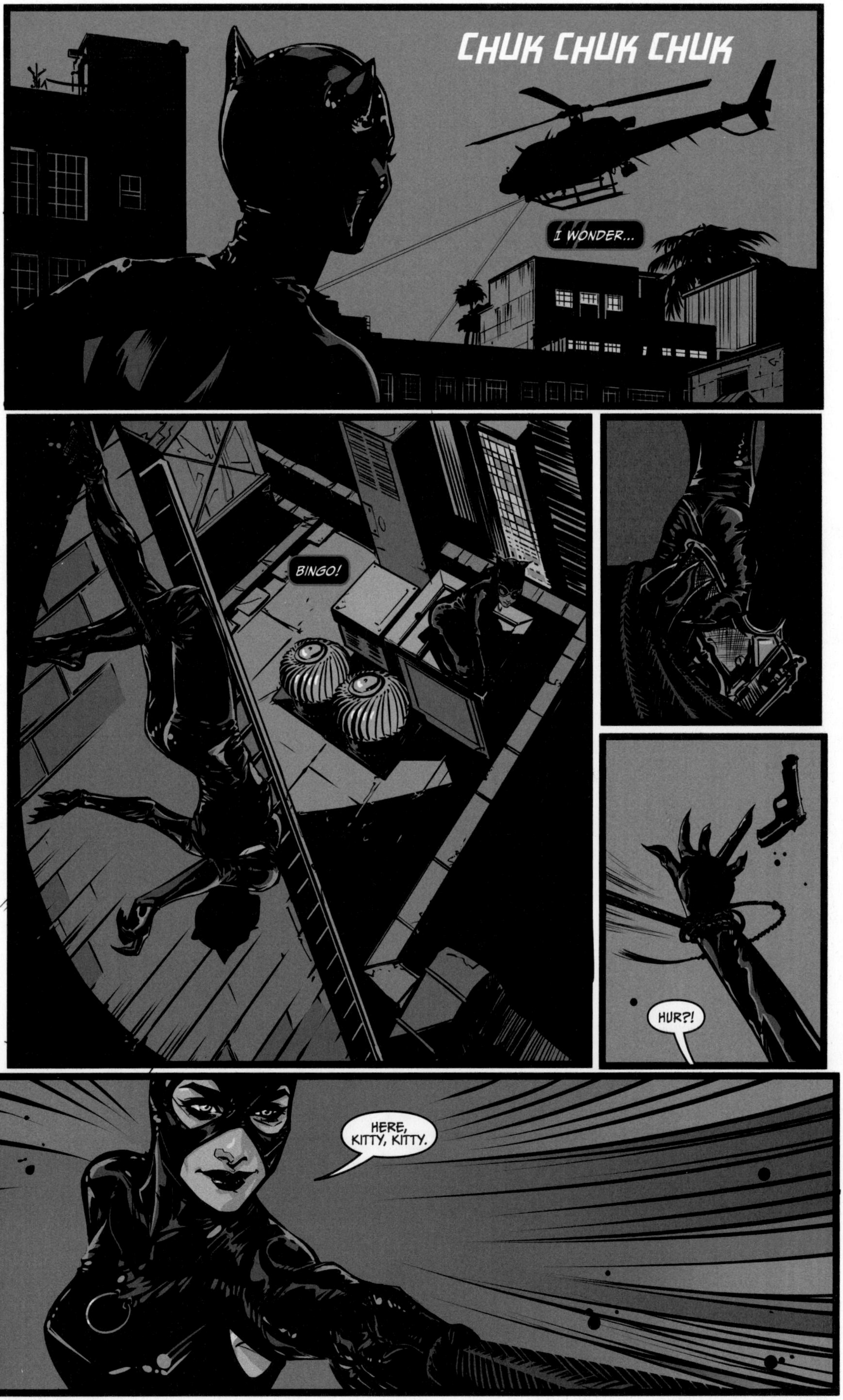
CHUK CHUK CHUK
I WONDER...
BINGO!
HUR?!
HERE, KITTY, KITTY.

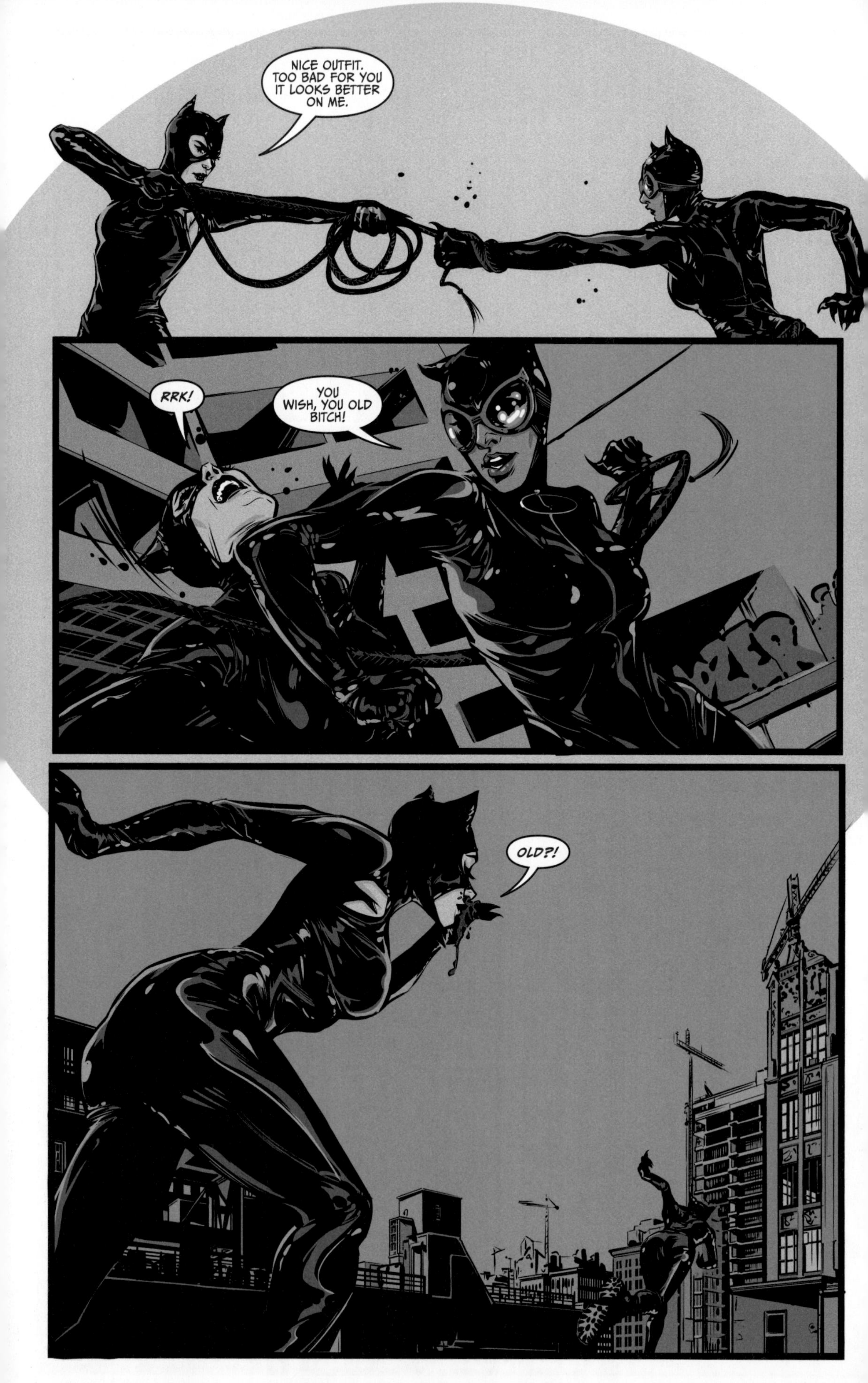
NICE OUTFIT. TOO BAD FOR YOU IT LOOKS BETTER ON ME.
RRK!
YOU WISH, YOU OLD BITCH!
OLD?!

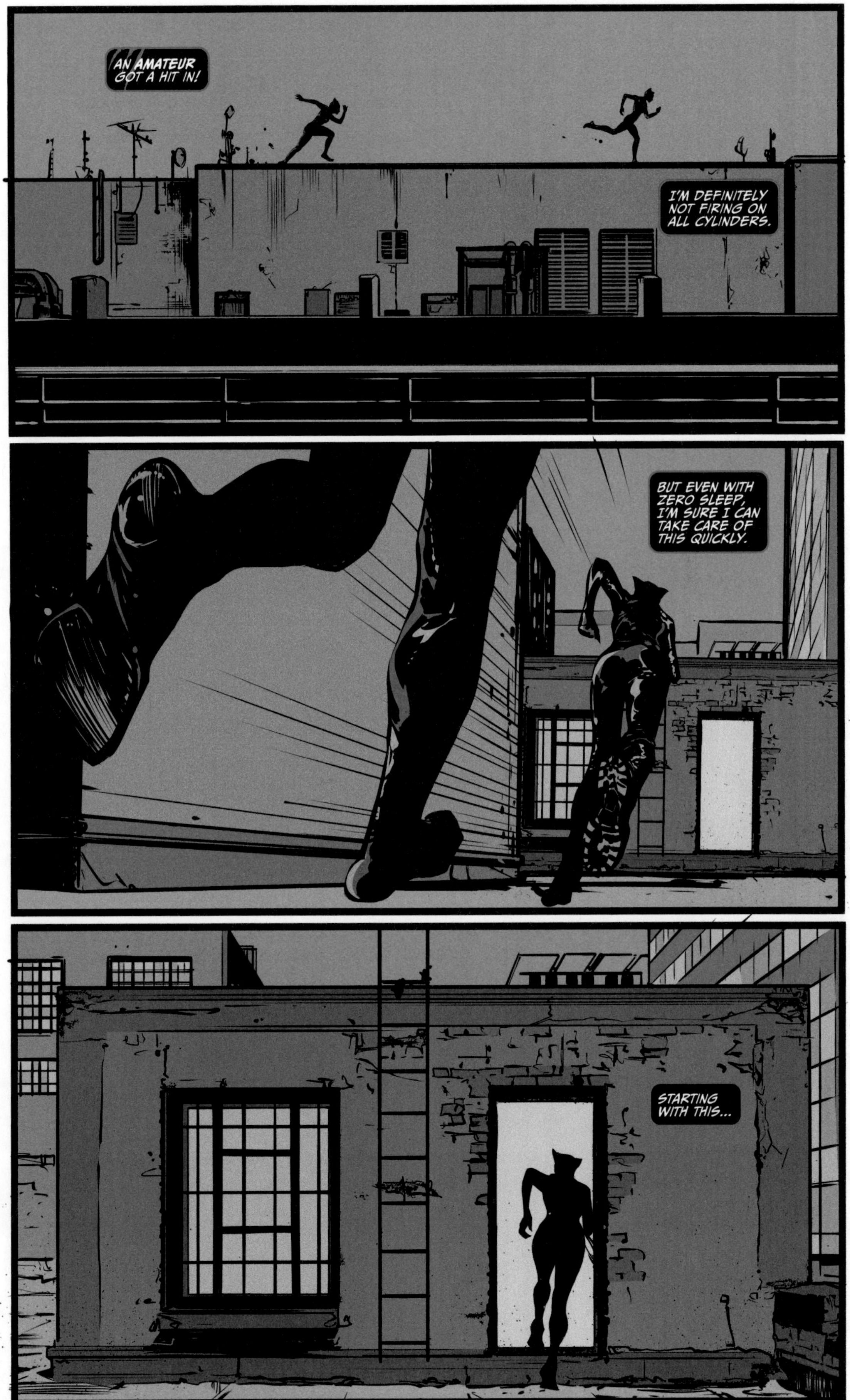
AN AMATEUR GOT A HIT IN!
I'M DEFINITELY NOT FIRING ON ALL CYLINDERS.
BUT EVEN WITH ZERO SLEEP, I'M SURE I CAN TAKE CARE OF THIS QUICKLY.
STARTING WITH THIS...

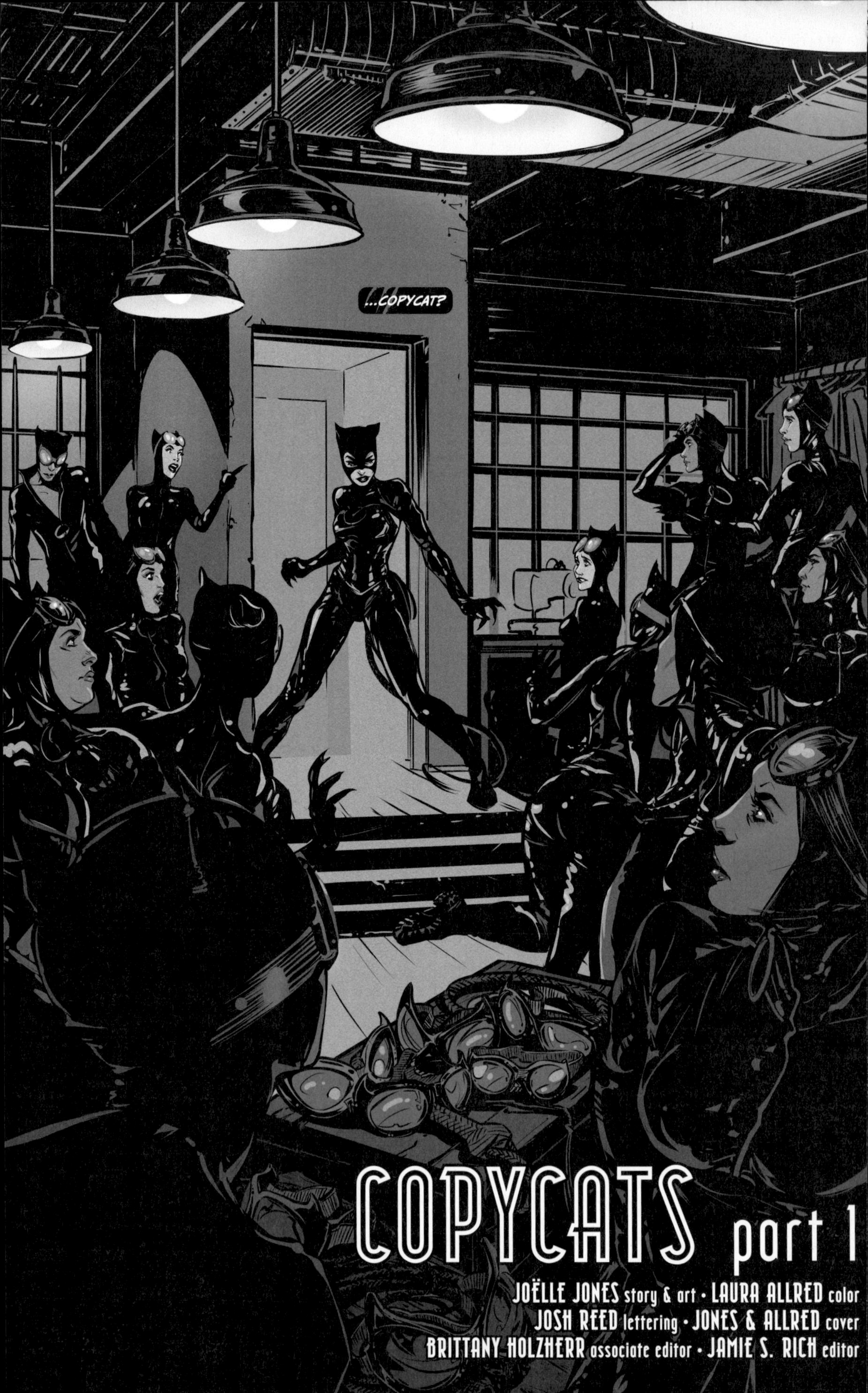
...COPYCAT?
COPYCATS part 1
JOËLLE JONES story & art • LAURA ALLRED color
JOSH REED lettering • JONES & ALLRED cover
BRITTANY HOLZHERR associate editor • JAMIE S. RICH editor

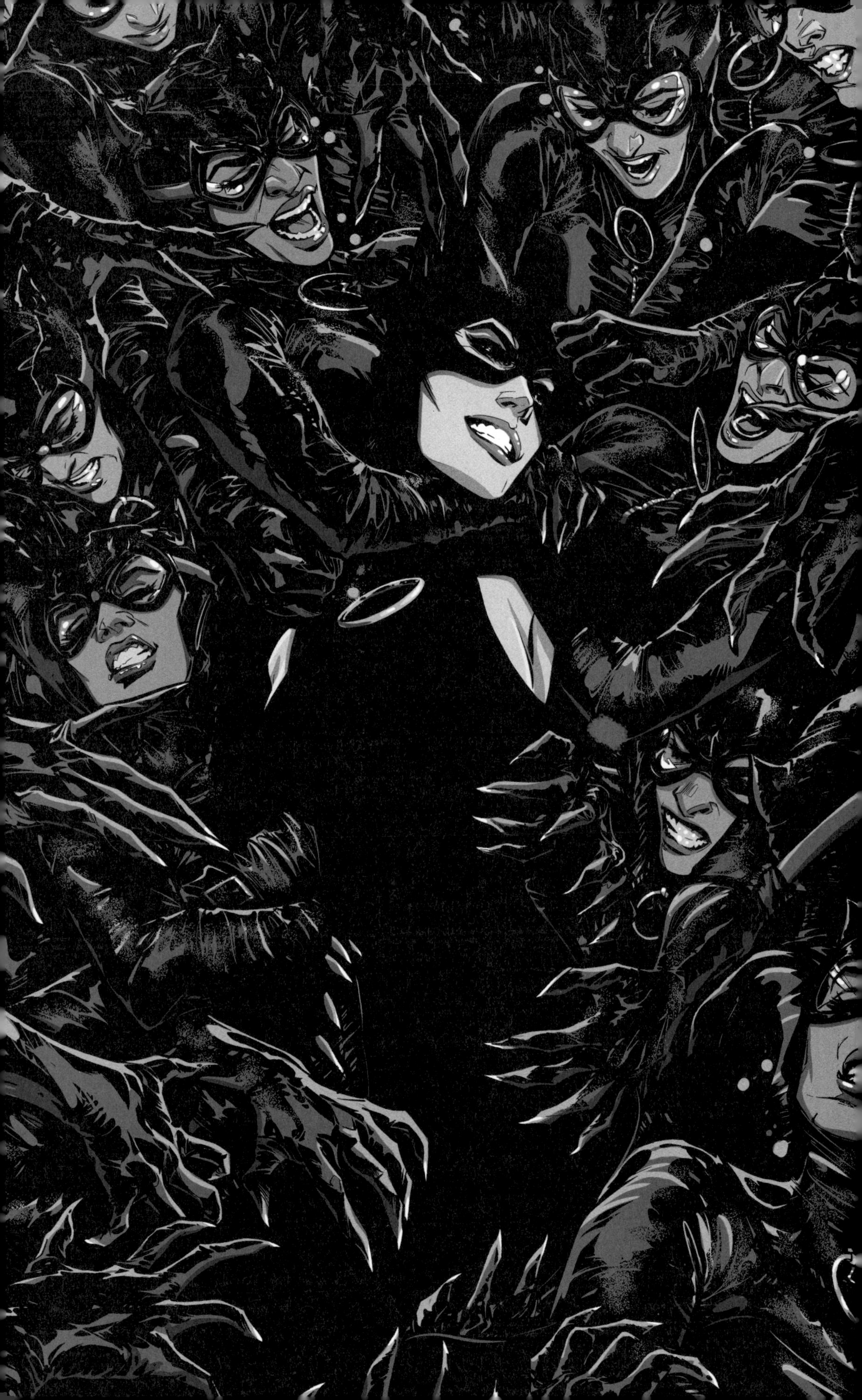

CATWOMAN
#2

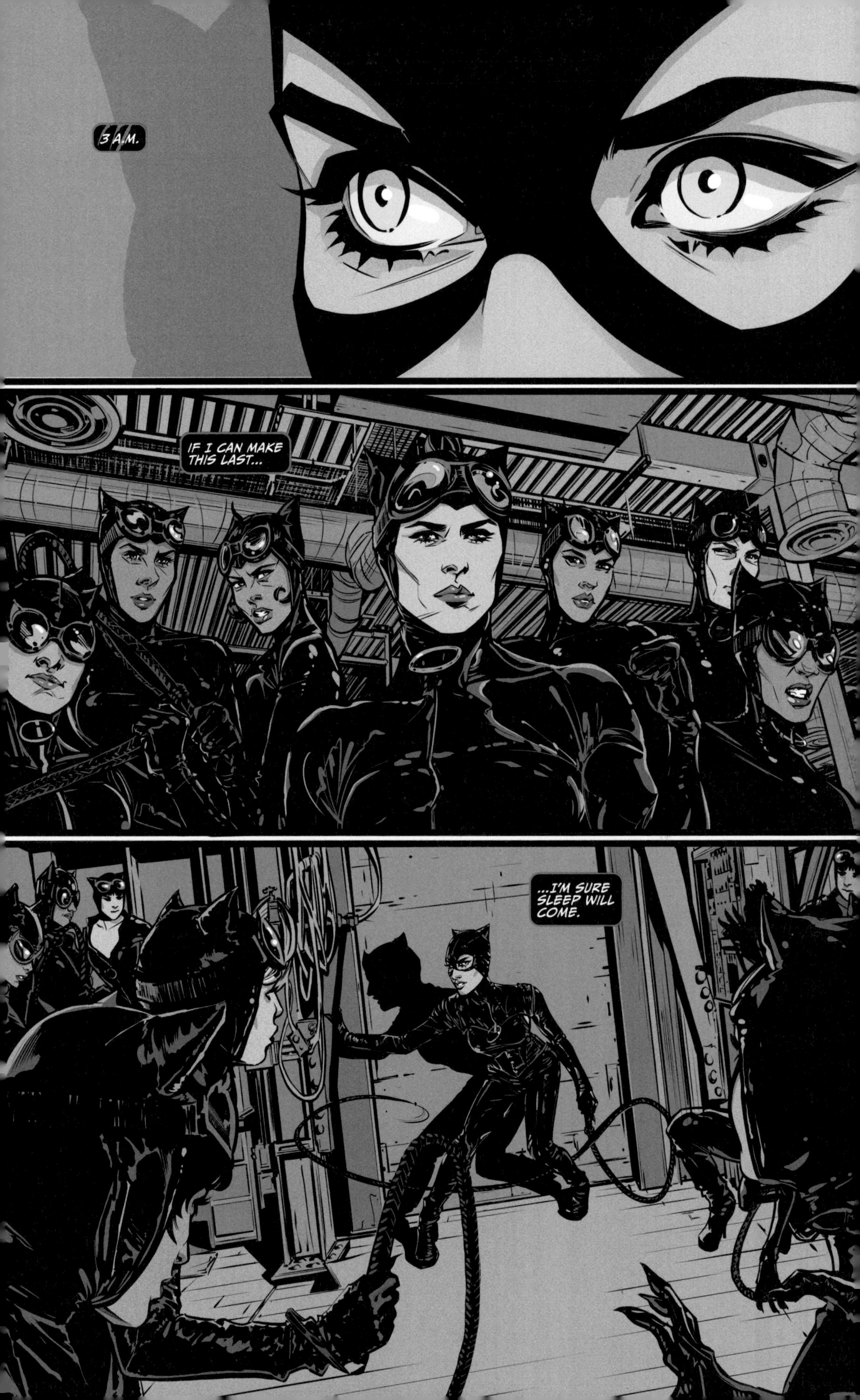
3 A.M.
IF I CAN MAKE THIS LAST...
...I'M SURE SLEEP WILL COME.

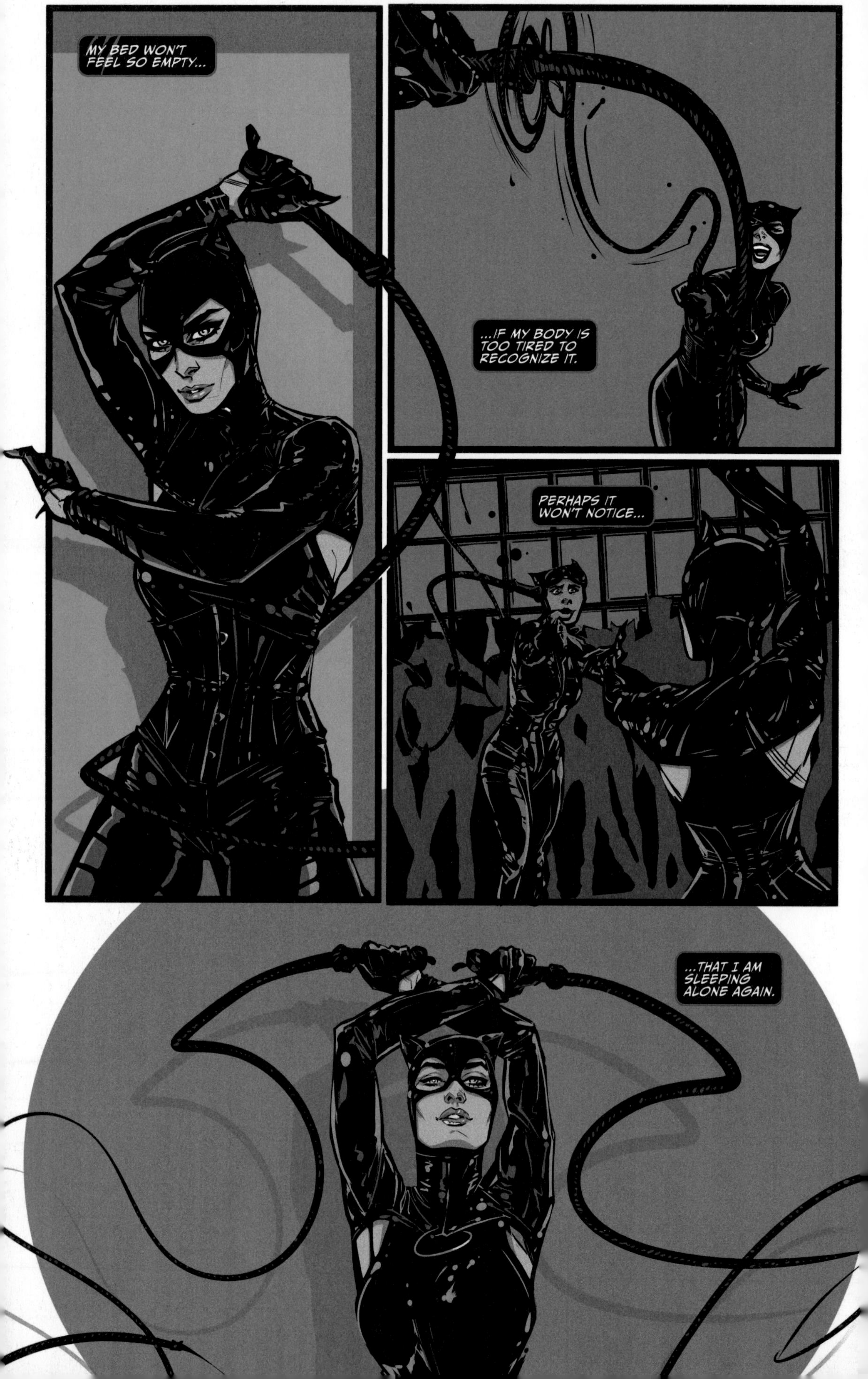
MY BED WON'T FEEL SO EMPTY...
...IF MY BODY IS TOO TIRED TO RECOGNIZE IT.
PERHAPS IT WON'T NOTICE...
...THAT I AM SLEEPING ALONE AGAIN.

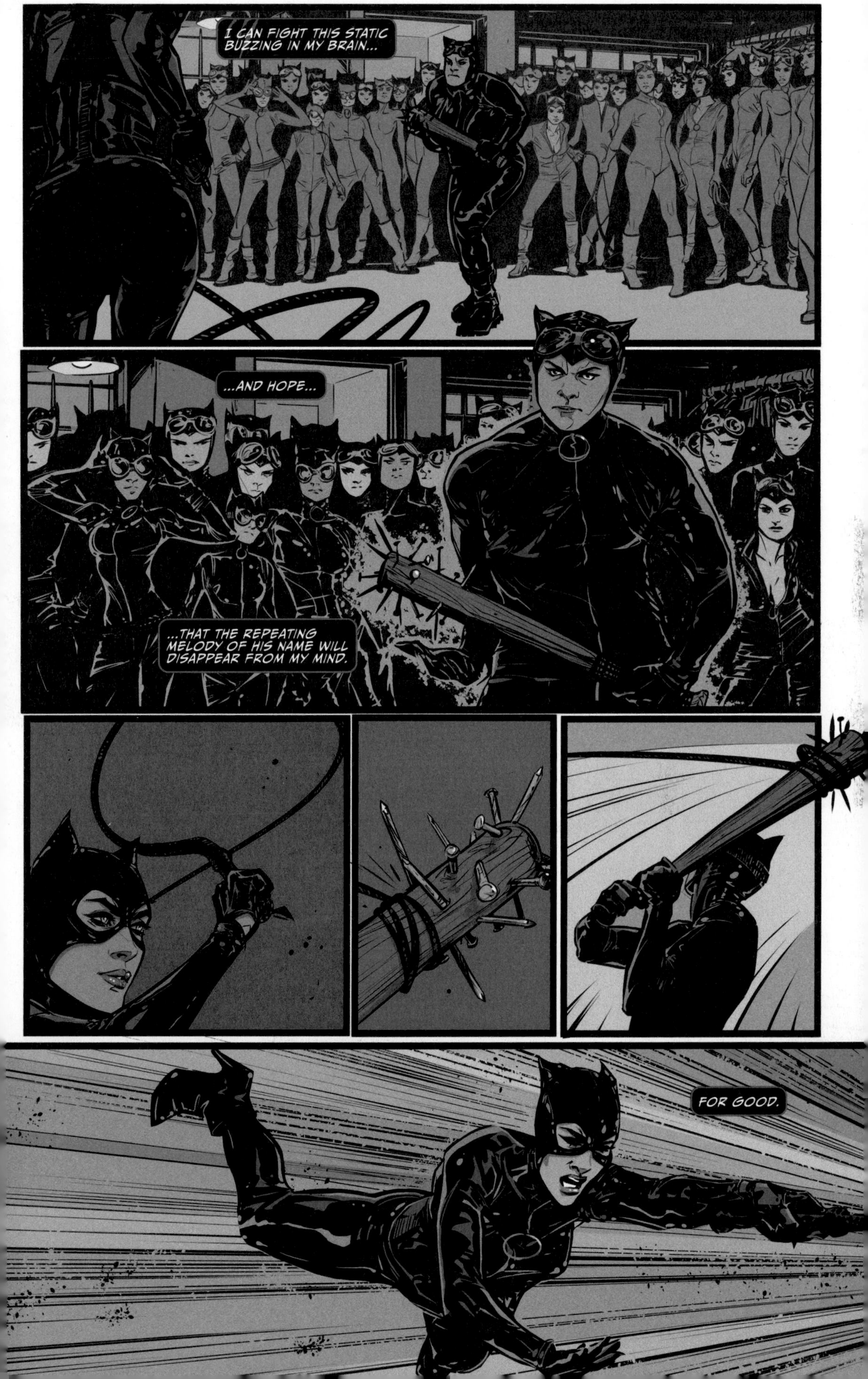
I CAN FIGHT THIS STATIC BUZZING IN MY BRAIN...
...AND HOPE...
...THAT THE REPEATING MELODY OF HIS NAME WILL DISAPPEAR FROM MY MIND.
FOR GOOD.

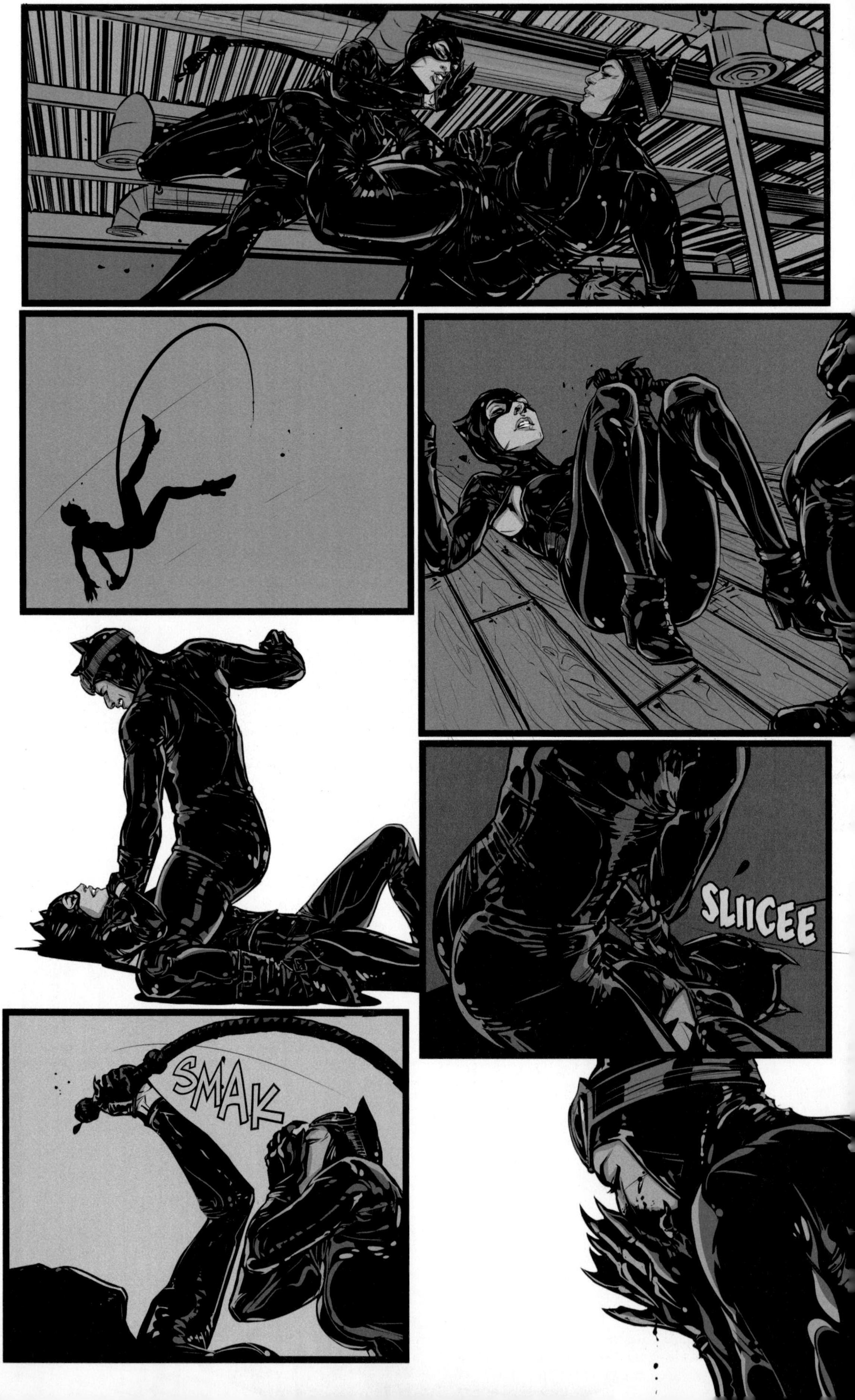
SLIICEE
SMAK

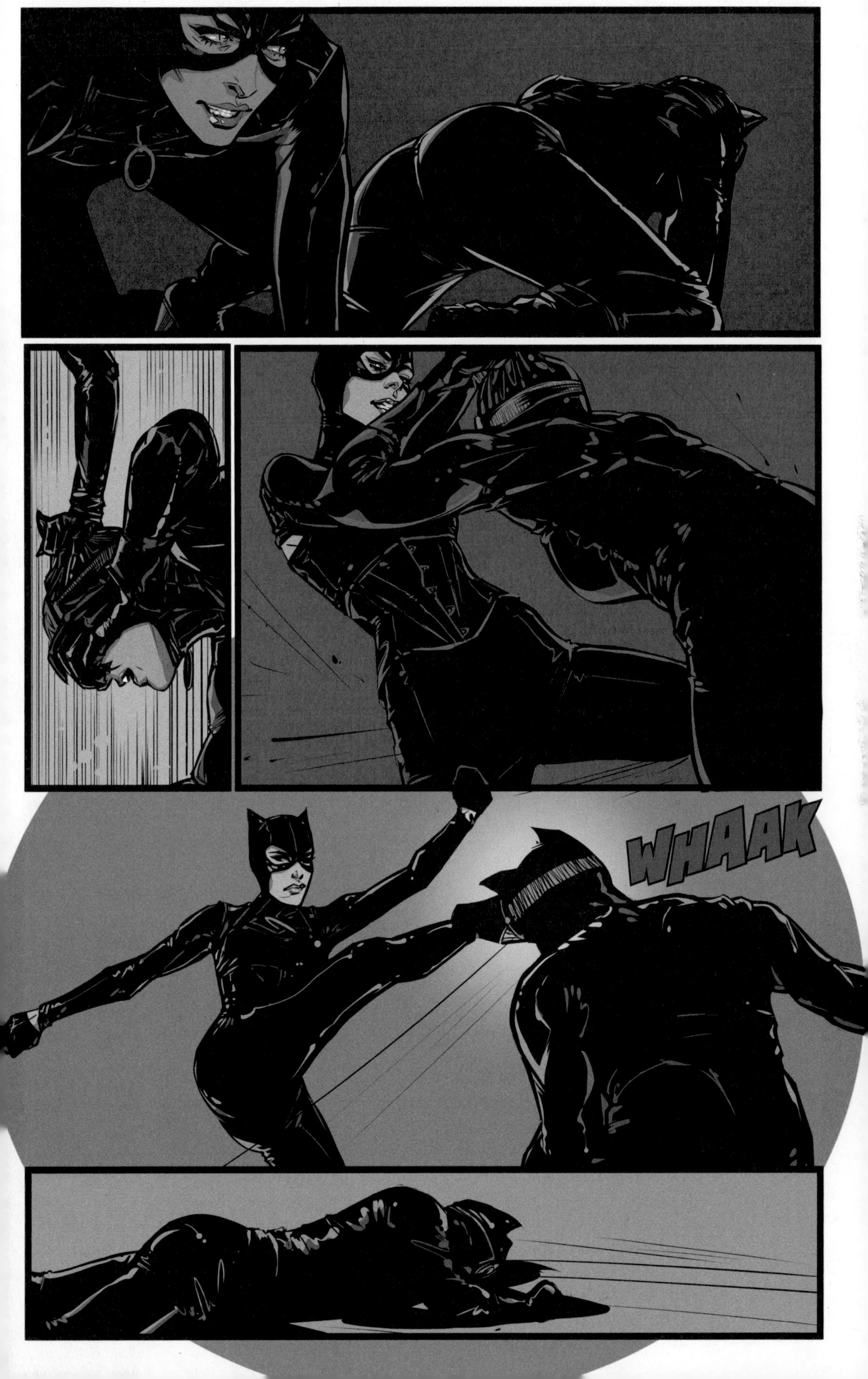
WHAAK

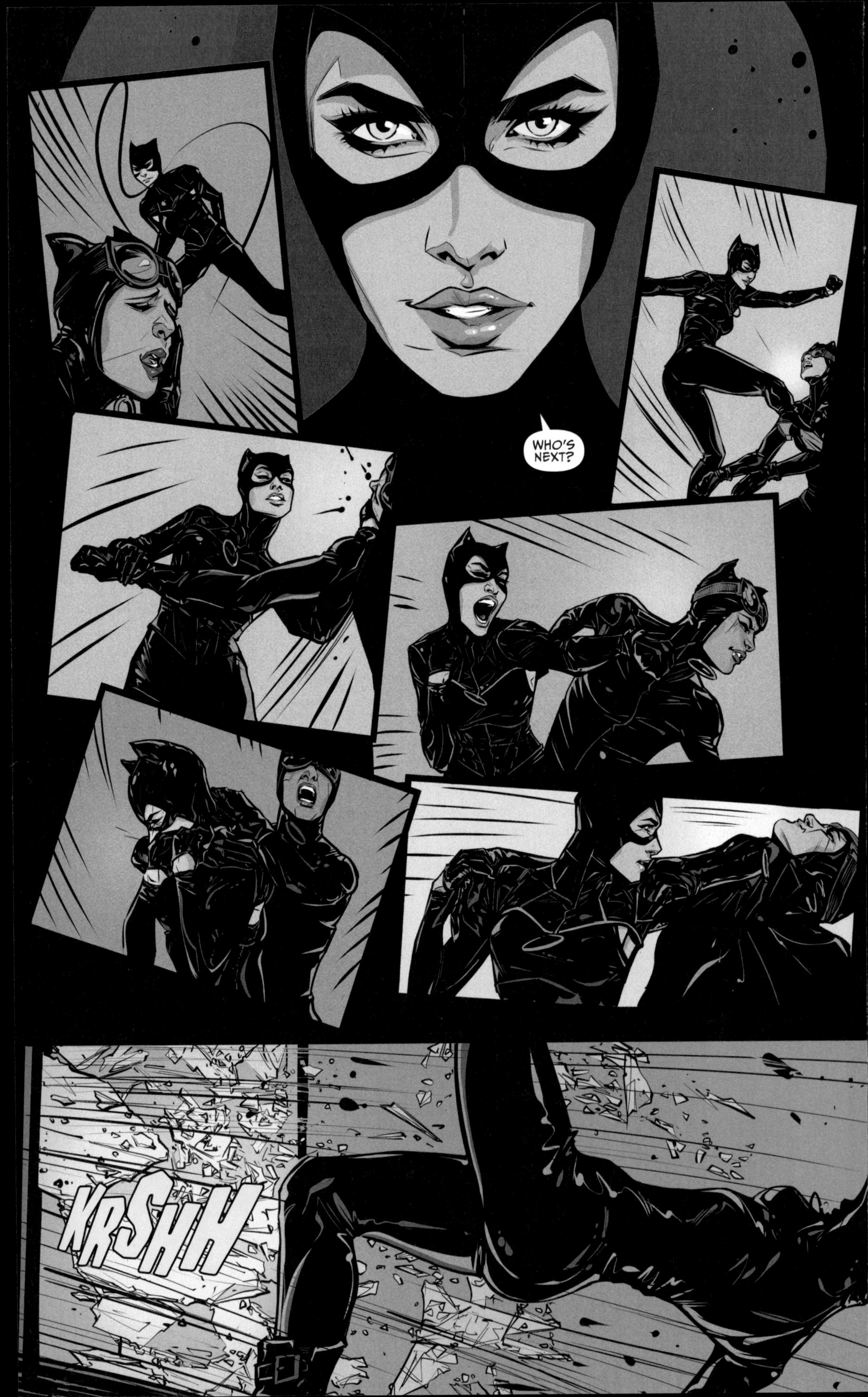
WHO'S NEXT?
KRSHH

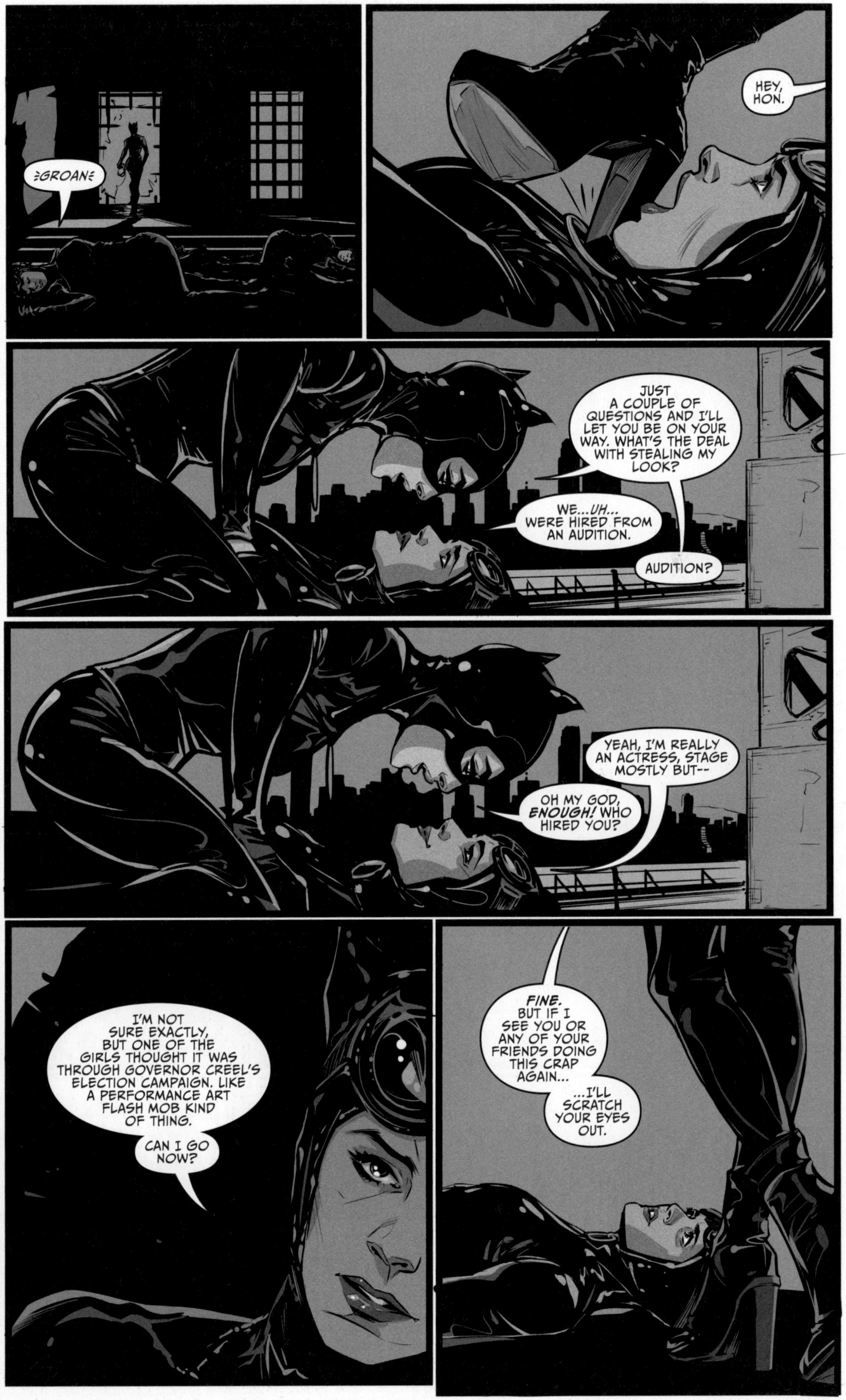
GROAN
HEY, HON.
JUST A COUPLE OF QUESTIONS AND I'LL LET YOU BE ON YOUR WAY. WHAT'S THE DEAL WITH STEALING MY LOOK?
WE...UH... WERE HIRED FROM AN AUDITION.
AUDITION?
YEAH, I'M REALLY AN ACTRESS, STAGE MOSTLY BUT--
OH MY GOD, ENOUGH! WHO HIRED YOU?
I'M NOT SURE EXACTLY, BUT ONE OF THE GIRLS THOUGHT IT WAS THROUGH GOVERNOR CREEL'S ELECTION CAMPAIGN. LIKE A PERFORMANCE ART FLASH MOB KIND OF THING.
CAN I GO NOW?
FINE. BUT IF I SEE YOU OR ANY OF YOUR FRIENDS DOING THIS CRAP AGAIN...
...I'LL SCRATCH YOUR EYES OUT.

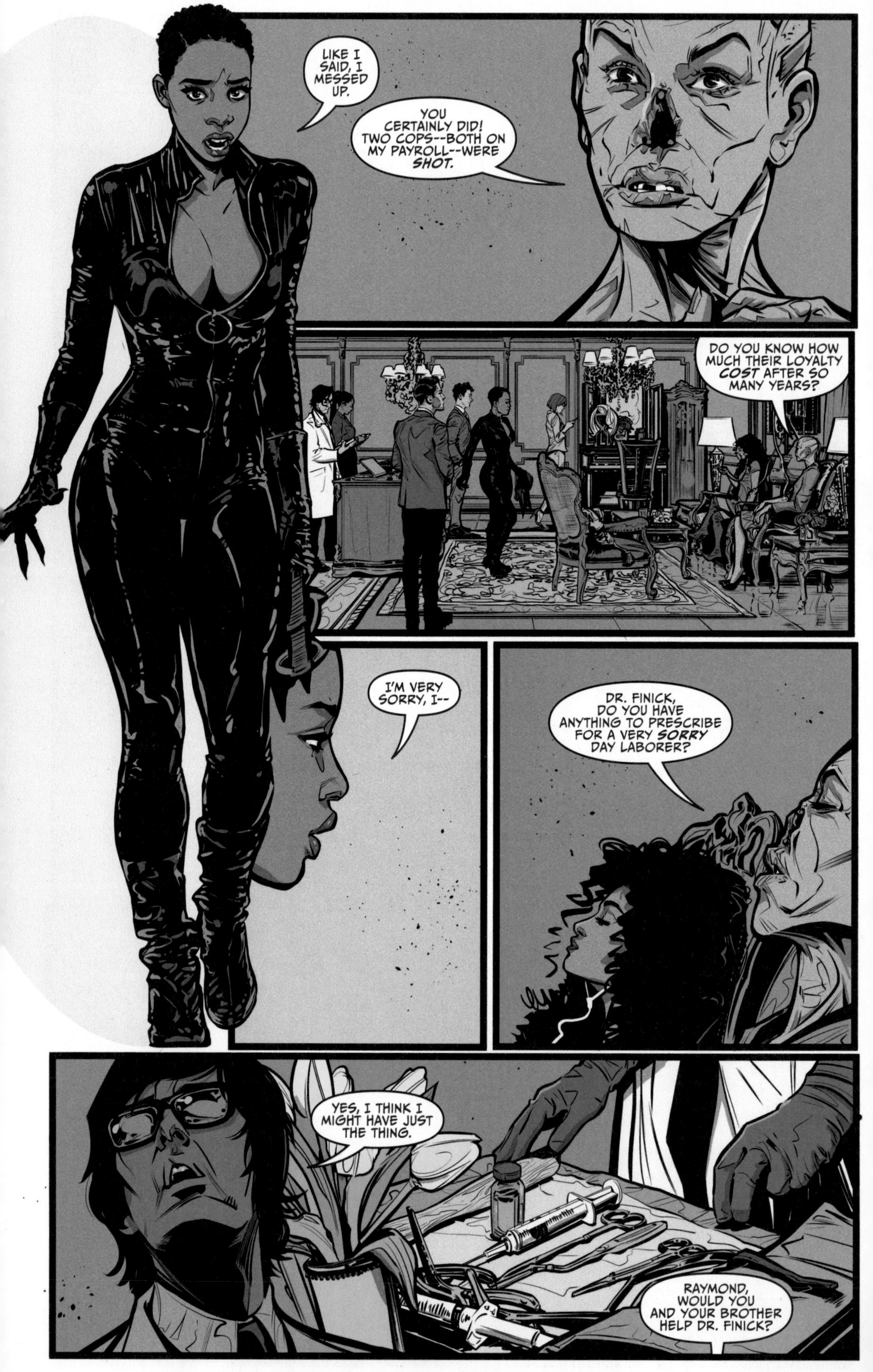
LIKE I SAID, I MESSED UP.
YOU CERTAINLY DID! TWO COPS--BOTH ON MY PAYROLL--WERE *SHOT.*
DO YOU KNOW HOW MUCH THEIR LOYALTY *COST* AFTER SO MANY YEARS?
I'M VERY SORRY, I--
DR. FINICK, DO YOU HAVE ANYTHING TO PRESCRIBE FOR A VERY *SORRY* DAY LABORER?
YES, I THINK I MIGHT HAVE JUST THE THING.
RAYMOND, WOULD YOU AND YOUR BROTHER HELP DR. FINICK?

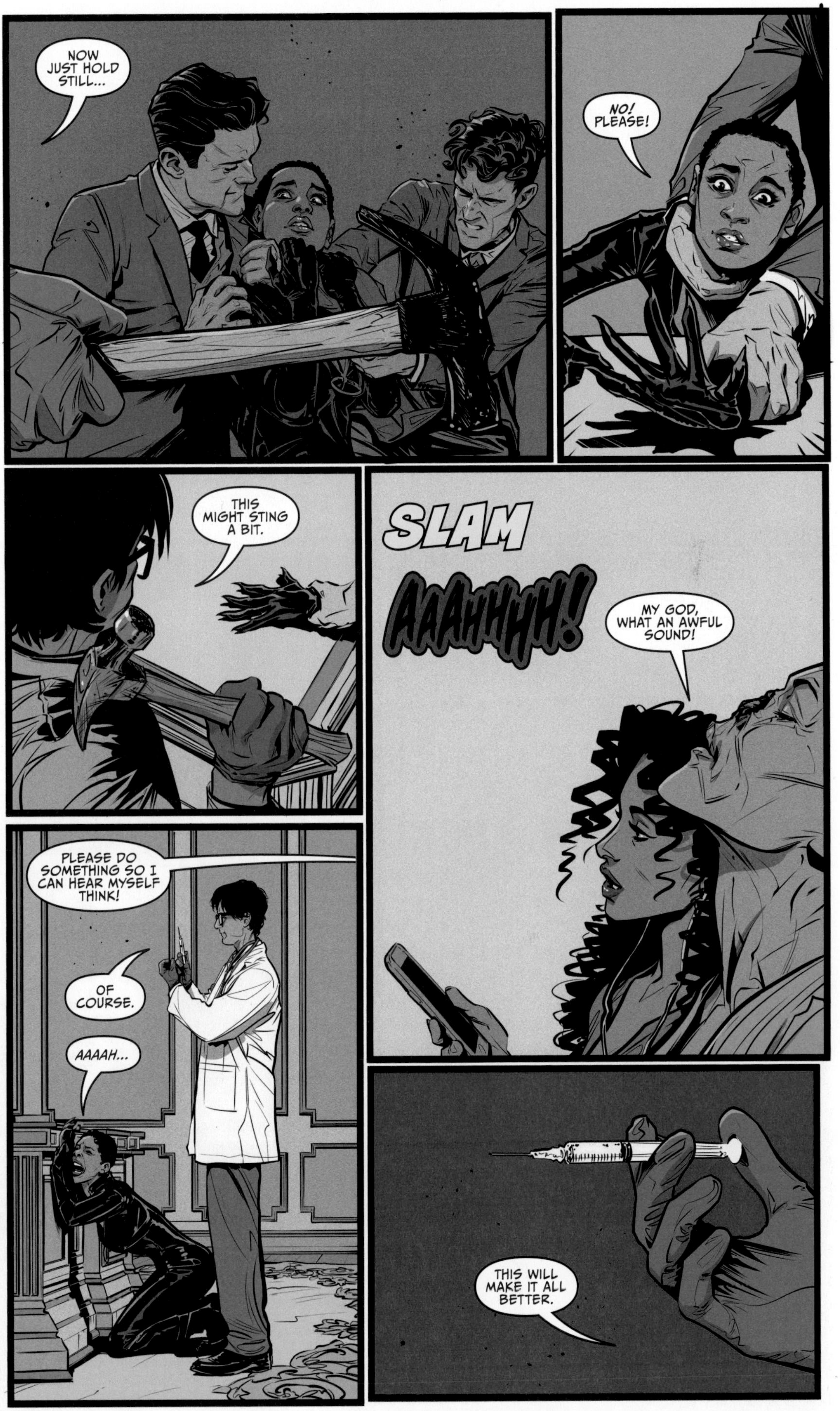
NOW JUST HOLD STILL...
NO! PLEASE!
THIS MIGHT STING A BIT.
SLAM
AAAHHHH!
MY GOD, WHAT AN AWFUL SOUND!
PLEASE DO SOMETHING SO I CAN HEAR MYSELF THINK!
OF COURSE.
AAAAH...
THIS WILL MAKE IT ALL BETTER.

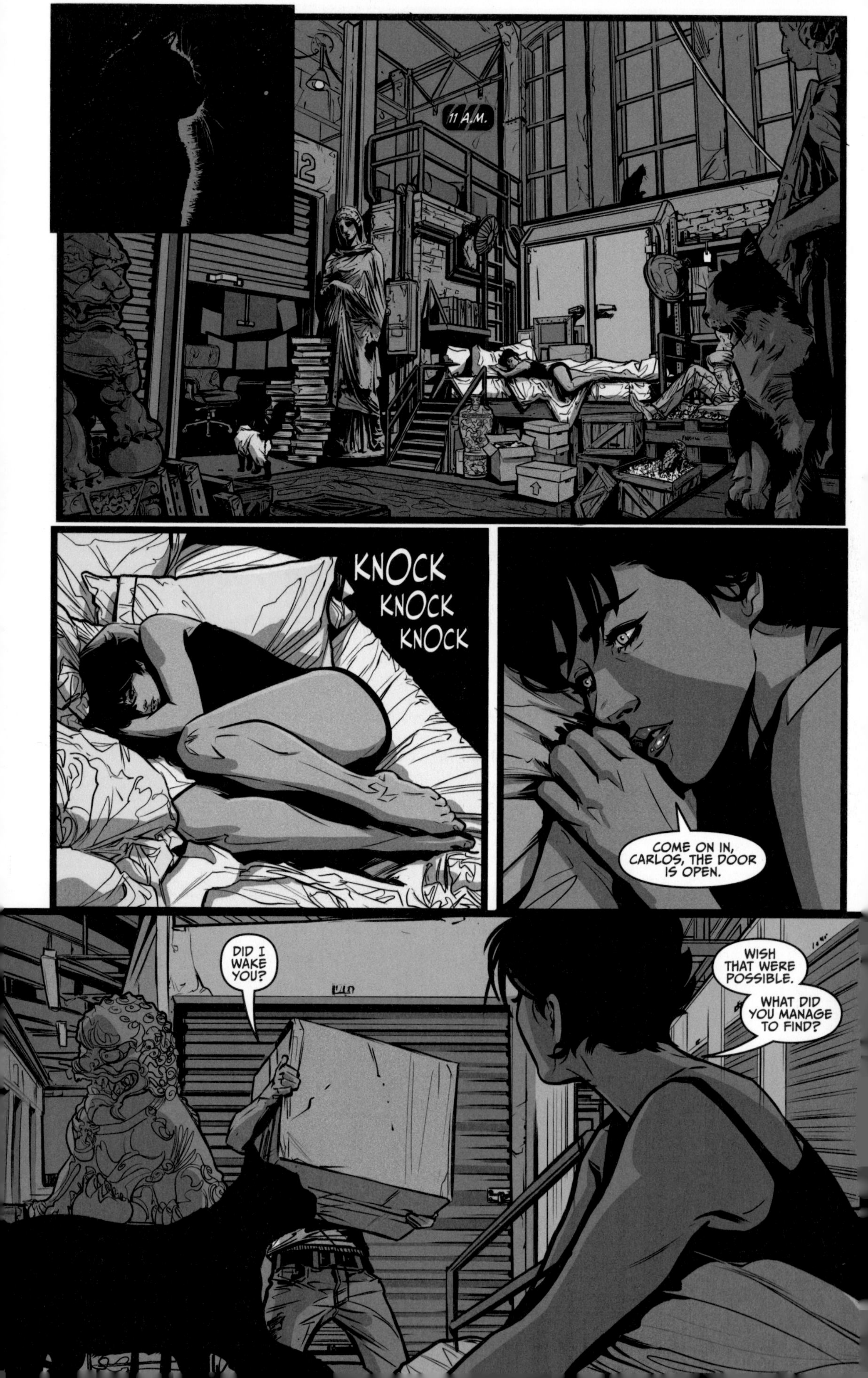
11 A.M.
KNOCK KNOCK KNOCK
COME ON IN, CARLOS, THE DOOR IS OPEN.
DID I WAKE YOU?
WISH THAT WERE POSSIBLE.
WHAT DID YOU MANAGE TO FIND?

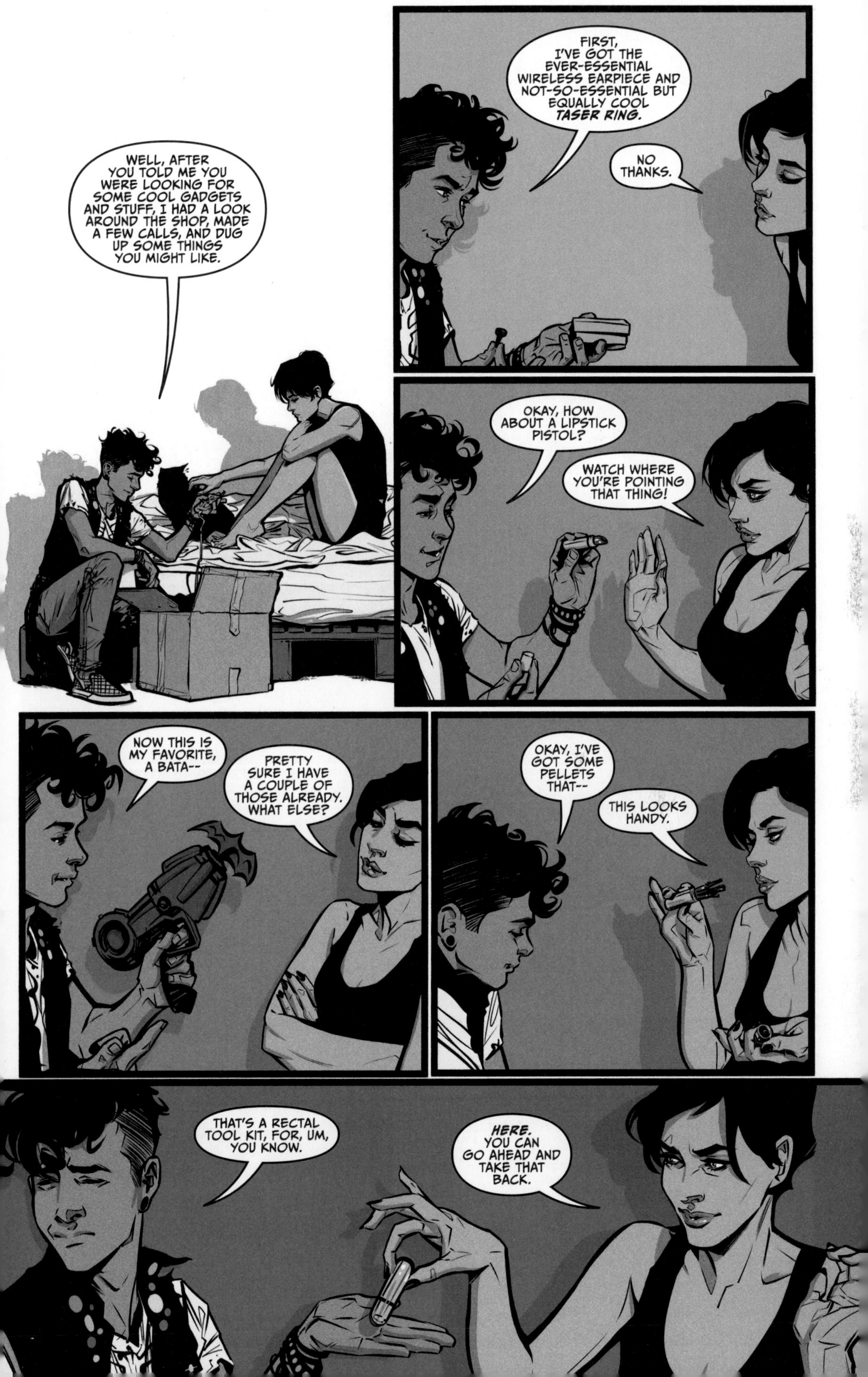
WELL, AFTER YOU TOLD ME YOU WERE LOOKING FOR SOME COOL GADGETS AND STUFF, I HAD A LOOK AROUND THE SHOP, MADE A FEW CALLS, AND DUG UP SOME THINGS YOU MIGHT LIKE.
FIRST, I'VE GOT THE EVER-ESSENTIAL WIRELESS EARPIECE AND NOT-SO-ESSENTIAL BUT EQUALLY COOL ***TASER RING.***
NO THANKS.
OKAY, HOW ABOUT A LIPSTICK PISTOL?
WATCH WHERE YOU'RE POINTING THAT THING!
NOW THIS IS MY FAVORITE, A BATA--
PRETTY SURE I HAVE A COUPLE OF THOSE ALREADY. WHAT ELSE?
OKAY, I'VE GOT SOME PELLETS THAT--
THIS LOOKS HANDY.
THAT'S A RECTAL TOOL KIT, FOR, UM, YOU KNOW.
HERE. YOU CAN GO AHEAD AND TAKE THAT BACK.

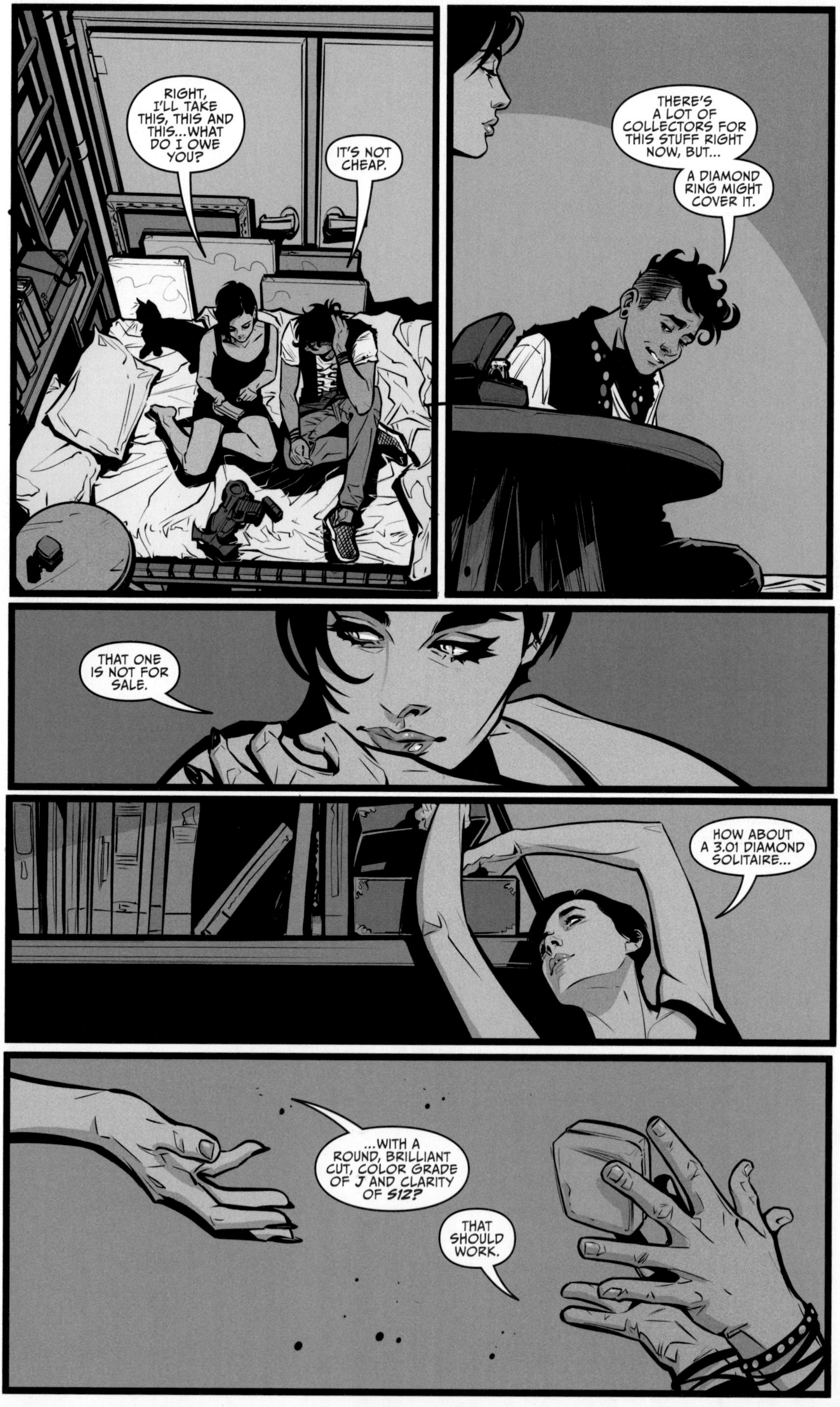
RIGHT, I'LL TAKE THIS, THIS AND THIS...WHAT DO I OWE YOU?
IT'S NOT CHEAP.
THERE'S A LOT OF COLLECTORS FOR THIS STUFF RIGHT NOW, BUT...
A DIAMOND RING MIGHT COVER IT.
THAT ONE IS NOT FOR SALE.
HOW ABOUT A 3.01 DIAMOND SOLITAIRE...
...WITH A ROUND, BRILLIANT CUT, COLOR GRADE OF J AND CLARITY OF SI2?
THAT SHOULD WORK.

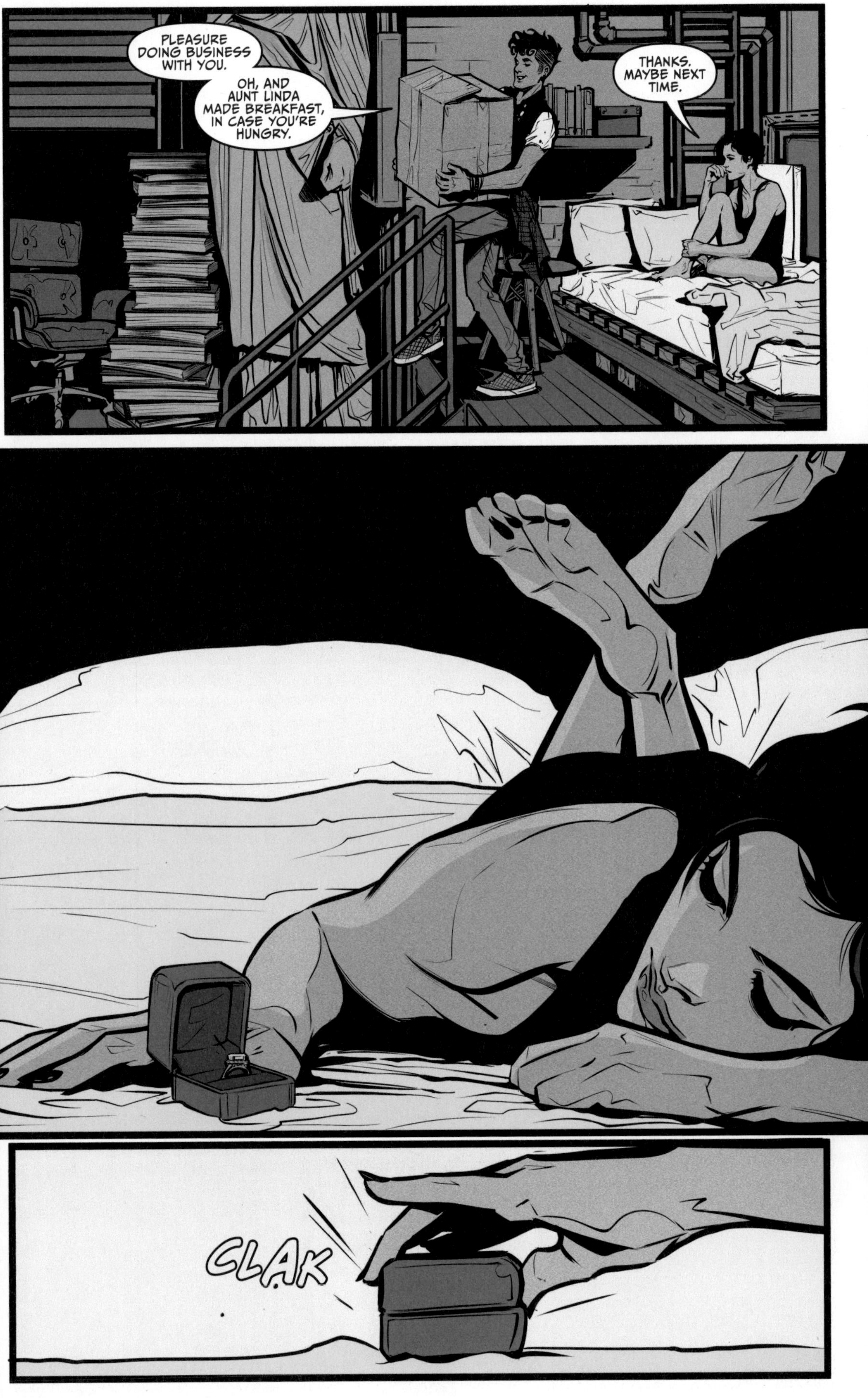
PLEASURE DOING BUSINESS WITH YOU.
OH, AND AUNT LINDA MADE BREAKFAST, IN CASE YOU'RE HUNGRY.
THANKS. MAYBE NEXT TIME.
CLAK

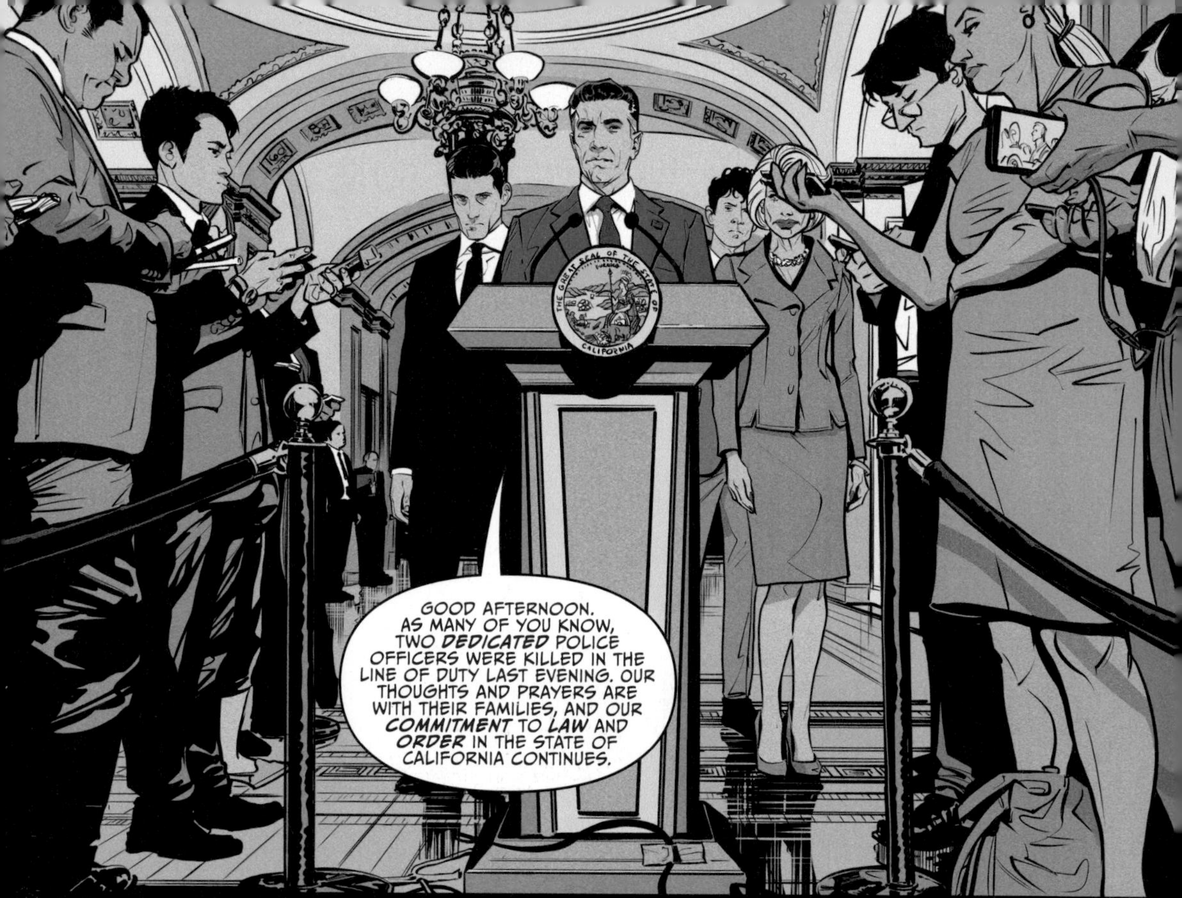
GOOD AFTERNOON. AS MANY OF YOU KNOW, TWO DEDICATED POLICE OFFICERS WERE KILLED IN THE LINE OF DUTY LAST EVENING. OUR THOUGHTS AND PRAYERS ARE WITH THEIR FAMILIES, AND OUR COMMITMENT TO LAW AND ORDER IN THE STATE OF CALIFORNIA CONTINUES.

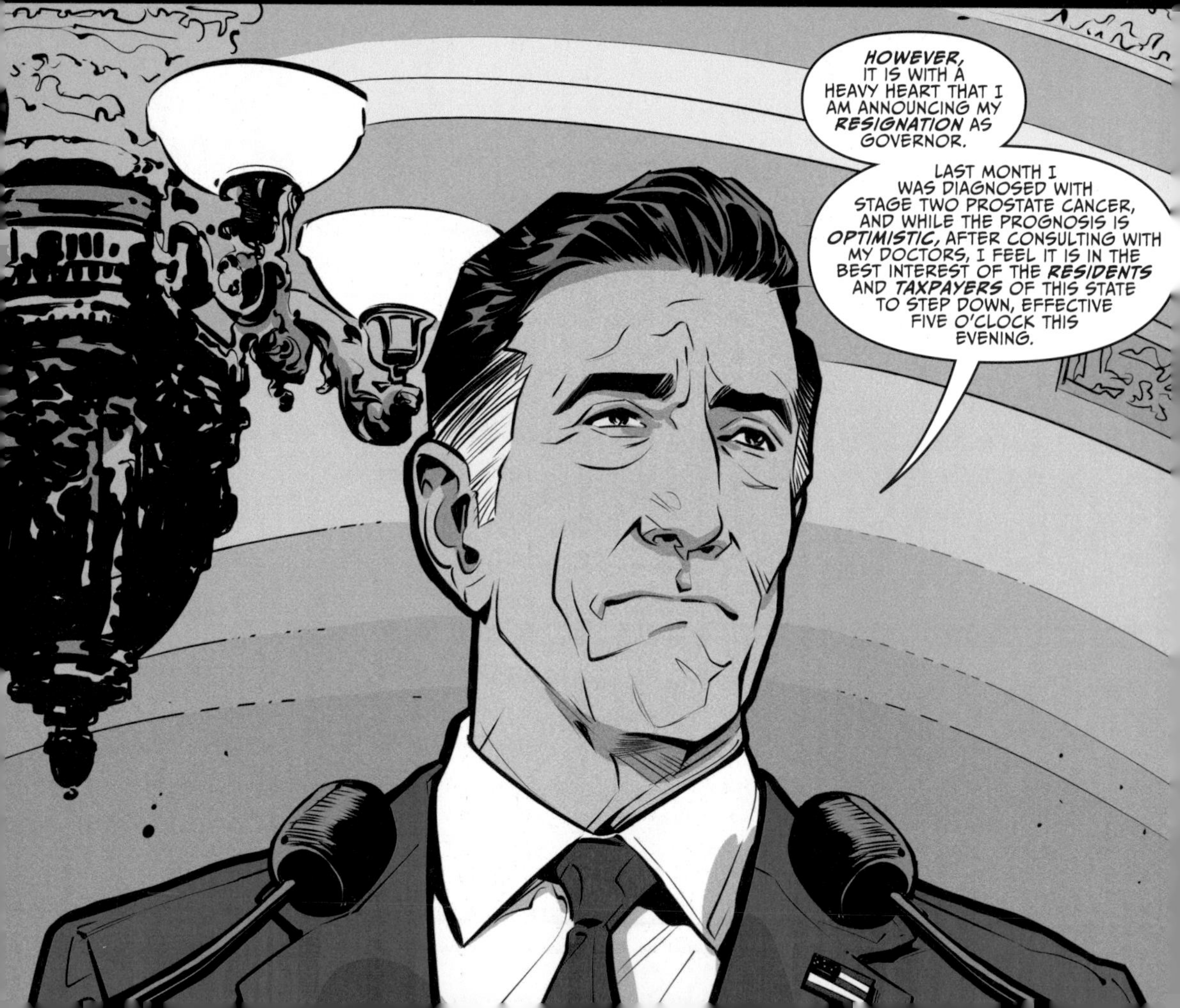
HOWEVER, IT IS WITH A HEAVY HEART THAT I AM ANNOUNCING MY RESIGNATION AS GOVERNOR.
LAST MONTH I WAS DIAGNOSED WITH STAGE TWO PROSTATE CANCER, AND WHILE THE PROGNOSIS IS OPTIMISTIC, AFTER CONSULTING WITH MY DOCTORS, I FEEL IT IS IN THE BEST INTEREST OF THE RESIDENTS AND TAXPAYERS OF THIS STATE TO STEP DOWN, EFFECTIVE FIVE O'CLOCK THIS EVENING.

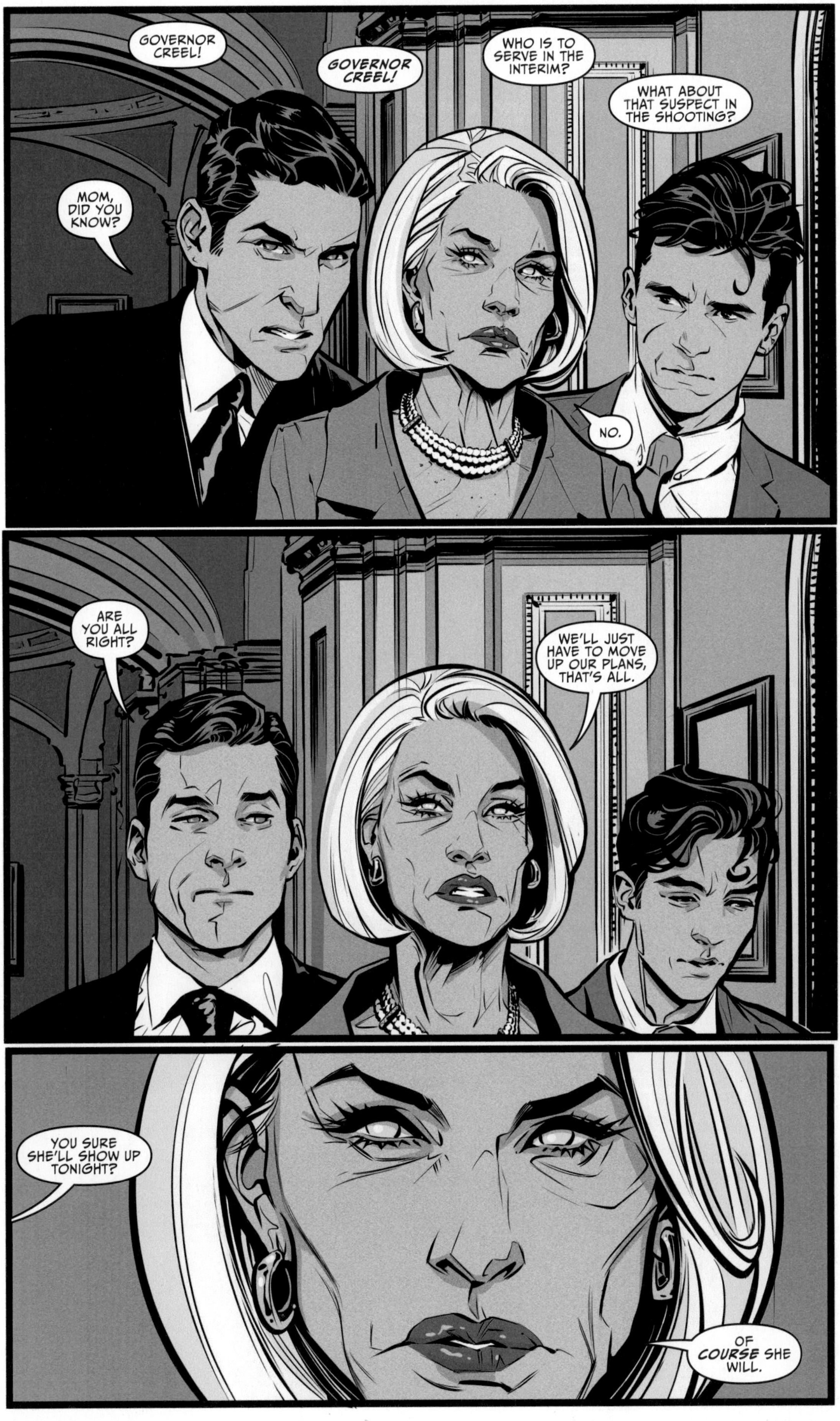
GOVERNOR CREEL!
GOVERNOR CREEL!
WHO IS TO SERVE IN THE INTERIM?
WHAT ABOUT THAT SUSPECT IN THE SHOOTING?
MOM, DID YOU KNOW?
NO.
ARE YOU ALL RIGHT?
WE'LL JUST HAVE TO MOVE UP OUR PLANS, THAT'S ALL.
YOU SURE SHE'LL SHOW UP TONIGHT?
OF COURSE SHE WILL.

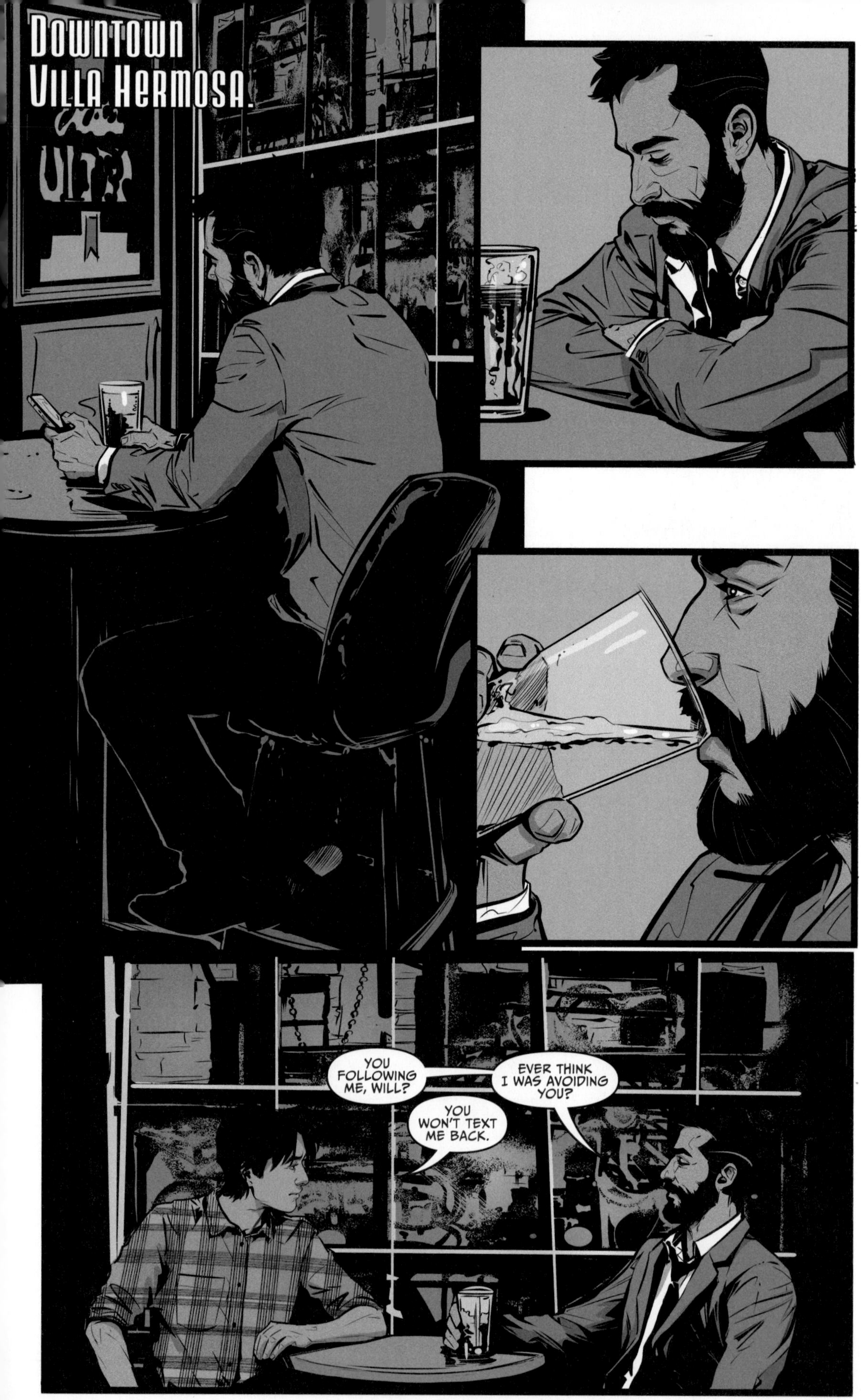
DOWNTOWN VILLA HERMOSA.
ULTRA
YOU FOLLOWING ME, WILL?
EVER THINK I WAS AVOIDING YOU?
YOU WON'T TEXT ME BACK.

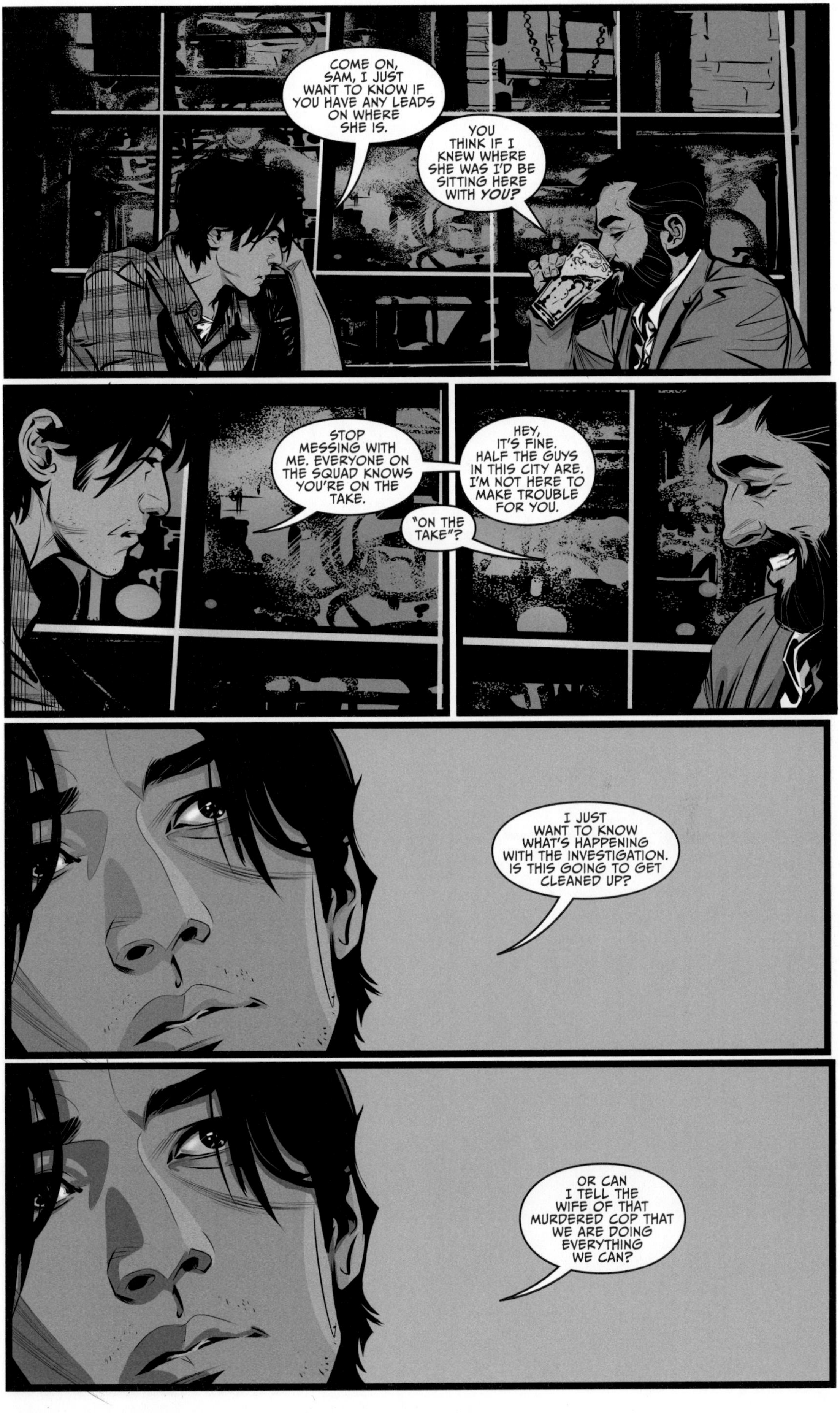
COME ON, SAM, I JUST WANT TO KNOW IF YOU HAVE ANY LEADS ON WHERE SHE IS.
YOU THINK IF I KNEW WHERE SHE WAS I'D BE SITTING HERE WITH YOU?
STOP MESSING WITH ME. EVERYONE ON THE SQUAD KNOWS YOU'RE ON THE TAKE.
"ON THE TAKE"?
HEY, IT'S FINE. HALF THE GUYS IN THIS CITY ARE. I'M NOT HERE TO MAKE TROUBLE FOR YOU.
I JUST WANT TO KNOW WHAT'S HAPPENING WITH THE INVESTIGATION. IS THIS GOING TO GET CLEANED UP?
OR CAN I TELL THE WIFE OF THAT MURDERED COP THAT WE ARE DOING EVERYTHING WE CAN?

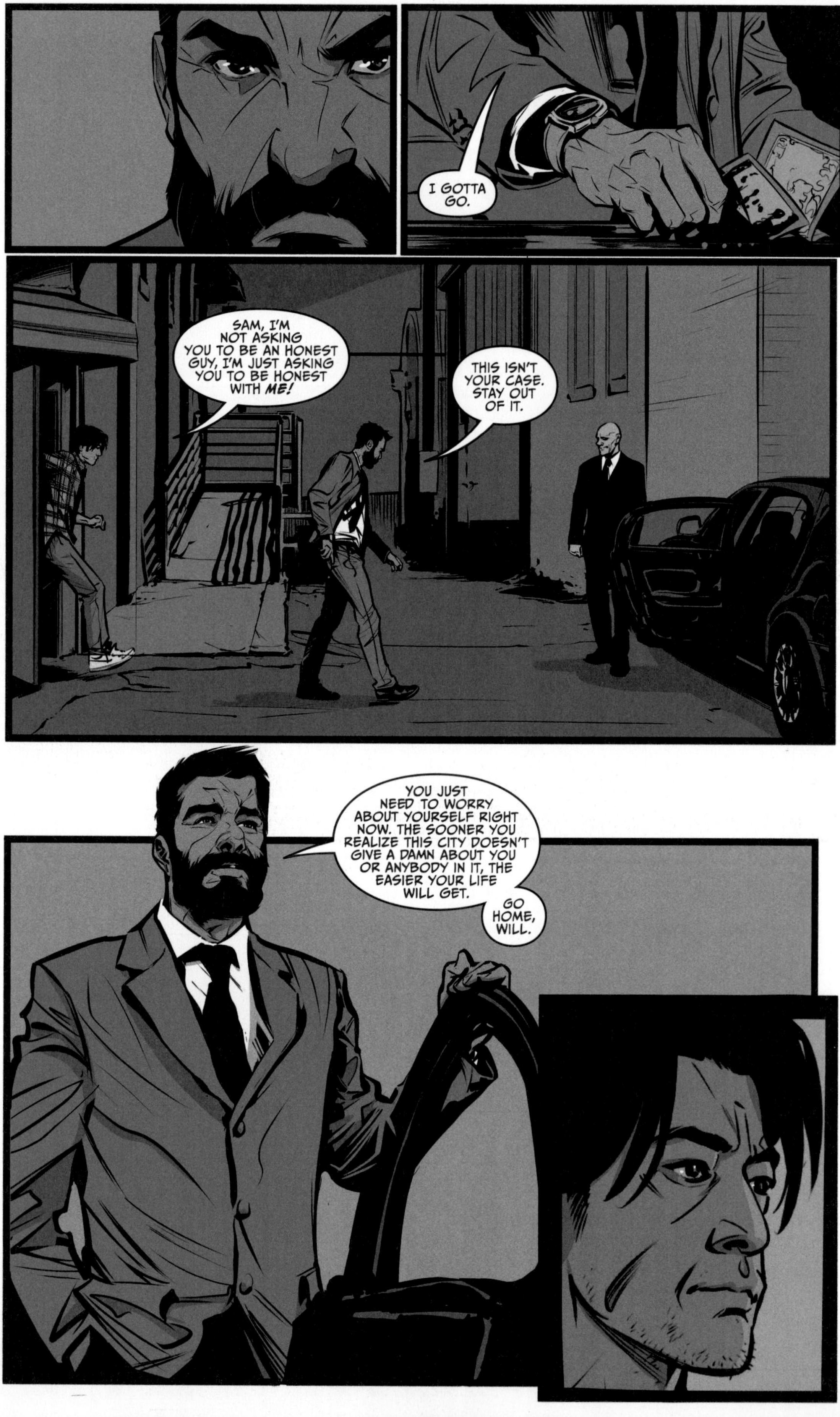
I GOTTA GO.
SAM, I'M NOT ASKING YOU TO BE AN HONEST GUY, I'M JUST ASKING YOU TO BE HONEST WITH *ME!*
THIS ISN'T YOUR CASE. STAY OUT OF IT.
YOU JUST NEED TO WORRY ABOUT YOURSELF RIGHT NOW. THE SOONER YOU REALIZE THIS CITY DOESN'T GIVE A DAMN ABOUT YOU OR ANYBODY IN IT, THE EASIER YOUR LIFE WILL GET.
GO HOME, WILL.

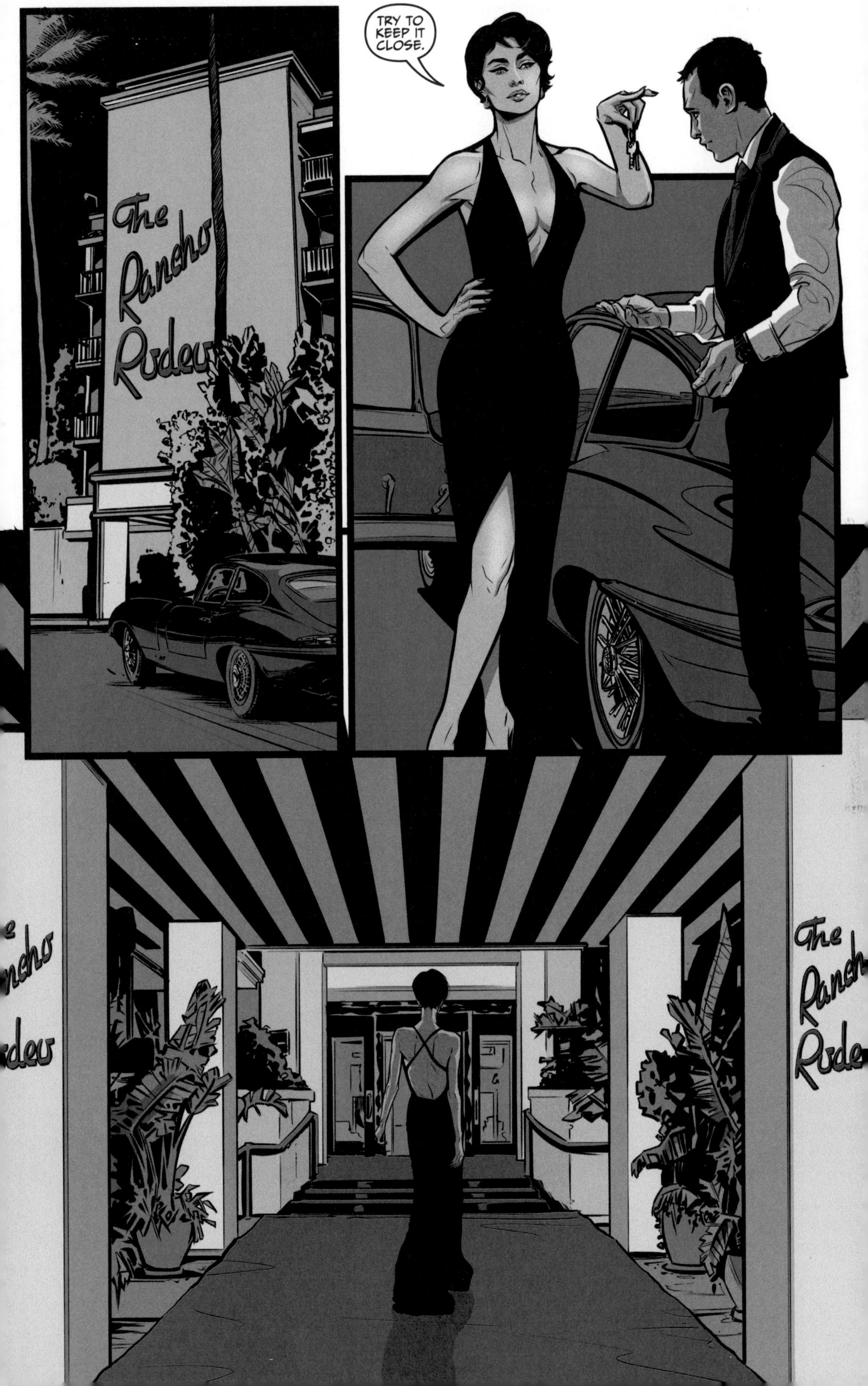
The Rancho Rodeo
TRY TO KEEP IT CLOSE.
The Rancho Rodeo

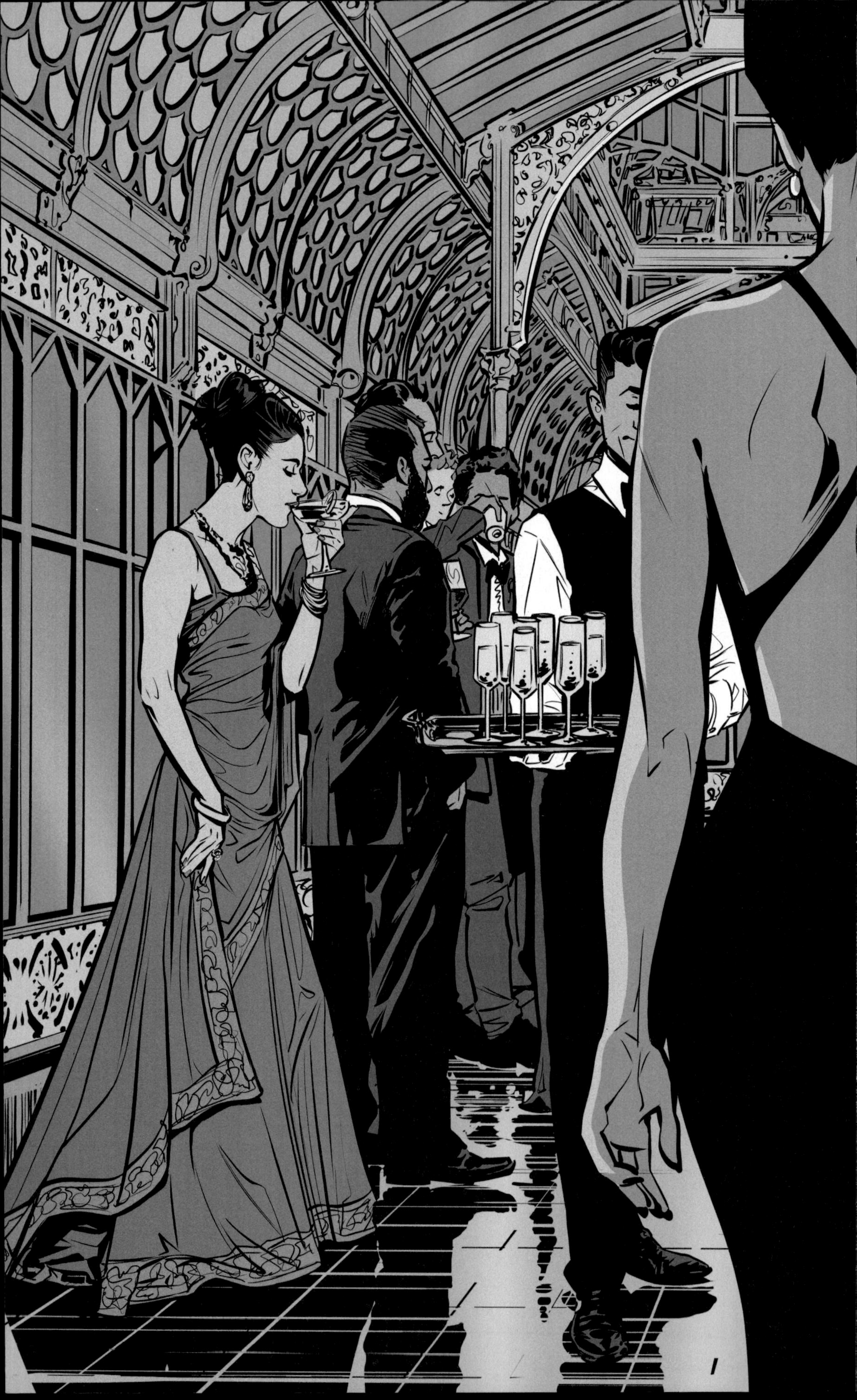

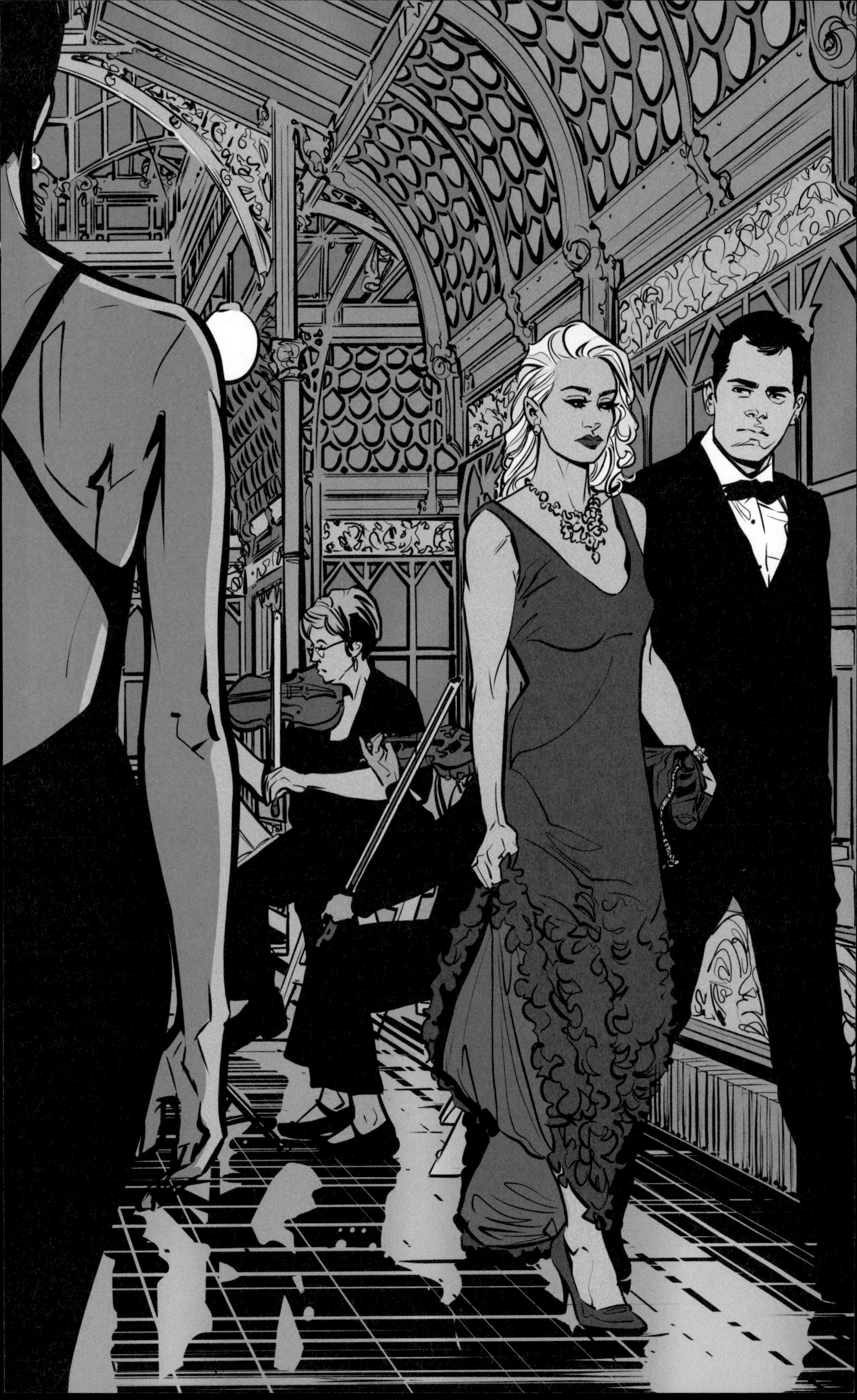

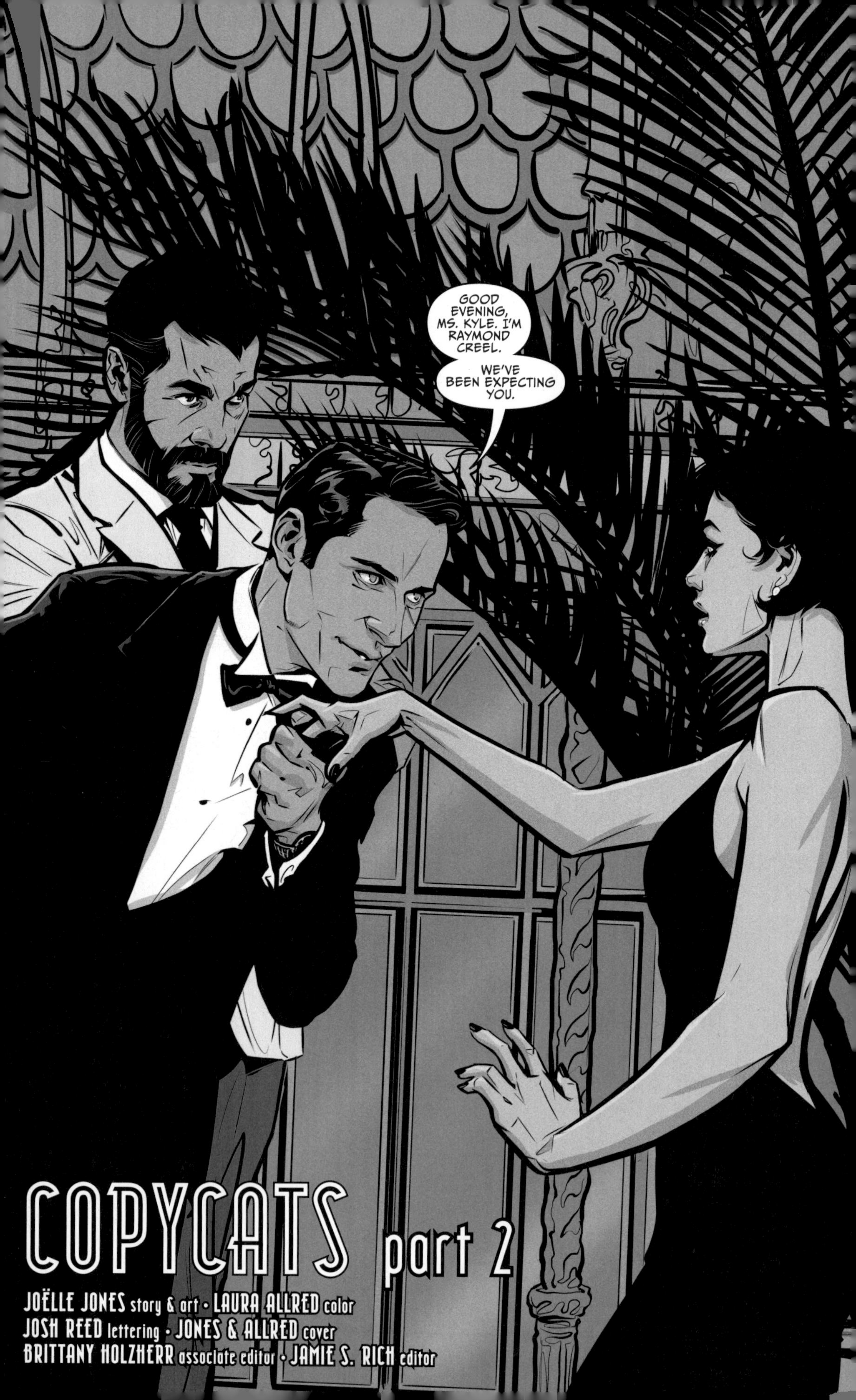
GOOD EVENING, MS. KYLE. I'M RAYMOND CREEL.
WE'VE BEEN EXPECTING YOU.
COPYCATS part 2
JOËLLE JONES story & art • LAURA ALLRED color
JOSH REED lettering • JONES & ALLRED cover
BRITTANY HOLZHERR associate editor • JAMIE S. RICH editor

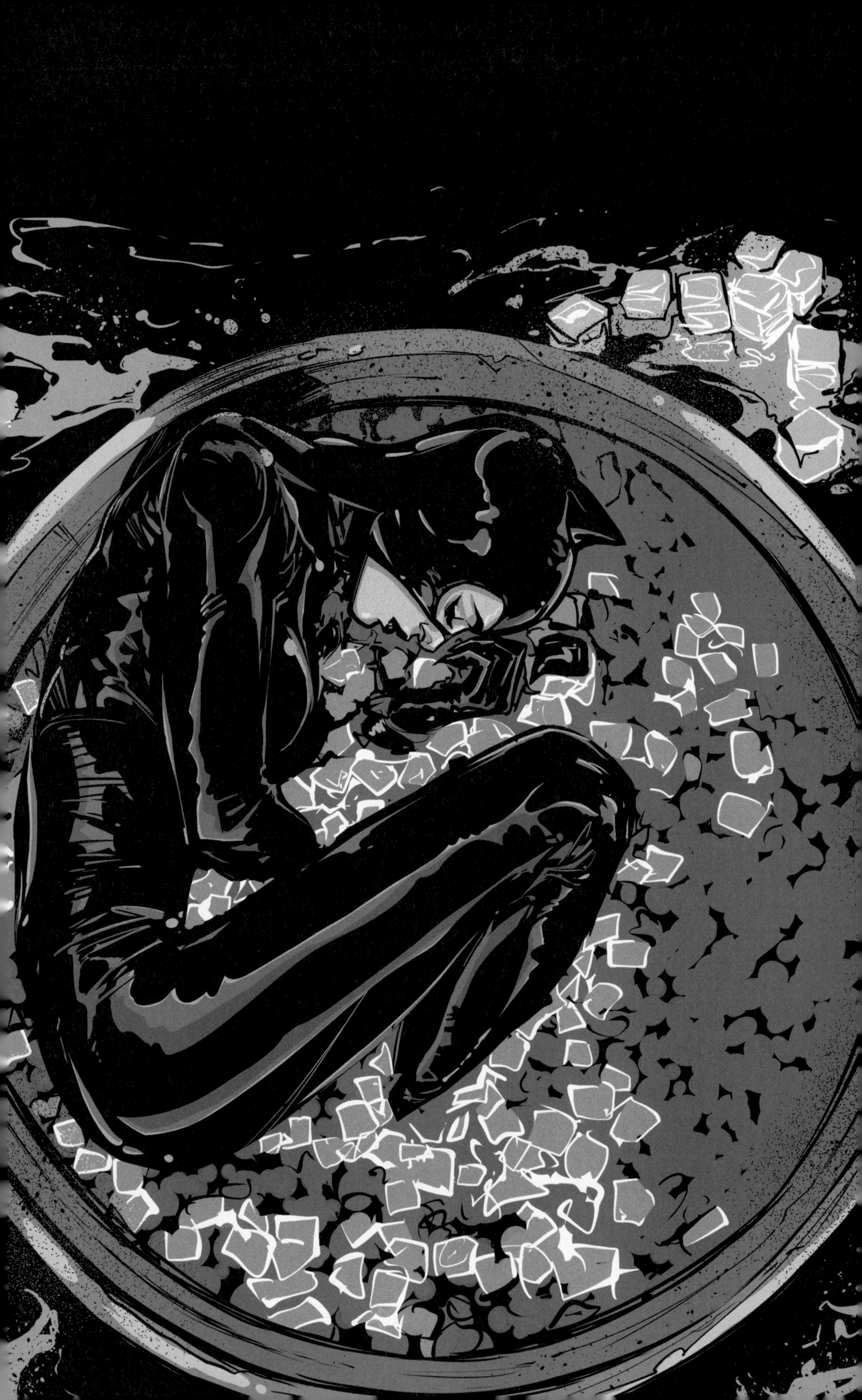

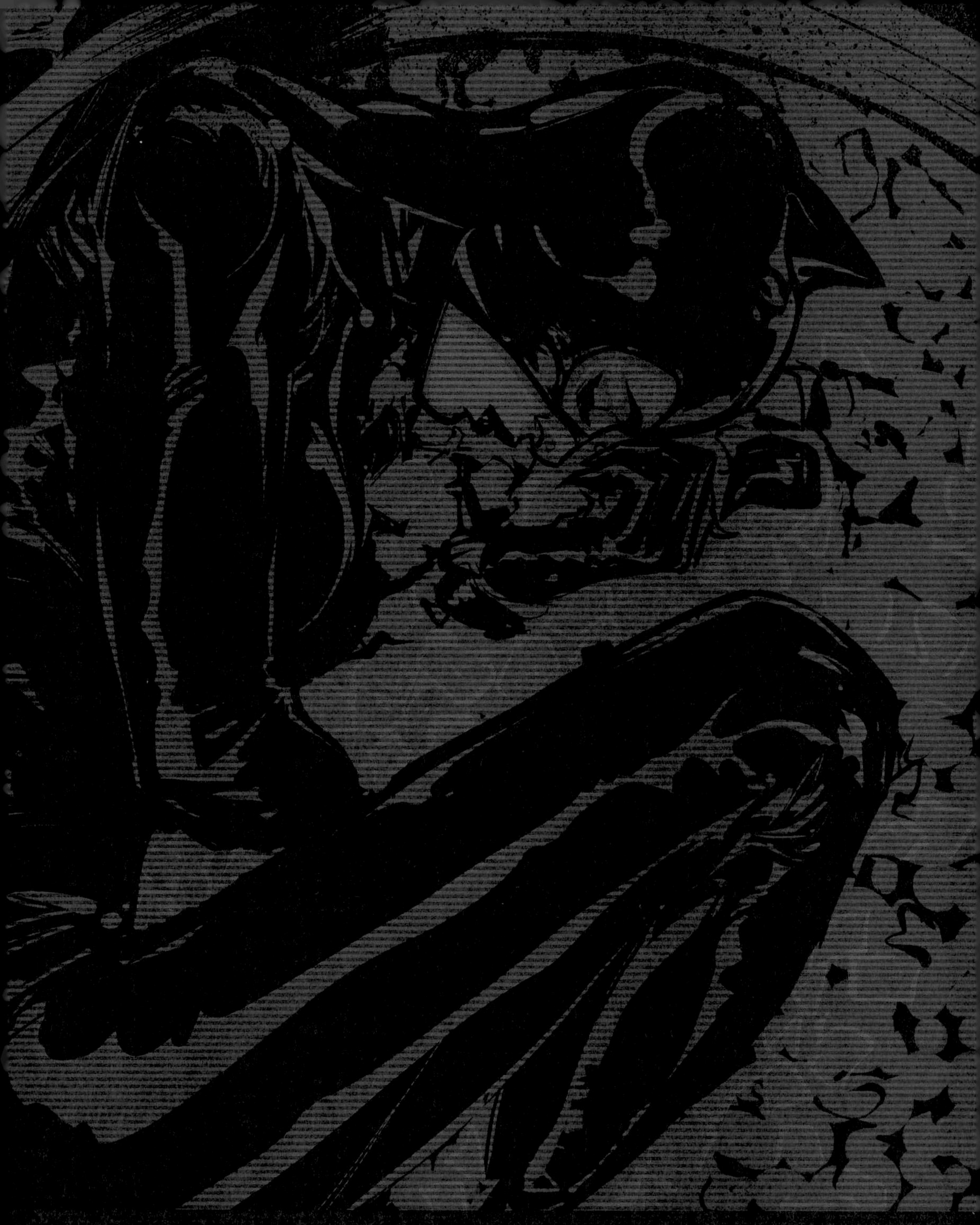

CATWOMAN

#3

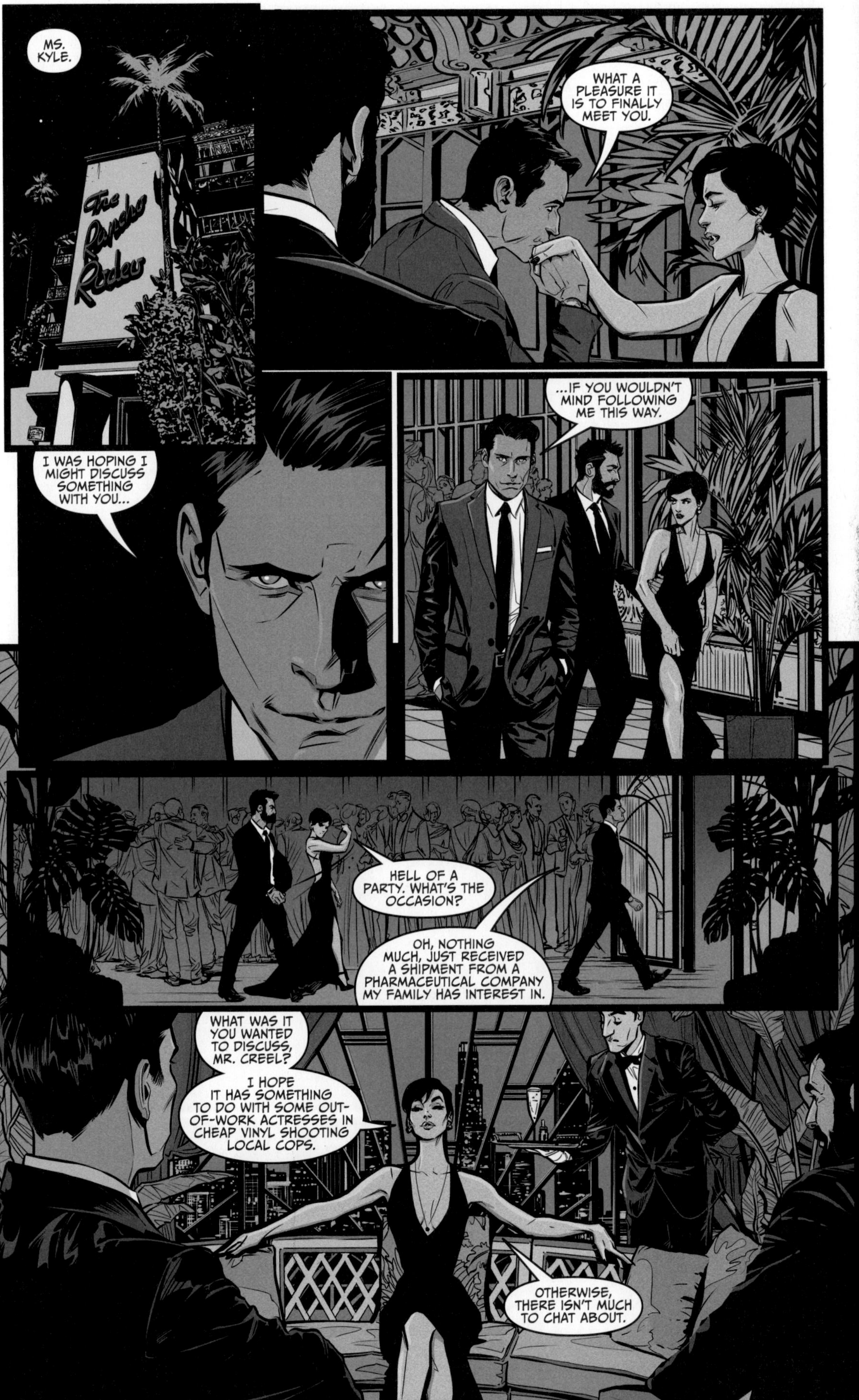

MS. KYLE.
WHAT A PLEASURE IT IS TO FINALLY MEET YOU.
I WAS HOPING I MIGHT DISCUSS SOMETHING WITH YOU...
...IF YOU WOULDN'T MIND FOLLOWING ME THIS WAY.
HELL OF A PARTY. WHAT'S THE OCCASION?
OH, NOTHING MUCH, JUST RECEIVED A SHIPMENT FROM A PHARMACEUTICAL COMPANY MY FAMILY HAS INTEREST IN.
WHAT WAS IT YOU WANTED TO DISCUSS, MR. CREEL?
I HOPE IT HAS SOMETHING TO DO WITH SOME OUT-OF-WORK ACTRESSES IN CHEAP VINYL SHOOTING LOCAL COPS.
OTHERWISE, THERE ISN'T MUCH TO CHAT ABOUT.

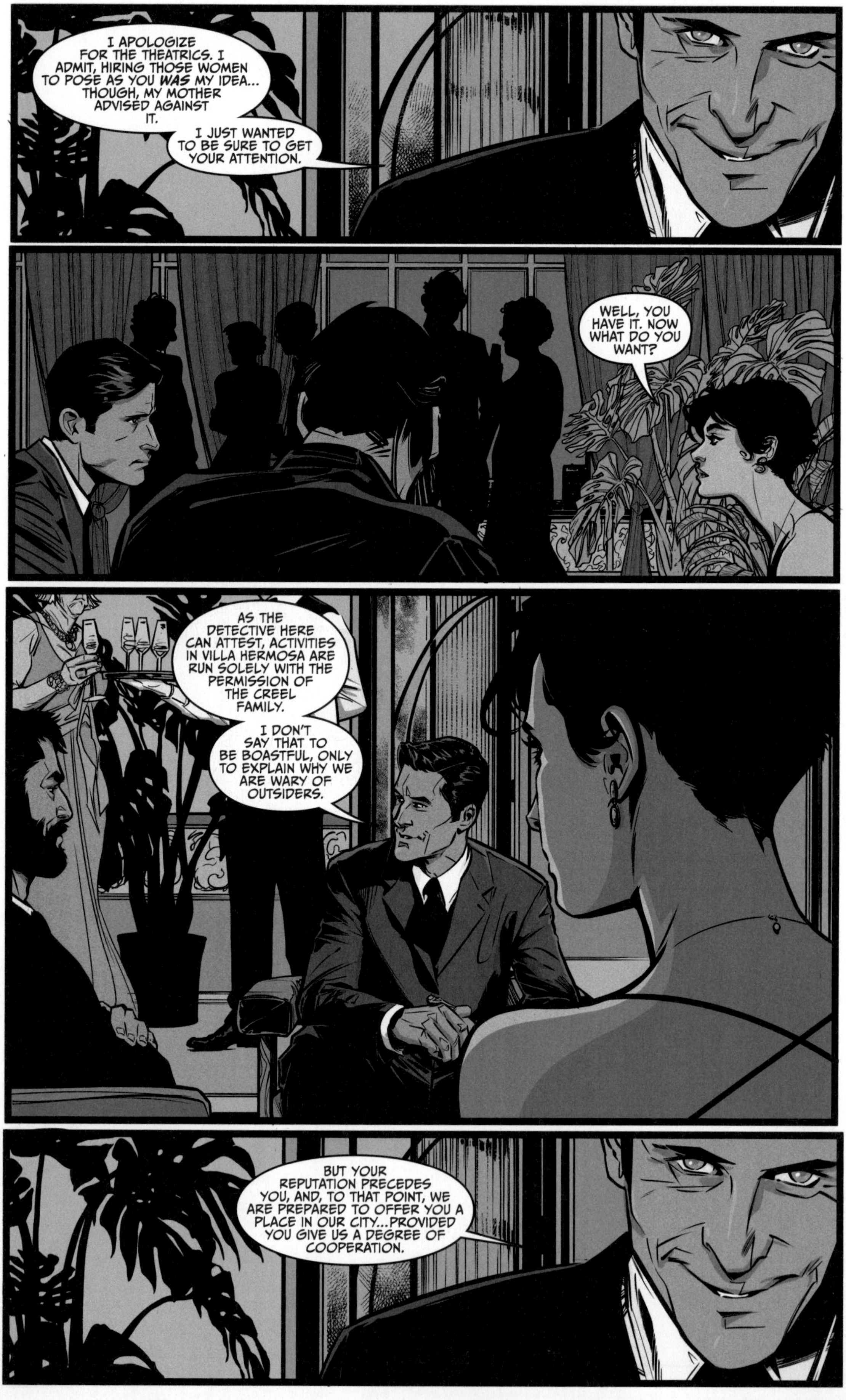
I APOLOGIZE FOR THE THEATRICS. I ADMIT, HIRING THOSE WOMEN TO POSE AS YOU *WAS* MY IDEA... THOUGH, MY MOTHER ADVISED AGAINST IT.
I JUST WANTED TO BE SURE TO GET YOUR ATTENTION.
WELL, YOU HAVE IT. NOW WHAT DO YOU WANT?
AS THE DETECTIVE HERE CAN ATTEST, ACTIVITIES IN VILLA HERMOSA ARE RUN SOLELY WITH THE PERMISSION OF THE CREEL FAMILY.
I DON'T SAY THAT TO BE BOASTFUL, ONLY TO EXPLAIN WHY WE ARE WARY OF OUTSIDERS.
BUT YOUR REPUTATION PRECEDES YOU, AND, TO THAT POINT, WE ARE PREPARED TO OFFER YOU A PLACE IN OUR CITY...PROVIDED YOU GIVE US A DEGREE OF COOPERATION.

COPYCATS part 3

JOËLLE JONES story & art (P.1-8, 14-22) FERNANDO BLANCO art (P.9-13)
LAURA ALLRED color (P 1-8 14-22) JOHN KALISZ color (P 9-13)
JOSH REED lettering JONES & ALLRED cover
BRITTANY HOLZHERR associate editor JAMIE S. RICH editor

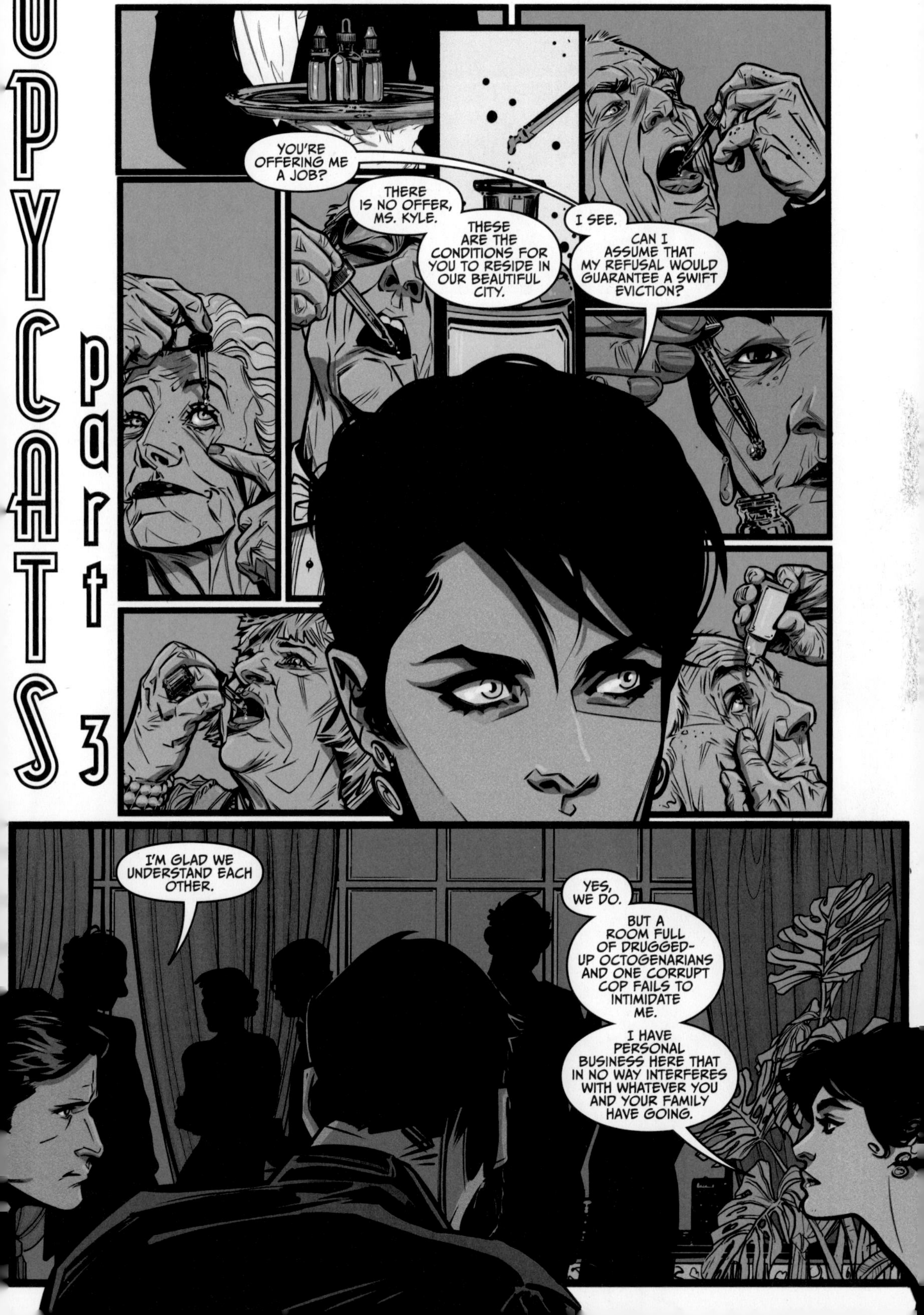
YOU'RE OFFERING ME A JOB?
THERE IS NO OFFER, MS. KYLE.
THESE ARE THE CONDITIONS FOR YOU TO RESIDE IN OUR BEAUTIFUL CITY.
I SEE.
CAN I ASSUME THAT MY REFUSAL WOULD GUARANTEE A SWIFT EVICTION?
I'M GLAD WE UNDERSTAND EACH OTHER.
YES, WE DO.
BUT A ROOM FULL OF DRUGGED-UP OCTOGENARIANS AND ONE CORRUPT COP FAILS TO INTIMIDATE ME.
I HAVE PERSONAL BUSINESS HERE THAT IN NO WAY INTERFERES WITH WHATEVER YOU AND YOUR FAMILY HAVE GOING.

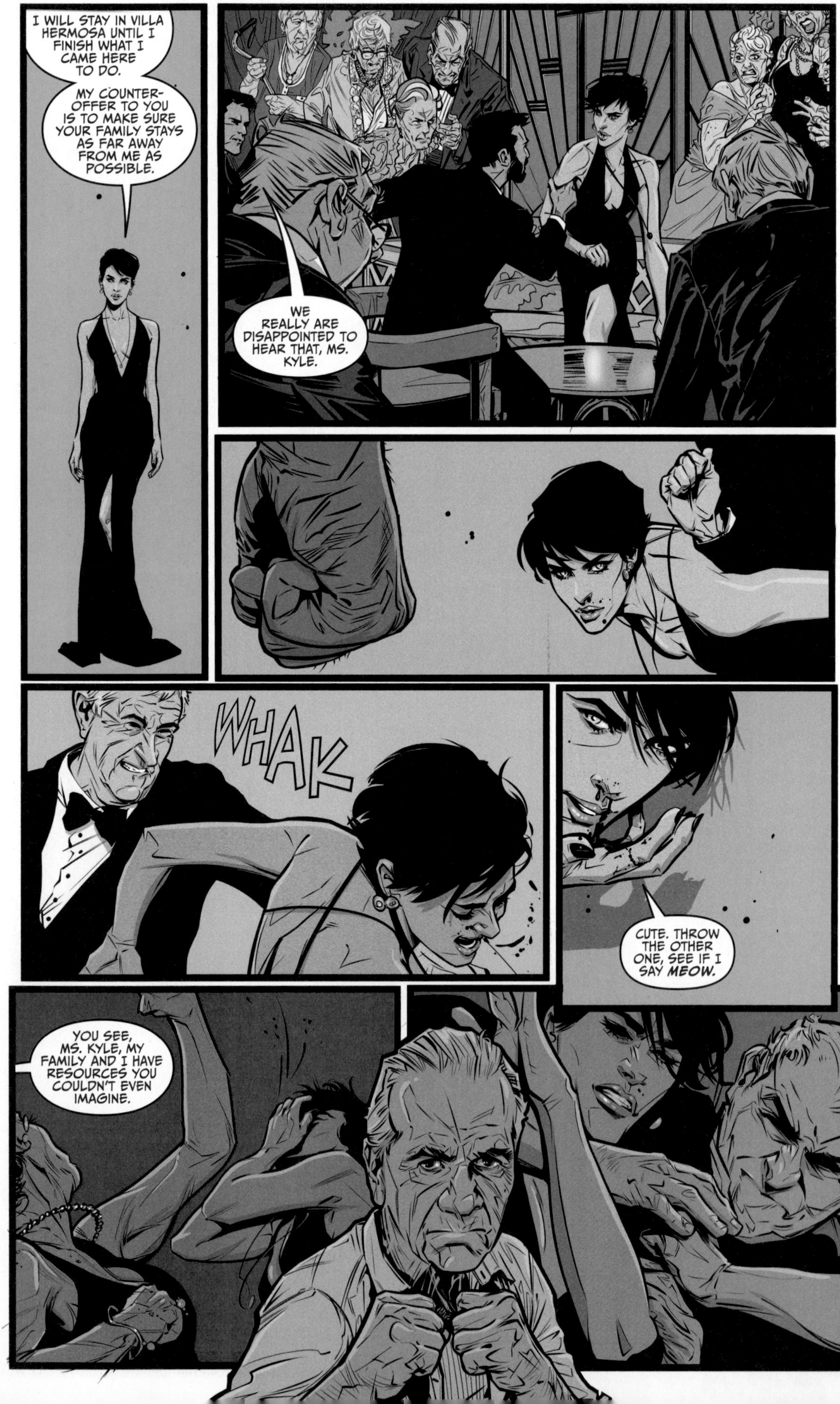
I WILL STAY IN VILLA HERMOSA UNTIL I FINISH WHAT I CAME HERE TO DO.
MY COUNTER-OFFER TO YOU IS TO MAKE SURE YOUR FAMILY STAYS AS FAR AWAY FROM ME AS POSSIBLE.
WE REALLY ARE DISAPPOINTED TO HEAR THAT, MS. KYLE.
WHAK
CUTE. THROW THE OTHER ONE, SEE IF I SAY MEOW.
YOU SEE, MS. KYLE, MY FAMILY AND I HAVE RESOURCES YOU COULDN'T EVEN IMAGINE.

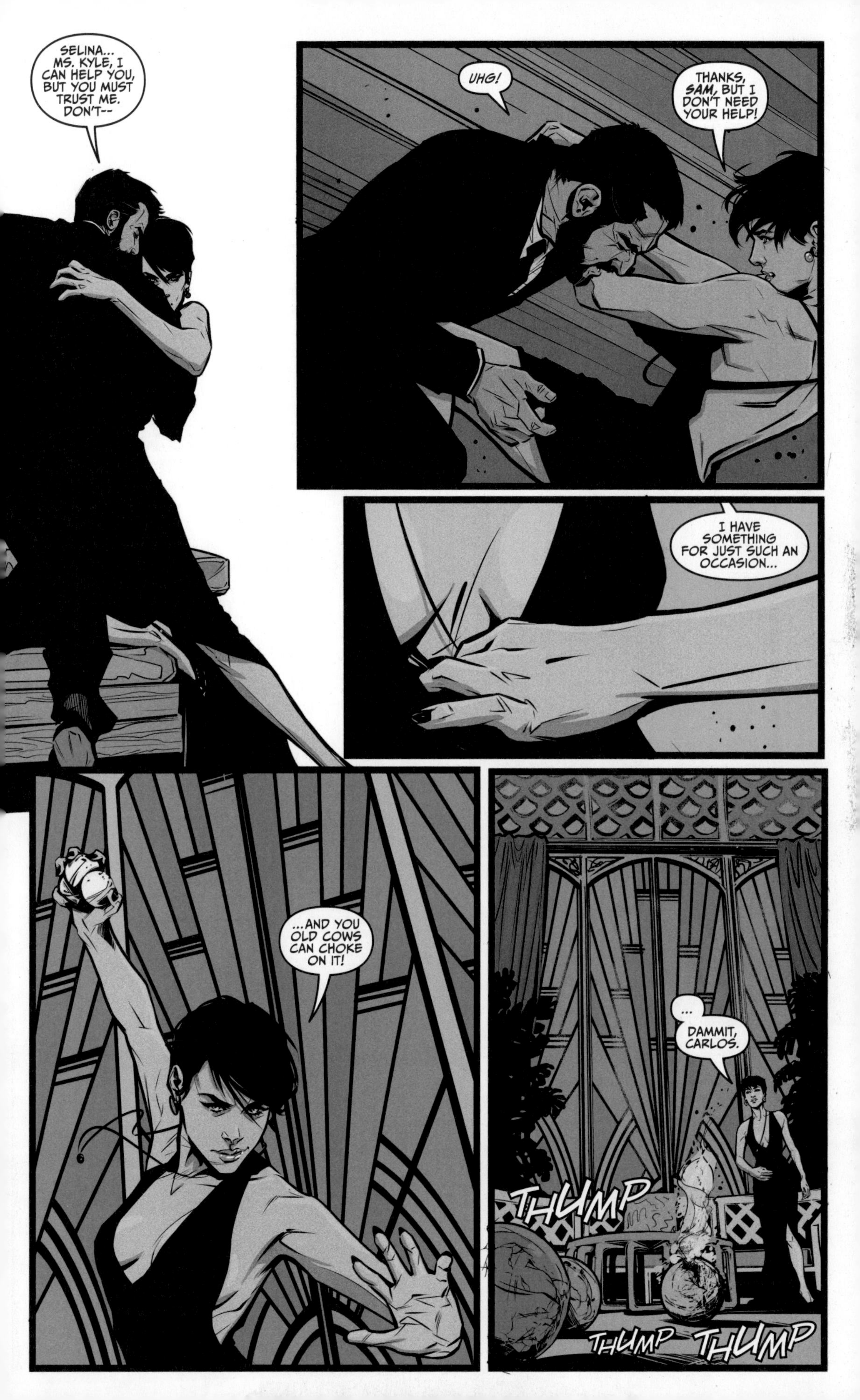
SELINA... MS. KYLE, I CAN HELP YOU, BUT YOU MUST TRUST ME. DON'T--
UHG!
THANKS, SAM, BUT I DON'T NEED YOUR HELP!
I HAVE SOMETHING FOR JUST SUCH AN OCCASION...
...AND YOU OLD COWS CAN CHOKE ON IT!
...
DAMMIT, CARLOS.
THUMP
THUMP THUMP

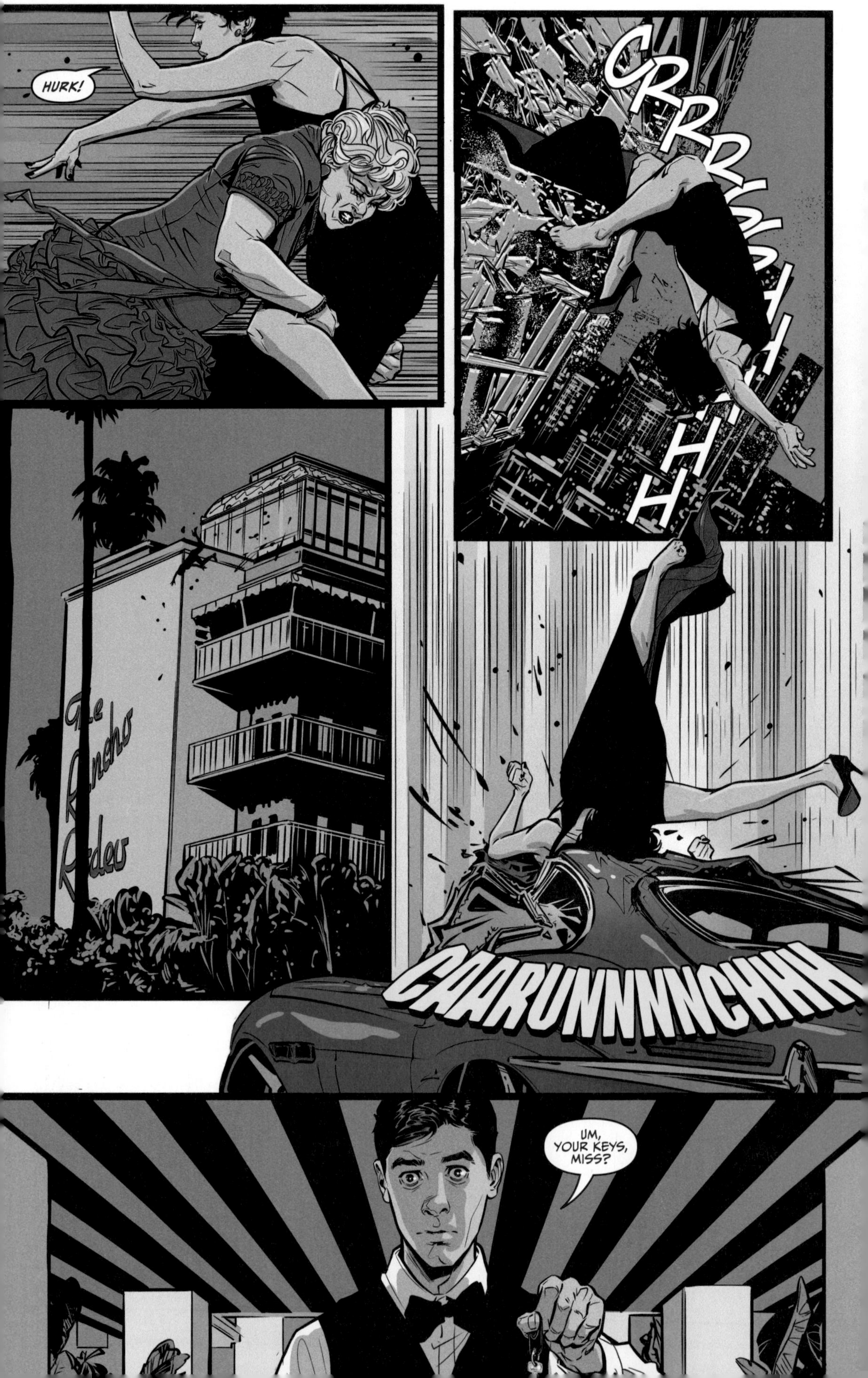
HURK!
CRRRAAAAASHHHHH
CAARUNNNNCHHH
The Rancho Rodeo
UM, YOUR KEYS, MISS?

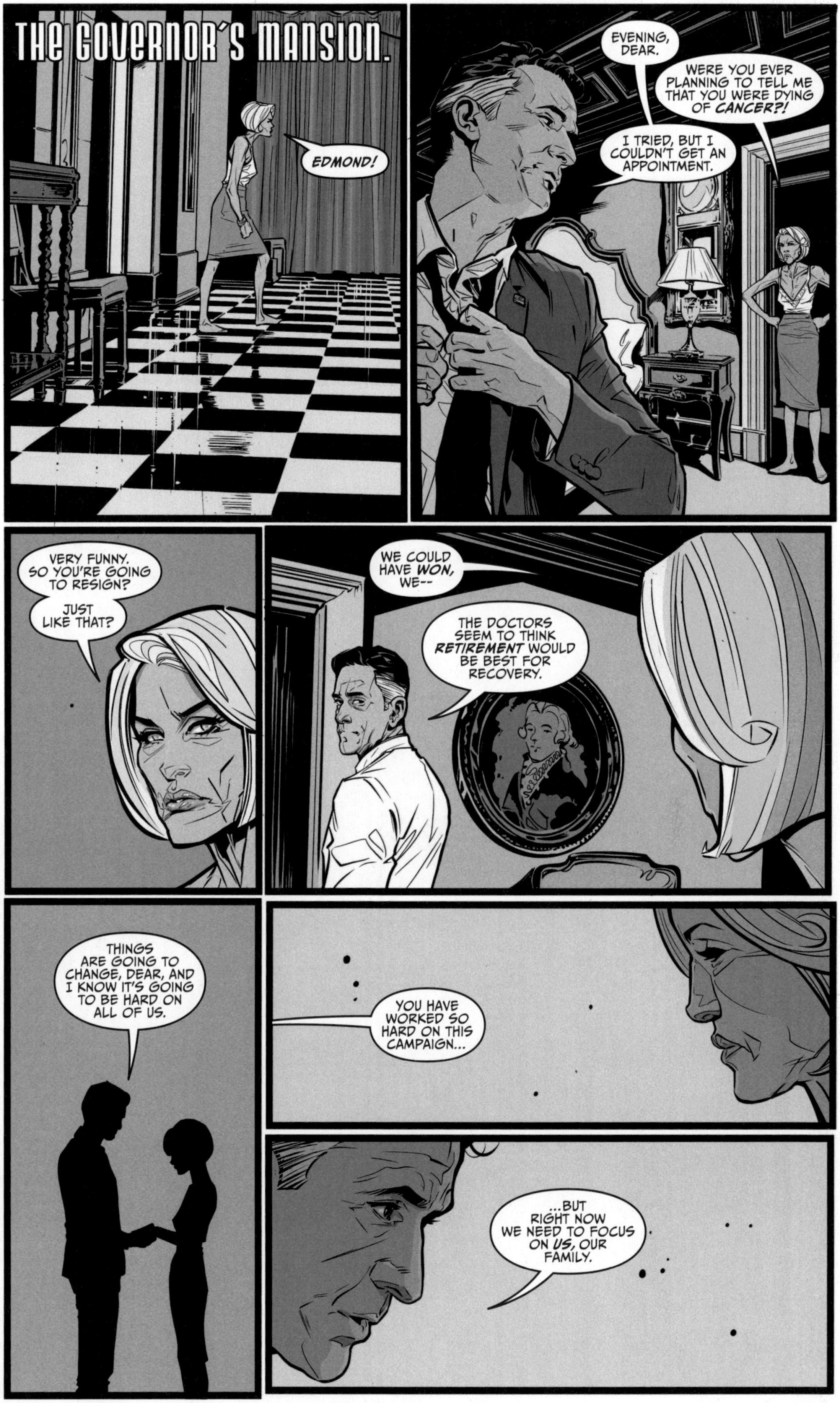
THE GOVERNOR'S MANSION.
EDMOND!
EVENING, DEAR.
WERE YOU EVER PLANNING TO TELL ME THAT YOU WERE DYING OF CANCER?!
I TRIED, BUT I COULDN'T GET AN APPOINTMENT.
VERY FUNNY. SO YOU'RE GOING TO RESIGN?
JUST LIKE THAT?
WE COULD HAVE WON, WE--
THE DOCTORS SEEM TO THINK RETIREMENT WOULD BE BEST FOR RECOVERY.
THINGS ARE GOING TO CHANGE, DEAR, AND I KNOW IT'S GOING TO BE HARD ON ALL OF US.
YOU HAVE WORKED SO HARD ON THIS CAMPAIGN...
...BUT RIGHT NOW WE NEED TO FOCUS ON US, OUR FAMILY.

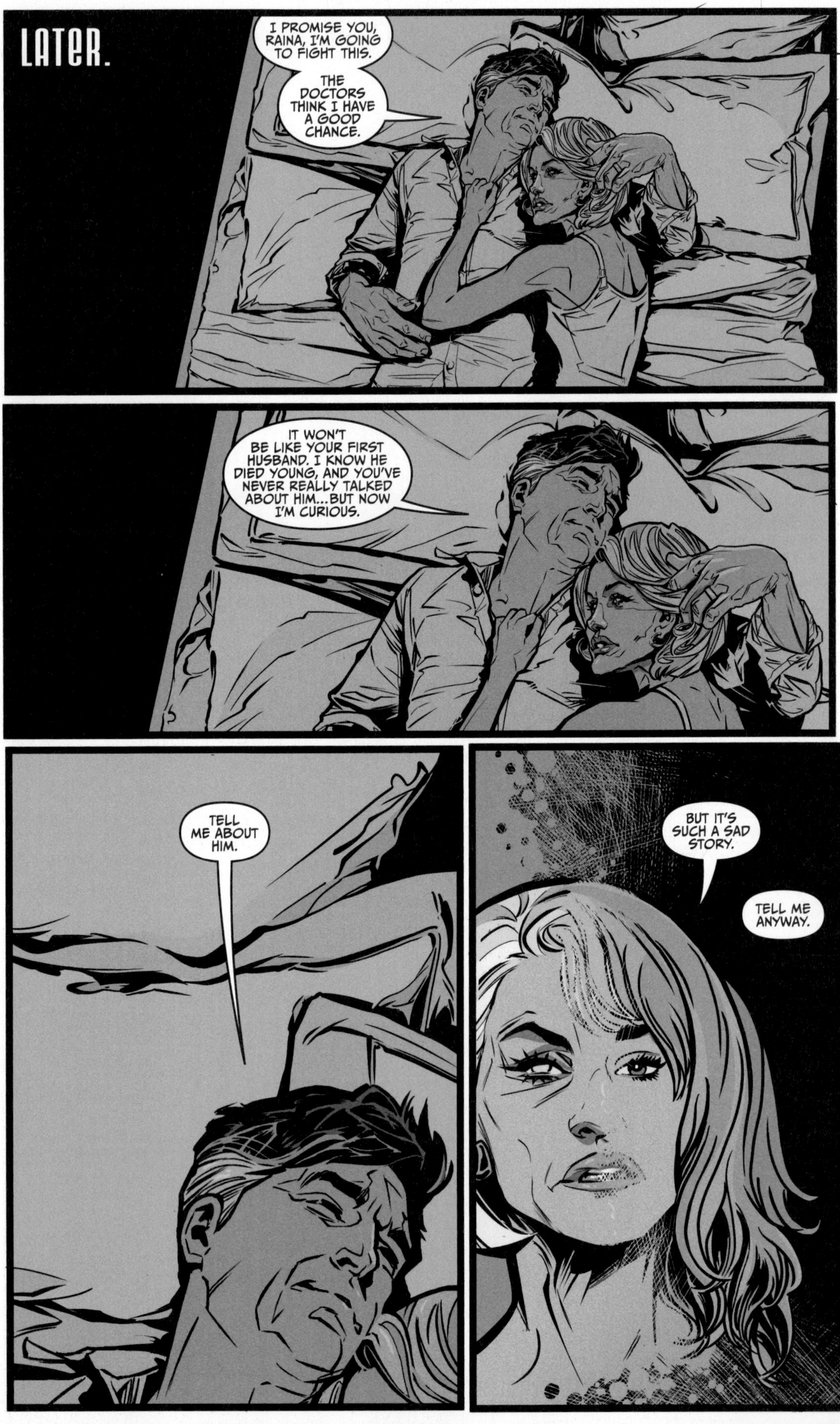
LATER.
I PROMISE YOU, RAINA, I'M GOING TO FIGHT THIS.
THE DOCTORS THINK I HAVE A GOOD CHANCE.
IT WON'T BE LIKE YOUR FIRST HUSBAND. I KNOW HE DIED YOUNG, AND YOU'VE NEVER REALLY TALKED ABOUT HIM...BUT NOW I'M CURIOUS.
TELL ME ABOUT HIM.
BUT IT'S SUCH A SAD STORY.
TELL ME ANYWAY.

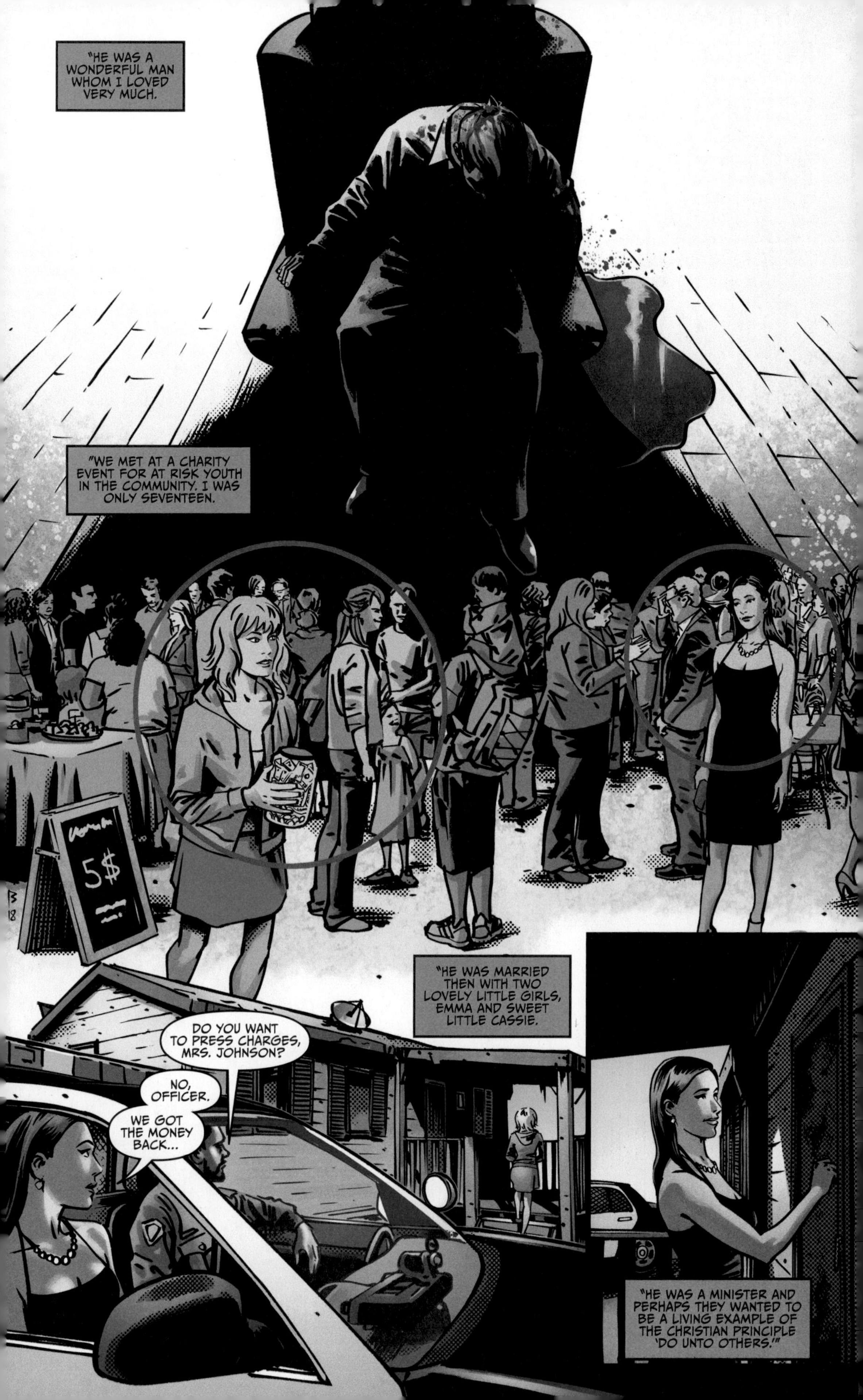
"HE WAS A WONDERFUL MAN WHOM I LOVED VERY MUCH.
"WE MET AT A CHARITY EVENT FOR AT RISK YOUTH IN THE COMMUNITY. I WAS ONLY SEVENTEEN.
5$
"HE WAS MARRIED THEN WITH TWO LOVELY LITTLE GIRLS, EMMA AND SWEET LITTLE CASSIE.
DO YOU WANT TO PRESS CHARGES, MRS. JOHNSON?
NO, OFFICER.
WE GOT THE MONEY BACK...
"HE WAS A MINISTER AND PERHAPS THEY WANTED TO BE A LIVING EXAMPLE OF THE CHRISTIAN PRINCIPLE 'DO UNTO OTHERS.'"

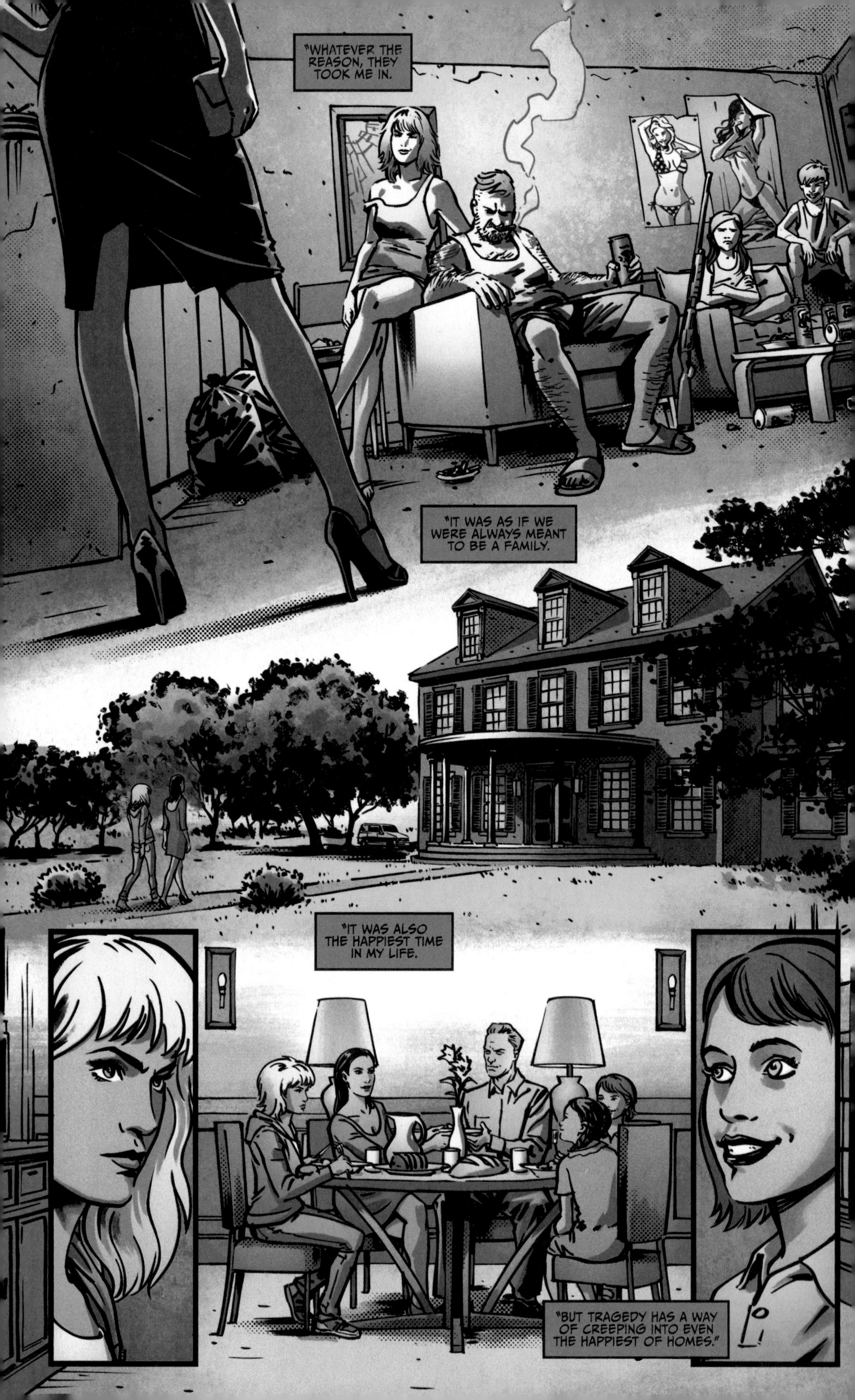
"WHATEVER THE REASON, THEY TOOK ME IN.
"IT WAS AS IF WE WERE ALWAYS MEANT TO BE A FAMILY.
"IT WAS ALSO THE HAPPIEST TIME IN MY LIFE.
"BUT TRAGEDY HAS A WAY OF CREEPING INTO EVEN THE HAPPIEST OF HOMES."

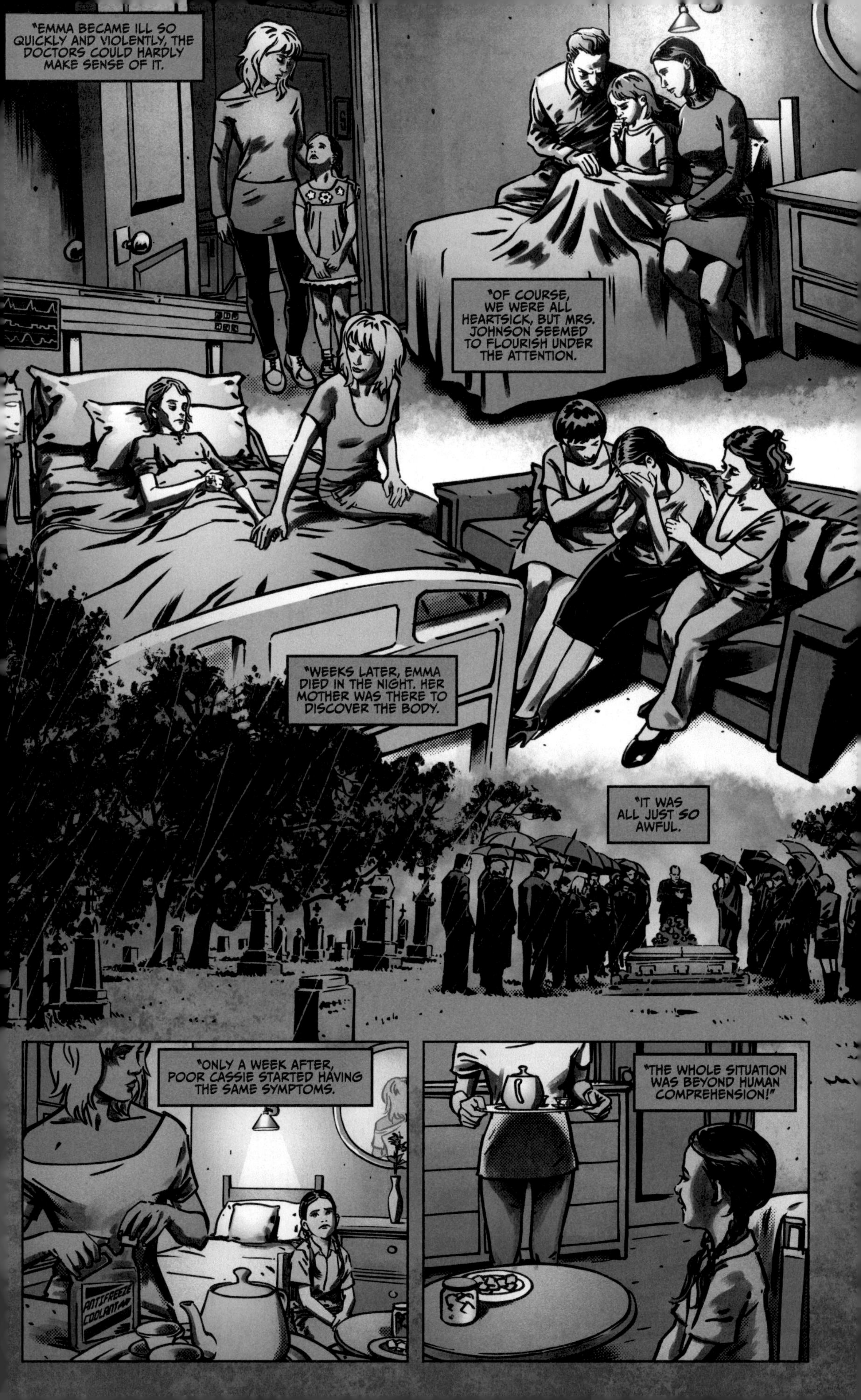
"EMMA BECAME ILL SO QUICKLY AND VIOLENTLY, THE DOCTORS COULD HARDLY MAKE SENSE OF IT.
"OF COURSE, WE WERE ALL HEARTSICK, BUT MRS. JOHNSON SEEMED TO FLOURISH UNDER THE ATTENTION.
"WEEKS LATER, EMMA DIED IN THE NIGHT. HER MOTHER WAS THERE TO DISCOVER THE BODY.
"IT WAS ALL JUST SO AWFUL.
"ONLY A WEEK AFTER, POOR CASSIE STARTED HAVING THE SAME SYMPTOMS.
ANTIFREEZE COOLANT
"THE WHOLE SITUATION WAS BEYOND HUMAN COMPREHENSION!"

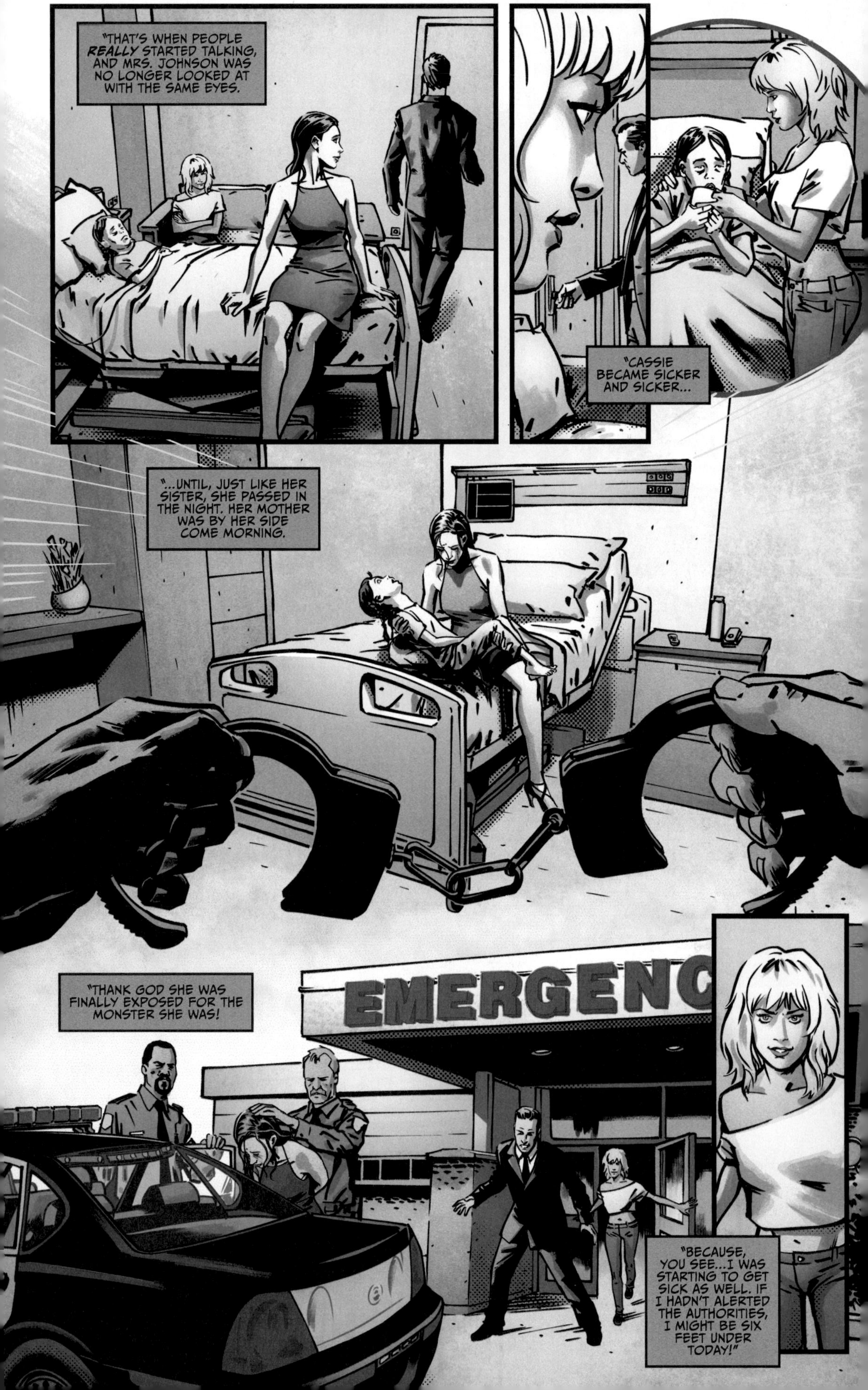
"THAT'S WHEN PEOPLE REALLY STARTED TALKING, AND MRS. JOHNSON WAS NO LONGER LOOKED AT WITH THE SAME EYES.
"CASSIE BECAME SICKER AND SICKER...
"...UNTIL, JUST LIKE HER SISTER, SHE PASSED IN THE NIGHT. HER MOTHER WAS BY HER SIDE COME MORNING.
"THANK GOD SHE WAS FINALLY EXPOSED FOR THE MONSTER SHE WAS!
EMERGENC
"BECAUSE, YOU SEE...I WAS STARTING TO GET SICK AS WELL. IF I HADN'T ALERTED THE AUTHORITIES, I MIGHT BE SIX FEET UNDER TODAY!"

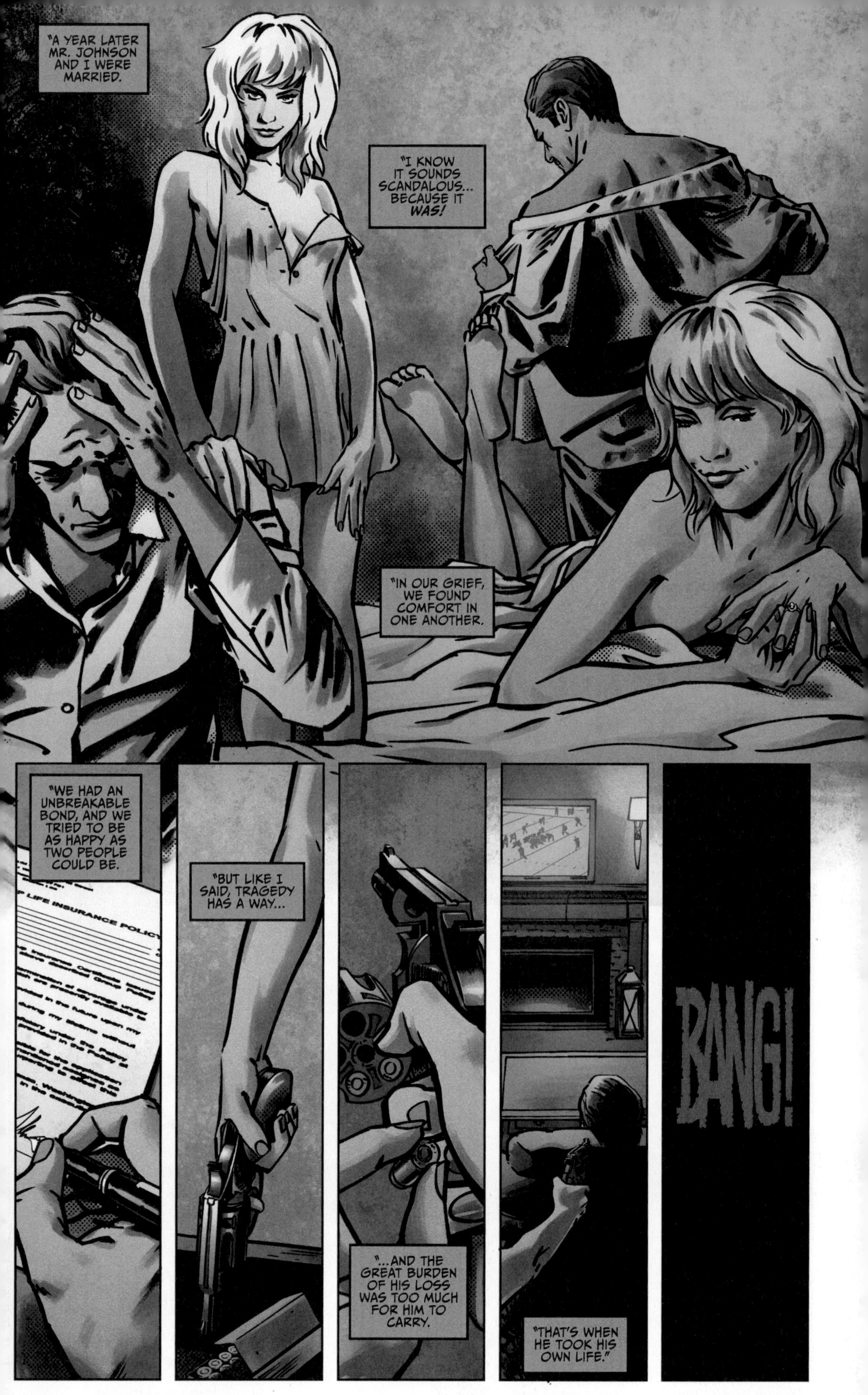
"A YEAR LATER MR. JOHNSON AND I WERE MARRIED.
"I KNOW IT SOUNDS SCANDALOUS... BECAUSE IT WAS!
"IN OUR GRIEF, WE FOUND COMFORT IN ONE ANOTHER.
"WE HAD AN UNBREAKABLE BOND, AND WE TRIED TO BE AS HAPPY AS TWO PEOPLE COULD BE.
LIFE INSURANCE POLICY
"BUT LIKE I SAID, TRAGEDY HAS A WAY...
"...AND THE GREAT BURDEN OF HIS LOSS WAS TOO MUCH FOR HIM TO CARRY.
"THAT'S WHEN HE TOOK HIS OWN LIFE."
BANG!

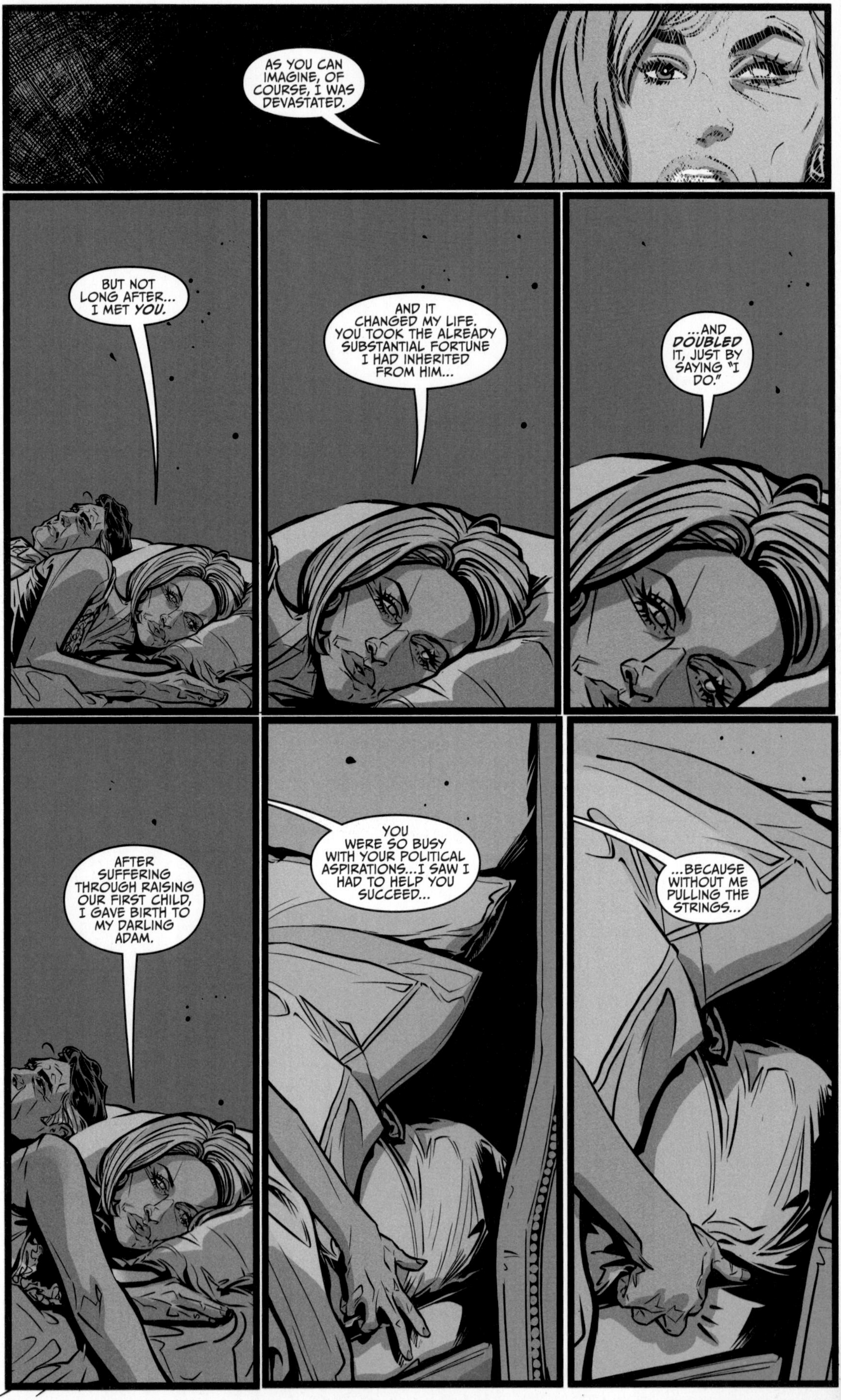
AS YOU CAN IMAGINE, OF COURSE, I WAS DEVASTATED.
BUT NOT LONG AFTER... I MET YOU.
AND IT CHANGED MY LIFE. YOU TOOK THE ALREADY SUBSTANTIAL FORTUNE I HAD INHERITED FROM HIM...
...AND DOUBLED IT, JUST BY SAYING "I DO."
AFTER SUFFERING THROUGH RAISING OUR FIRST CHILD, I GAVE BIRTH TO MY DARLING ADAM.
YOU WERE SO BUSY WITH YOUR POLITICAL ASPIRATIONS...I SAW I HAD TO HELP YOU SUCCEED...
...BECAUSE WITHOUT ME PULLING THE STRINGS...

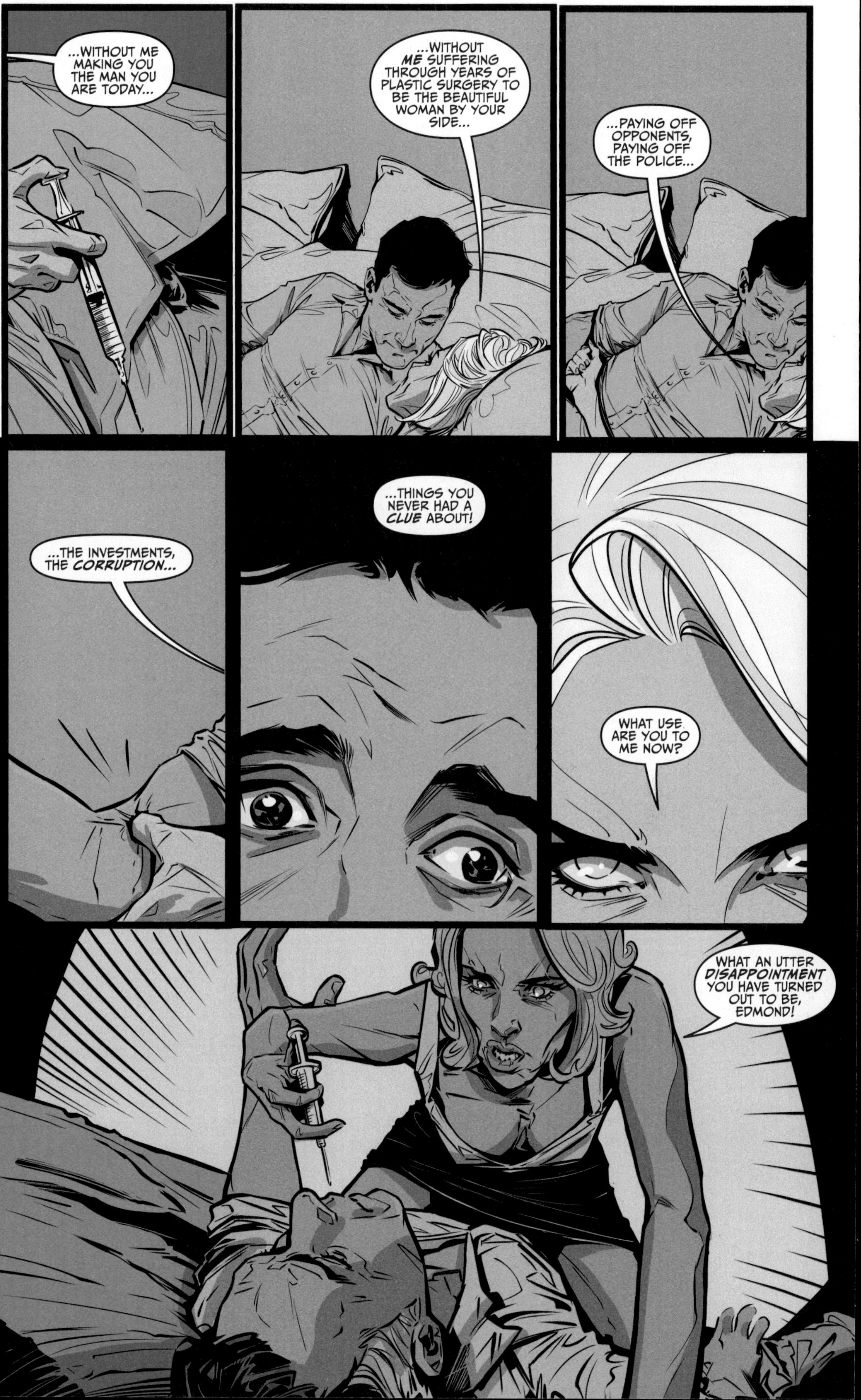
...WITHOUT ME MAKING YOU THE MAN YOU ARE TODAY...
...WITHOUT *ME* SUFFERING THROUGH YEARS OF PLASTIC SURGERY TO BE THE BEAUTIFUL WOMAN BY YOUR SIDE...
...PAYING OFF OPPONENTS, PAYING OFF THE POLICE...
...THE INVESTMENTS, THE *CORRUPTION*...
...THINGS YOU NEVER HAD A *CLUE* ABOUT!
WHAT USE ARE YOU TO ME NOW?
WHAT AN UTTER *DISAPPOINTMENT* YOU HAVE TURNED OUT TO BE, EDMOND!

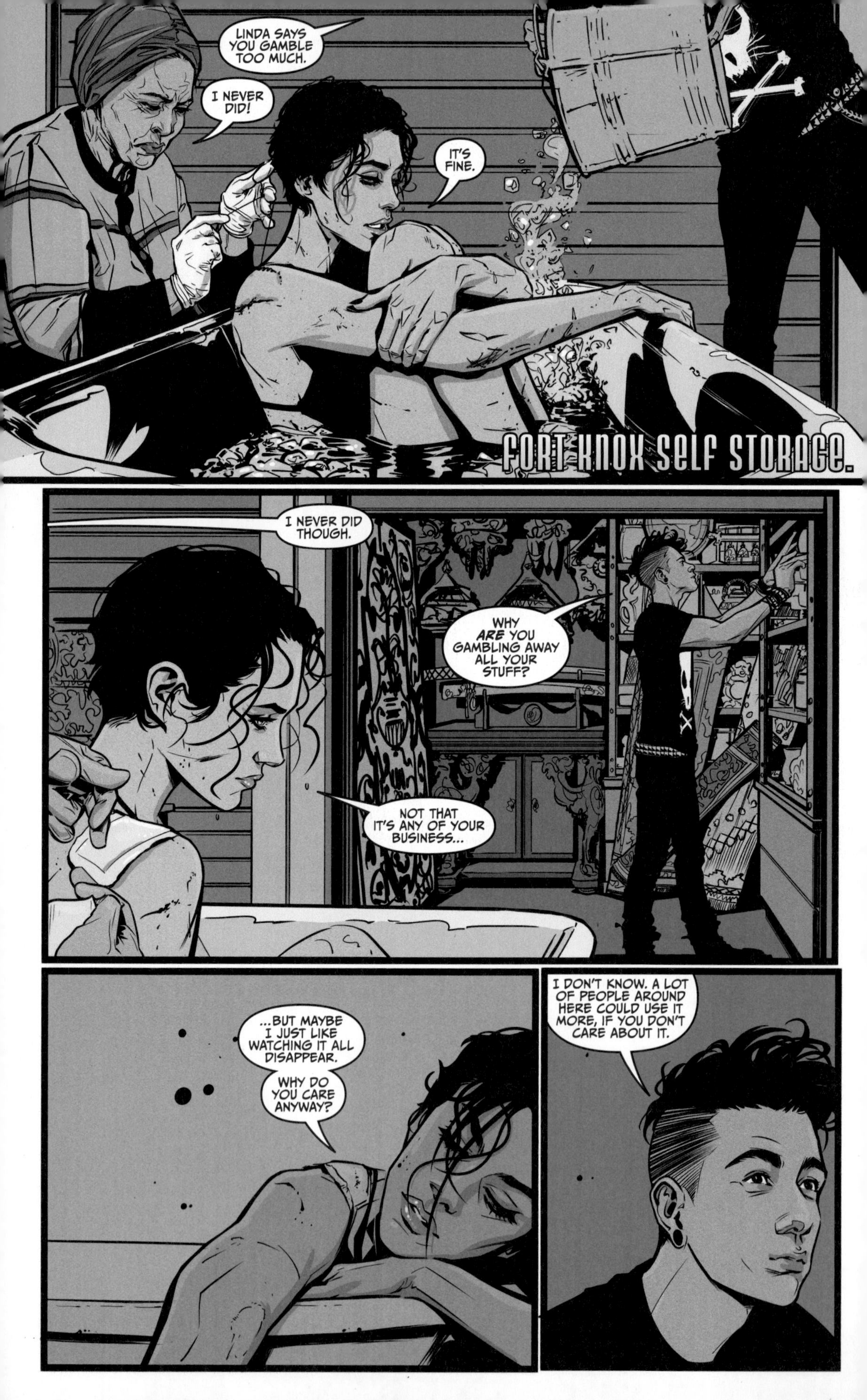
LINDA SAYS YOU GAMBLE TOO MUCH.
I NEVER DID!
IT'S FINE.
FORT KNOX SELF STORAGE.
I NEVER DID THOUGH.
WHY *ARE* YOU GAMBLING AWAY ALL YOUR STUFF?
NOT THAT IT'S ANY OF YOUR BUSINESS...
...BUT MAYBE I JUST LIKE WATCHING IT ALL DISAPPEAR.
WHY DO YOU CARE ANYWAY?
I DON'T KNOW. A LOT OF PEOPLE AROUND HERE COULD USE IT MORE, IF YOU DON'T CARE ABOUT IT.

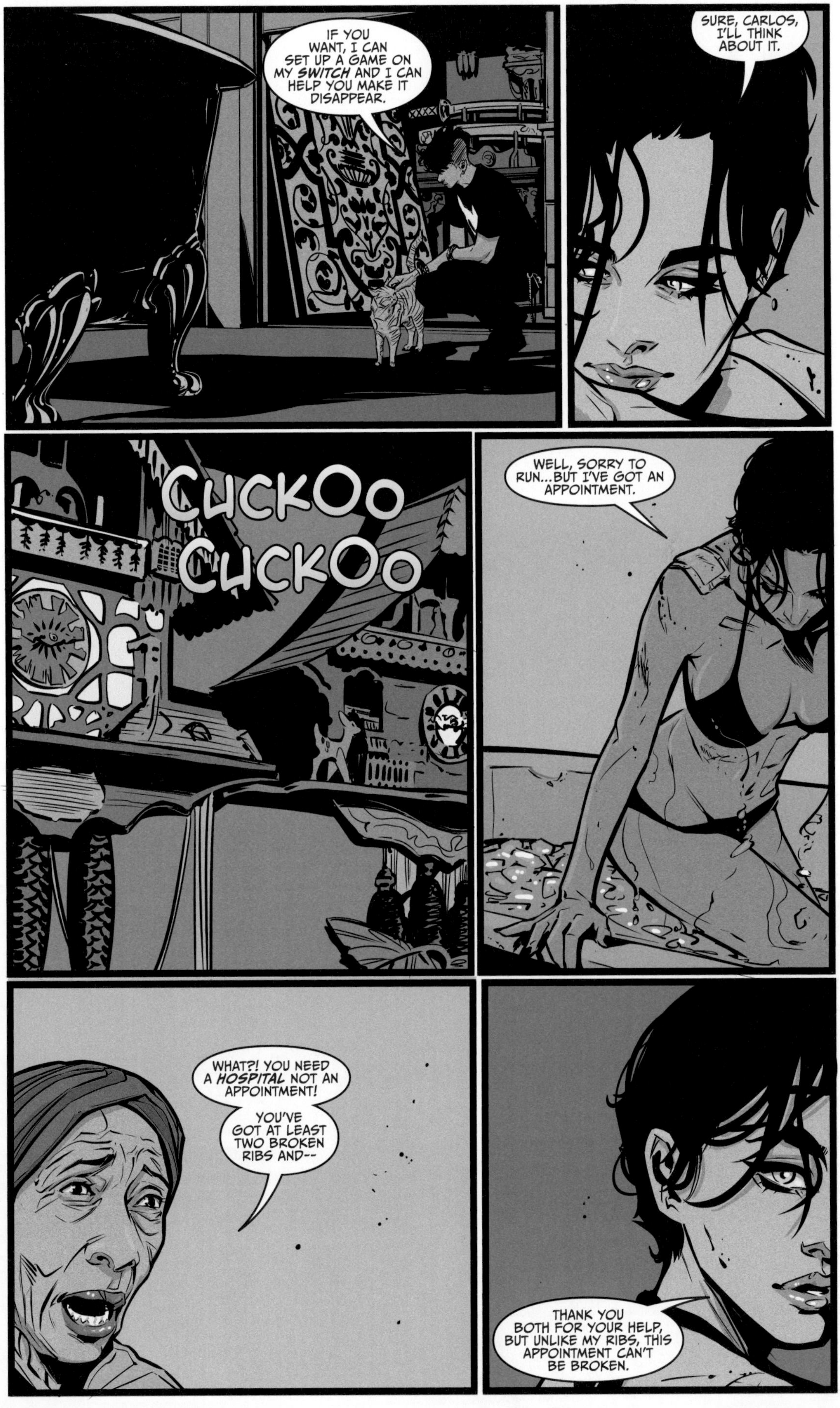
IF YOU WANT, I CAN SET UP A GAME ON MY SWITCH AND I CAN HELP YOU MAKE IT DISAPPEAR.
SURE, CARLOS, I'LL THINK ABOUT IT.
CUCKOO CUCKOO
WELL, SORRY TO RUN...BUT I'VE GOT AN APPOINTMENT.
WHAT?! YOU NEED A HOSPITAL NOT AN APPOINTMENT!
YOU'VE GOT AT LEAST TWO BROKEN RIBS AND--
THANK YOU BOTH FOR YOUR HELP, BUT UNLIKE MY RIBS, THIS APPOINTMENT CAN'T BE BROKEN.

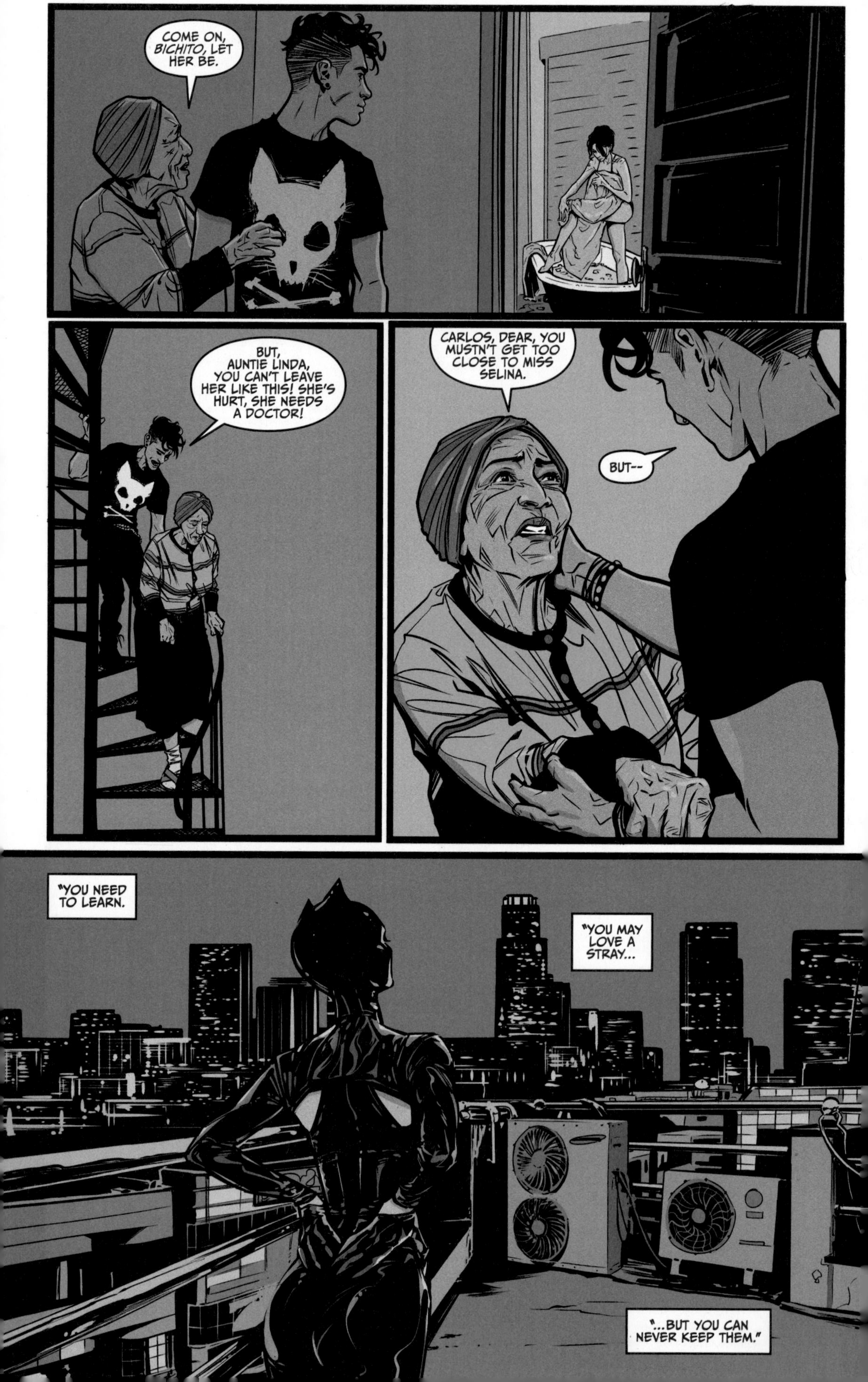

COME ON, *BICHITO*, LET HER BE.
BUT, AUNTIE LINDA, YOU CAN'T LEAVE HER LIKE THIS! SHE'S HURT, SHE NEEDS A DOCTOR!
CARLOS, DEAR, YOU MUSTN'T GET TOO CLOSE TO MISS SELINA.
BUT--
"YOU NEED TO LEARN.
"YOU MAY LOVE A STRAY...
"...BUT YOU CAN NEVER KEEP THEM."

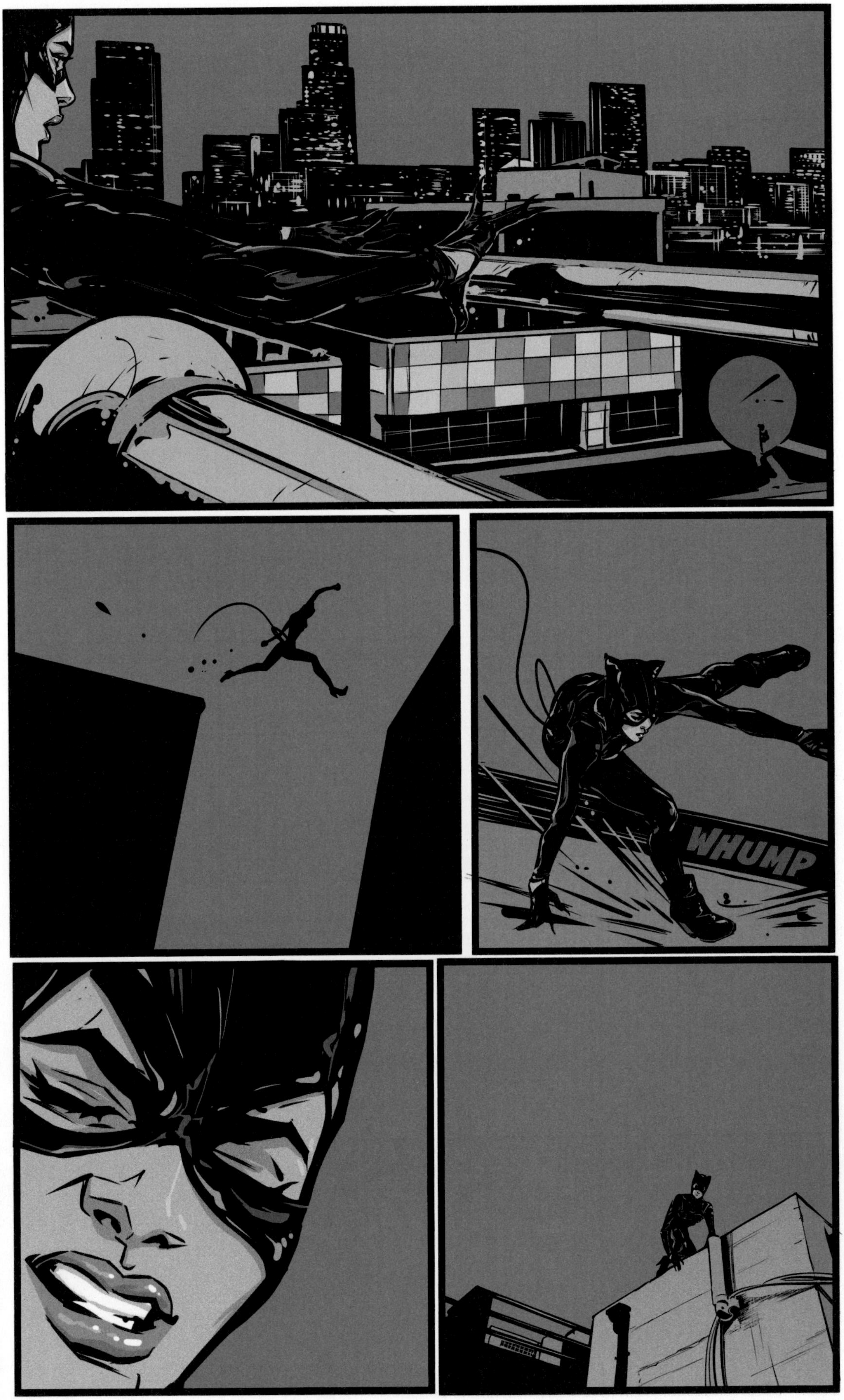
WHUMP

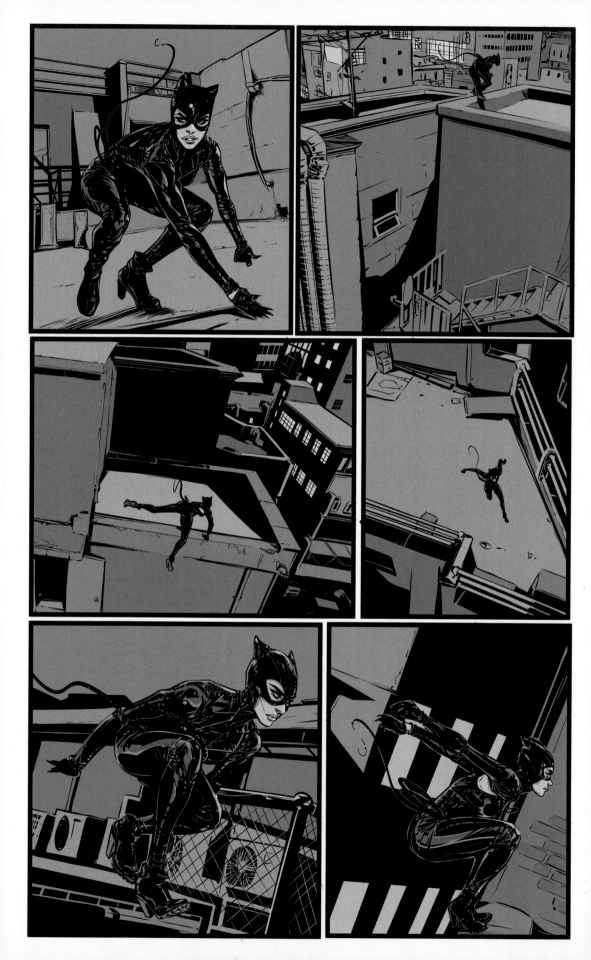

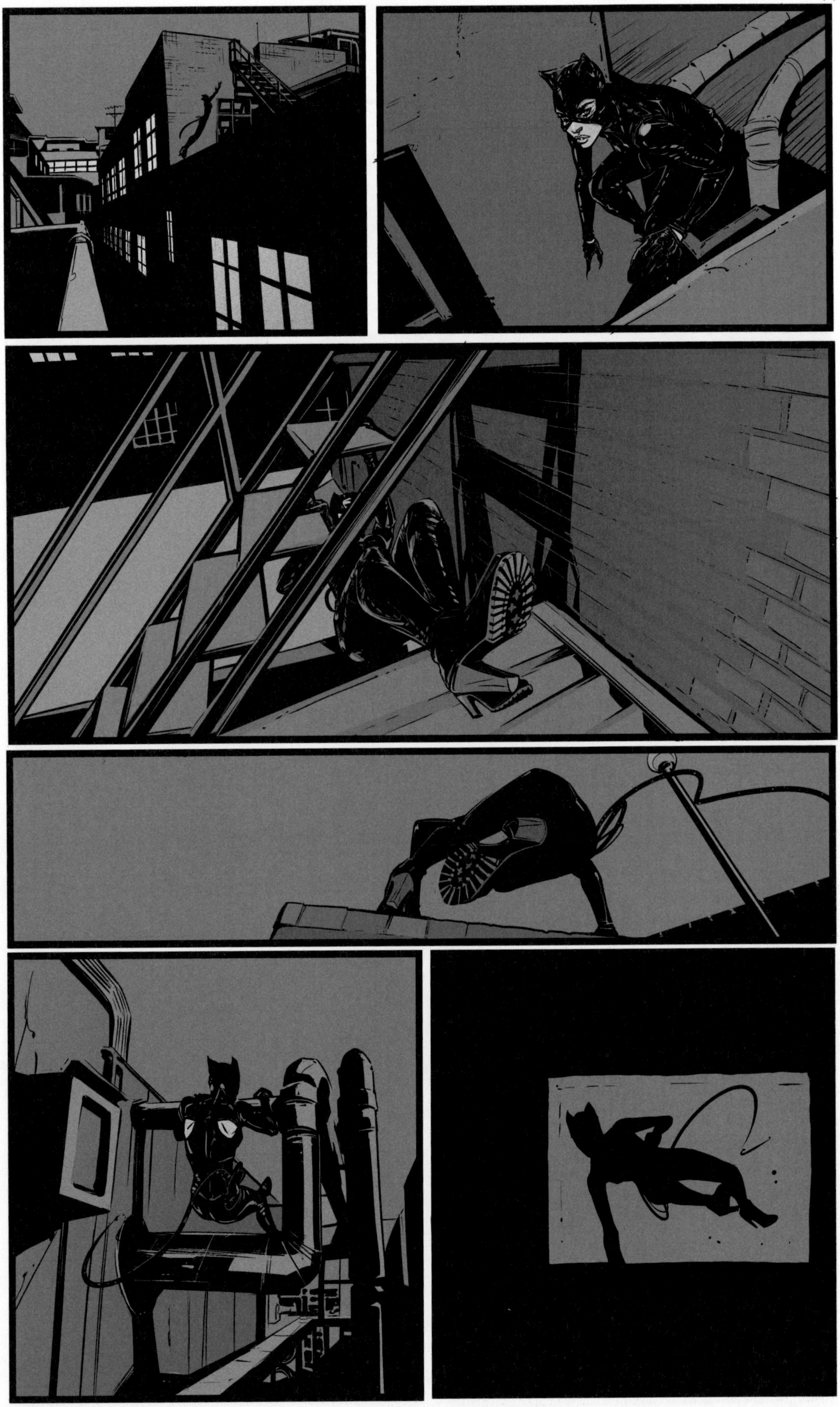

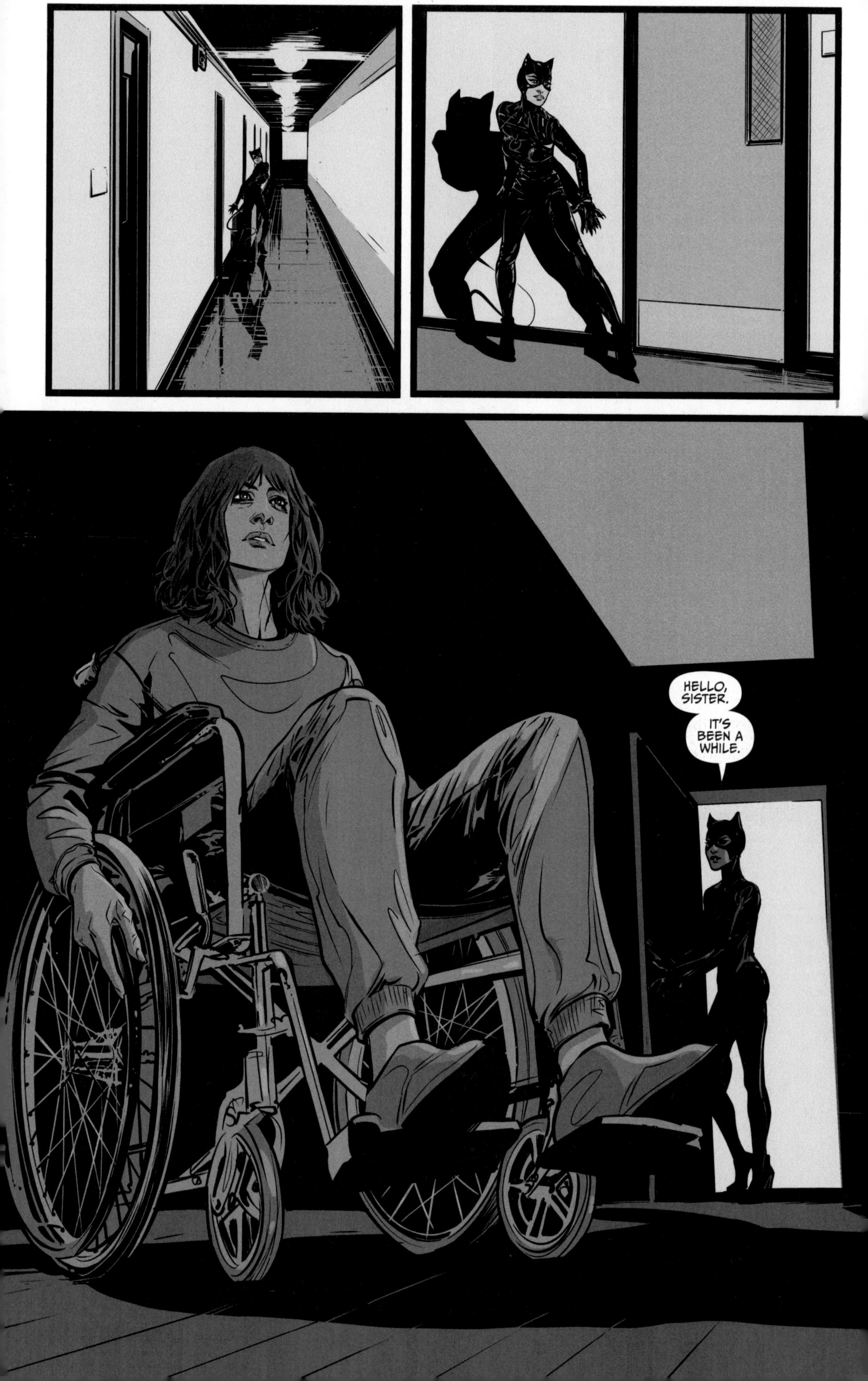
HELLO, SISTER.
IT'S BEEN A WHILE.

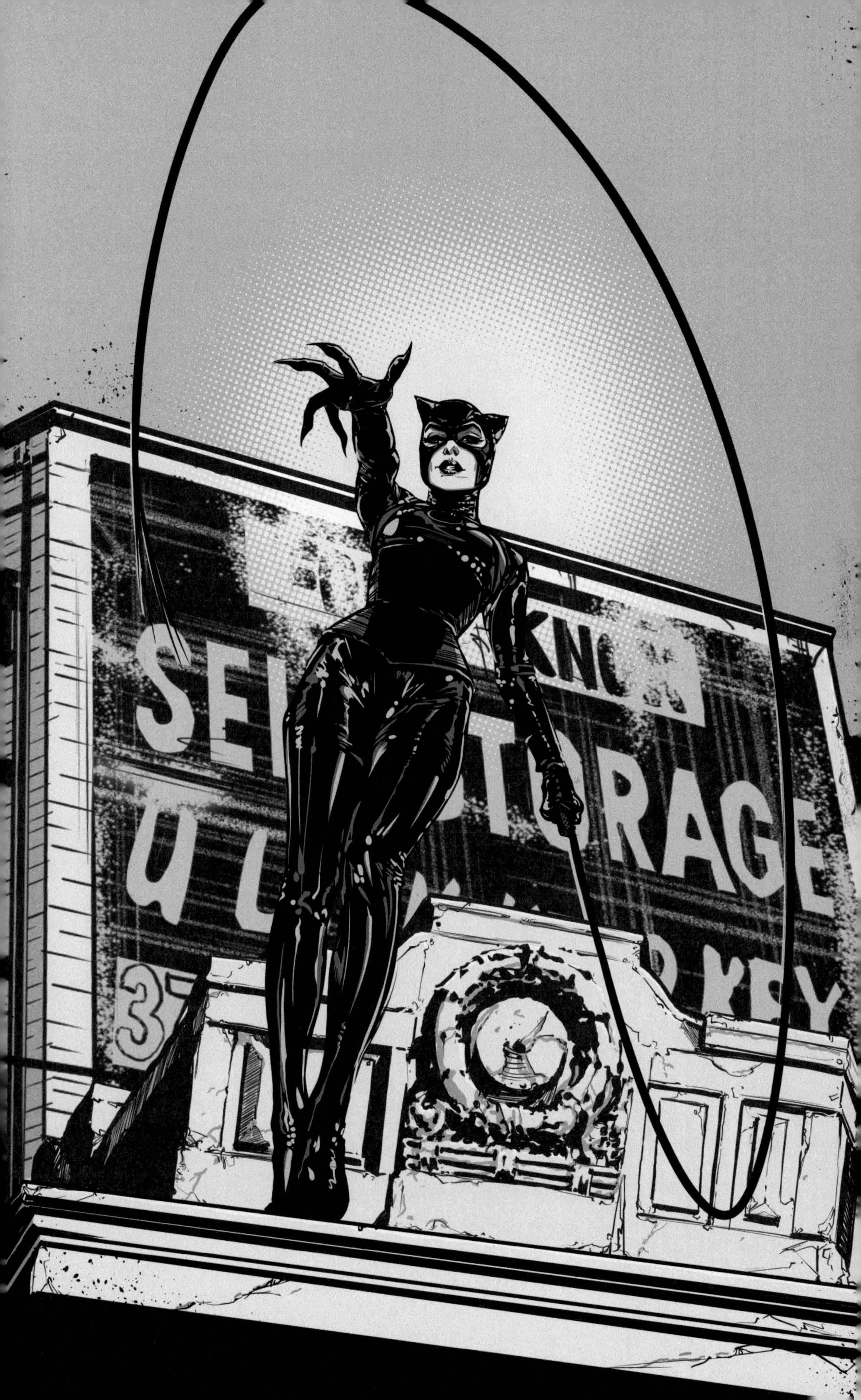
KNO
SE TORAGE
KEY
37

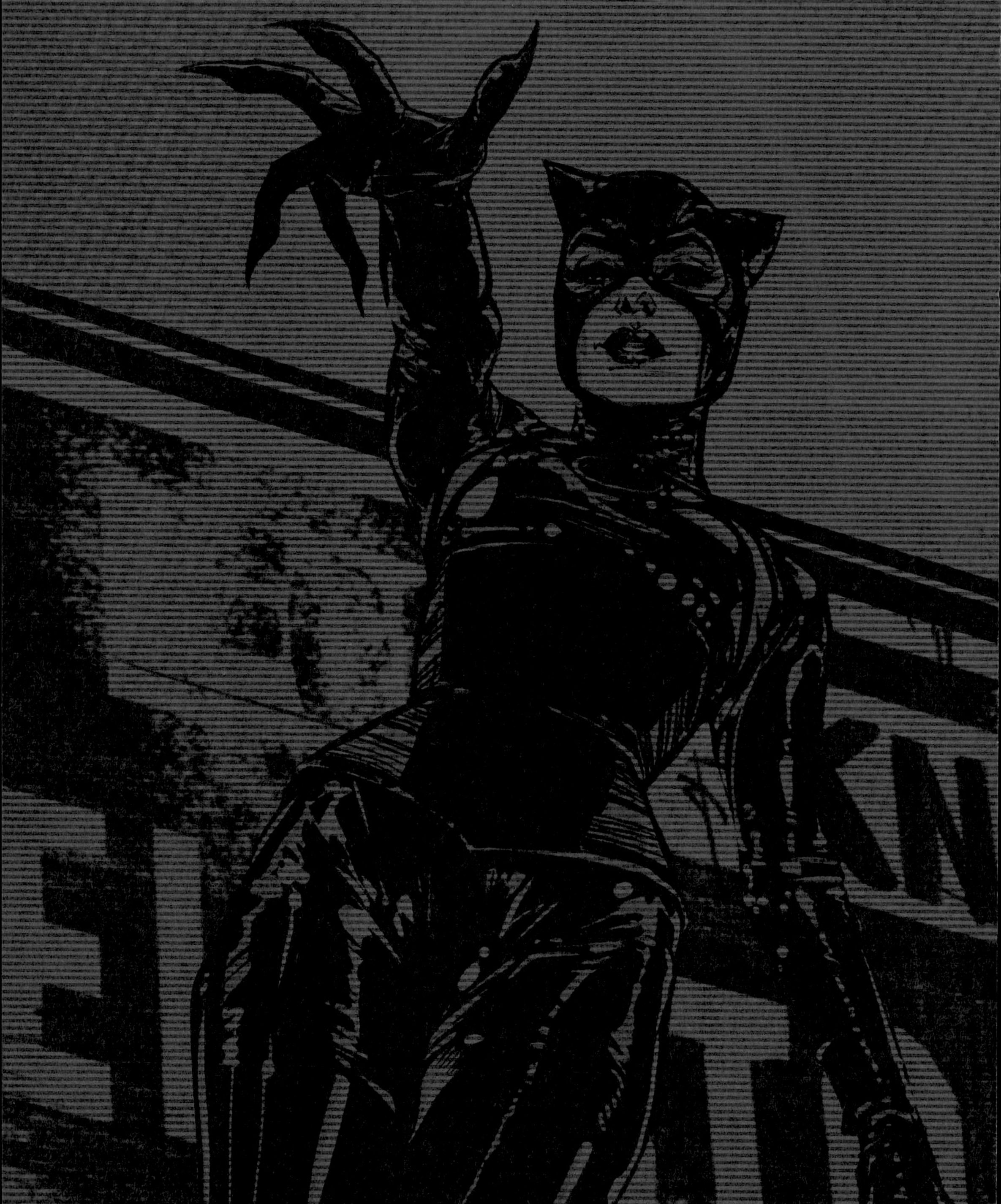

CATWOMAN
#4

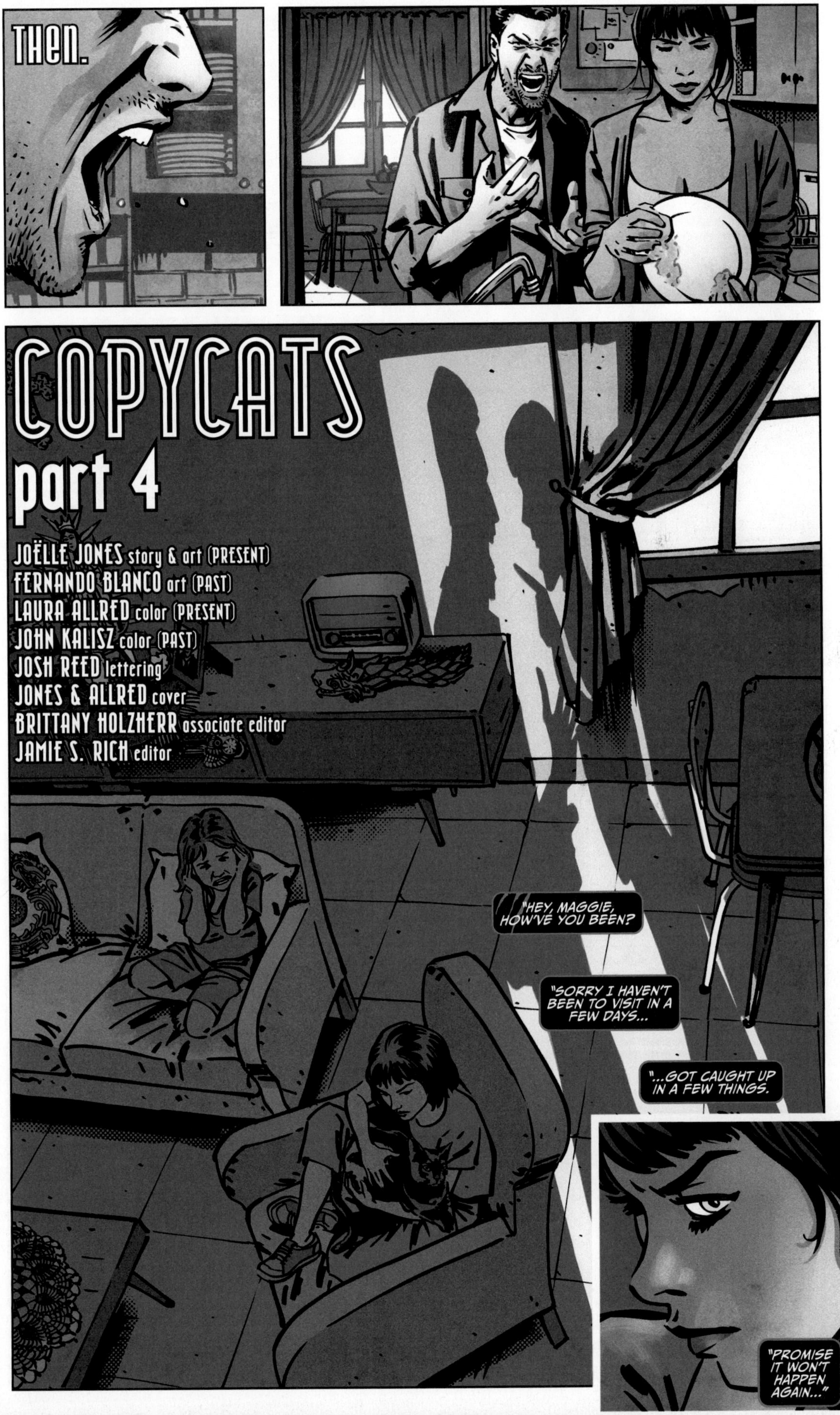
THEN.
COPYCATS
part 4
JOËLLE JONES story & art (PRESENT)
FERNANDO BLANCO art (PAST)
LAURA ALLRED color (PRESENT)
JOHN KALISZ color (PAST)
JOSH REED lettering
JONES & ALLRED cover
BRITTANY HOLZHERR associate editor
JAMIE S. RICH editor
"HEY, MAGGIE, HOW'VE YOU BEEN?
"SORRY I HAVEN'T BEEN TO VISIT IN A FEW DAYS...
"...GOT CAUGHT UP IN A FEW THINGS.
"PROMISE IT WON'T HAPPEN AGAIN..."

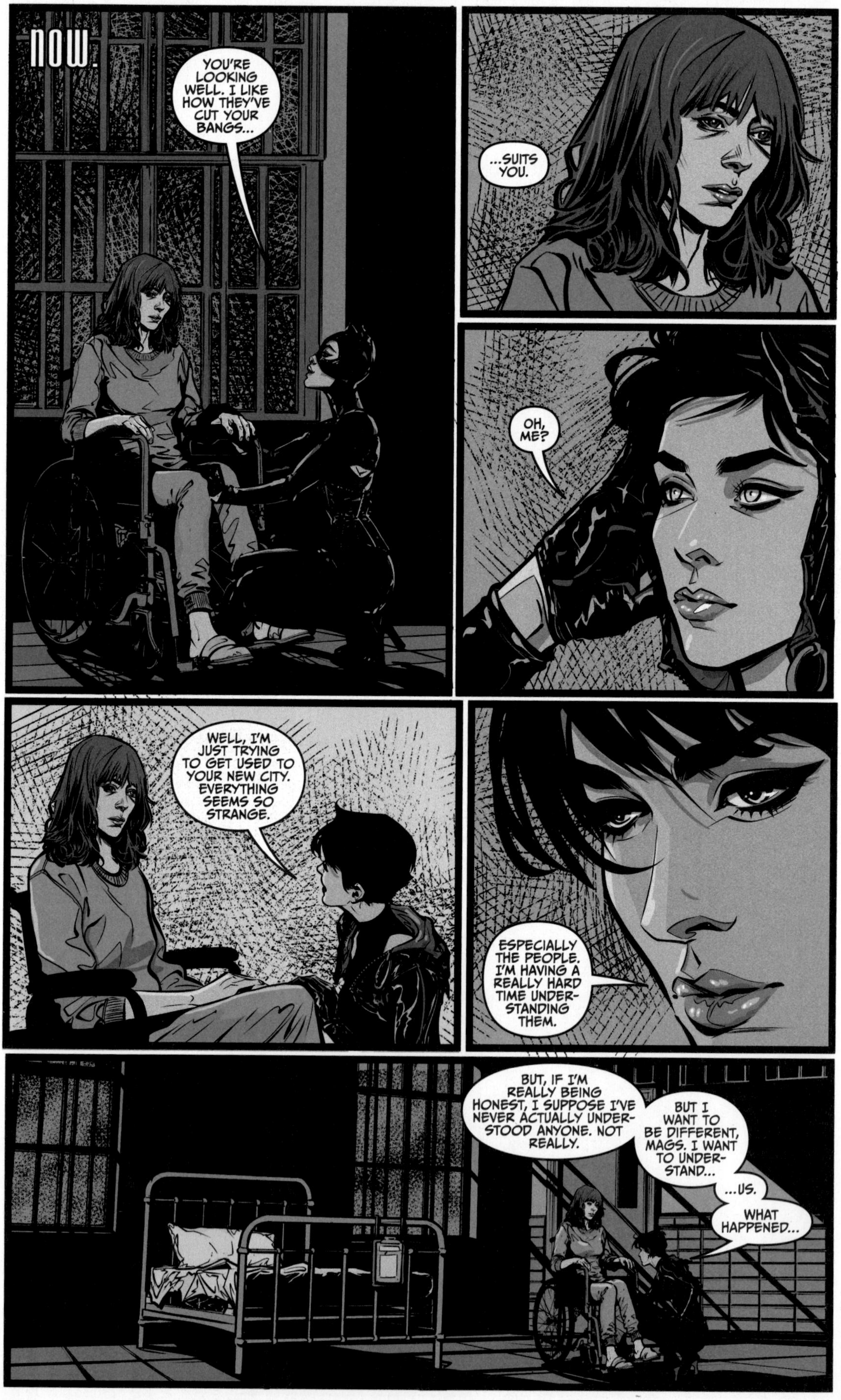
NOW.
YOU'RE LOOKING WELL. I LIKE HOW THEY'VE CUT YOUR BANGS...
...SUITS YOU.
OH, ME?
WELL, I'M JUST TRYING TO GET USED TO YOUR NEW CITY. EVERYTHING SEEMS SO STRANGE.
ESPECIALLY THE PEOPLE. I'M HAVING A REALLY HARD TIME UNDER-STANDING THEM.
BUT, IF I'M REALLY BEING HONEST, I SUPPOSE I'VE NEVER ACTUALLY UNDER-STOOD ANYONE. NOT REALLY.
BUT I WANT TO BE DIFFERENT, MAGS. I WANT TO UNDER-STAND...
...US.
WHAT HAPPENED...

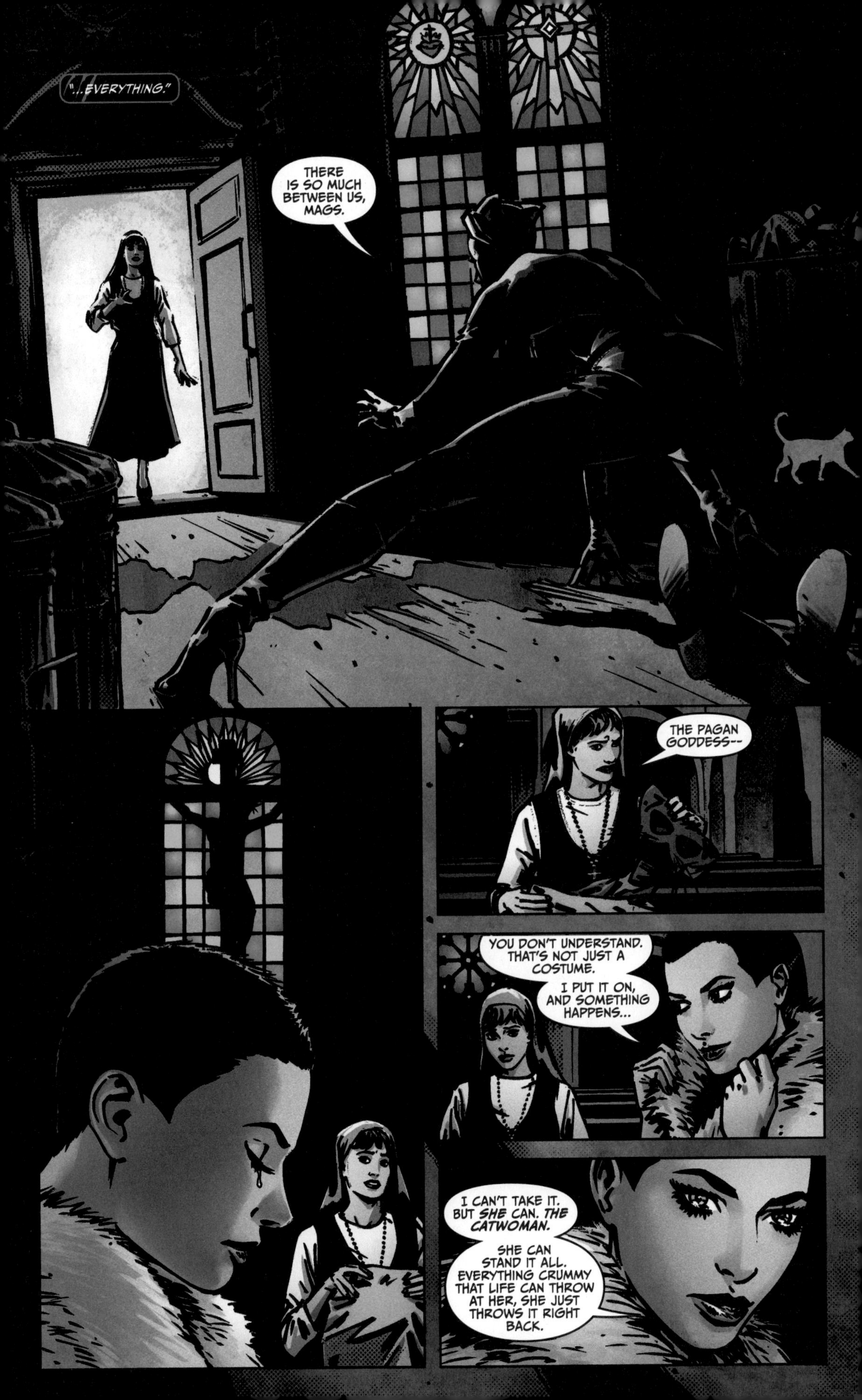
"...EVERYTHING."
THERE IS SO MUCH BETWEEN US, MAGS.
THE PAGAN GODDESS--
YOU DON'T UNDERSTAND. THAT'S NOT JUST A COSTUME.
I PUT IT ON, AND SOMETHING HAPPENS...
I CAN'T TAKE IT. BUT SHE CAN. THE CATWOMAN.
SHE CAN STAND IT ALL. EVERYTHING CRUMMY THAT LIFE CAN THROW AT HER, SHE JUST THROWS IT RIGHT BACK.

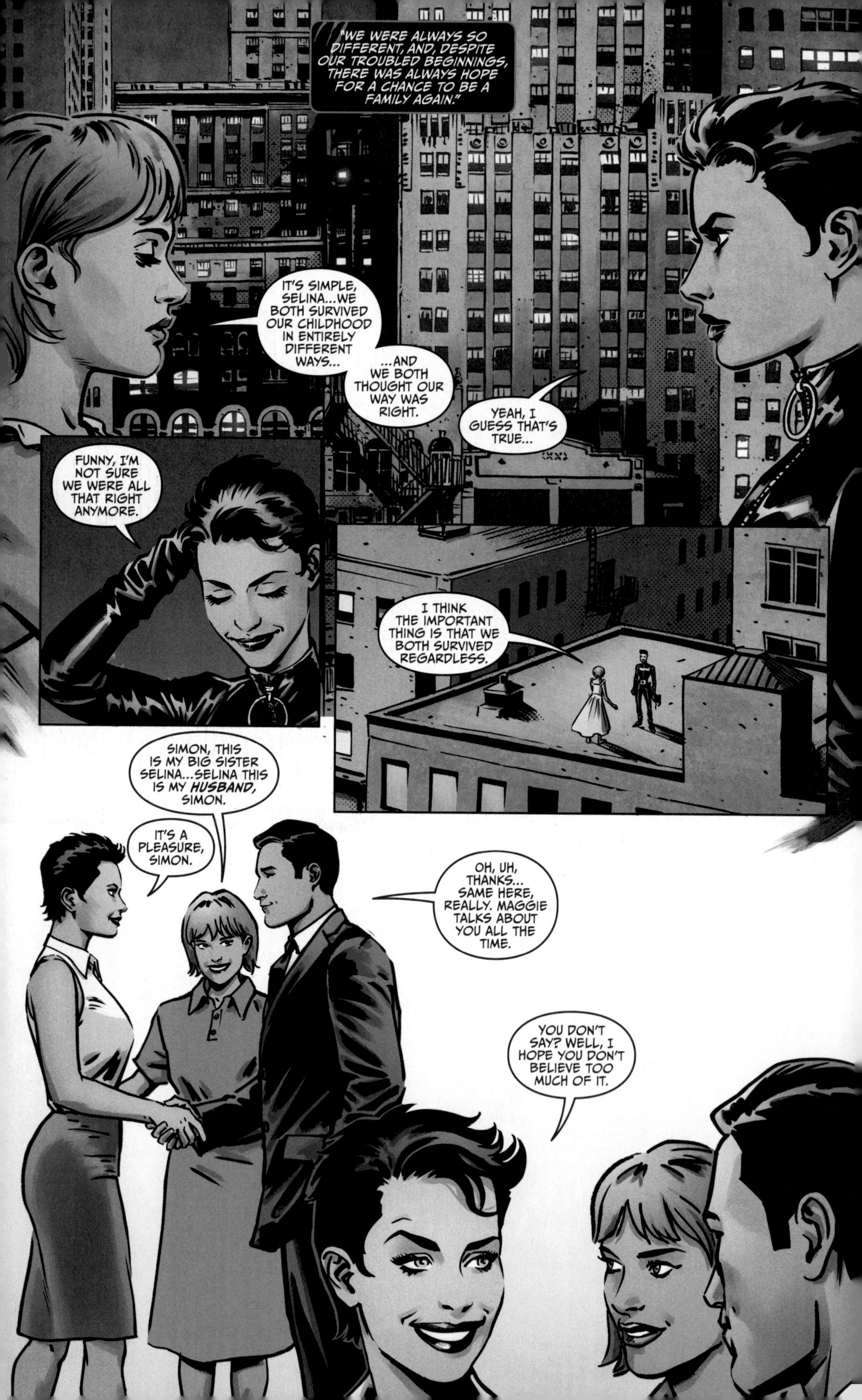
"WE WERE ALWAYS SO DIFFERENT, AND, DESPITE OUR TROUBLED BEGINNINGS, THERE WAS ALWAYS HOPE FOR A CHANCE TO BE A FAMILY AGAIN."
IT'S SIMPLE, SELINA...WE BOTH SURVIVED OUR CHILDHOOD IN ENTIRELY DIFFERENT WAYS...
...AND WE BOTH THOUGHT OUR WAY WAS RIGHT.
YEAH, I GUESS THAT'S TRUE...
FUNNY, I'M NOT SURE WE WERE ALL THAT RIGHT ANYMORE.
I THINK THE IMPORTANT THING IS THAT WE BOTH SURVIVED REGARDLESS.
SIMON, THIS IS MY BIG SISTER SELINA...SELINA THIS IS MY HUSBAND, SIMON.
IT'S A PLEASURE, SIMON.
OH, UH, THANKS... SAME HERE, REALLY. MAGGIE TALKS ABOUT YOU ALL THE TIME.
YOU DON'T SAY? WELL, I HOPE YOU DON'T BELIEVE TOO MUCH OF IT.

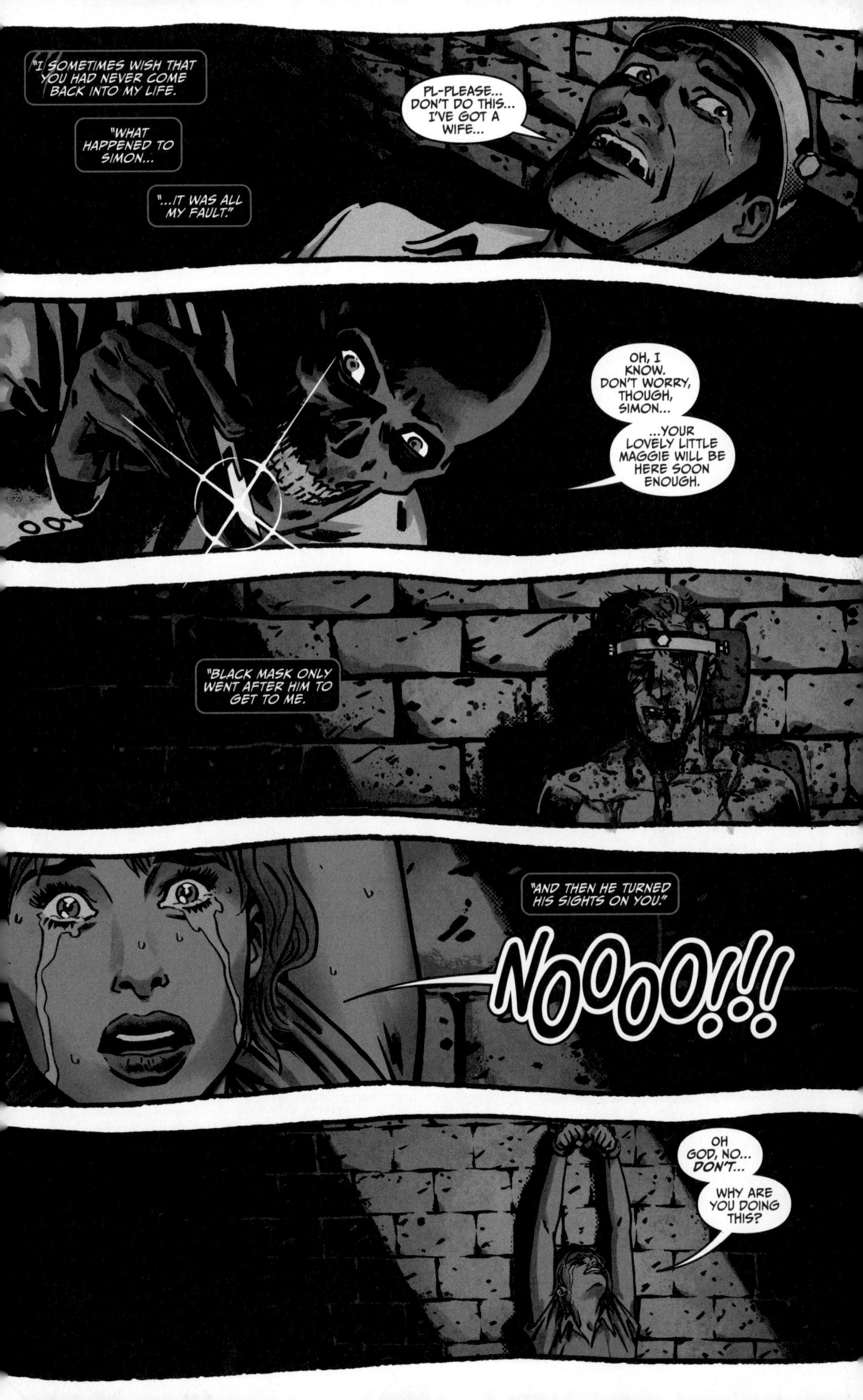
"I SOMETIMES WISH THAT YOU HAD NEVER COME BACK INTO MY LIFE.
"WHAT HAPPENED TO SIMON...
"...IT WAS ALL MY FAULT."
PL-PLEASE... DON'T DO THIS... I'VE GOT A WIFE...
OH, I KNOW. DON'T WORRY, THOUGH, SIMON...
...YOUR LOVELY LITTLE MAGGIE WILL BE HERE SOON ENOUGH.
"BLACK MASK ONLY WENT AFTER HIM TO GET TO ME.
"AND THEN HE TURNED HIS SIGHTS ON YOU."
NOOOOO!!!
OH GOD, NO... DON'T...
WHY ARE YOU DOING THIS?

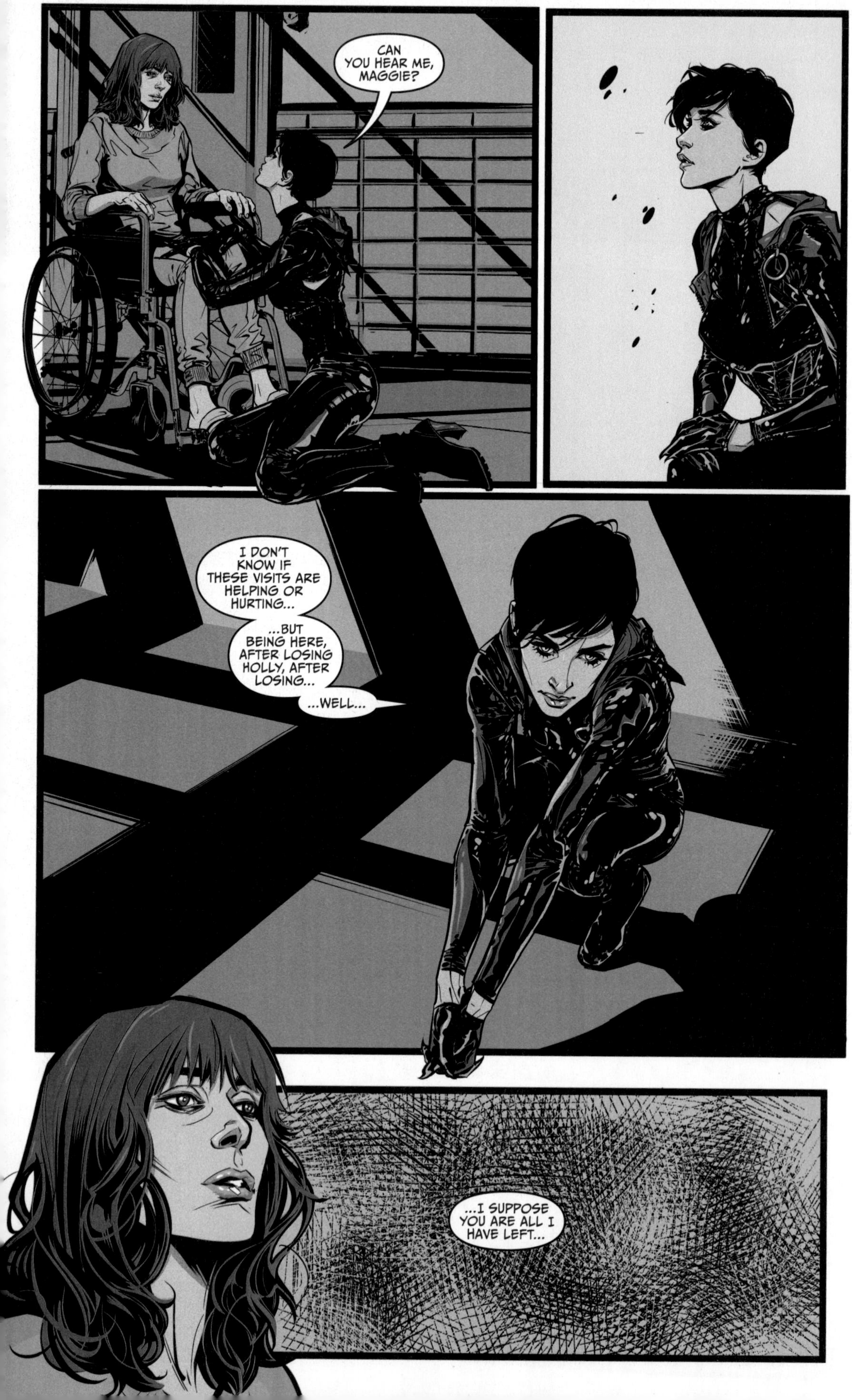
CAN YOU HEAR ME, MAGGIE?
I DON'T KNOW IF THESE VISITS ARE HELPING OR HURTING...
...BUT BEING HERE, AFTER LOSING HOLLY, AFTER LOSING...
...WELL...
...I SUPPOSE YOU ARE ALL I HAVE LEFT...

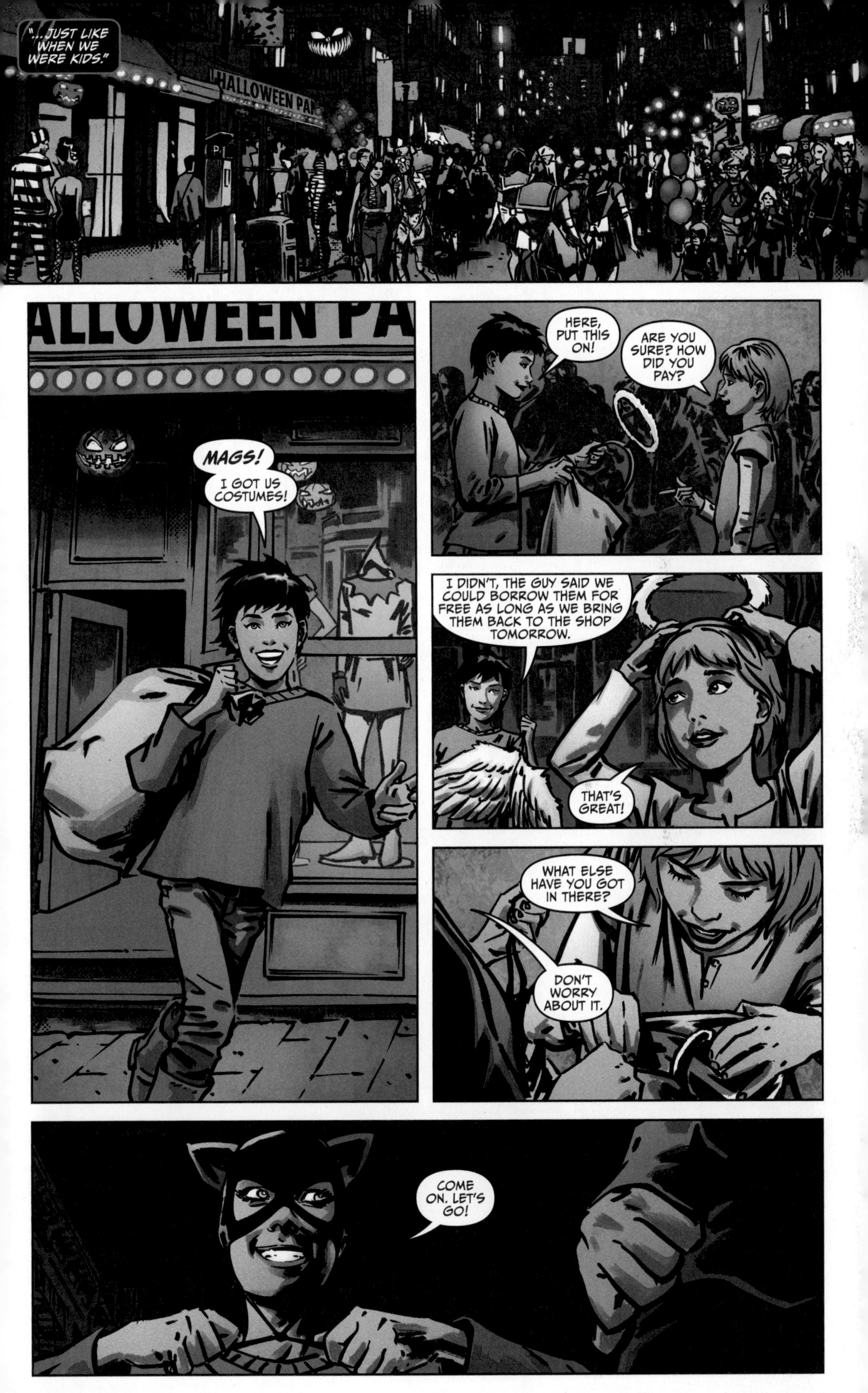
"...JUST LIKE WHEN WE WERE KIDS."
HALLOWEEN PA
ALLOWEEN PA
MAGS!
I GOT US COSTUMES!
HERE, PUT THIS ON!
ARE YOU SURE? HOW DID YOU PAY?
I DIDN'T, THE GUY SAID WE COULD BORROW THEM FOR FREE AS LONG AS WE BRING THEM BACK TO THE SHOP TOMORROW.
THAT'S GREAT!
WHAT ELSE HAVE YOU GOT IN THERE?
DON'T WORRY ABOUT IT.
COME ON. LET'S GO!

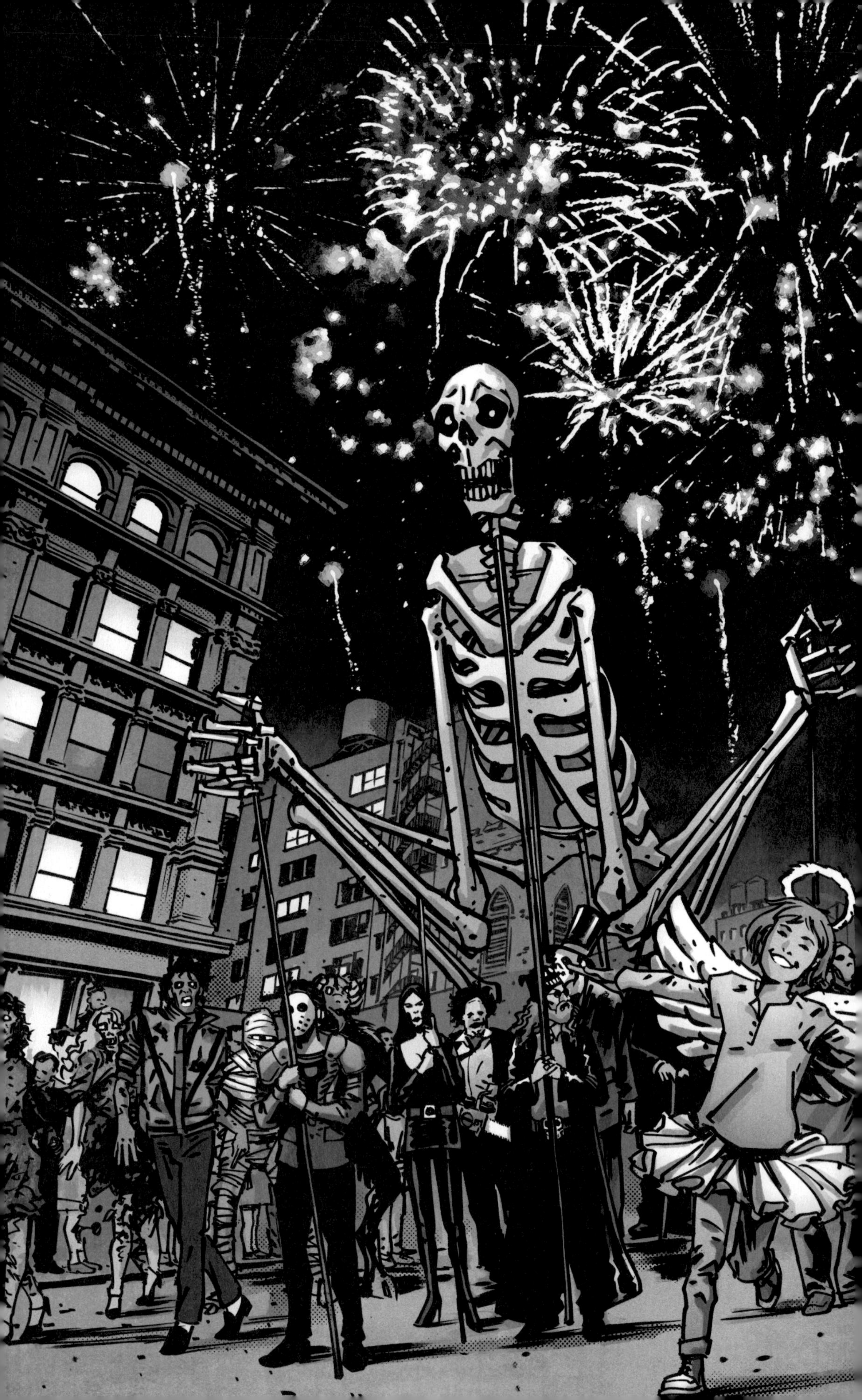

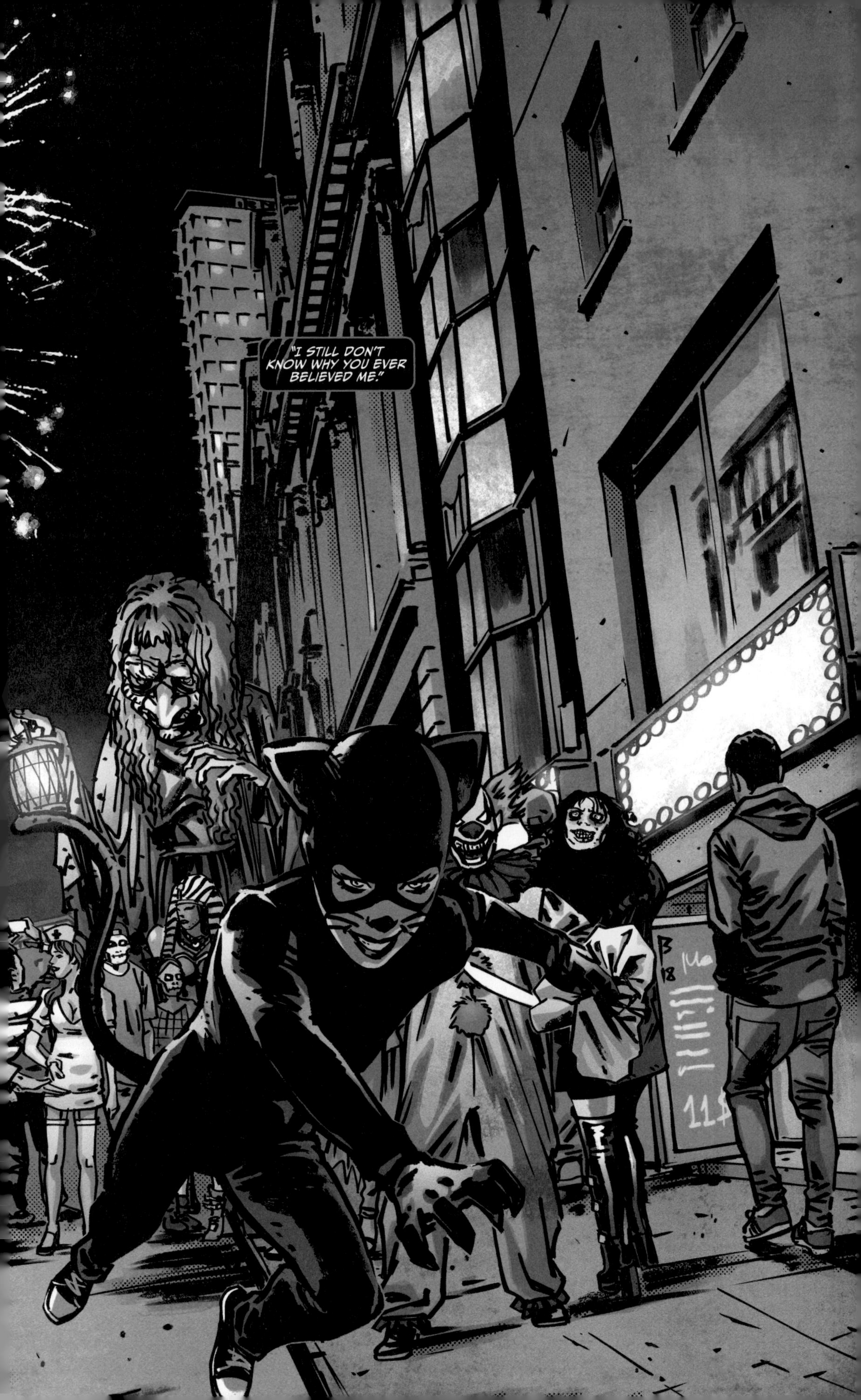
"I STILL DON'T KNOW WHY YOU EVER BELIEVED ME."
11$

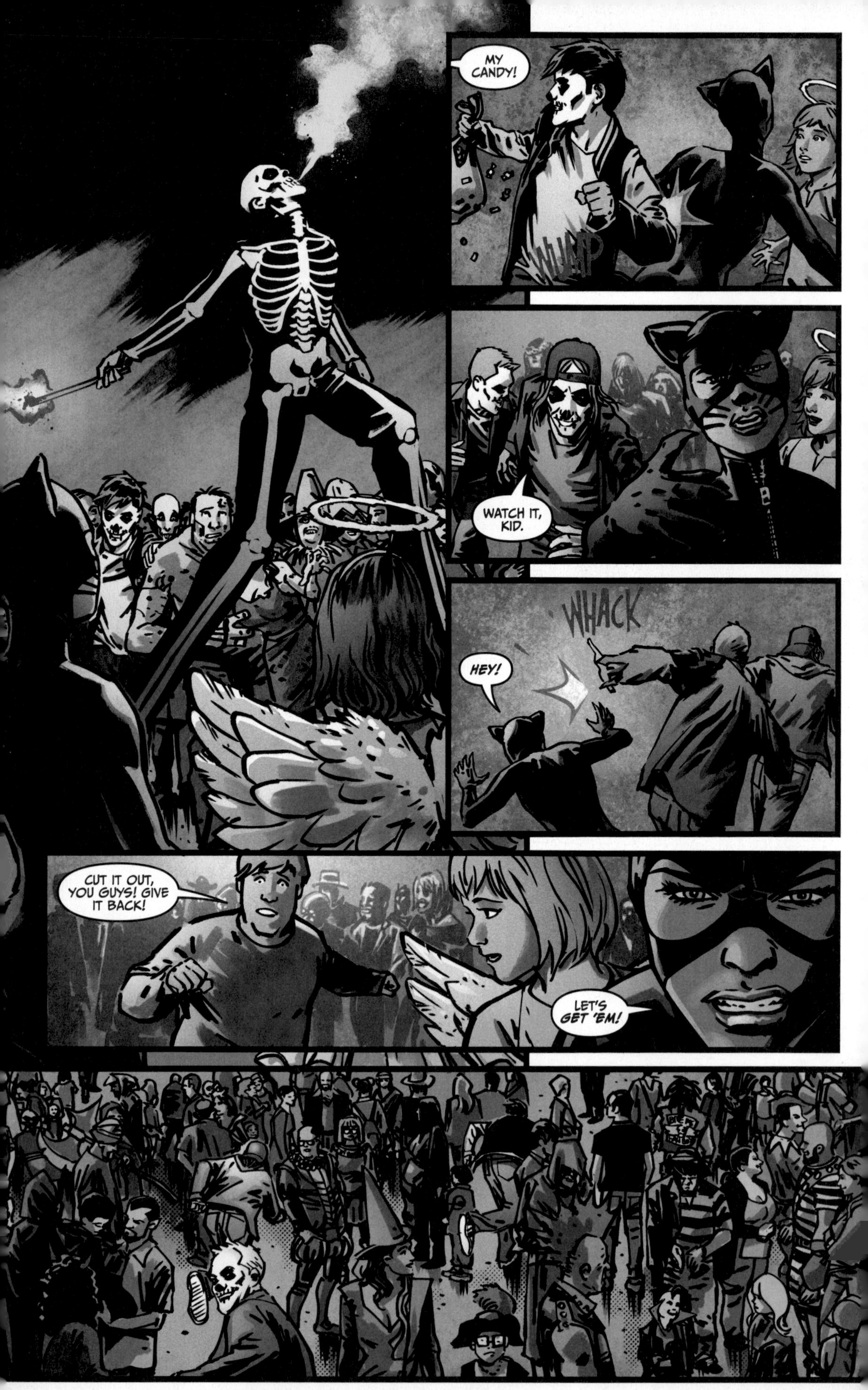
MY CANDY!
WUMP
WATCH IT, KID.
WHACK
HEY!
CUT IT OUT, YOU GUYS! GIVE IT BACK!
LET'S GET 'EM!

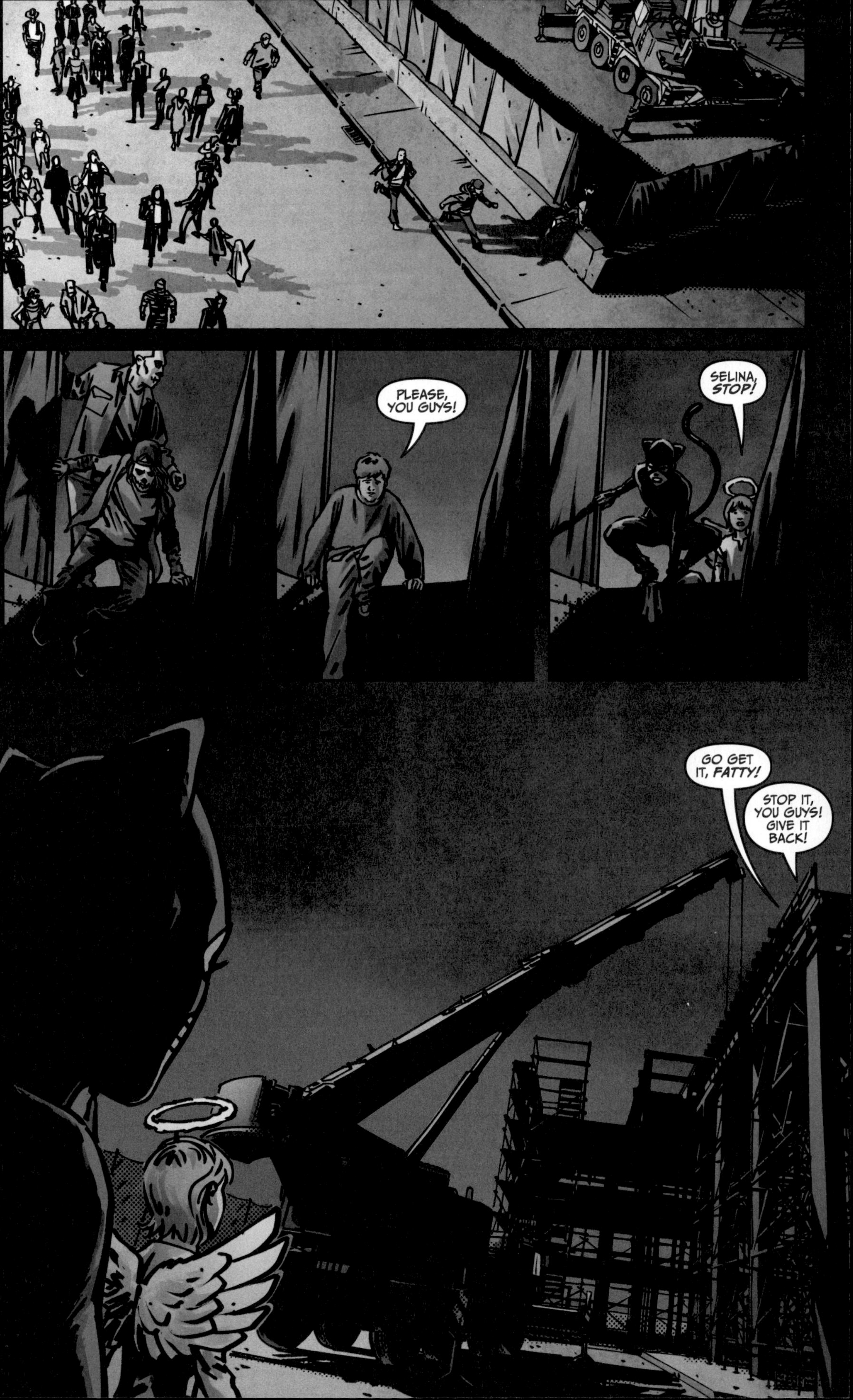
PLEASE, YOU GUYS!
SELINA, STOP!
GO GET IT, FATTY!
STOP IT, YOU GUYS! GIVE IT BACK!

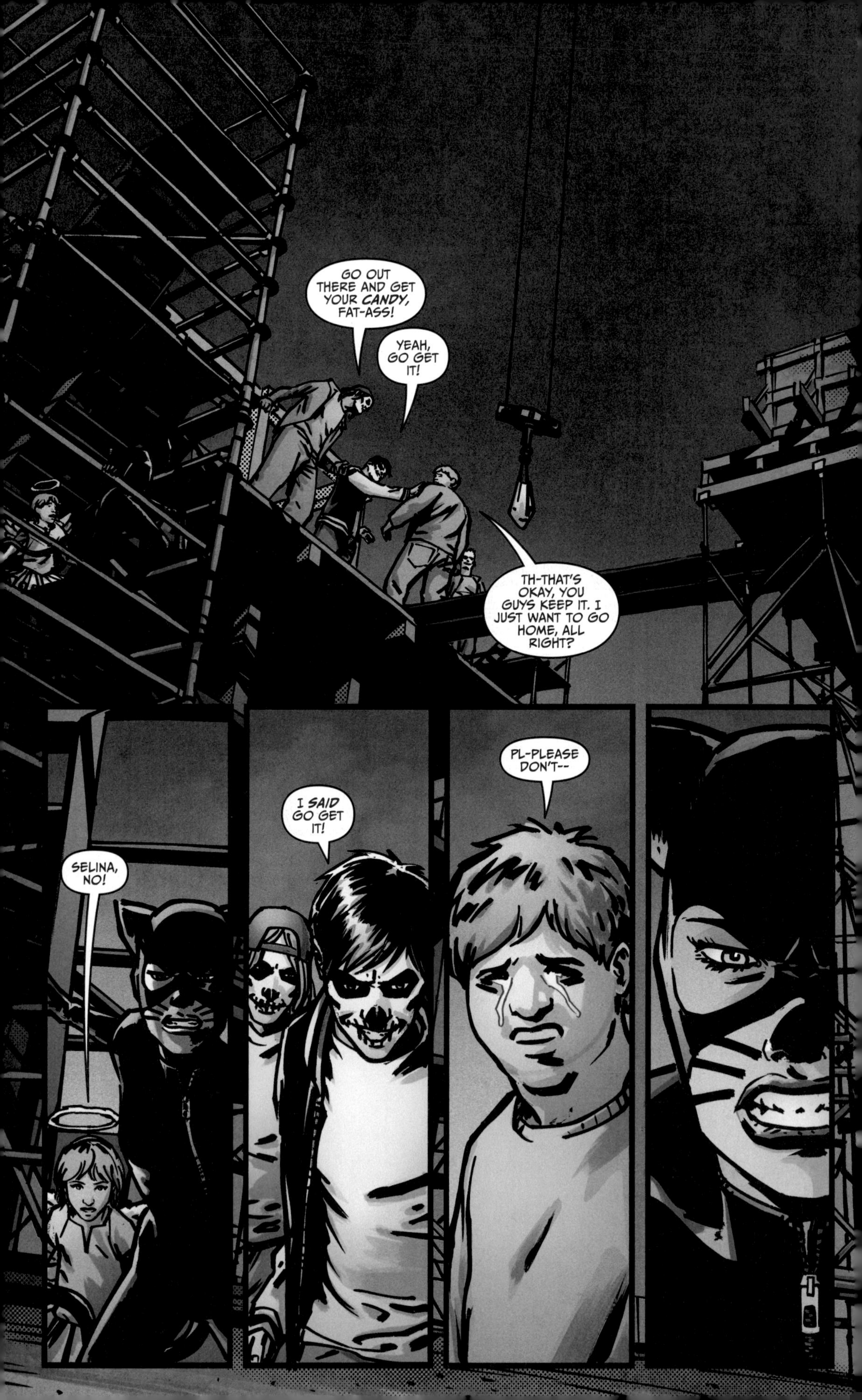
GO OUT THERE AND GET YOUR CANDY, FAT-ASS!
YEAH, GO GET IT!
TH-THAT'S OKAY, YOU GUYS KEEP IT. I JUST WANT TO GO HOME, ALL RIGHT?
SELINA, NO!
I SAID GO GET IT!
PL-PLEASE DON'T--

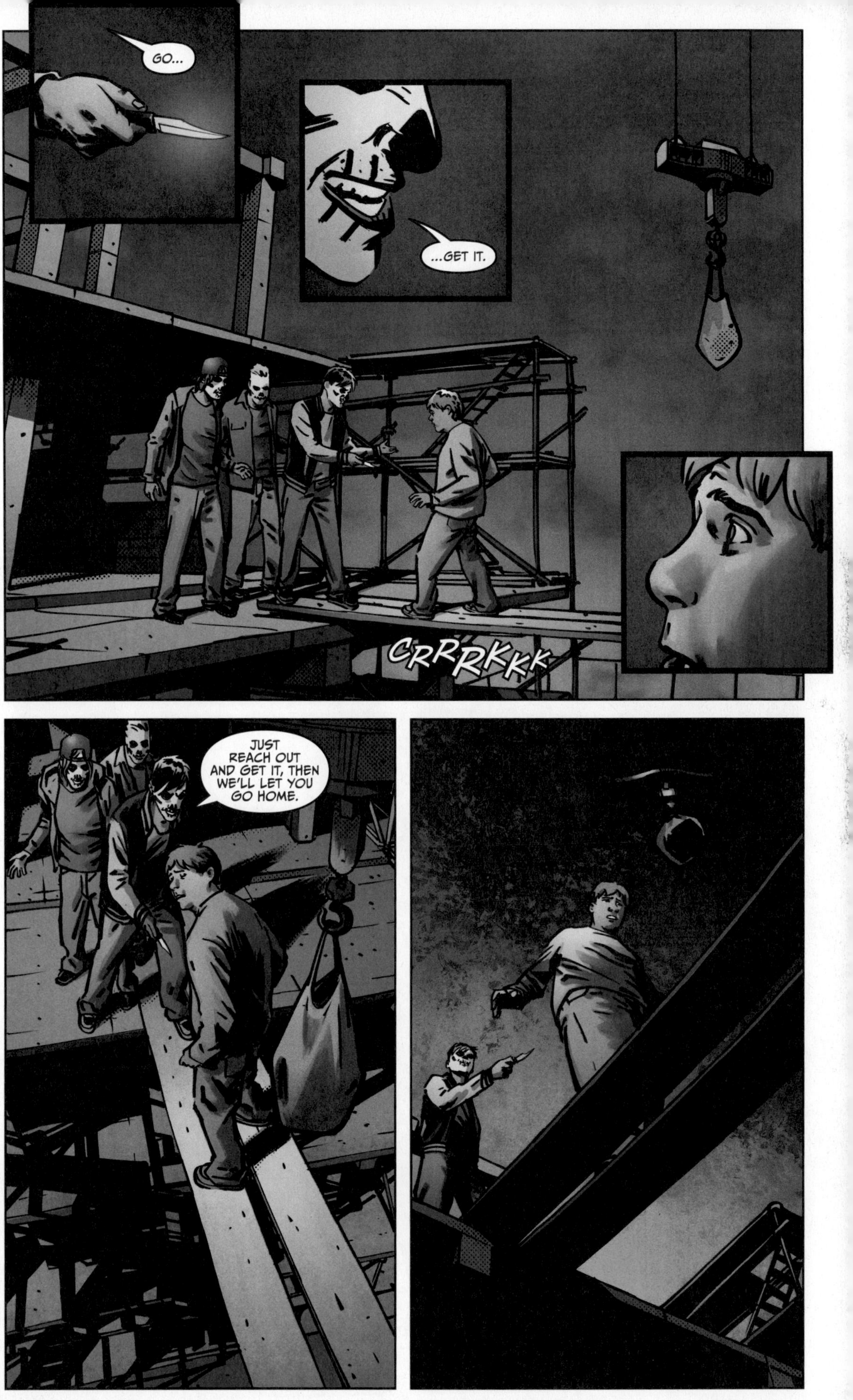
GO...
...GET IT.
CRRRKKK
JUST REACH OUT AND GET IT, THEN WE'LL LET YOU GO HOME.

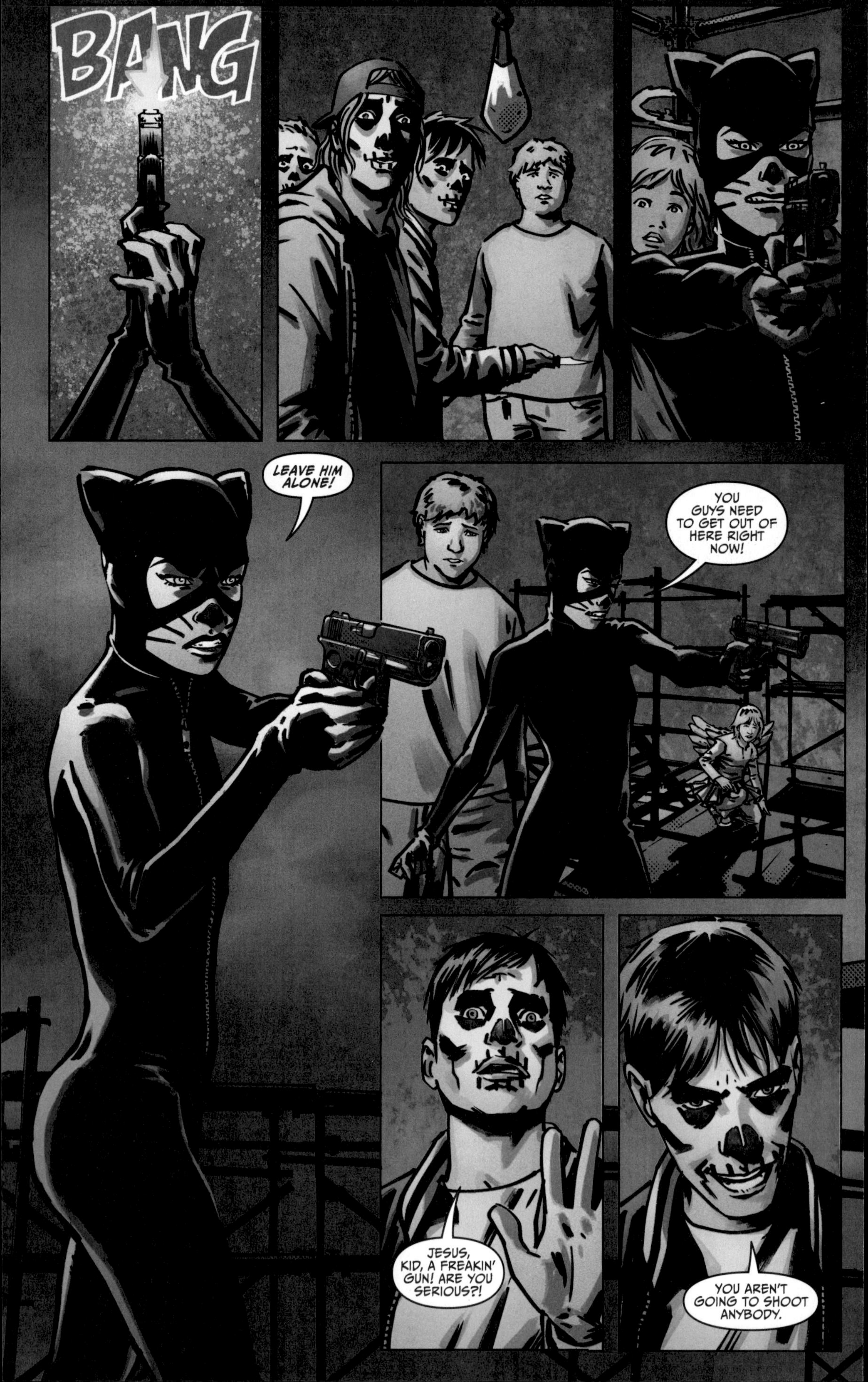
BANG
LEAVE HIM ALONE!
YOU GUYS NEED TO GET OUT OF HERE RIGHT NOW!
JESUS, KID, A FREAKIN' GUN! ARE YOU SERIOUS?!
YOU AREN'T GOING TO SHOOT ANYBODY.

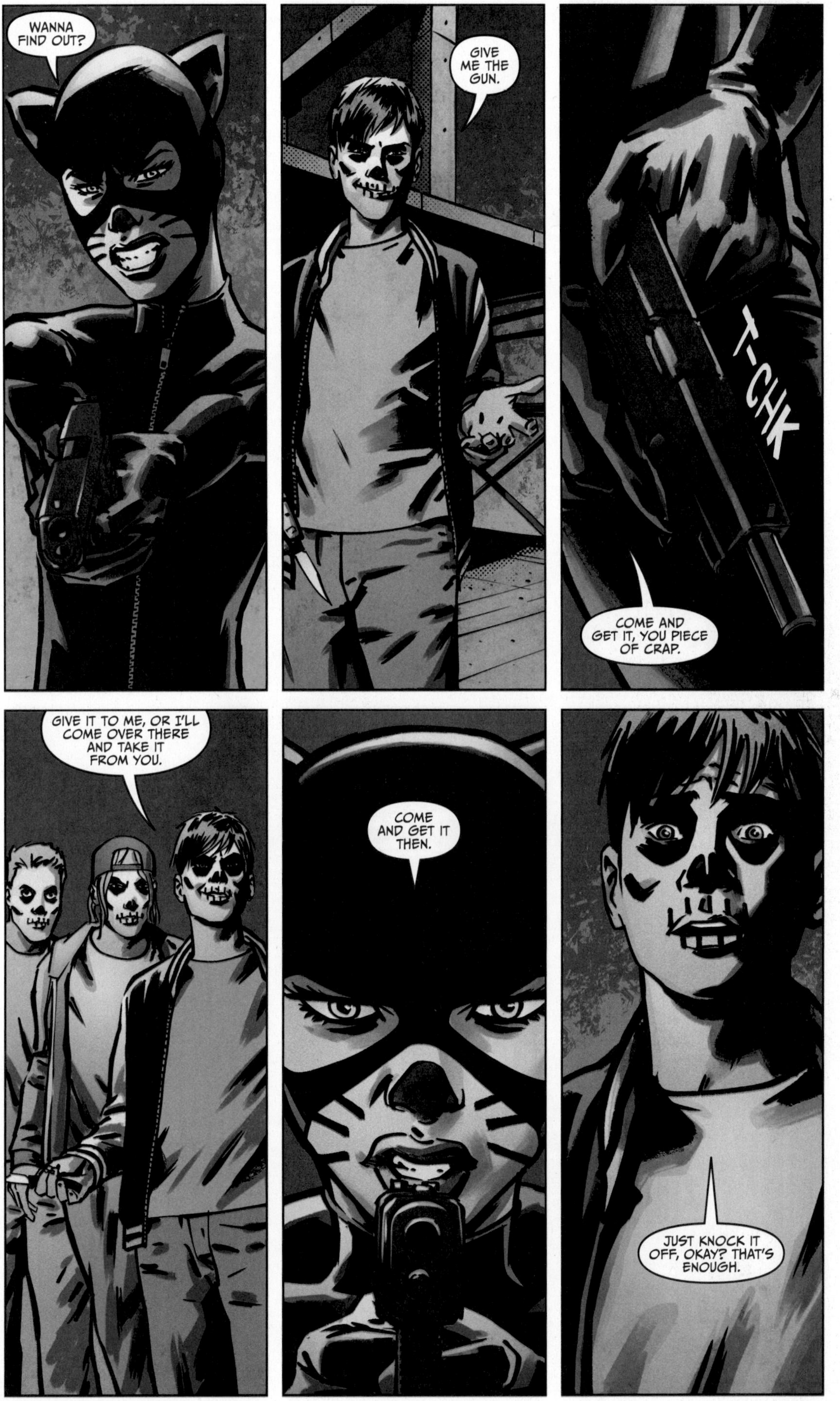
WANNA FIND OUT?
GIVE ME THE GUN.
T-CHK
COME AND GET IT, YOU PIECE OF CRAP.
GIVE IT TO ME, OR I'LL COME OVER THERE AND TAKE IT FROM YOU.
COME AND GET IT THEN.
JUST KNOCK IT OFF, OKAY? THAT'S ENOUGH.

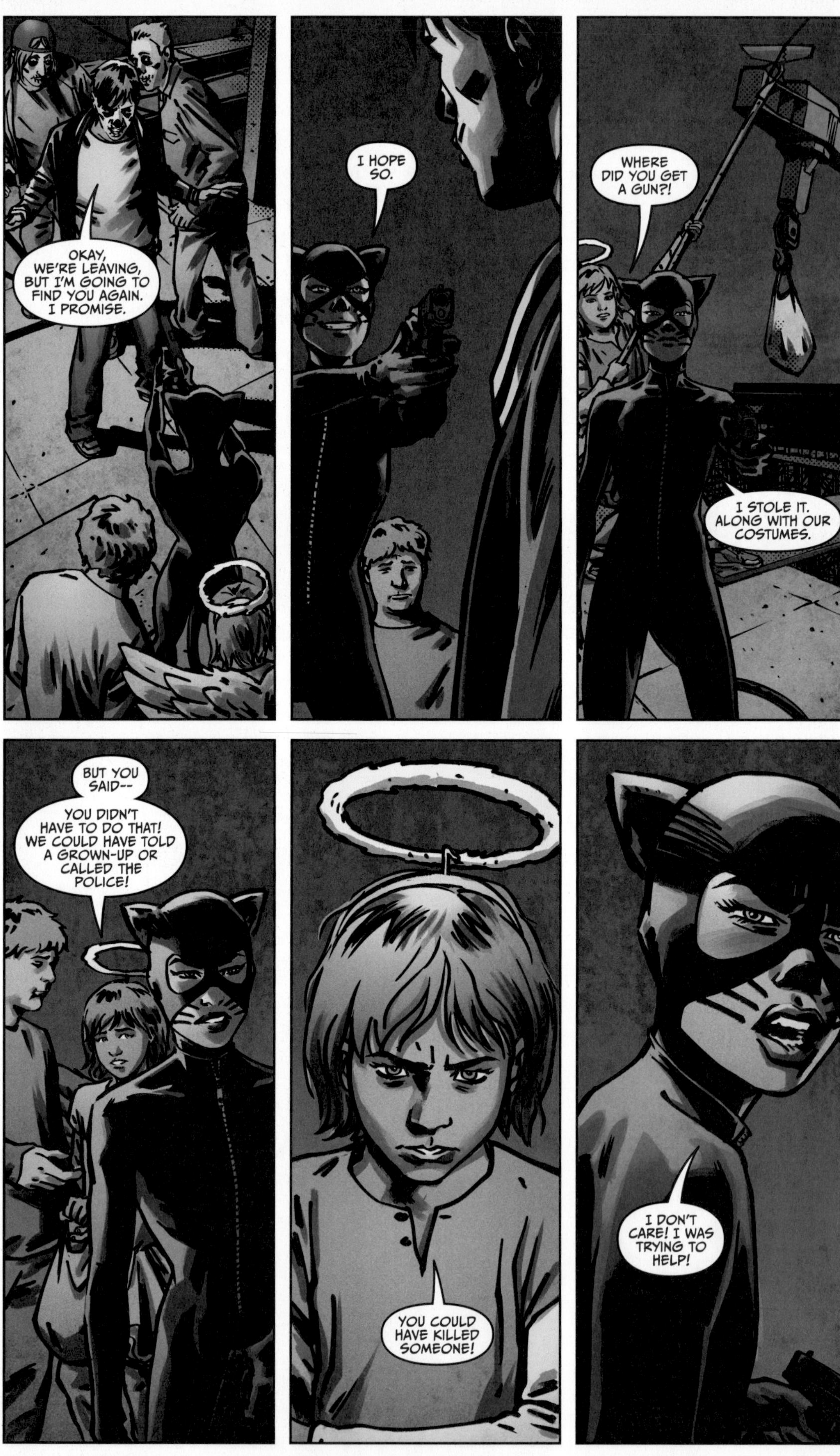
OKAY, WE'RE LEAVING, BUT I'M GOING TO FIND YOU AGAIN. I PROMISE.
I HOPE SO.
WHERE DID YOU GET A GUN?!
I STOLE IT. ALONG WITH OUR COSTUMES.
BUT YOU SAID--
YOU DIDN'T HAVE TO DO THAT! WE COULD HAVE TOLD A GROWN-UP OR CALLED THE POLICE!
YOU COULD HAVE KILLED SOMEONE!
I DON'T CARE! I WAS TRYING TO HELP!

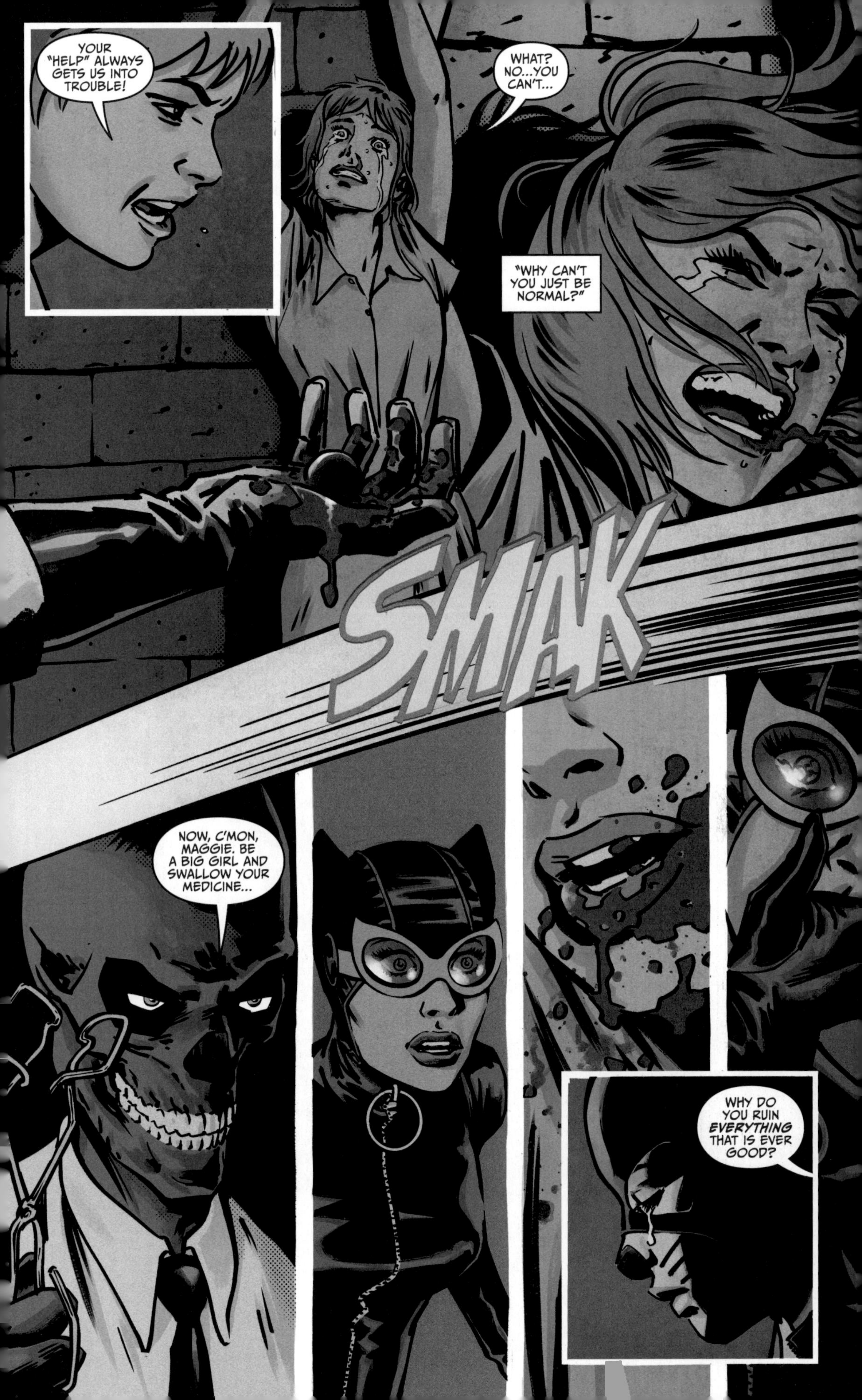
YOUR "HELP" ALWAYS GETS US INTO TROUBLE!
WHAT? NO...YOU CAN'T...
"WHY CAN'T YOU JUST BE NORMAL?"
SMAK
NOW, C'MON, MAGGIE. BE A BIG GIRL AND SWALLOW YOUR MEDICINE...
WHY DO YOU RUIN *EVERYTHING* THAT IS EVER GOOD?

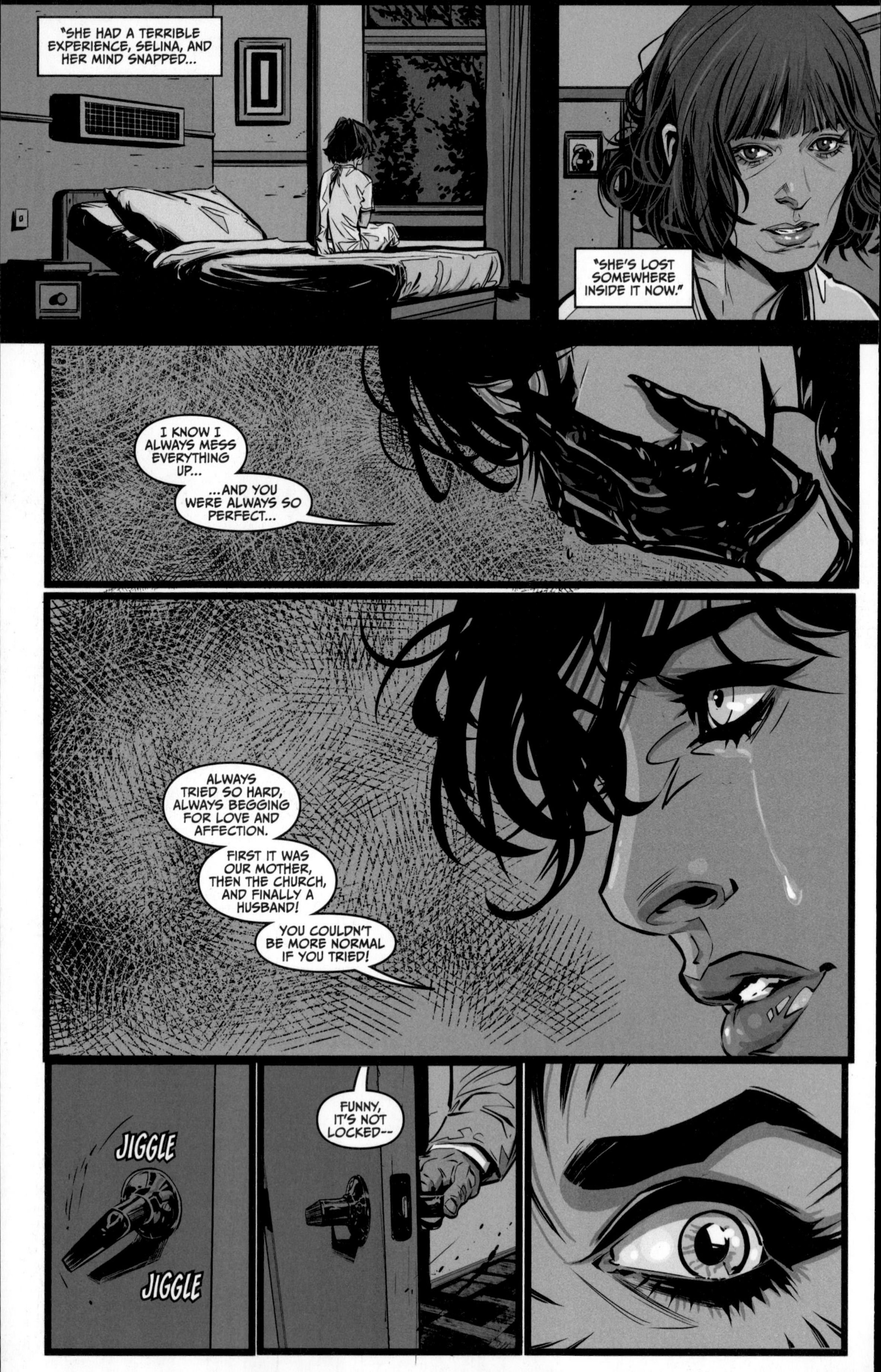
"SHE HAD A TERRIBLE EXPERIENCE, SELINA, AND HER MIND SNAPPED...
"SHE'S LOST SOMEWHERE INSIDE IT NOW."
I KNOW I ALWAYS MESS EVERYTHING UP...
...AND YOU WERE ALWAYS SO PERFECT...
ALWAYS TRIED SO HARD, ALWAYS BEGGING FOR LOVE AND AFFECTION.
FIRST IT WAS OUR MOTHER, THEN THE CHURCH, AND FINALLY A HUSBAND!
YOU COULDN'T BE MORE NORMAL IF YOU TRIED!
JIGGLE
JIGGLE
FUNNY, IT'S NOT LOCKED--

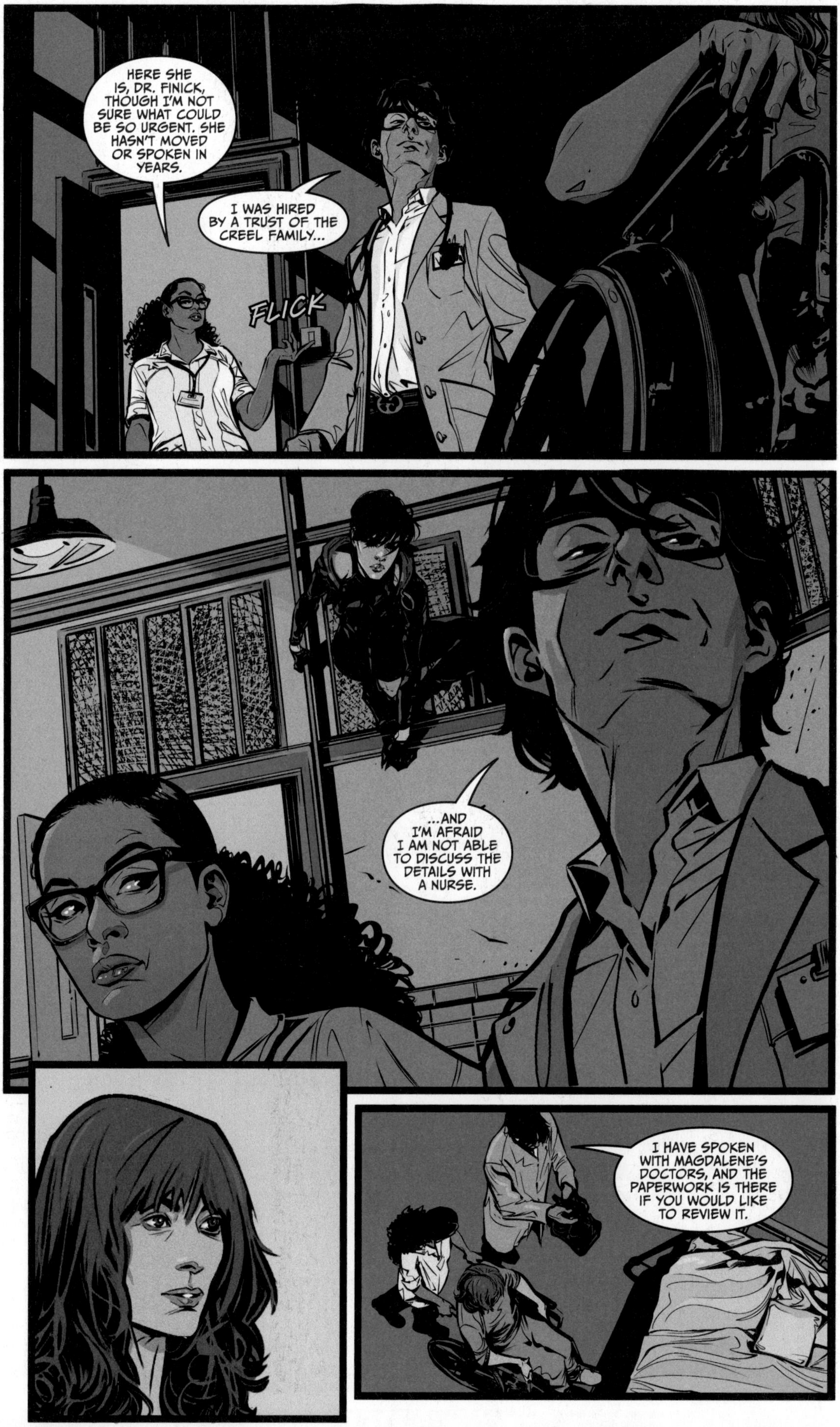
HERE SHE IS, DR. FINICK, THOUGH I'M NOT SURE WHAT COULD BE SO URGENT. SHE HASN'T MOVED OR SPOKEN IN YEARS.
I WAS HIRED BY A TRUST OF THE CREEL FAMILY...
FLICK
...AND I'M AFRAID I AM NOT ABLE TO DISCUSS THE DETAILS WITH A NURSE.
I HAVE SPOKEN WITH MAGDALENE'S DOCTORS, AND THE PAPERWORK IS THERE IF YOU WOULD LIKE TO REVIEW IT.

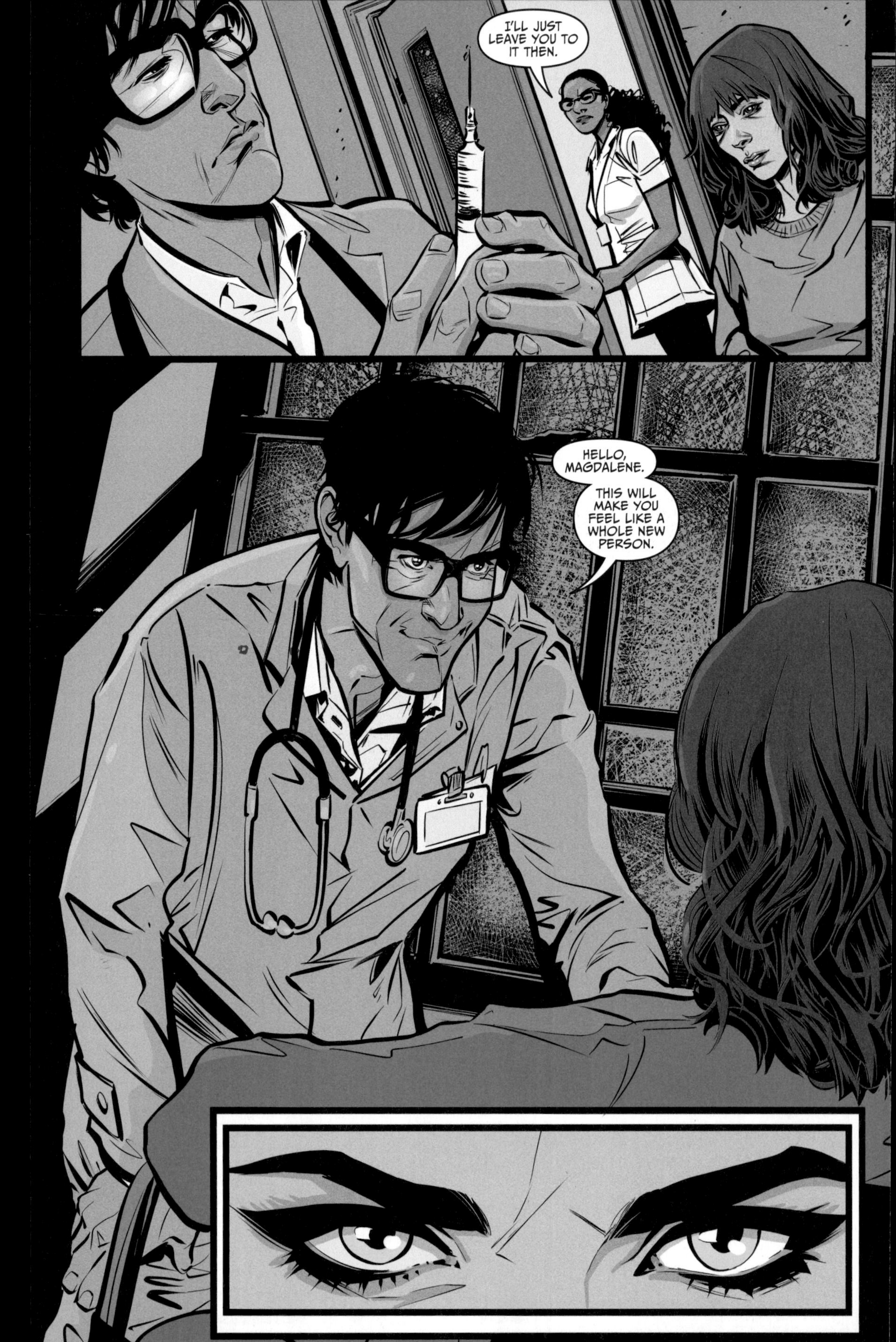
I'LL JUST LEAVE YOU TO IT THEN.
HELLO, MAGDALENE.
THIS WILL MAKE YOU FEEL LIKE A WHOLE NEW PERSON.

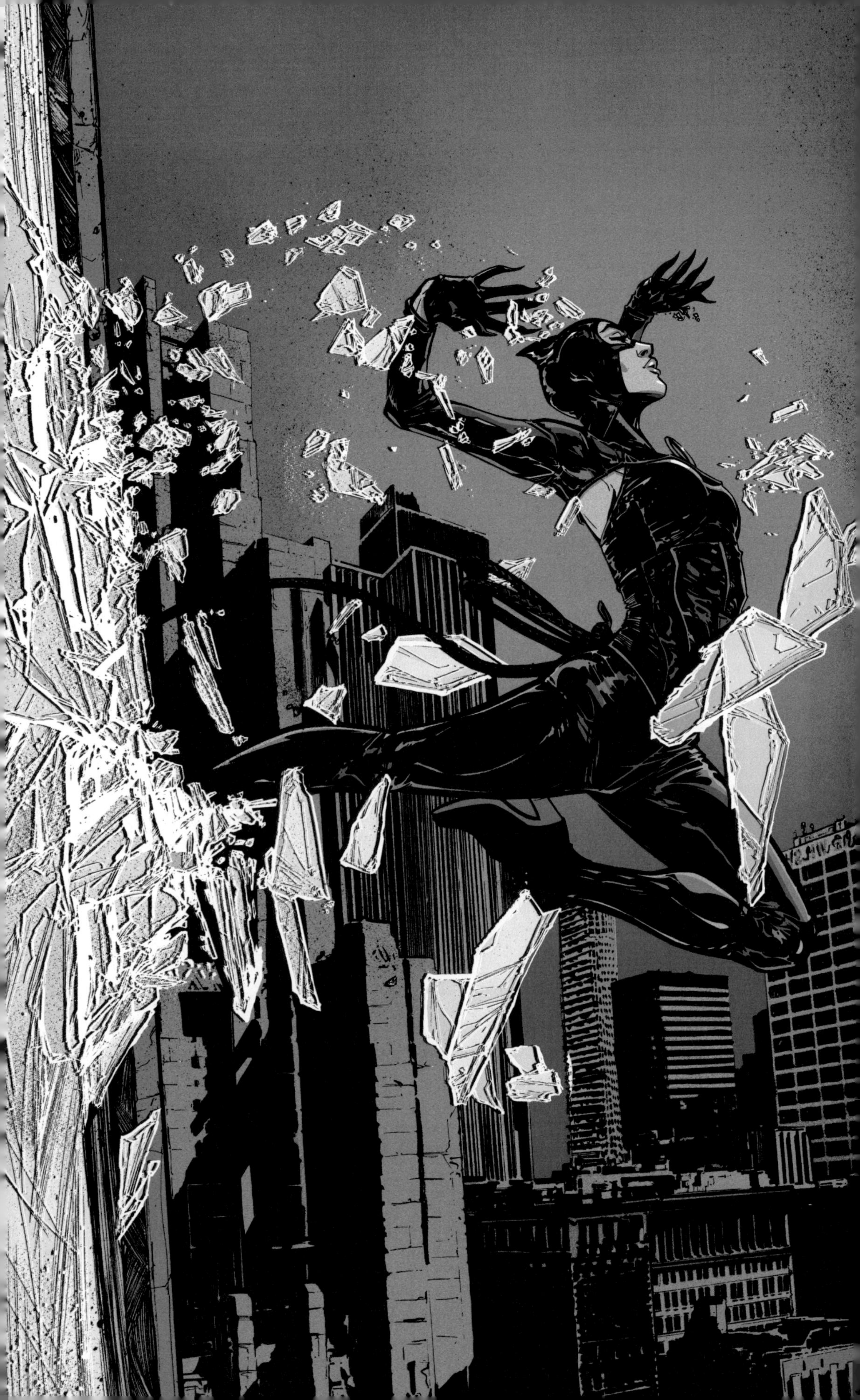

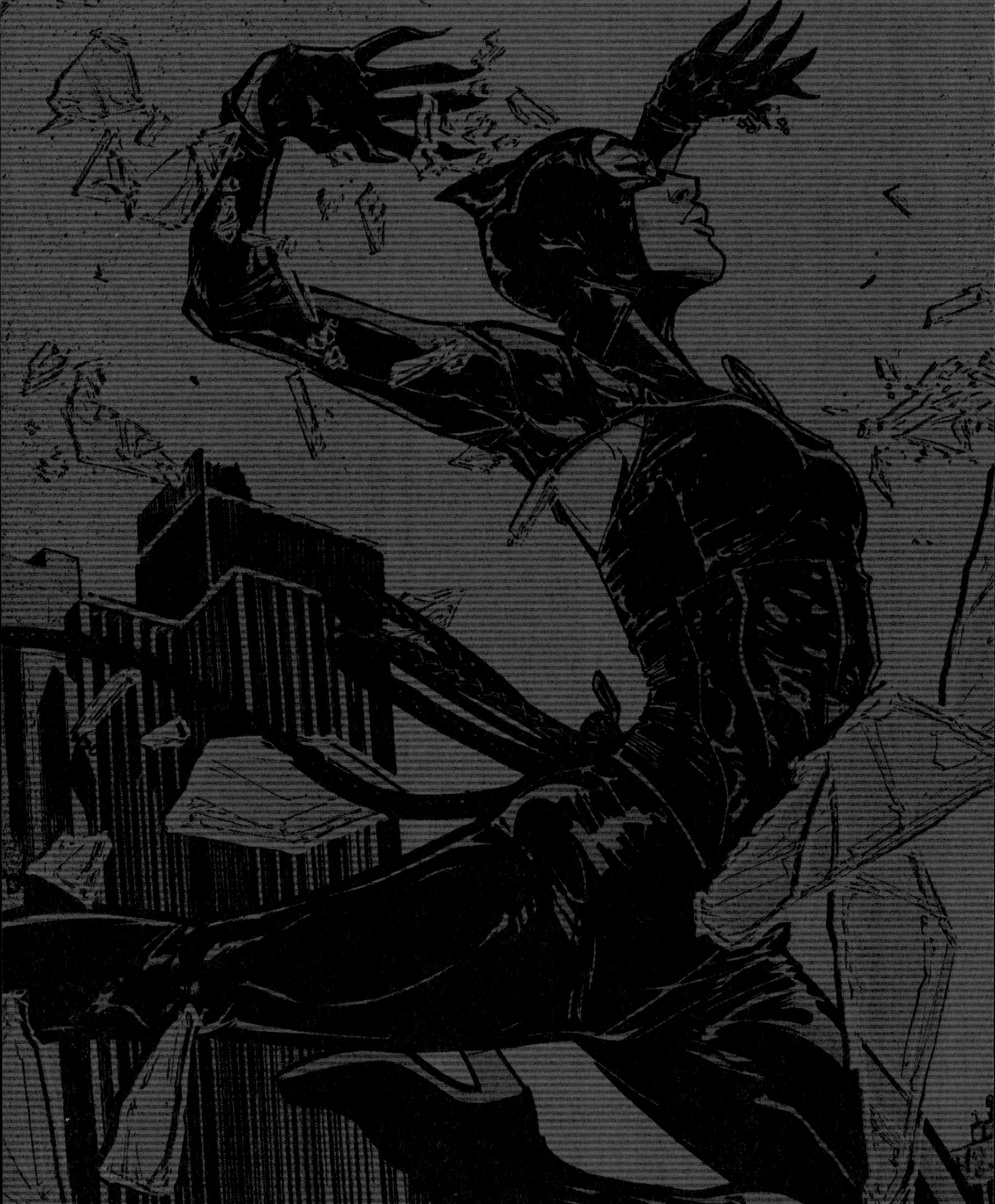

CATWOMAN
#5

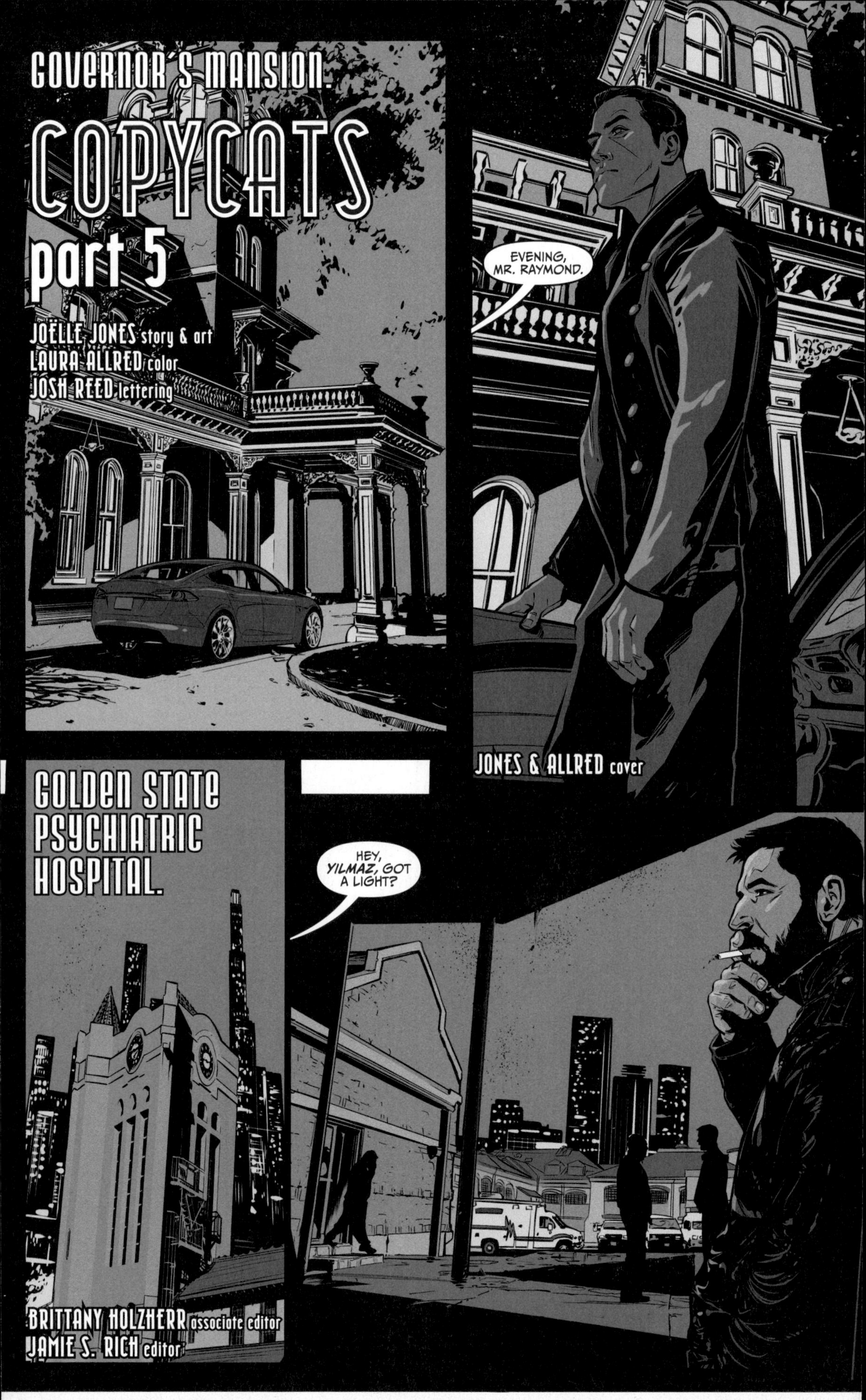
GOVERNOR'S MANSION.
COPYCATS
part 5
JOËLLE JONES story & art
LAURA ALLRED color
JOSH REED lettering
EVENING, MR. RAYMOND.
JONES & ALLRED cover
GOLDEN STATE PSYCHIATRIC HOSPITAL.
HEY, *YILMAZ,* GOT A LIGHT?
BRITTANY HOLZHERR associate editor
JAMIE S. RICH editor

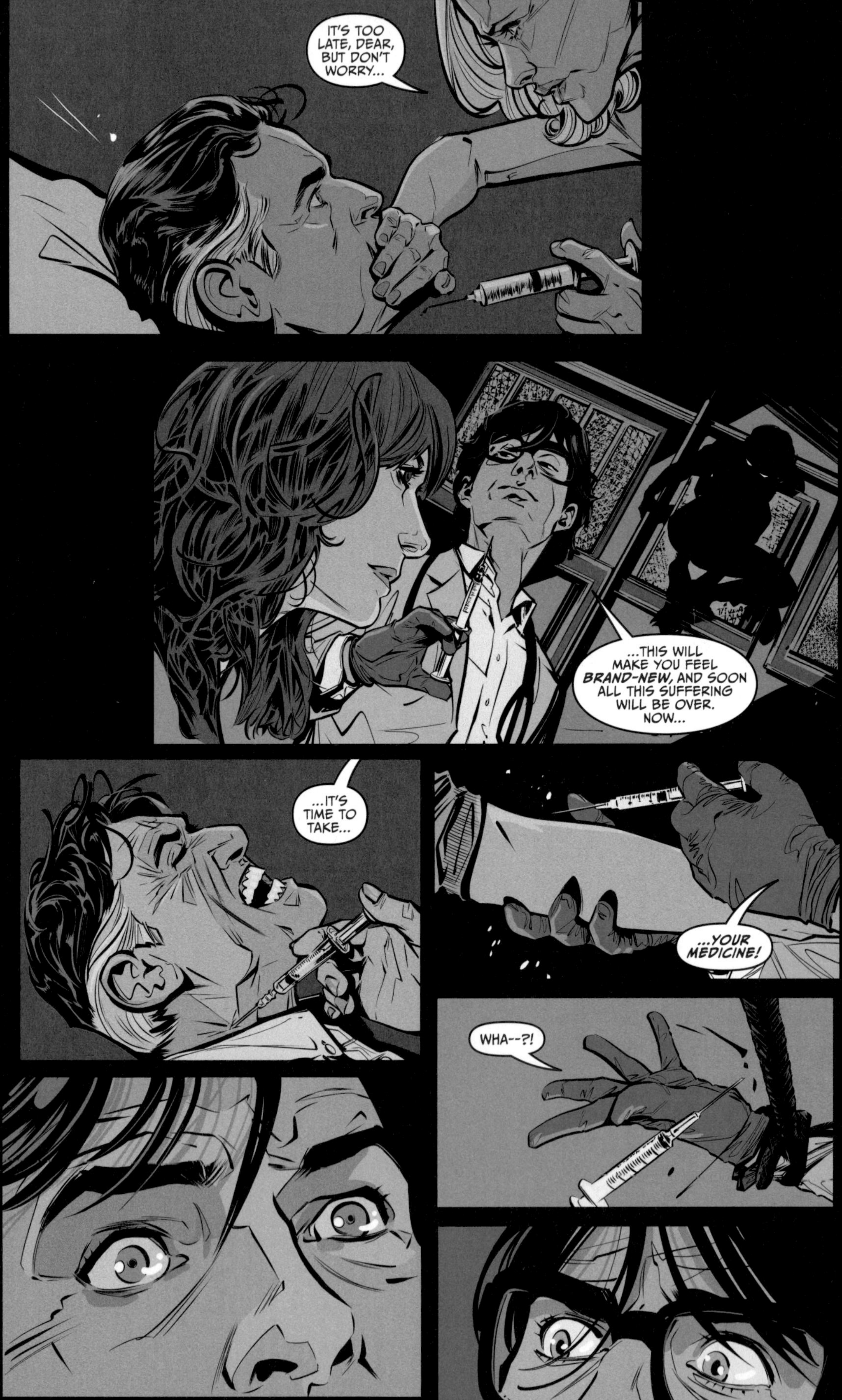
IT'S TOO LATE, DEAR, BUT DON'T WORRY...
...THIS WILL MAKE YOU FEEL *BRAND-NEW,* AND SOON ALL THIS SUFFERING WILL BE OVER. NOW...
...IT'S TIME TO TAKE...
...YOUR MEDICINE!
WHA--?!

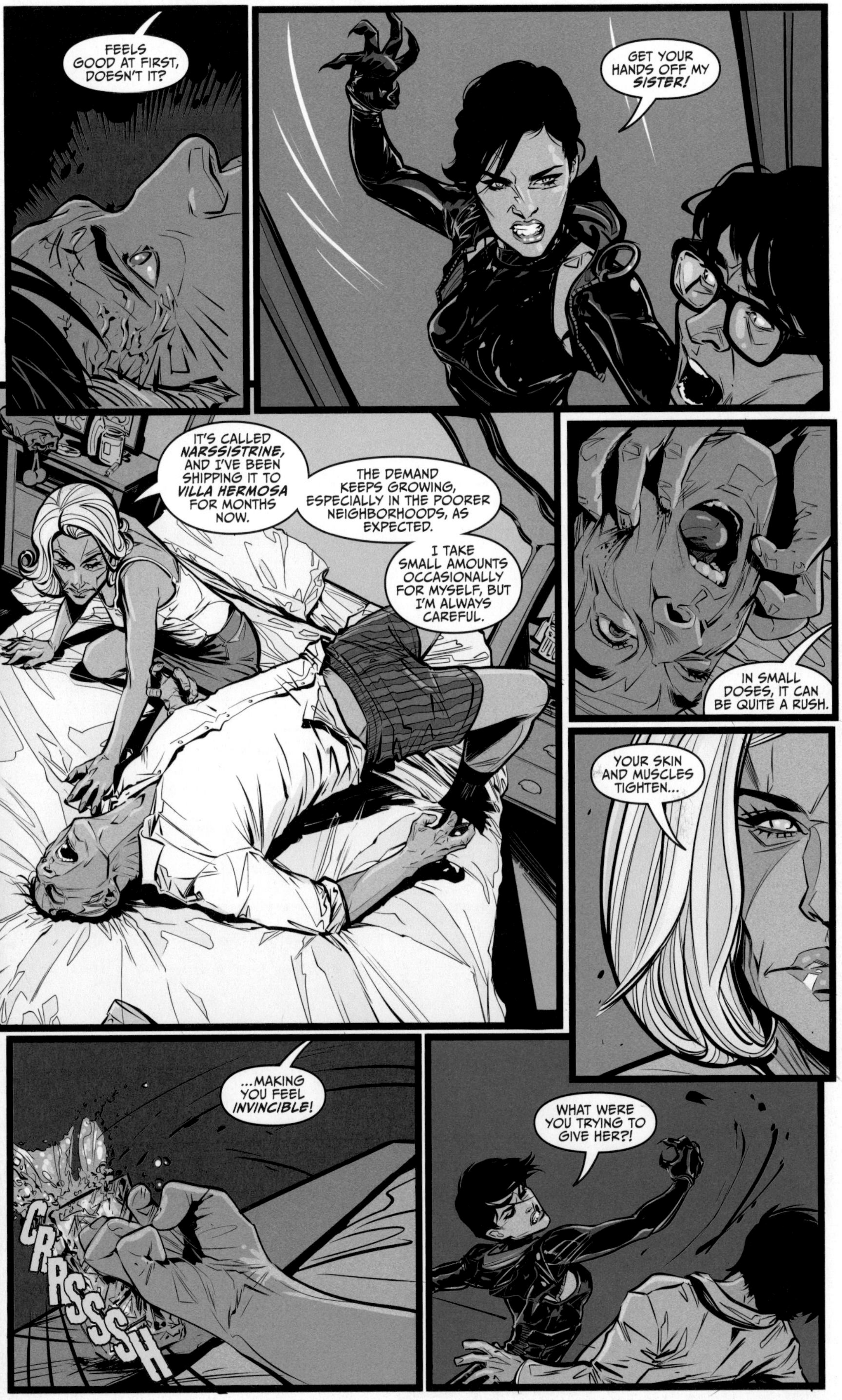
FEELS GOOD AT FIRST, DOESN'T IT?
GET YOUR HANDS OFF MY SISTER!
IT'S CALLED NARSSISTRINE, AND I'VE BEEN SHIPPING IT TO VILLA HERMOSA FOR MONTHS NOW.
THE DEMAND KEEPS GROWING, ESPECIALLY IN THE POORER NEIGHBORHOODS, AS EXPECTED.
I TAKE SMALL AMOUNTS OCCASIONALLY FOR MYSELF, BUT I'M ALWAYS CAREFUL.
IN SMALL DOSES, IT CAN BE QUITE A RUSH.
YOUR SKIN AND MUSCLES TIGHTEN...
...MAKING YOU FEEL INVINCIBLE!
CRRSSSSH
WHAT WERE YOU TRYING TO GIVE HER?!

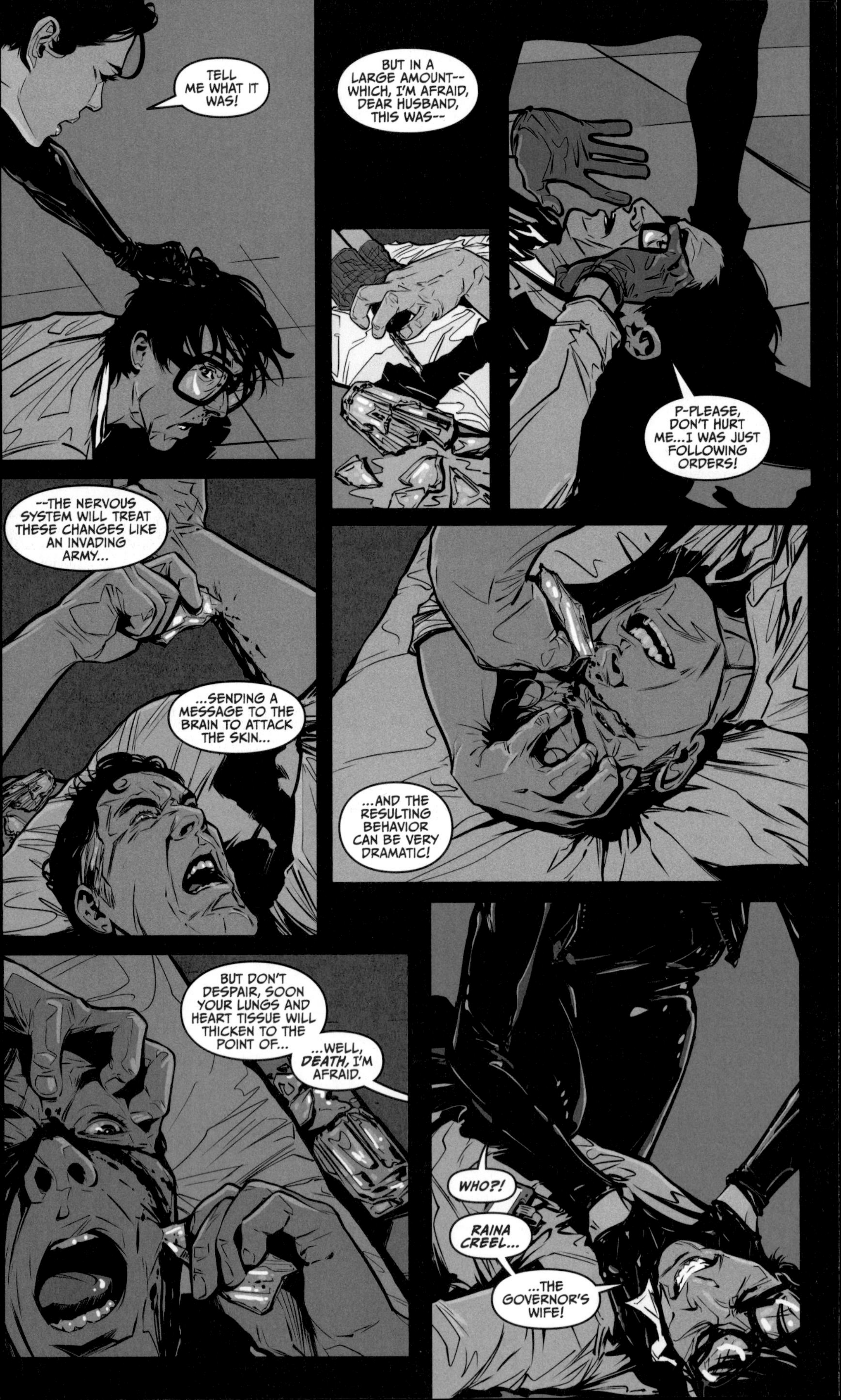
TELL ME WHAT IT WAS!
BUT IN A LARGE AMOUNT--WHICH, I'M AFRAID, DEAR HUSBAND, THIS WAS--
P-PLEASE, DON'T HURT ME...I WAS JUST FOLLOWING ORDERS!
--THE NERVOUS SYSTEM WILL TREAT THESE CHANGES LIKE AN INVADING ARMY...
...SENDING A MESSAGE TO THE BRAIN TO ATTACK THE SKIN...
...AND THE RESULTING BEHAVIOR CAN BE VERY DRAMATIC!
BUT DON'T DESPAIR, SOON YOUR LUNGS AND HEART TISSUE WILL THICKEN TO THE POINT OF...
...WELL, *DEATH*, I'M AFRAID.
WHO?!
RAINA CREEL...
...THE GOVERNOR'S WIFE!

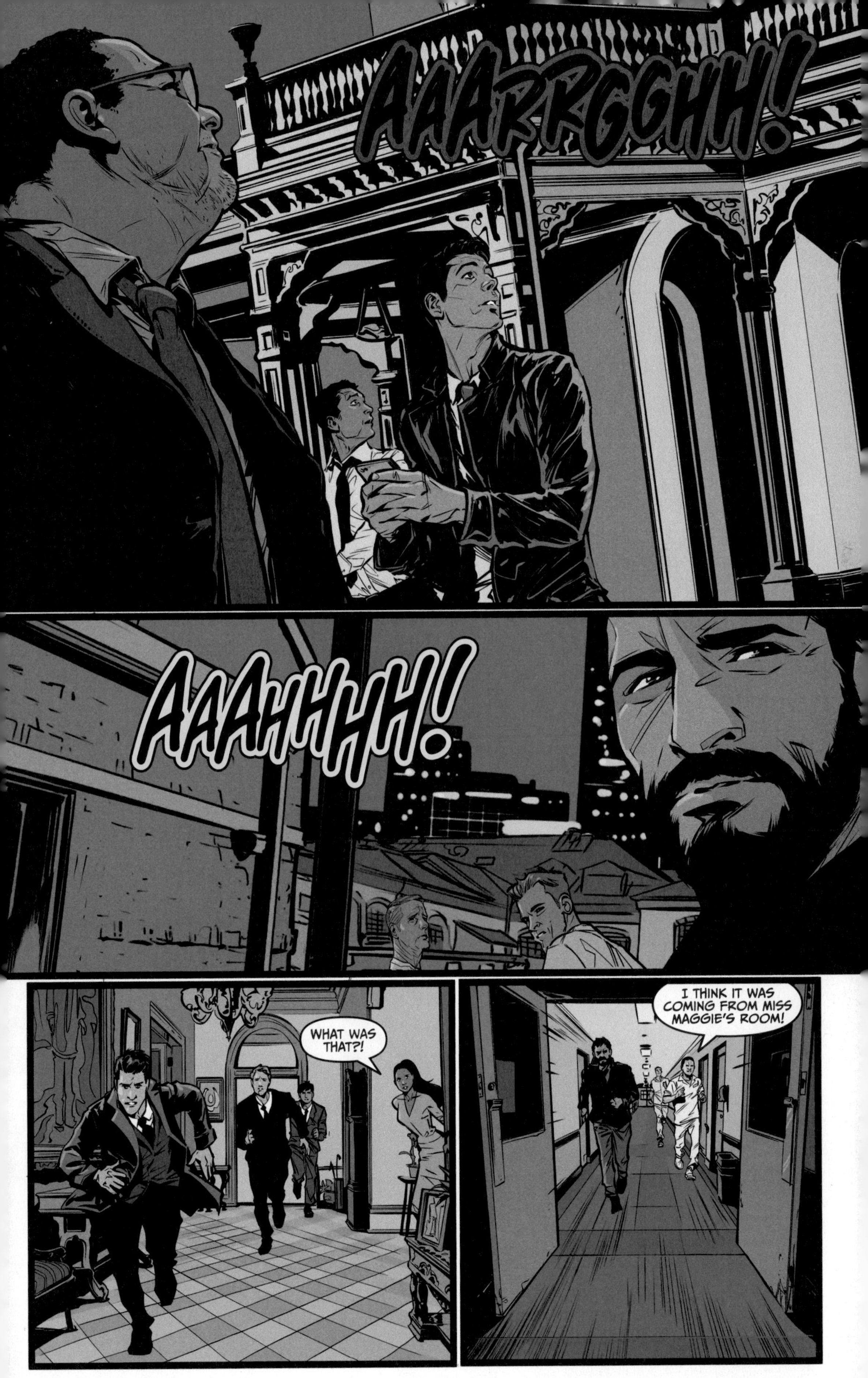
AAARRGGHH!
AAAHHHH!
WHAT WAS THAT?!
I THINK IT WAS COMING FROM MISS MAGGIE'S ROOM!

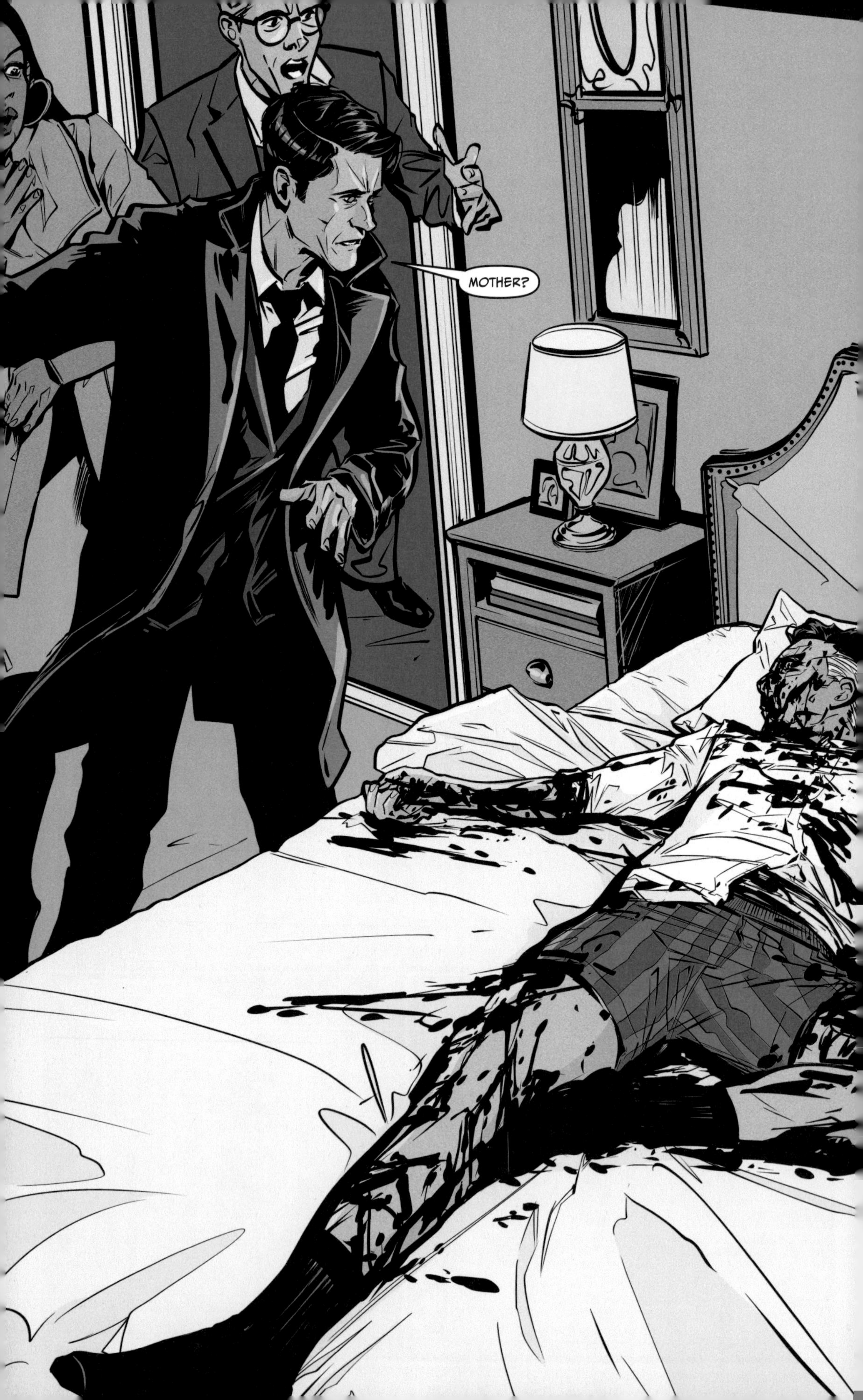
MOTHER?

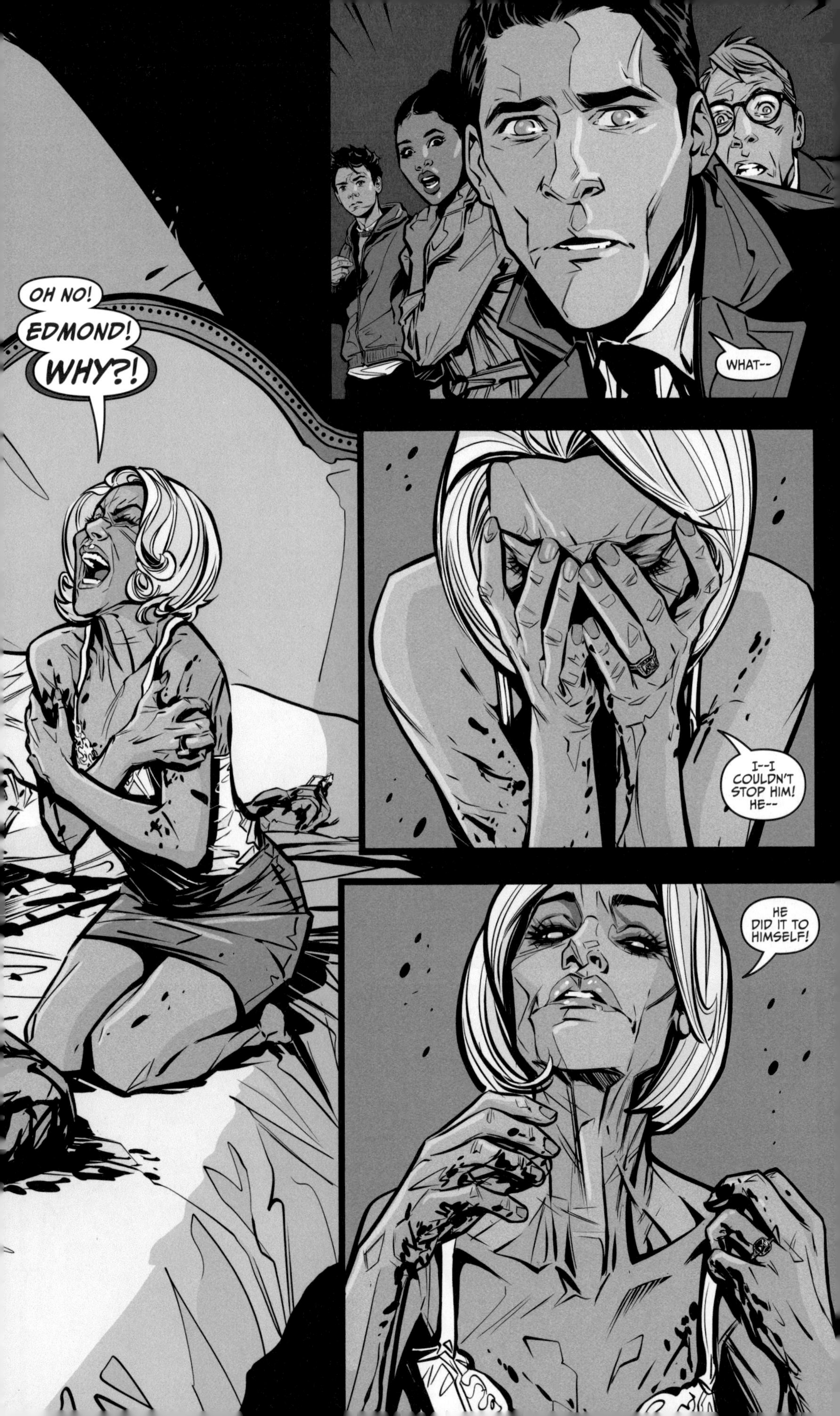

WHAT--
OH NO!
EDMOND!
WHY?!
I--I COULDN'T STOP HIM! HE--
HE DID IT TO HIMSELF!

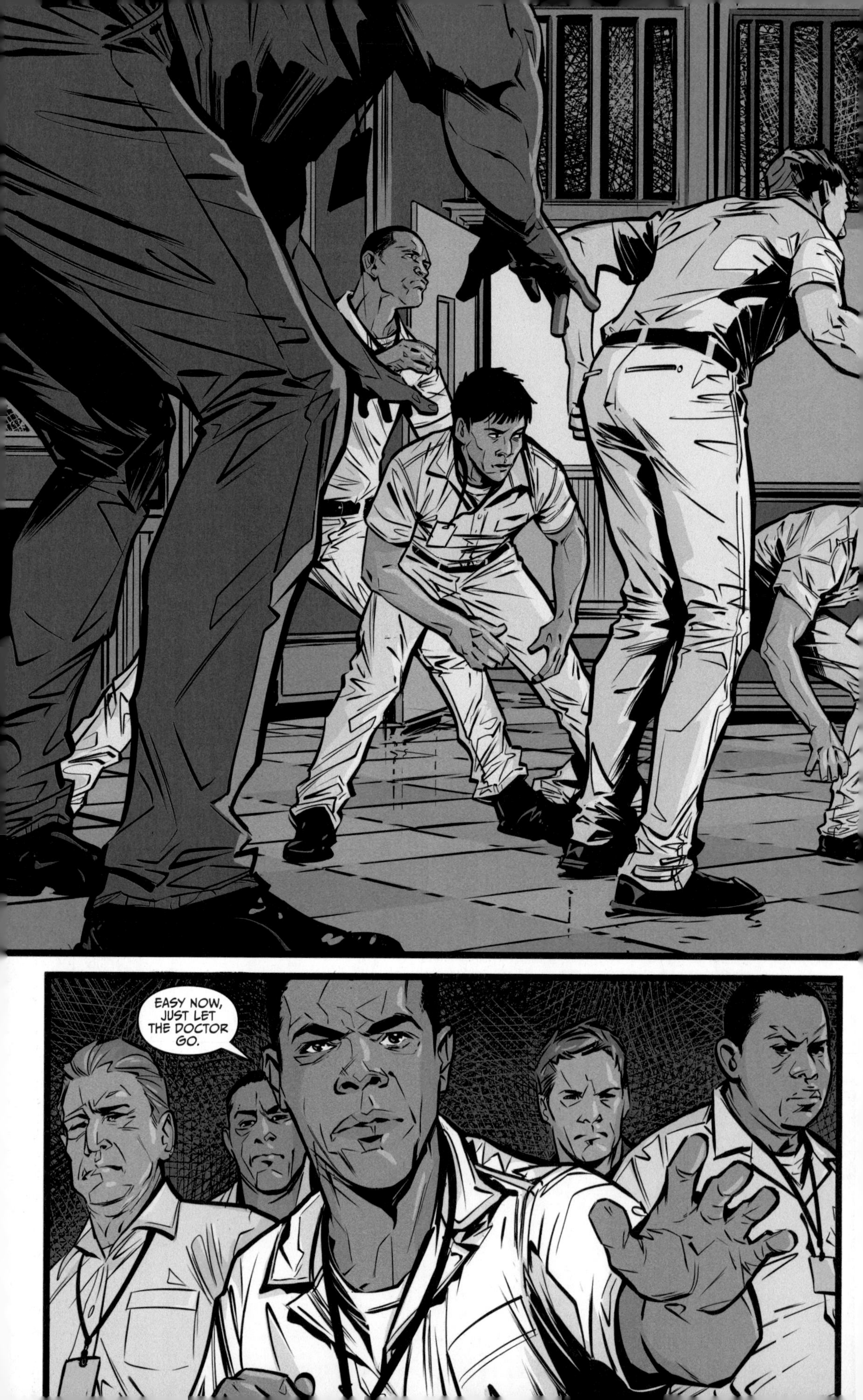
EASY NOW, JUST LET THE DOCTOR GO.

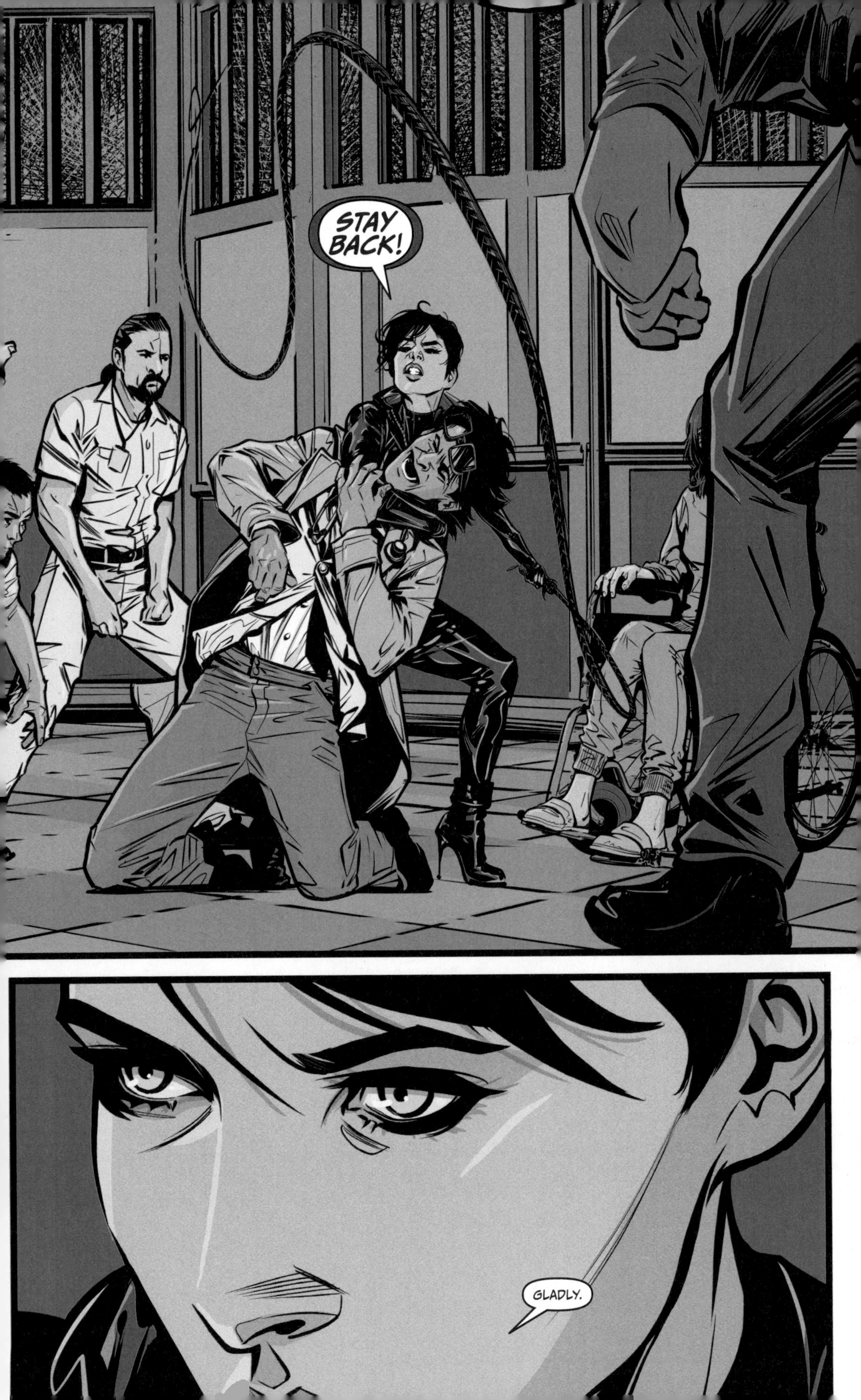
STAY BACK!
GLADLY.

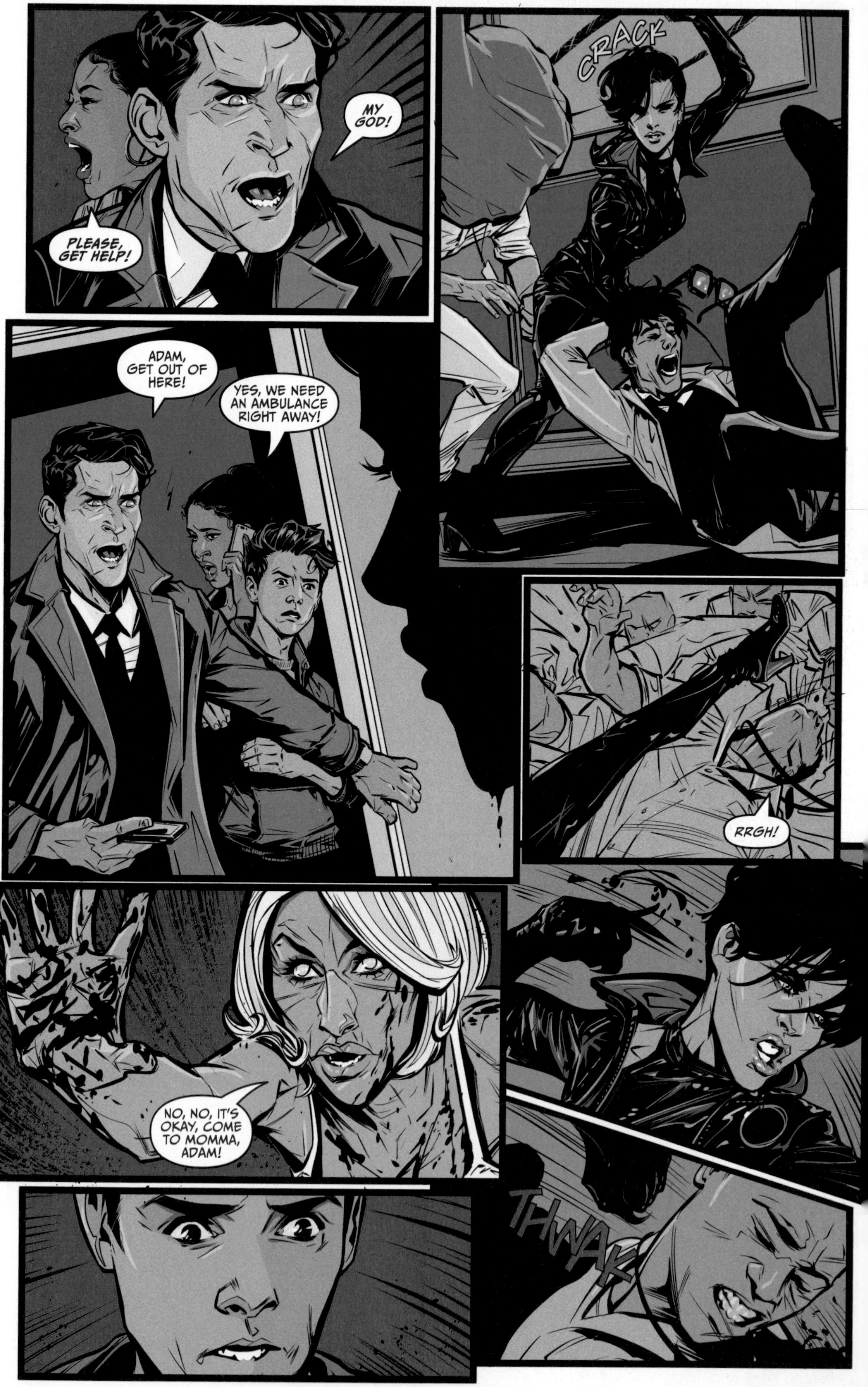
MY GOD!
PLEASE, GET HELP!
CRACK
ADAM, GET OUT OF HERE!
YES, WE NEED AN AMBULANCE RIGHT AWAY!
RRGH!
NO, NO, IT'S OKAY, COME TO MOMMA, ADAM!
THWAK

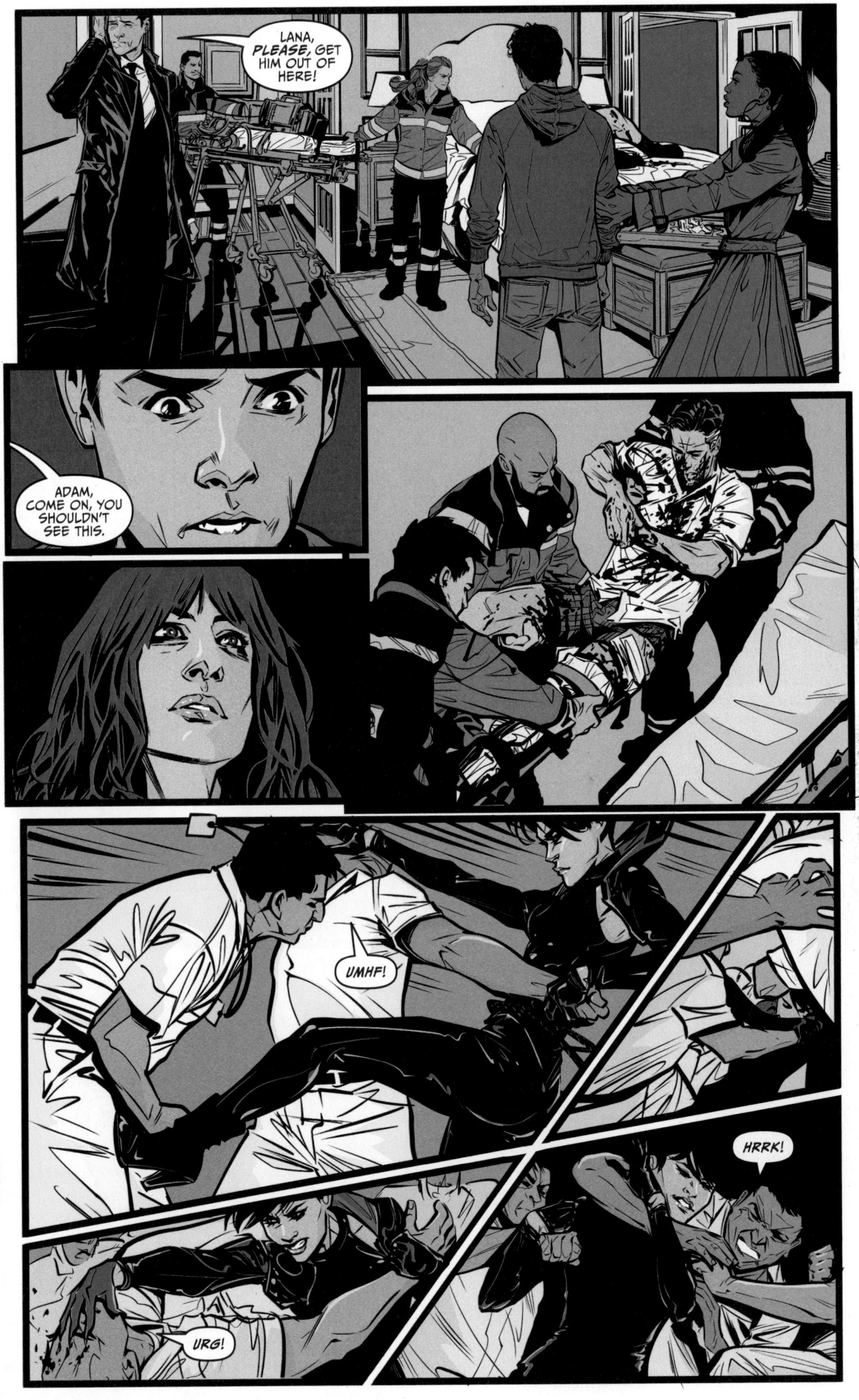
LANA, PLEASE, GET HIM OUT OF HERE!
ADAM, COME ON, YOU SHOULDN'T SEE THIS.
UMHF!
HRRK!
URG!

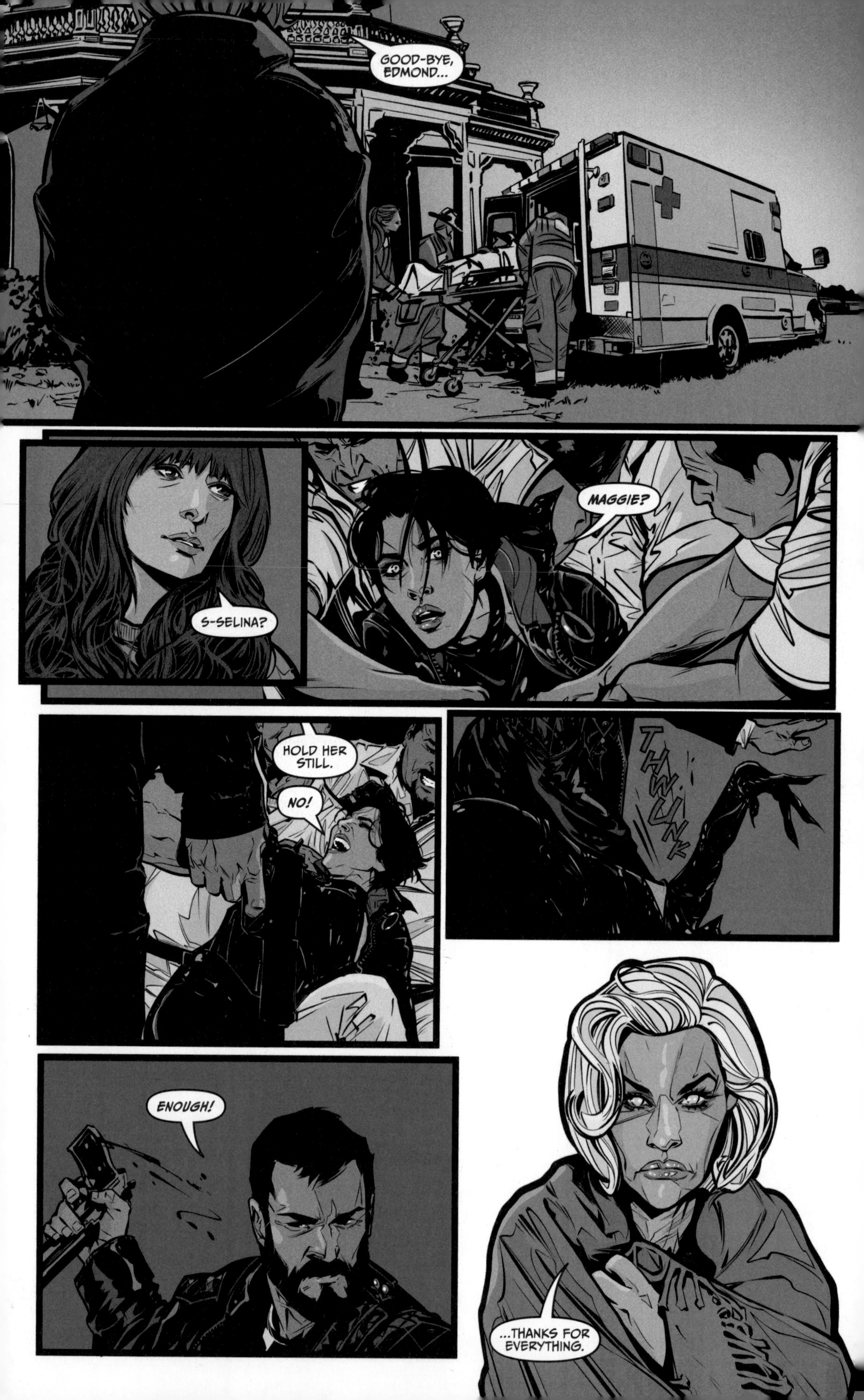
GOOD-BYE, EDMOND...
S-SELINA?
MAGGIE?
HOLD HER STILL.
NO!
THWUNK
ENOUGH!
...THANKS FOR EVERYTHING.

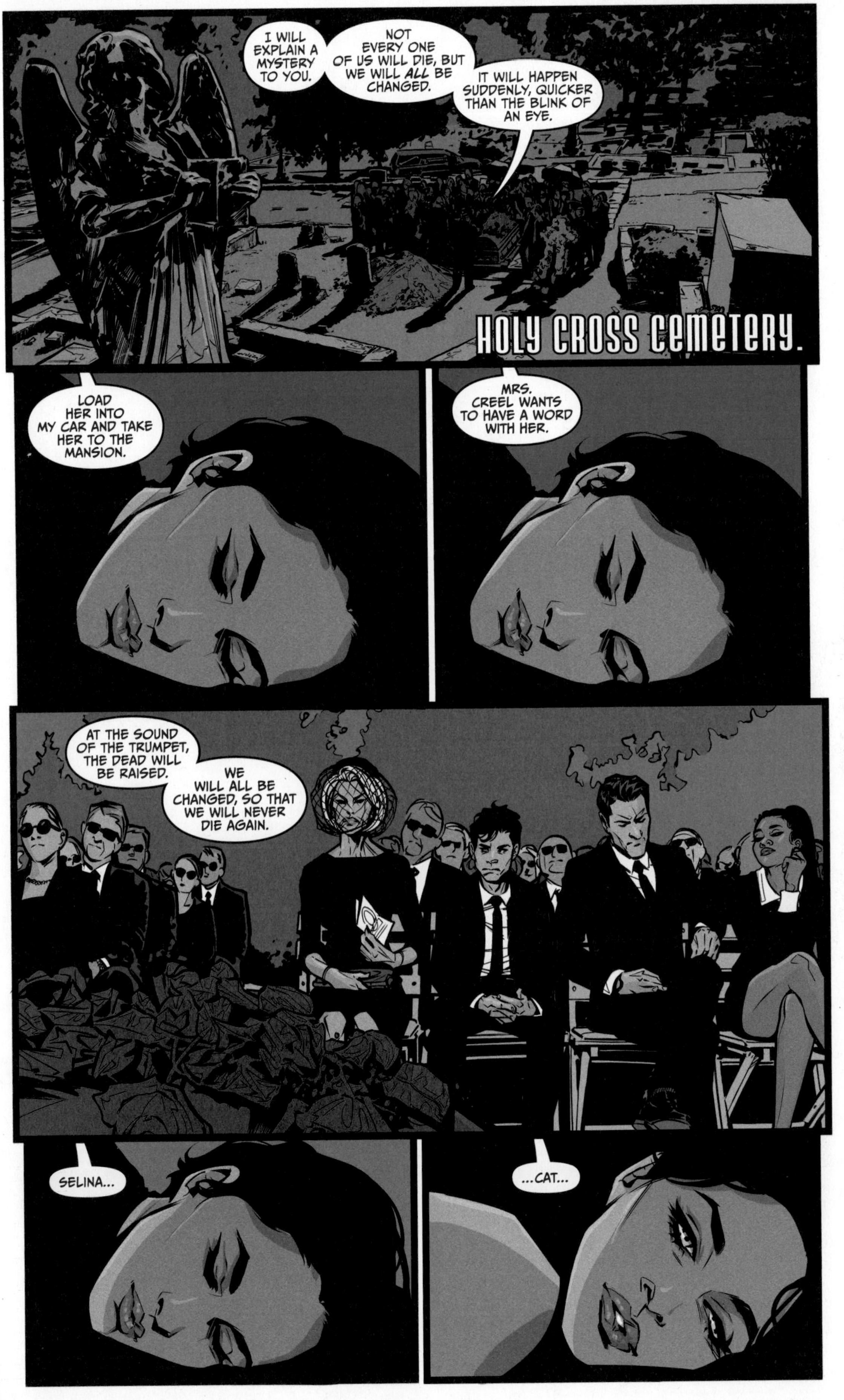
I WILL EXPLAIN A MYSTERY TO YOU.
NOT EVERY ONE OF US WILL DIE, BUT WE WILL *ALL* BE CHANGED.
IT WILL HAPPEN SUDDENLY, QUICKER THAN THE BLINK OF AN EYE.
HOLY CROSS CEMETERY.
LOAD HER INTO MY CAR AND TAKE HER TO THE MANSION.
MRS. CREEL WANTS TO HAVE A WORD WITH HER.
AT THE SOUND OF THE TRUMPET, THE DEAD WILL BE RAISED.
WE WILL ALL BE CHANGED, SO THAT WE WILL NEVER DIE AGAIN.
SELINA...
...CAT...

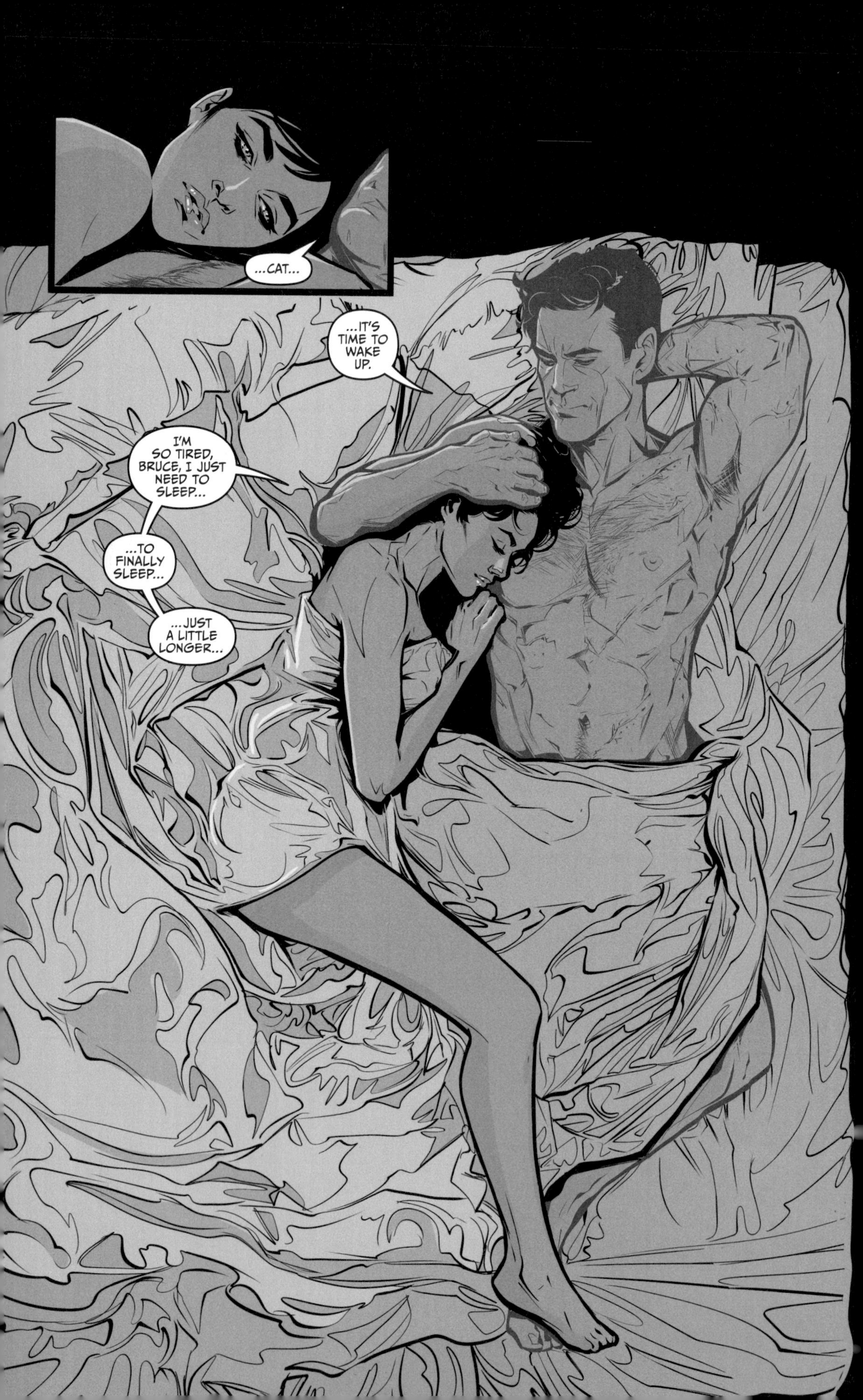
...CAT...
...IT'S TIME TO WAKE UP.
I'M SO TIRED, BRUCE, I JUST NEED TO SLEEP...
...TO FINALLY SLEEP...
...JUST A LITTLE LONGER...

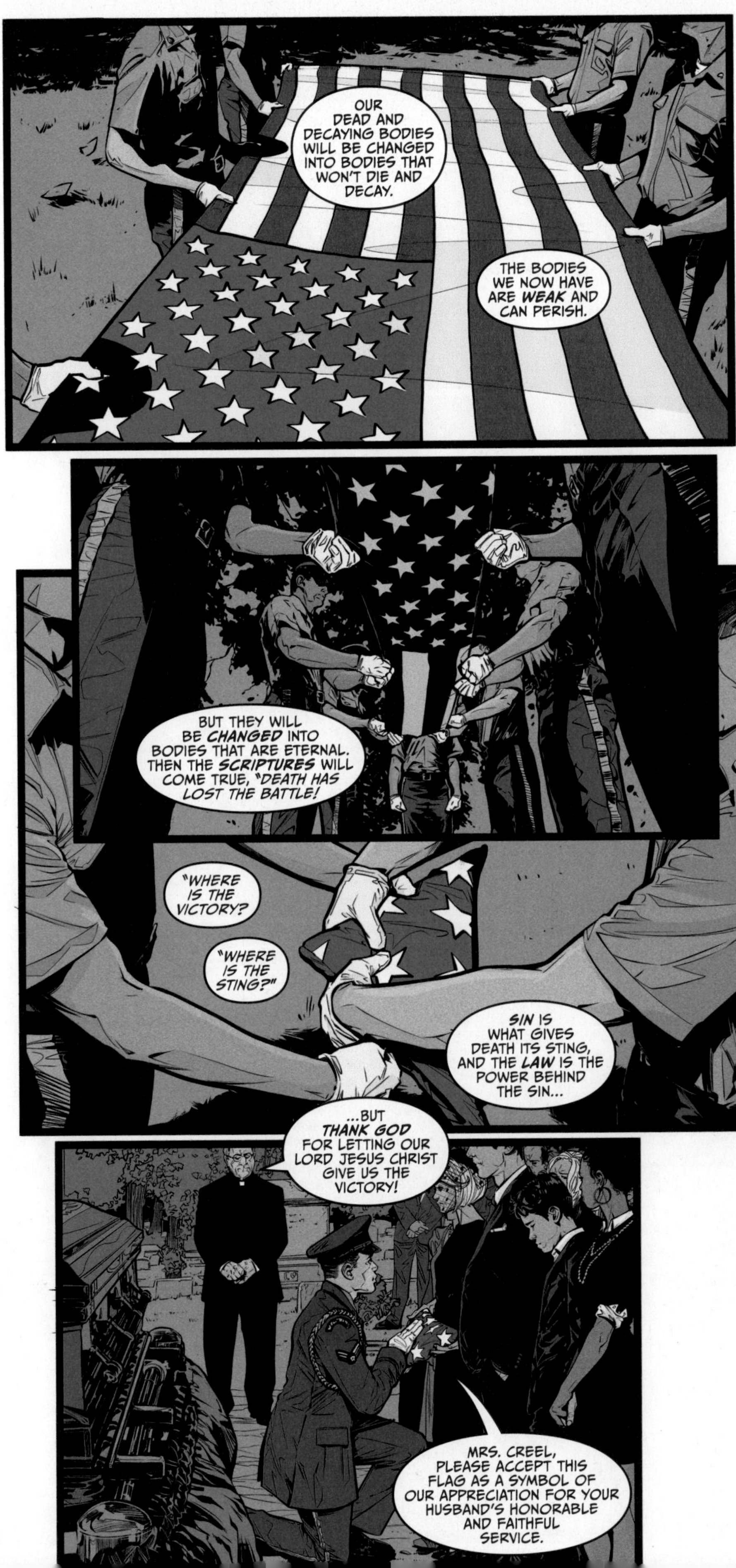
OUR DEAD AND DECAYING BODIES WILL BE CHANGED INTO BODIES THAT WON'T DIE AND DECAY.
THE BODIES WE NOW HAVE ARE *WEAK* AND CAN PERISH.
BUT THEY WILL BE *CHANGED* INTO BODIES THAT ARE ETERNAL. THEN THE *SCRIPTURES* WILL COME TRUE, "*DEATH HAS LOST THE BATTLE!*
"*WHERE IS THE VICTORY?*
"*WHERE IS THE STING?*"
SIN IS WHAT GIVES DEATH ITS STING, AND THE *LAW* IS THE POWER BEHIND THE SIN...
...BUT *THANK GOD* FOR LETTING OUR LORD JESUS CHRIST GIVE US THE VICTORY!
MRS. CREEL, PLEASE ACCEPT THIS FLAG AS A SYMBOL OF OUR APPRECIATION FOR YOUR HUSBAND'S HONORABLE AND FAITHFUL SERVICE.

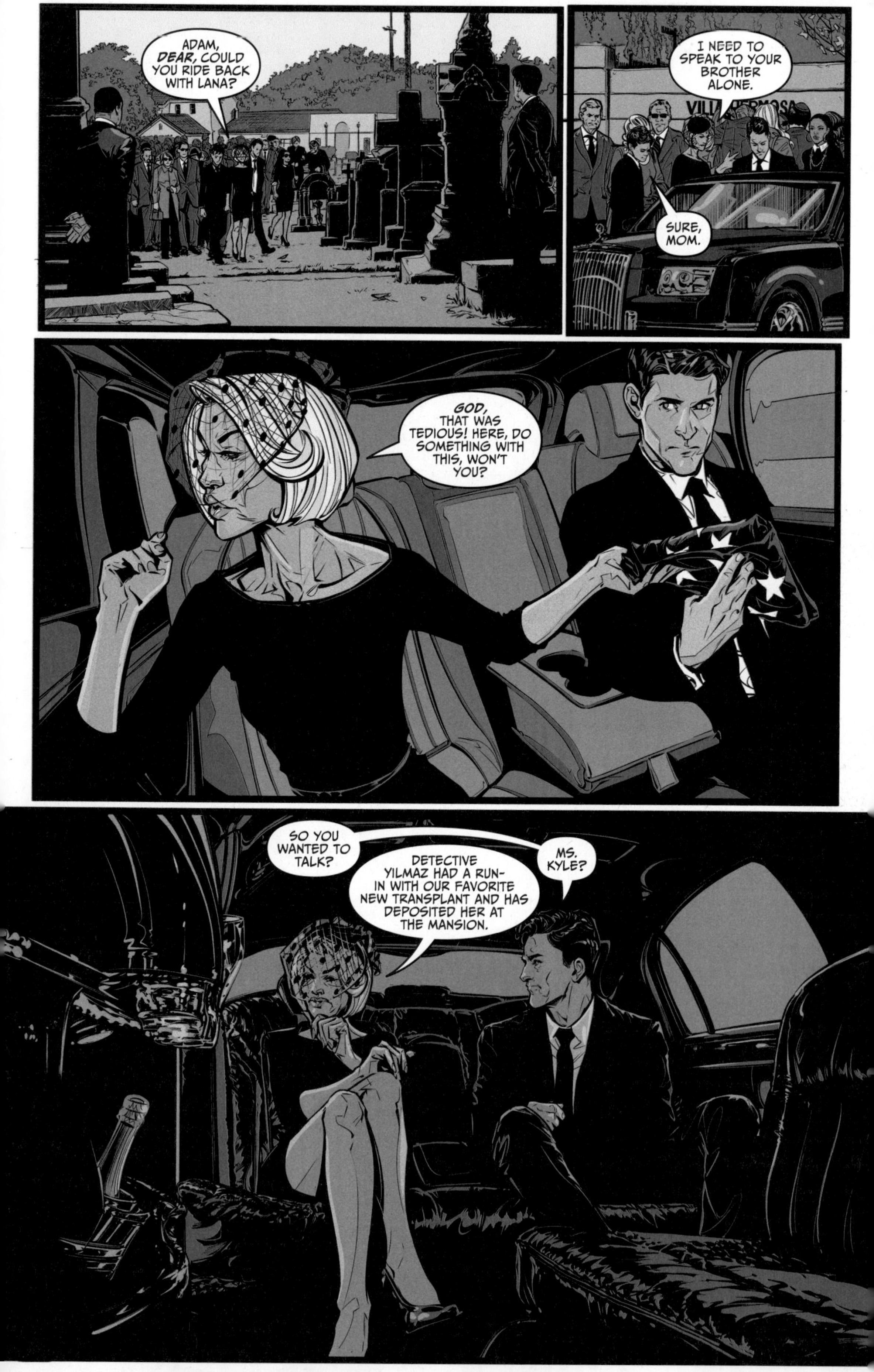
ADAM, DEAR, COULD YOU RIDE BACK WITH LANA?
I NEED TO SPEAK TO YOUR BROTHER ALONE.
SURE, MOM.
GOD, THAT WAS TEDIOUS! HERE, DO SOMETHING WITH THIS, WON'T YOU?
SO YOU WANTED TO TALK?
MS. KYLE?
DETECTIVE YILMAZ HAD A RUN-IN WITH OUR FAVORITE NEW TRANSPLANT AND HAS DEPOSITED HER AT THE MANSION.

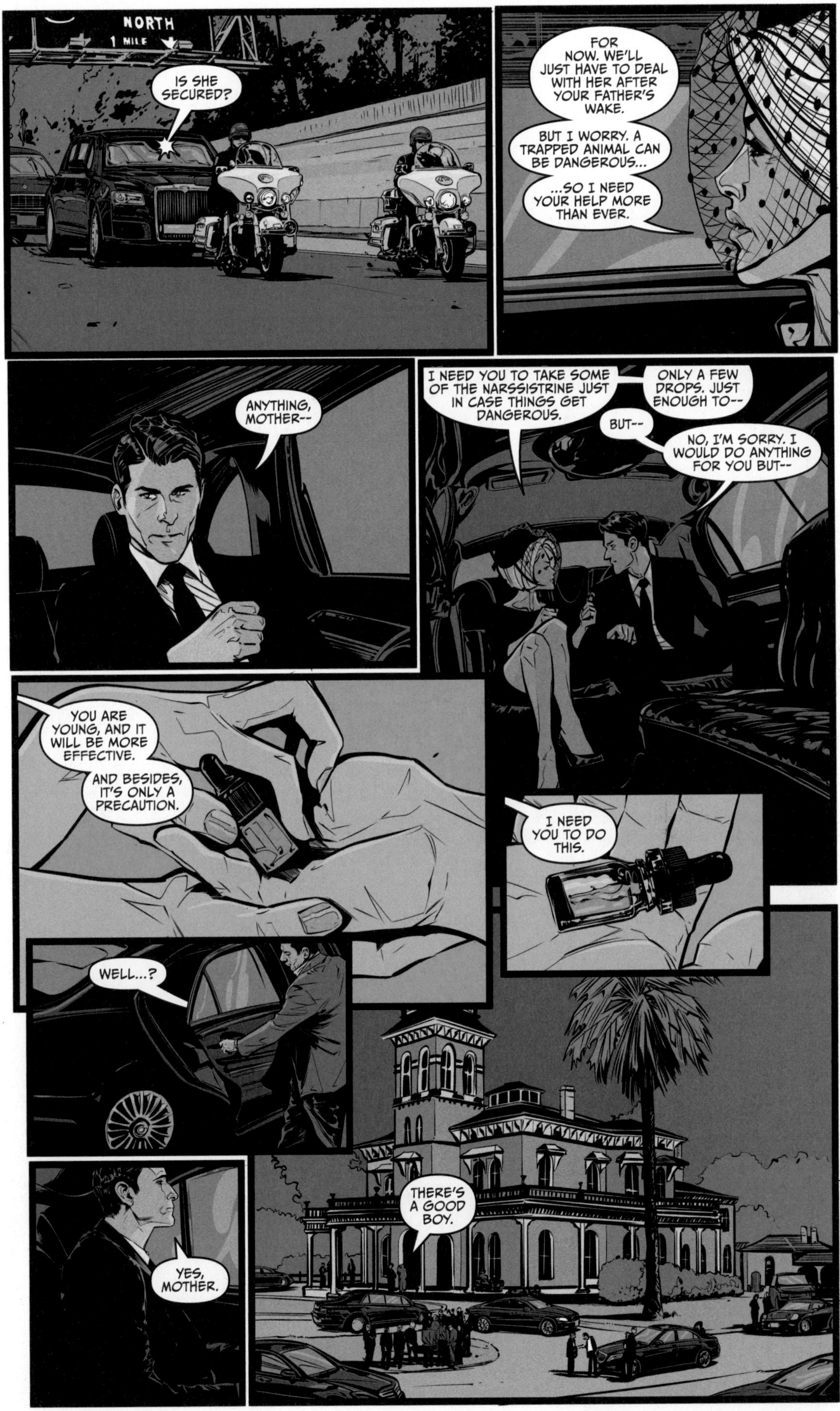
NORTH
1 MILE
IS SHE SECURED?
FOR NOW. WE'LL JUST HAVE TO DEAL WITH HER AFTER YOUR FATHER'S WAKE.
BUT I WORRY. A TRAPPED ANIMAL CAN BE DANGEROUS...
...SO I NEED YOUR HELP MORE THAN EVER.
ANYTHING, MOTHER--
I NEED YOU TO TAKE SOME OF THE NARSSISTRINE JUST IN CASE THINGS GET DANGEROUS.
ONLY A FEW DROPS. JUST ENOUGH TO--
BUT--
NO, I'M SORRY. I WOULD DO ANYTHING FOR YOU BUT--
YOU ARE YOUNG, AND IT WILL BE MORE EFFECTIVE.
AND BESIDES, IT'S ONLY A PRECAUTION.
I NEED YOU TO DO THIS.
WELL...?
YES, MOTHER.
THERE'S A GOOD BOY.

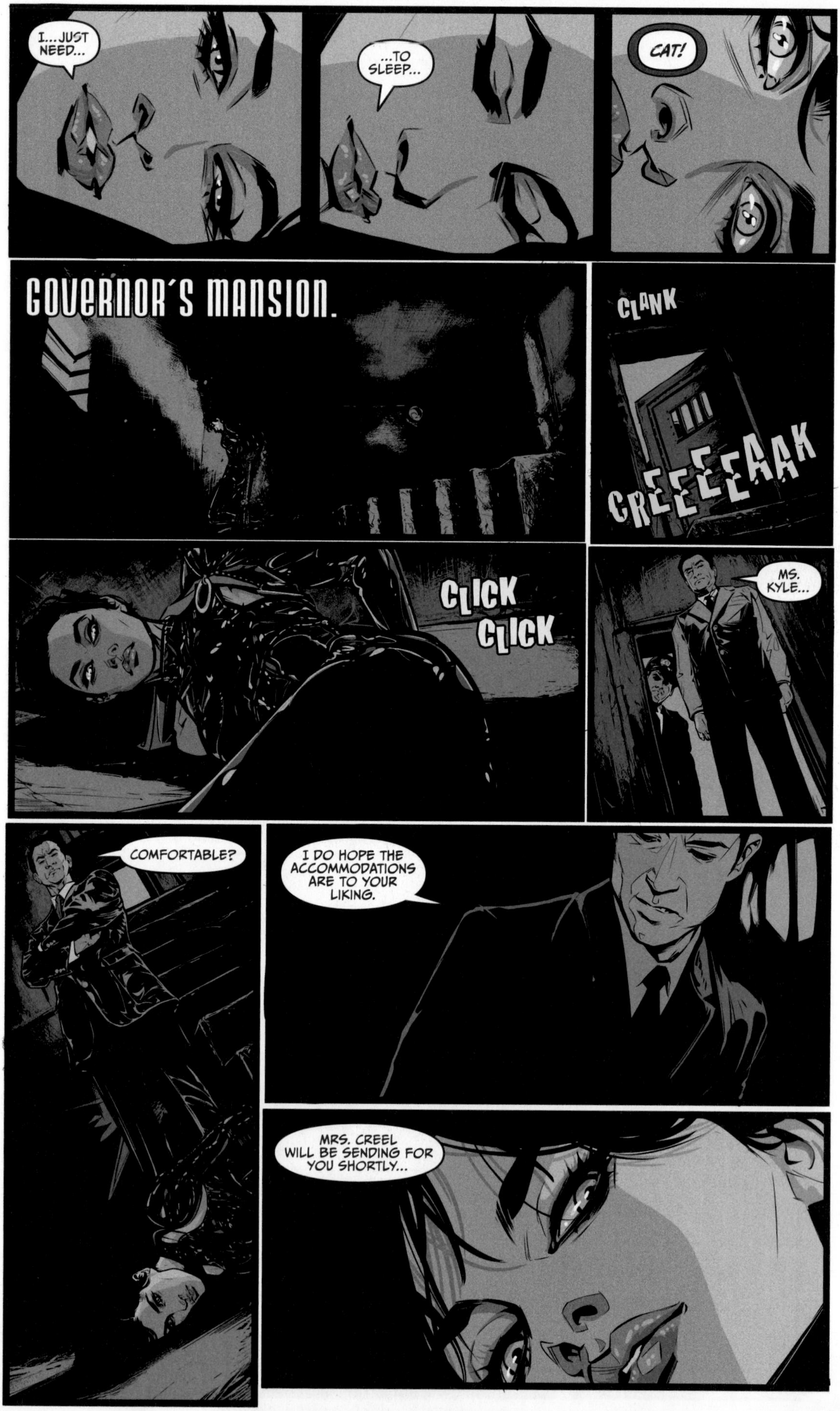
I...JUST NEED...
...TO SLEEP...
CAT!
GOVERNOR´S MANSION.
CLANK
CREEEEAAK
CLICK
CLICK
MS. KYLE...
COMFORTABLE?
I DO HOPE THE ACCOMMODATIONS ARE TO YOUR LIKING.
MRS. CREEL WILL BE SENDING FOR YOU SHORTLY...

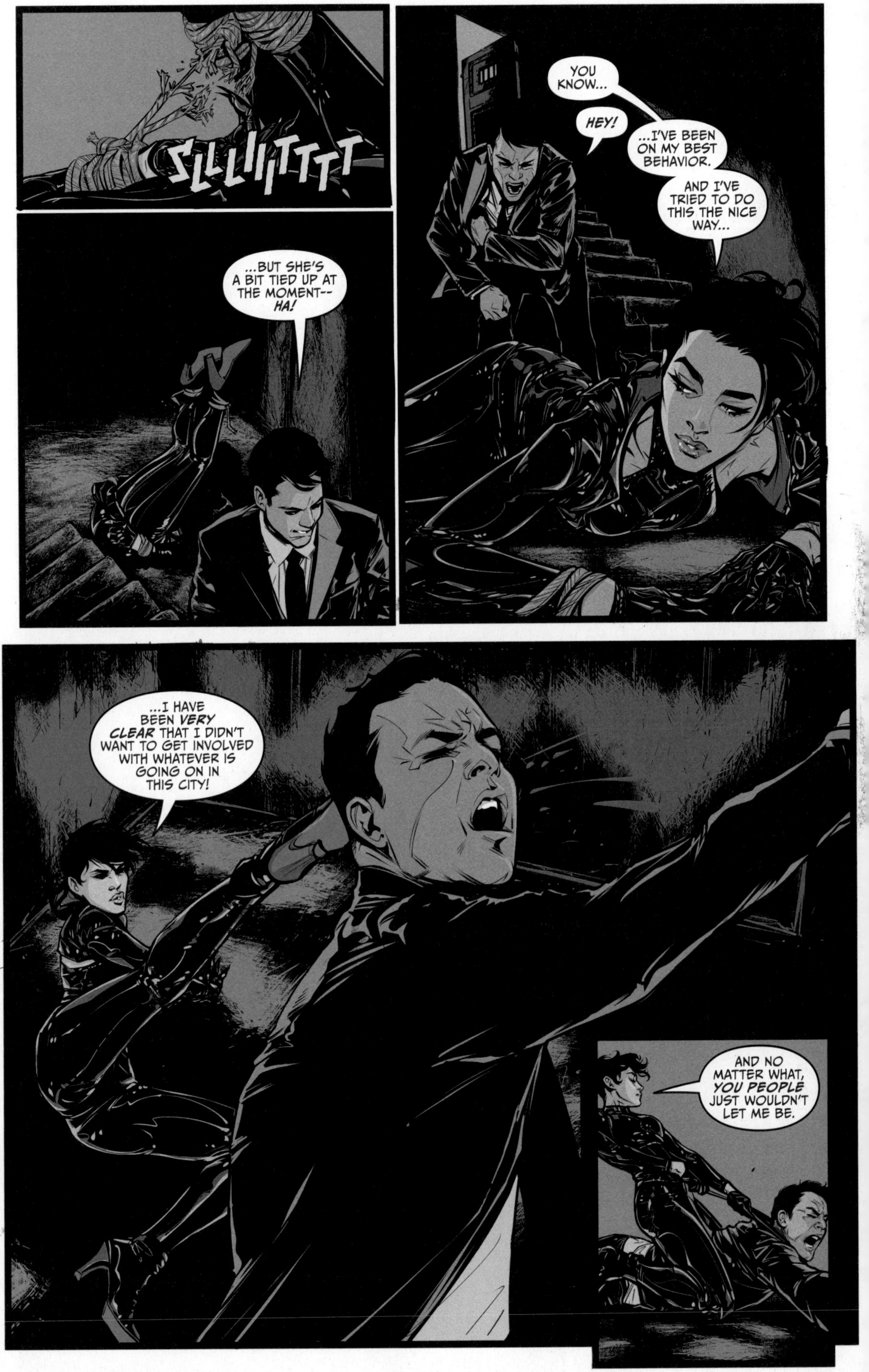
SLLIIITTTT
YOU KNOW...
HEY!
...I'VE BEEN ON MY BEST BEHAVIOR.
AND I'VE TRIED TO DO THIS THE NICE WAY...
...BUT SHE'S A BIT TIED UP AT THE MOMENT-- HA!
...I HAVE BEEN VERY CLEAR THAT I DIDN'T WANT TO GET INVOLVED WITH WHATEVER IS GOING ON IN THIS CITY!
AND NO MATTER WHAT, YOU PEOPLE JUST WOULDN'T LET ME BE.

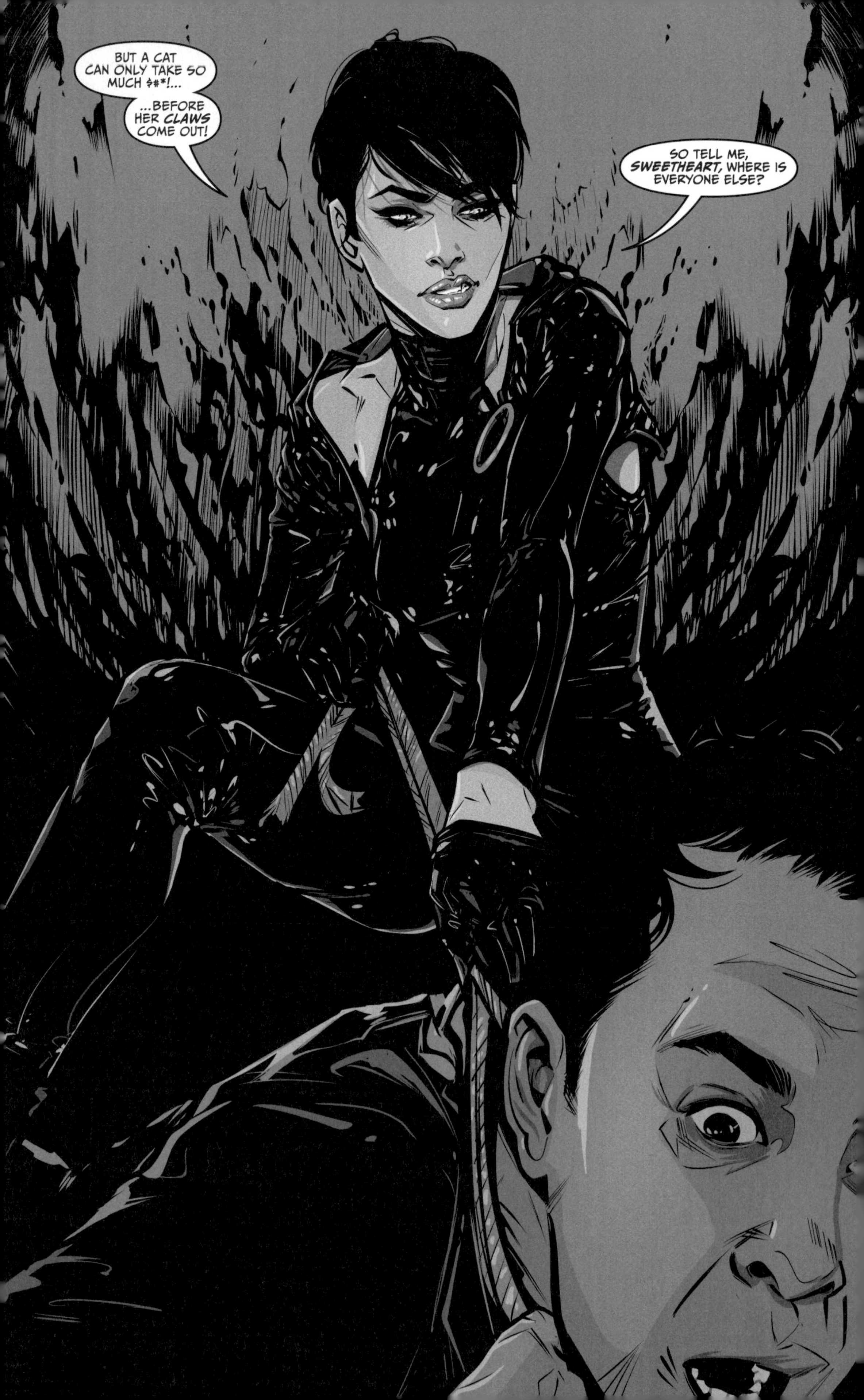
BUT A CAT CAN ONLY TAKE SO MUCH $#*!...
...BEFORE HER CLAWS COME OUT!
SO TELL ME, SWEETHEART, WHERE IS EVERYONE ELSE?

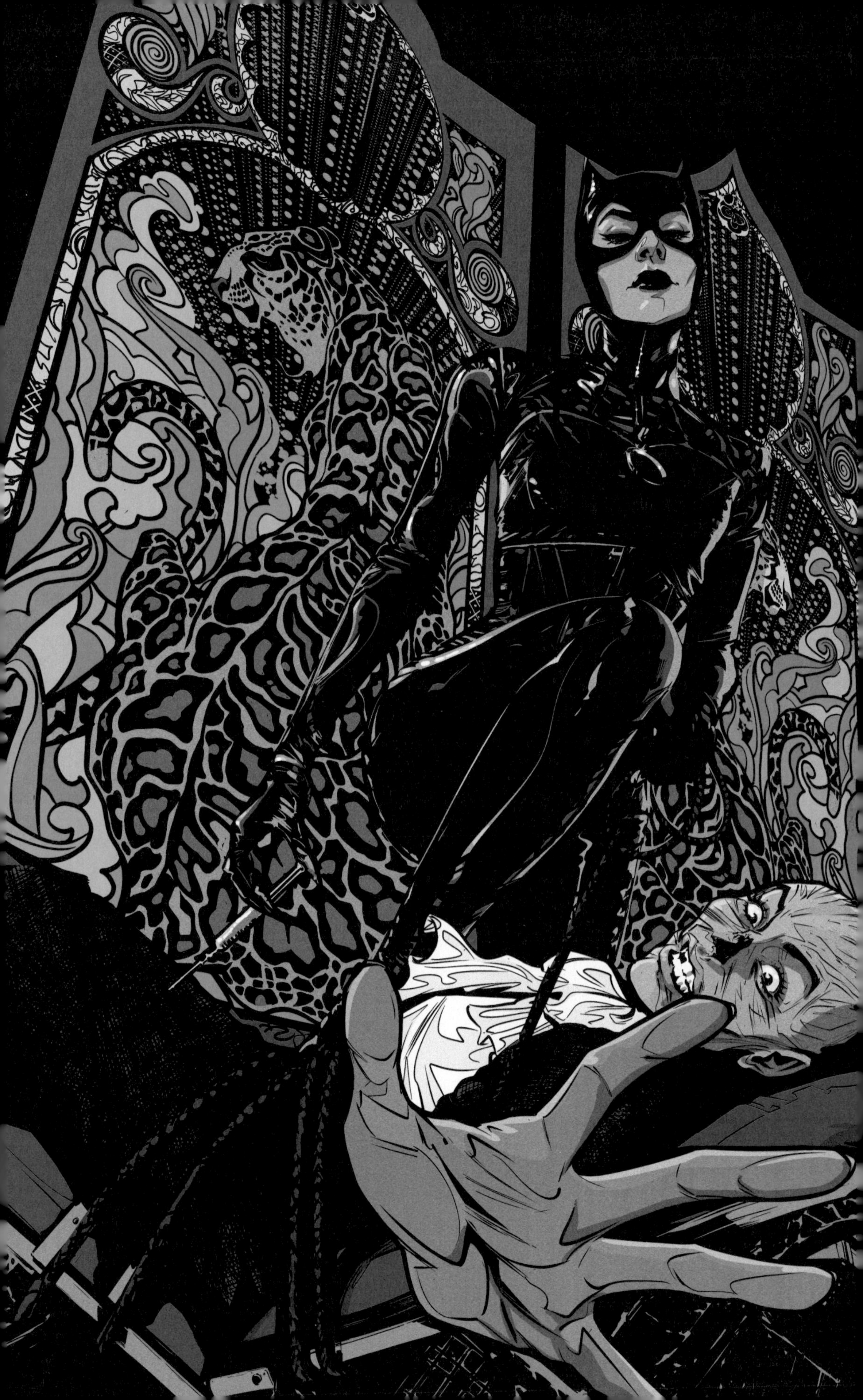

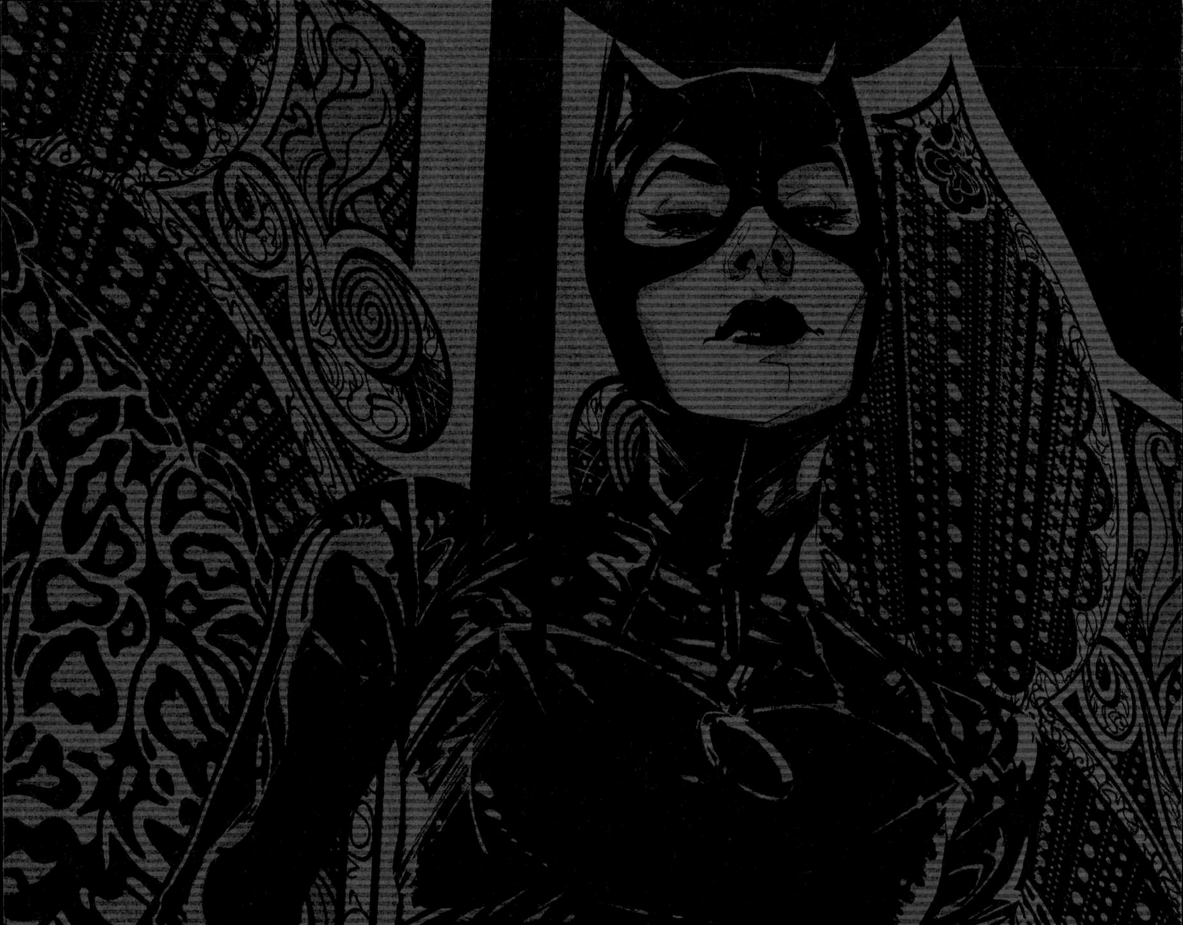

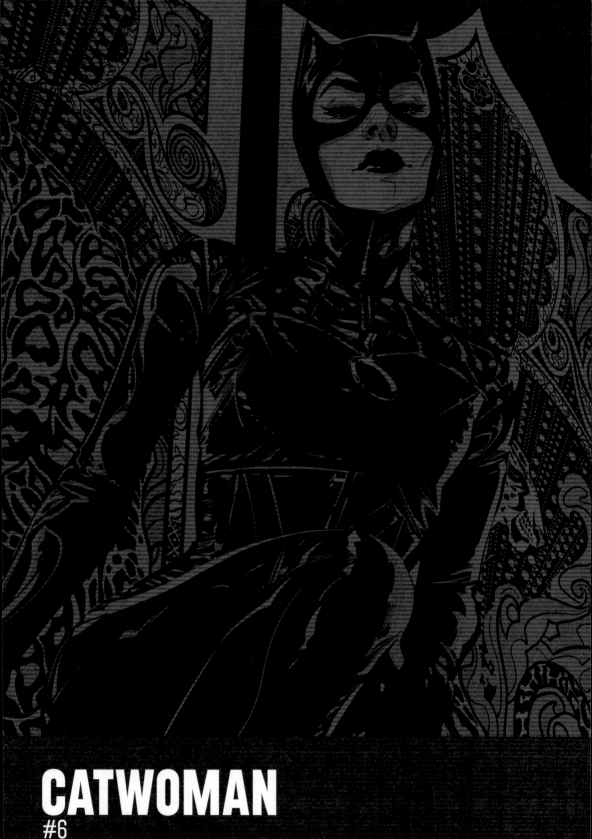

CATWOMAN
#6

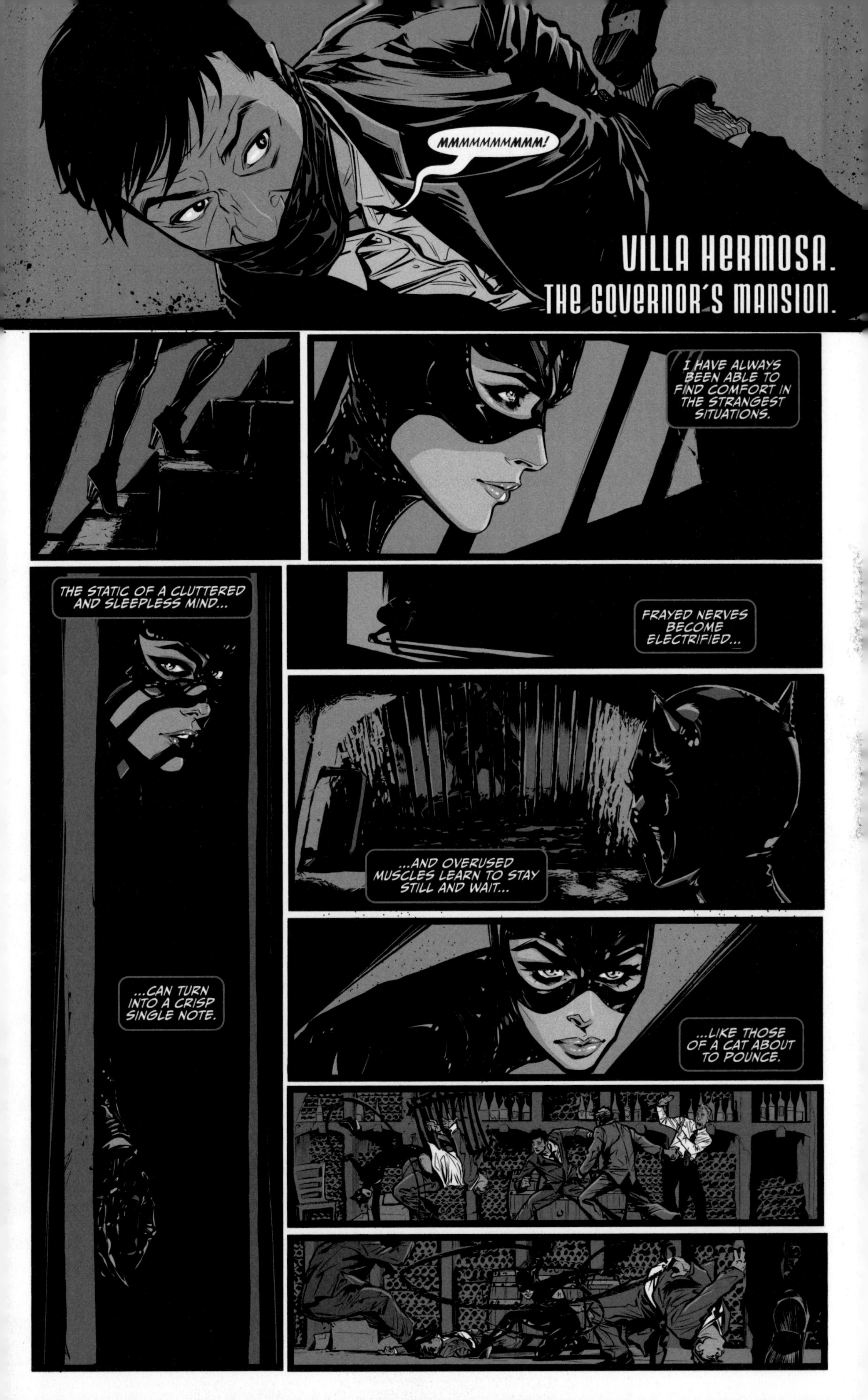
MMMMMMMMMM!
VILLA HERMOSA.
THE GOVERNOR'S MANSION.
I HAVE ALWAYS BEEN ABLE TO FIND COMFORT IN THE STRANGEST SITUATIONS.
THE STATIC OF A CLUTTERED AND SLEEPLESS MIND...
...CAN TURN INTO A CRISP SINGLE NOTE.
FRAYED NERVES BECOME ELECTRIFIED...
...AND OVERUSED MUSCLES LEARN TO STAY STILL AND WAIT...
...LIKE THOSE OF A CAT ABOUT TO POUNCE.

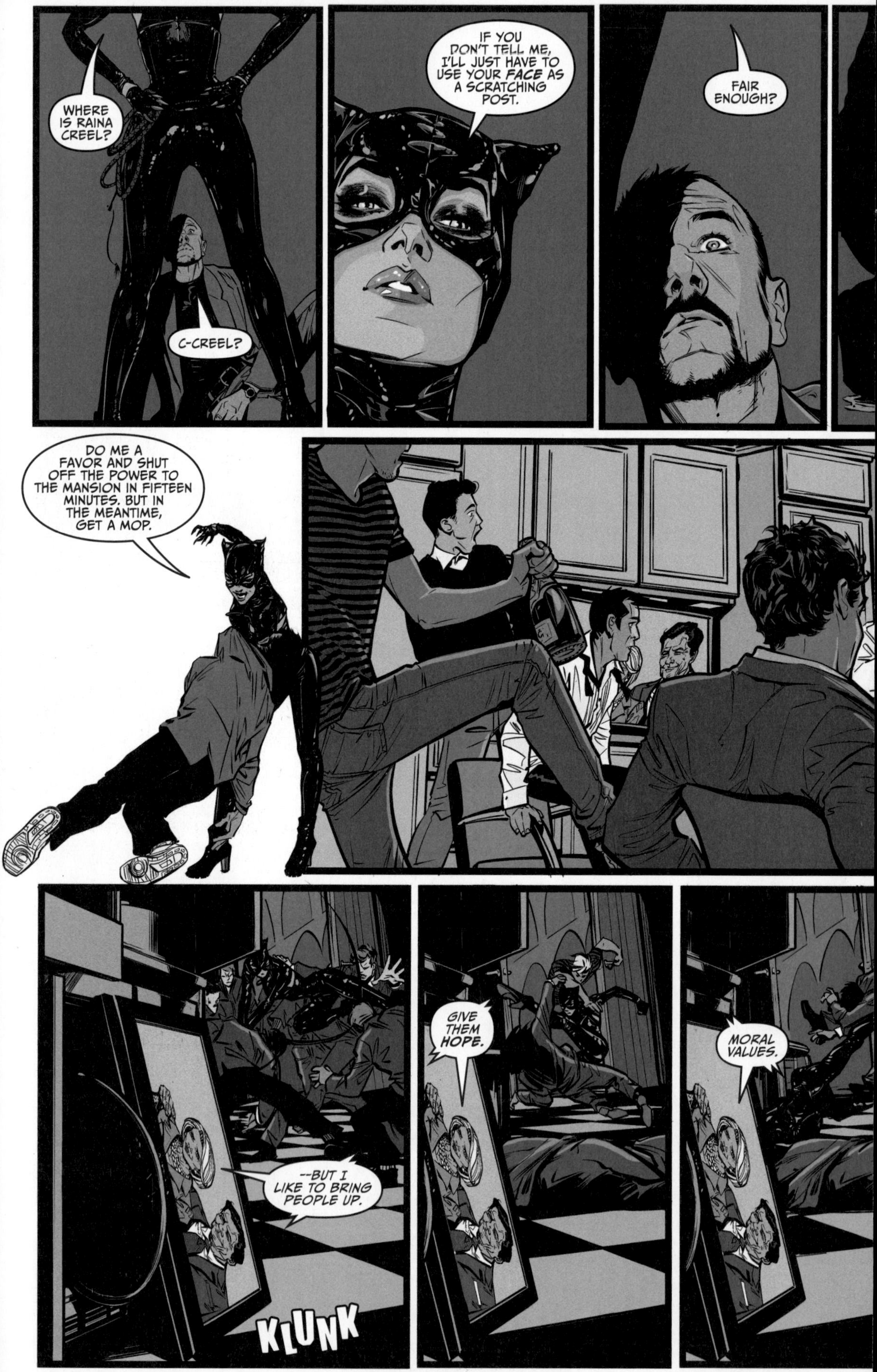
WHERE IS RAINA CREEL?
C-CREEL?
IF YOU DON'T TELL ME, I'LL JUST HAVE TO USE YOUR *FACE* AS A SCRATCHING POST.
FAIR ENOUGH?
DO ME A FAVOR AND SHUT OFF THE POWER TO THE MANSION IN FIFTEEN MINUTES. BUT IN THE MEANTIME, GET A MOP.
--BUT I LIKE TO BRING PEOPLE UP.
KLUNK
GIVE THEM *HOPE*.
MORAL VALUES.

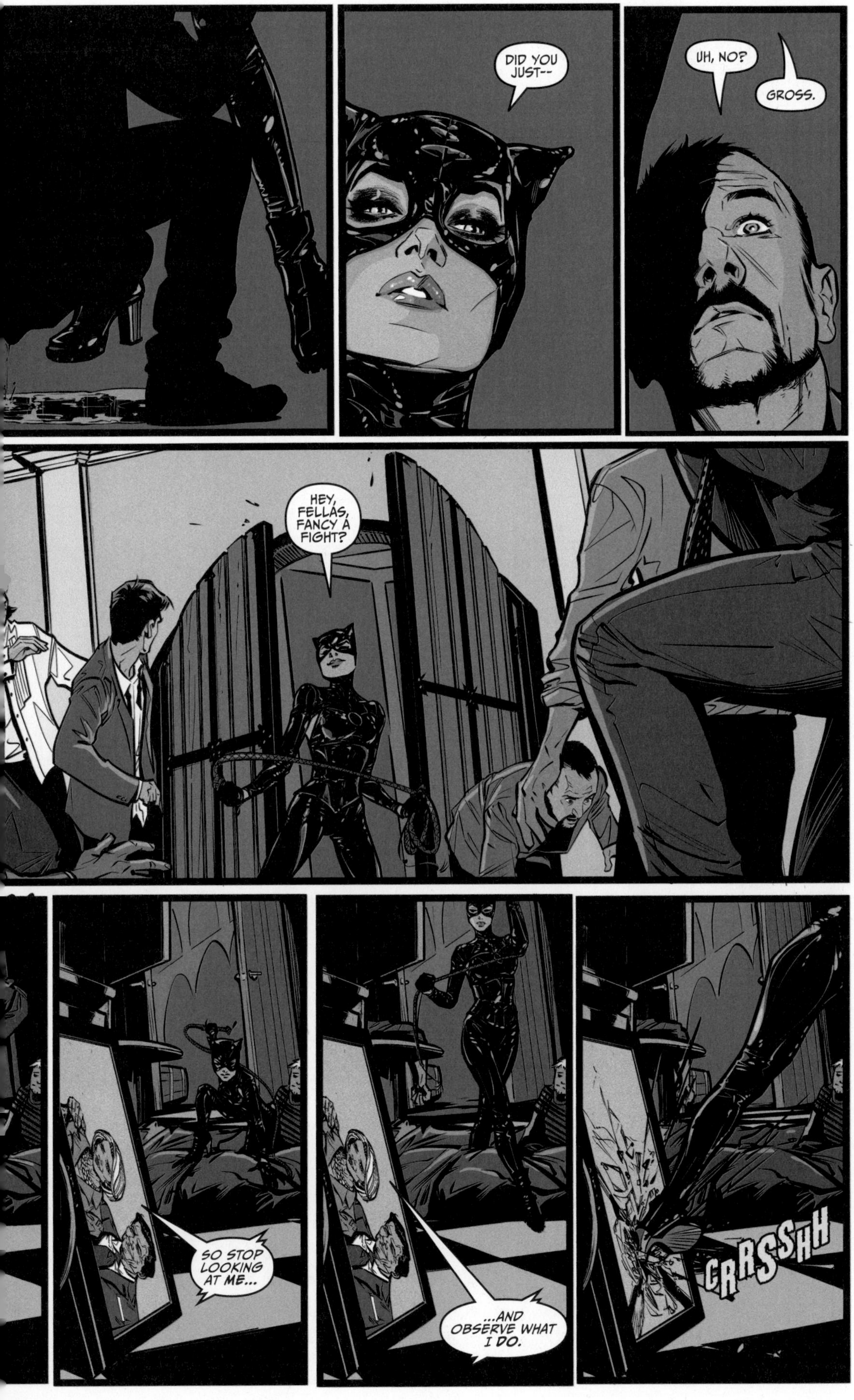
DID YOU JUST--
UH, NO?
GROSS.
HEY, FELLAS, FANCY A FIGHT?
SO STOP LOOKING AT ME...
...AND OBSERVE WHAT I DO.
CRRSSHH

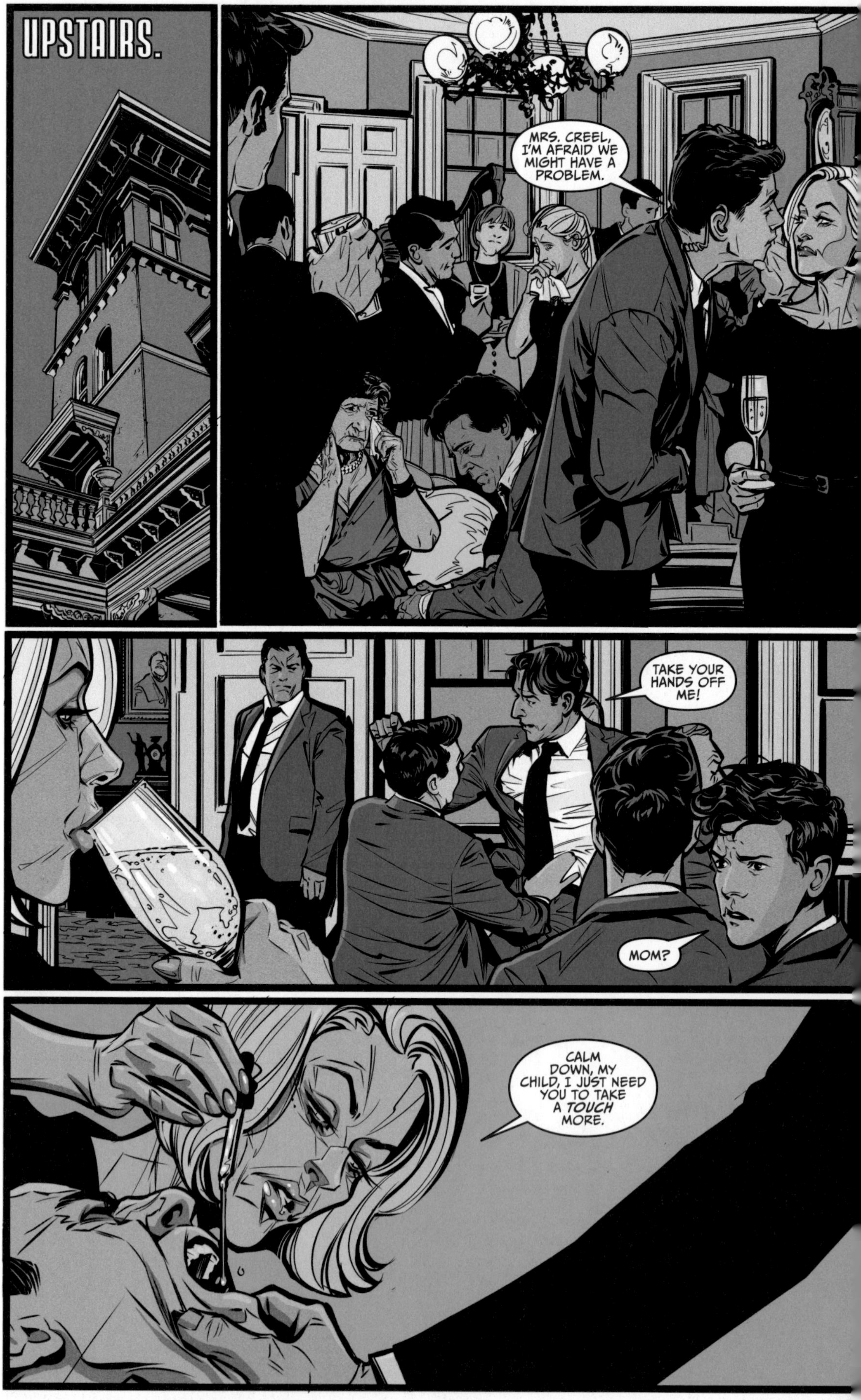
UPSTAIRS.
MRS. CREEL, I'M AFRAID WE MIGHT HAVE A PROBLEM.
TAKE YOUR HANDS OFF ME!
MOM?
CALM DOWN, MY CHILD, I JUST NEED YOU TO TAKE A *TOUCH* MORE.

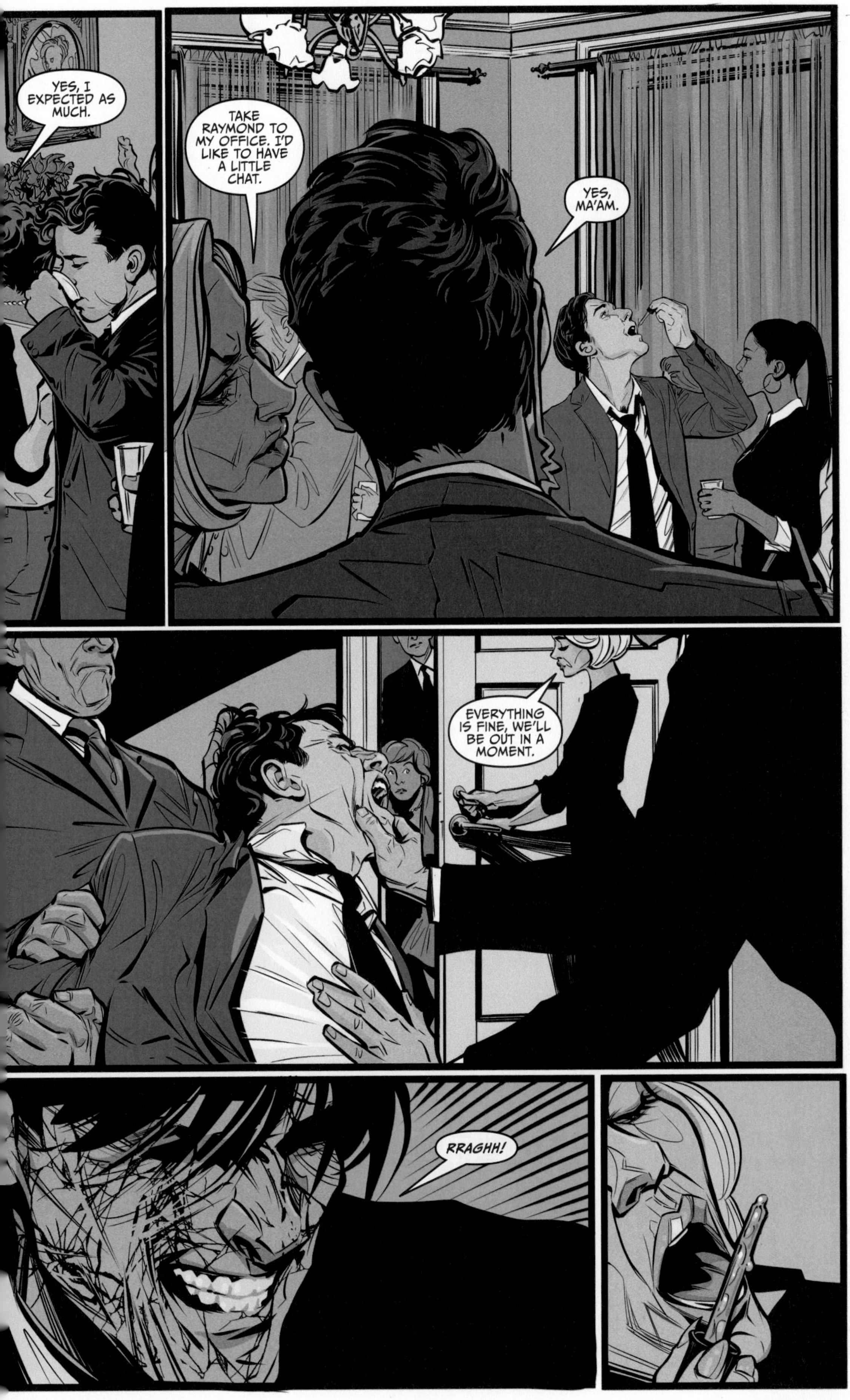
YES, I EXPECTED AS MUCH.
TAKE RAYMOND TO MY OFFICE. I'D LIKE TO HAVE A LITTLE CHAT.
YES, MA'AM.
EVERYTHING IS FINE, WE'LL BE OUT IN A MOMENT.
RRAGHH!

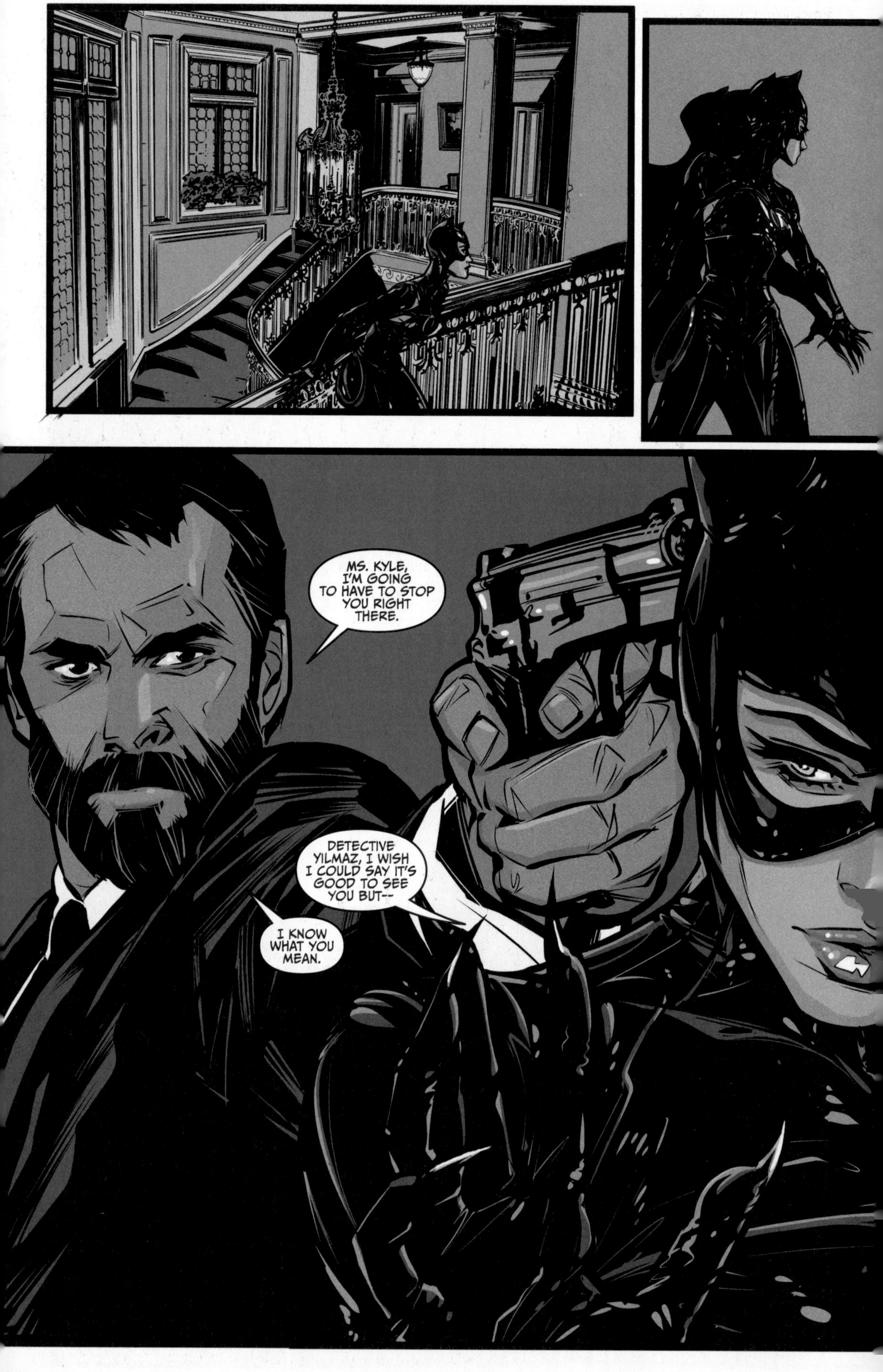
MS. KYLE, I'M GOING TO HAVE TO STOP YOU RIGHT THERE.
DETECTIVE YILMAZ, I WISH I COULD SAY IT'S GOOD TO SEE YOU BUT--
I KNOW WHAT YOU MEAN.

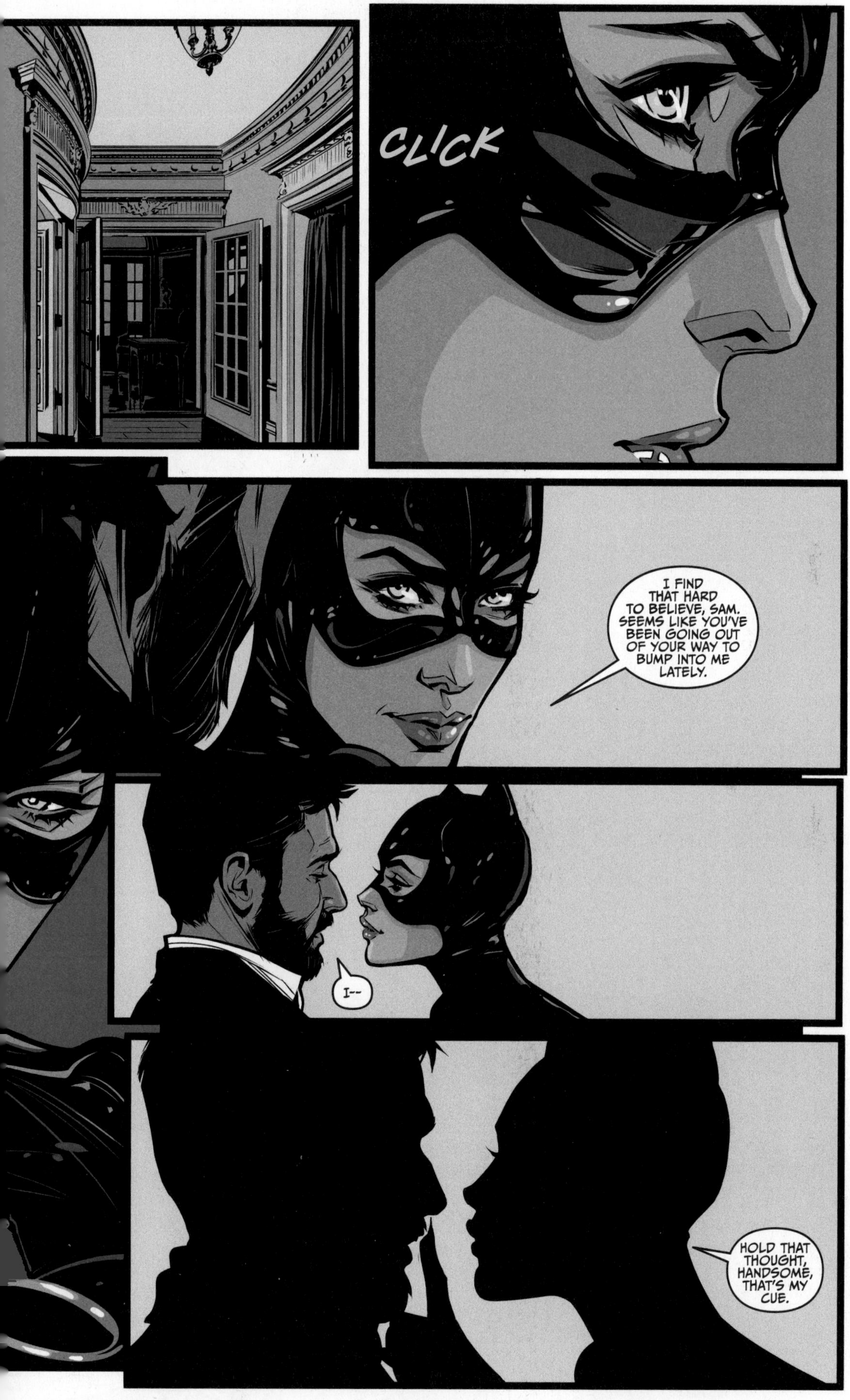
CLICK
I FIND THAT HARD TO BELIEVE, SAM. SEEMS LIKE YOU'VE BEEN GOING OUT OF YOUR WAY TO BUMP INTO ME LATELY.
I--
HOLD THAT THOUGHT, HANDSOME, THAT'S MY CUE.

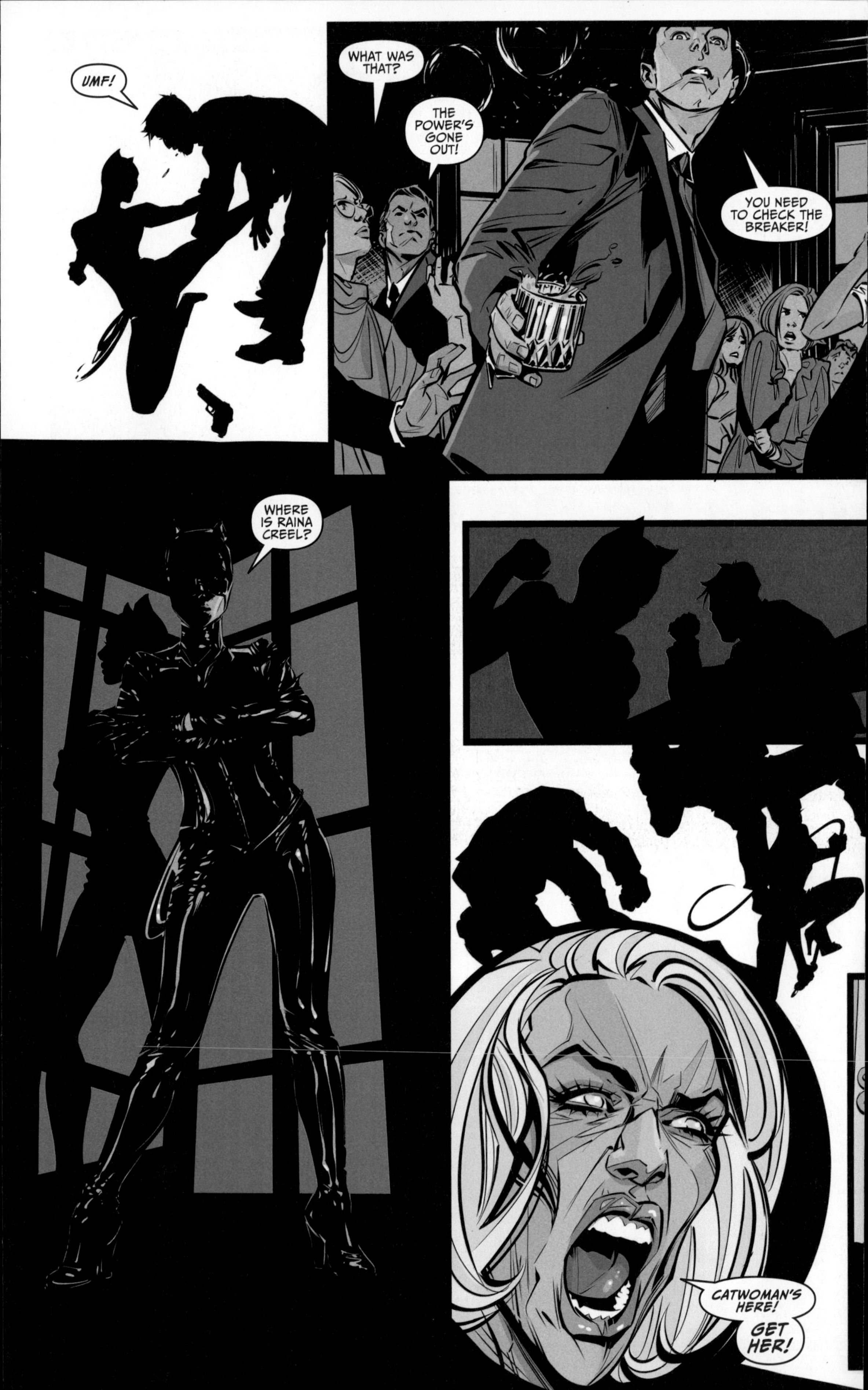
UMF!
WHAT WAS THAT?
THE POWER'S GONE OUT!
YOU NEED TO CHECK THE BREAKER!
WHERE IS RAINA CREEL?
CATWOMAN'S HERE!
GET HER!

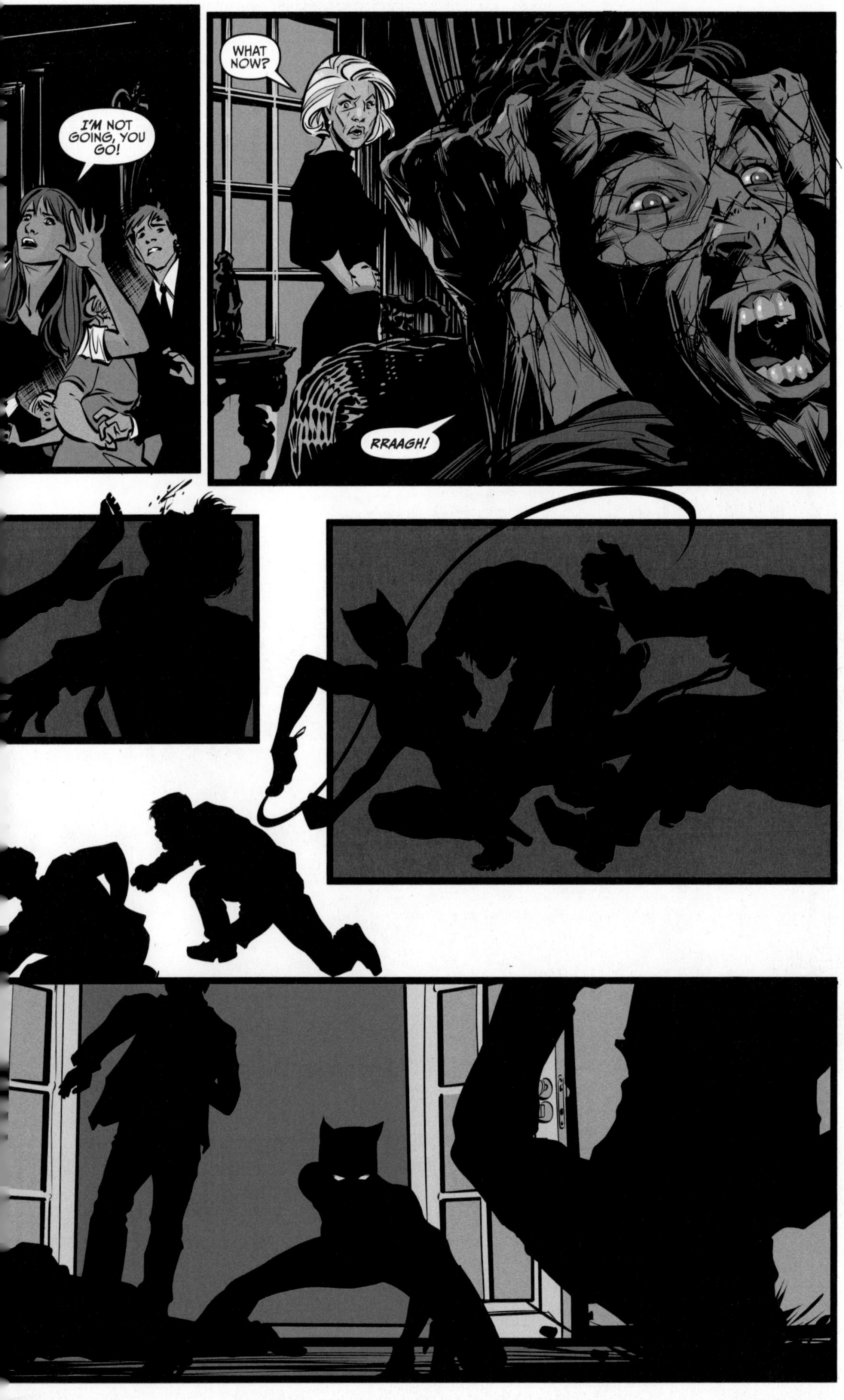
I'M NOT GOING, YOU GO!
WHAT NOW?
RRAAGH!

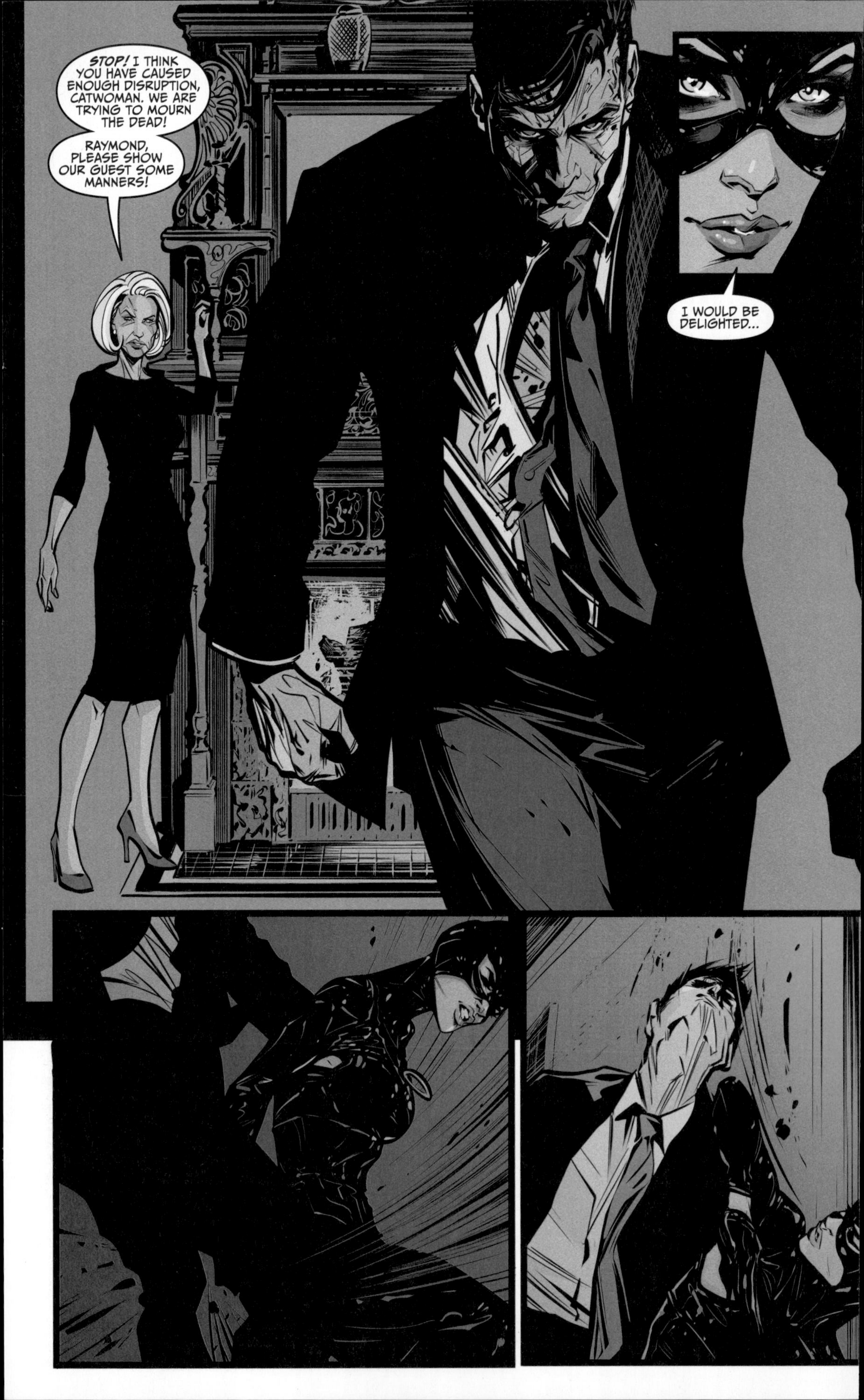
STOP! I THINK YOU HAVE CAUSED ENOUGH DISRUPTION, CATWOMAN. WE ARE TRYING TO MOURN THE DEAD!
RAYMOND, PLEASE SHOW OUR GUEST SOME MANNERS!
I WOULD BE DELIGHTED...

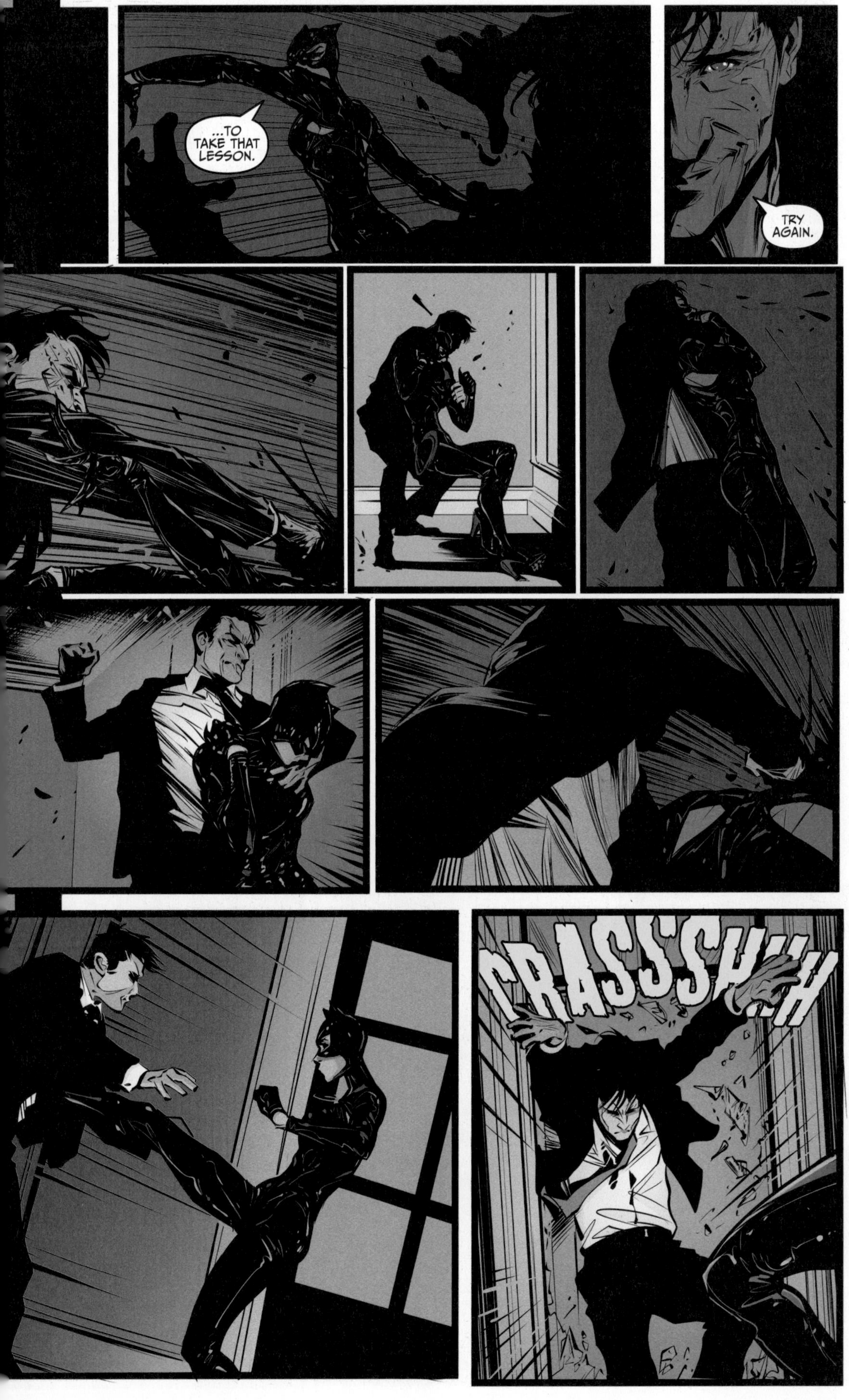
...TO TAKE THAT LESSON.
TRY AGAIN.
CRASSSHHH

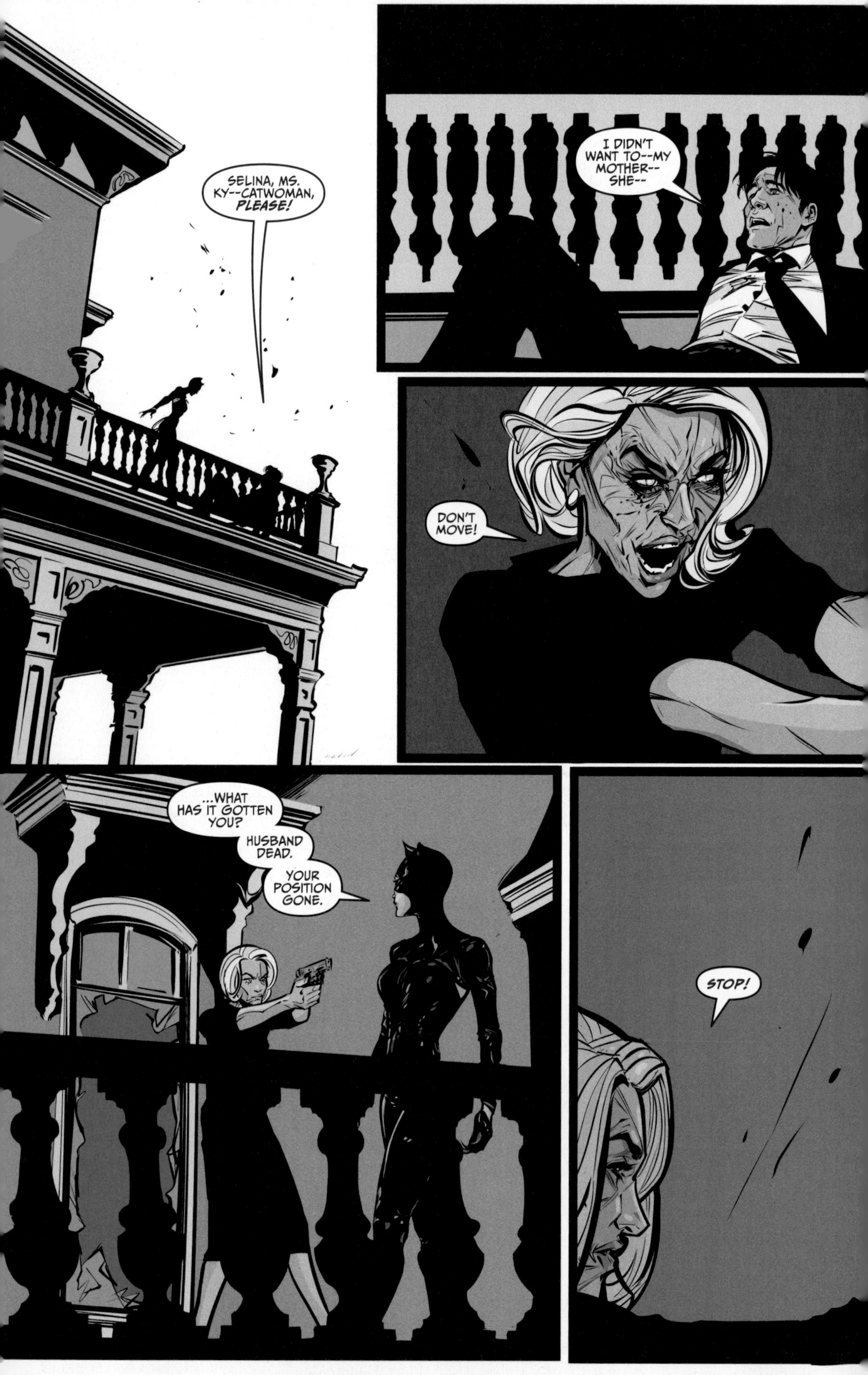
SELINA, MS. KY--CATWOMAN, PLEASE!
I DIDN'T WANT TO--MY MOTHER-- SHE--
DON'T MOVE!
...WHAT HAS IT GOTTEN YOU?
HUSBAND DEAD.
YOUR POSITION GONE.
STOP!

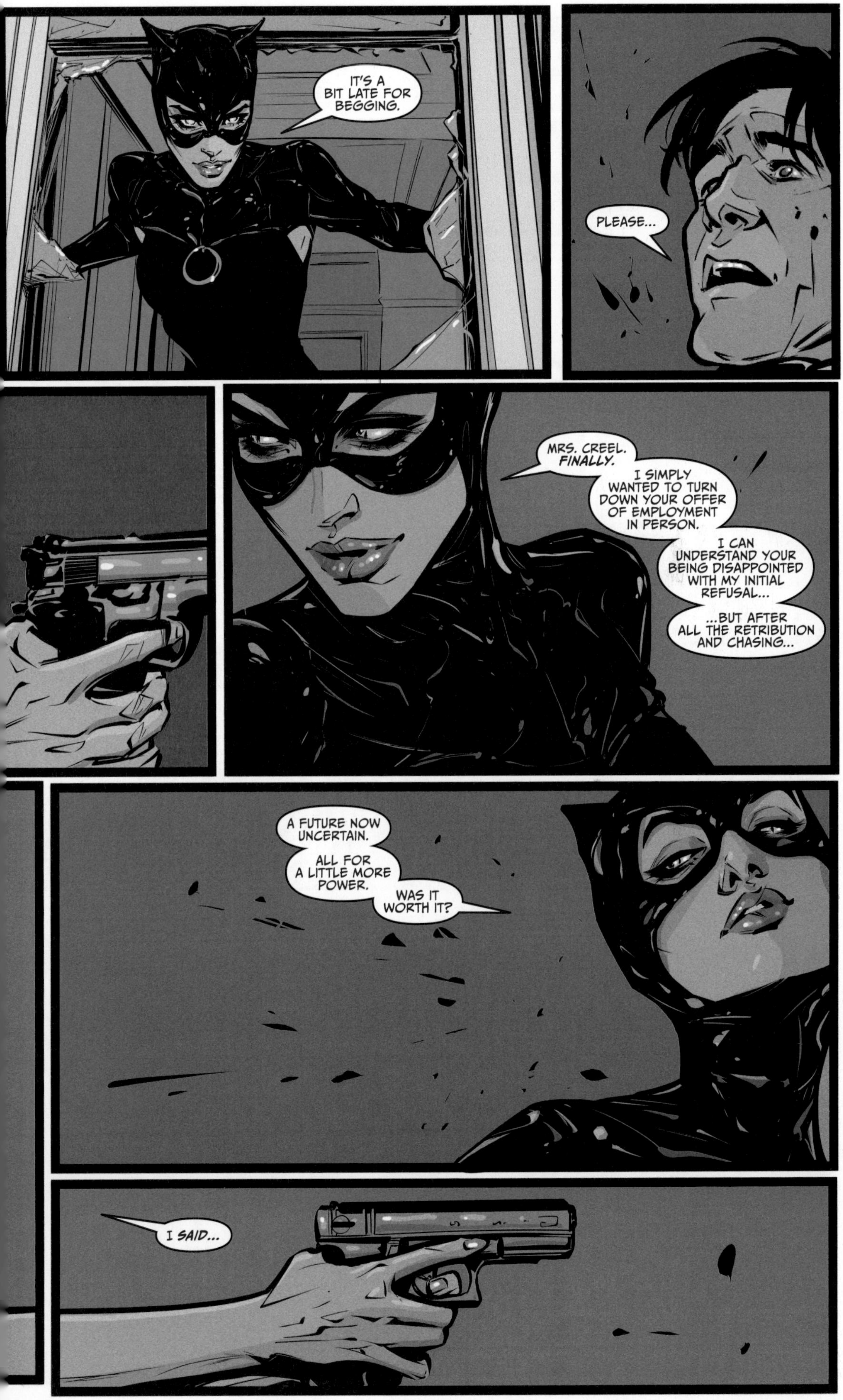
IT'S A BIT LATE FOR BEGGING.
PLEASE...
MRS. CREEL. *FINALLY.*
I SIMPLY WANTED TO TURN DOWN YOUR OFFER OF EMPLOYMENT IN PERSON.
I CAN UNDERSTAND YOUR BEING DISAPPOINTED WITH MY INITIAL REFUSAL...
...BUT AFTER ALL THE RETRIBUTION AND CHASING...
A FUTURE NOW UNCERTAIN.
ALL FOR A LITTLE MORE POWER.
WAS IT WORTH IT?
I *SAID*...

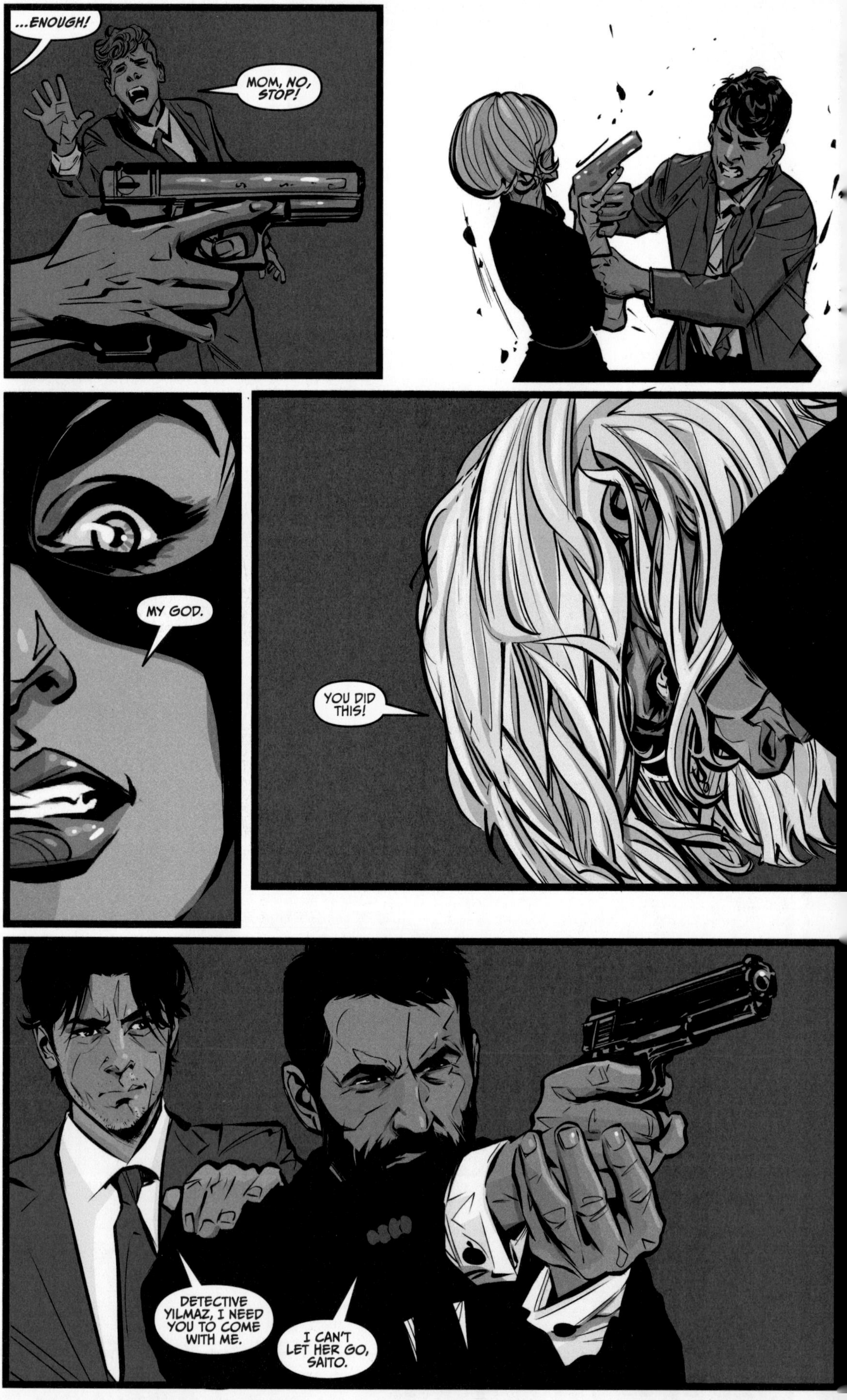
...ENOUGH!
MOM, NO, STOP!
MY GOD.
YOU DID THIS!
DETECTIVE YILMAZ, I NEED YOU TO COME WITH ME.
I CAN'T LET HER GO, SAITO.

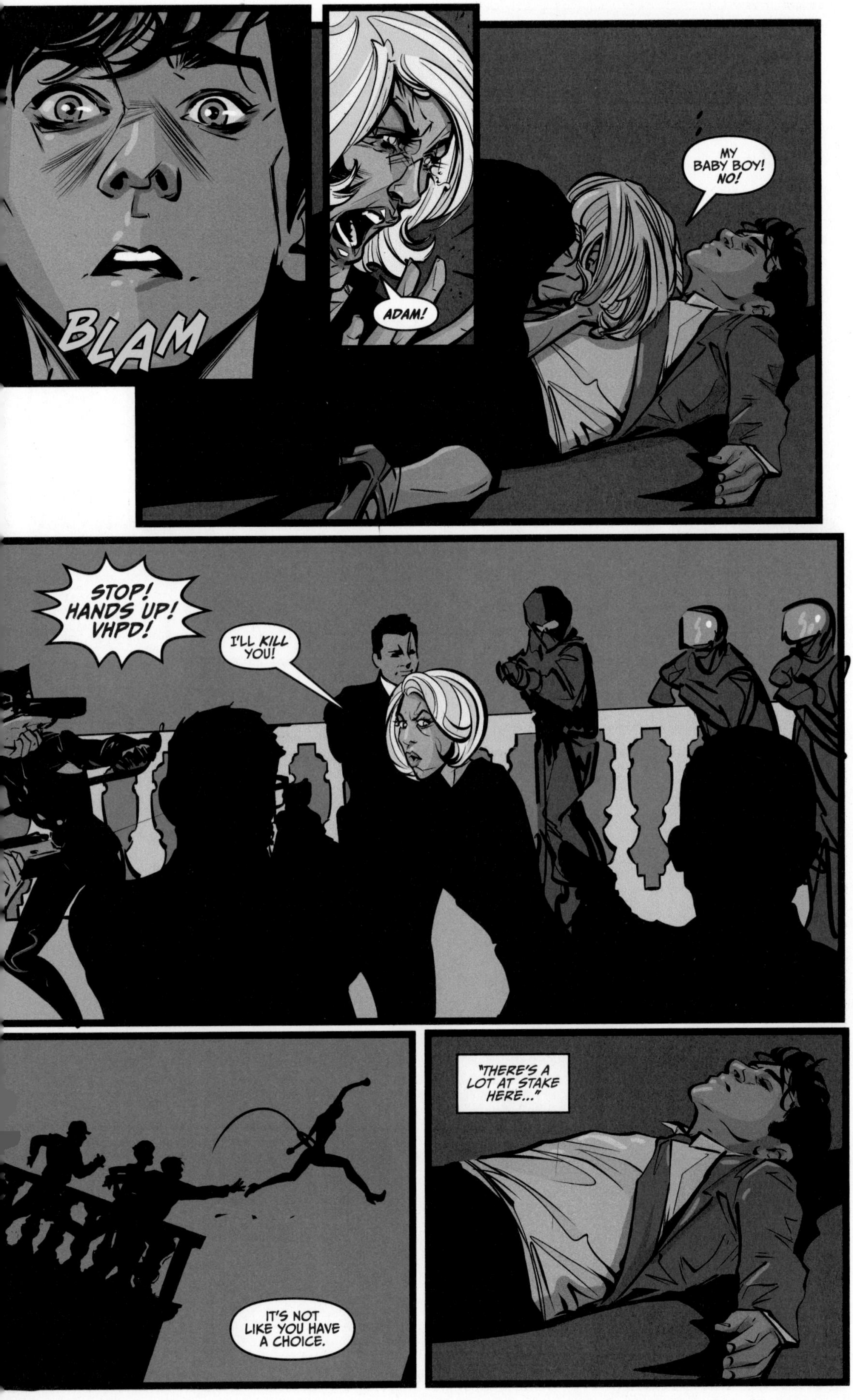
BLAM
ADAM!
MY BABY BOY! NO!
STOP! HANDS UP! VHPD!
I'LL KILL YOU!
IT'S NOT LIKE YOU HAVE A CHOICE.
"THERE'S A LOT AT STAKE HERE..."

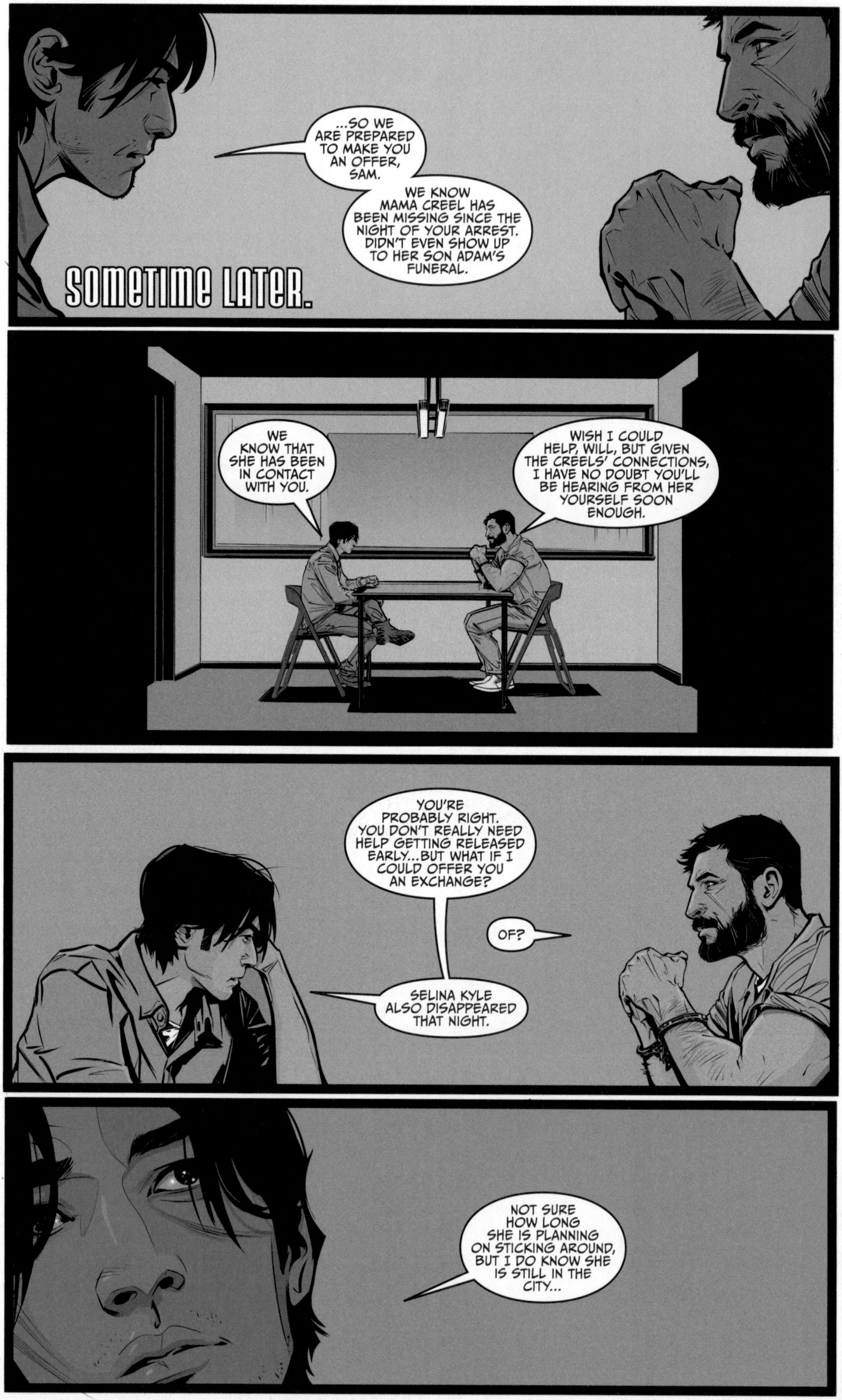
...SO WE ARE PREPARED TO MAKE YOU AN OFFER, SAM.
WE KNOW MAMA CREEL HAS BEEN MISSING SINCE THE NIGHT OF YOUR ARREST. DIDN'T EVEN SHOW UP TO HER SON ADAM'S FUNERAL.
SOMETIME LATER.
WE KNOW THAT SHE HAS BEEN IN CONTACT WITH YOU.
WISH I COULD HELP, WILL, BUT GIVEN THE CREELS' CONNECTIONS, I HAVE NO DOUBT YOU'LL BE HEARING FROM HER YOURSELF SOON ENOUGH.
YOU'RE PROBABLY RIGHT. YOU DON'T REALLY NEED HELP GETTING RELEASED EARLY...BUT WHAT IF I COULD OFFER YOU AN EXCHANGE?
OF?
SELINA KYLE ALSO DISAPPEARED THAT NIGHT.
NOT SURE HOW LONG SHE IS PLANNING ON STICKING AROUND, BUT I DO KNOW SHE IS STILL IN THE CITY...

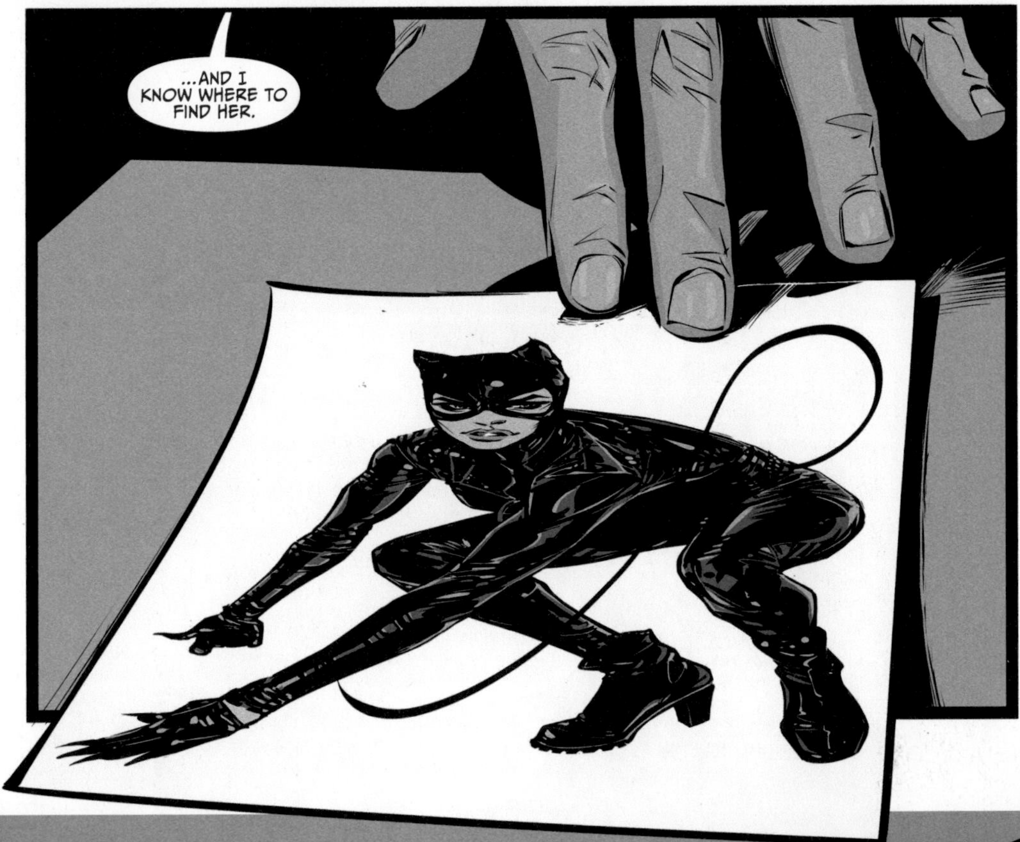
...AND I KNOW WHERE TO FIND HER.

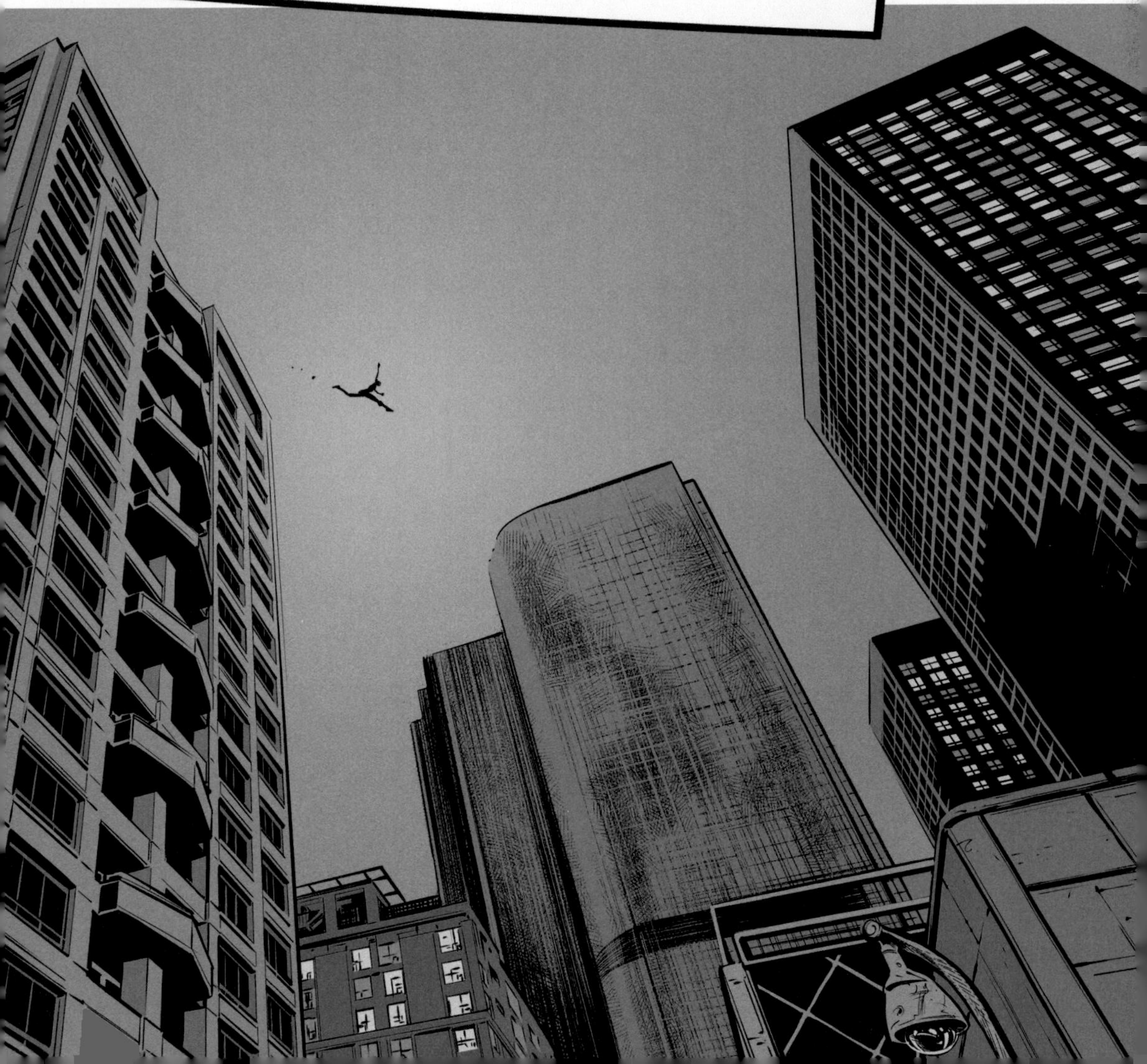

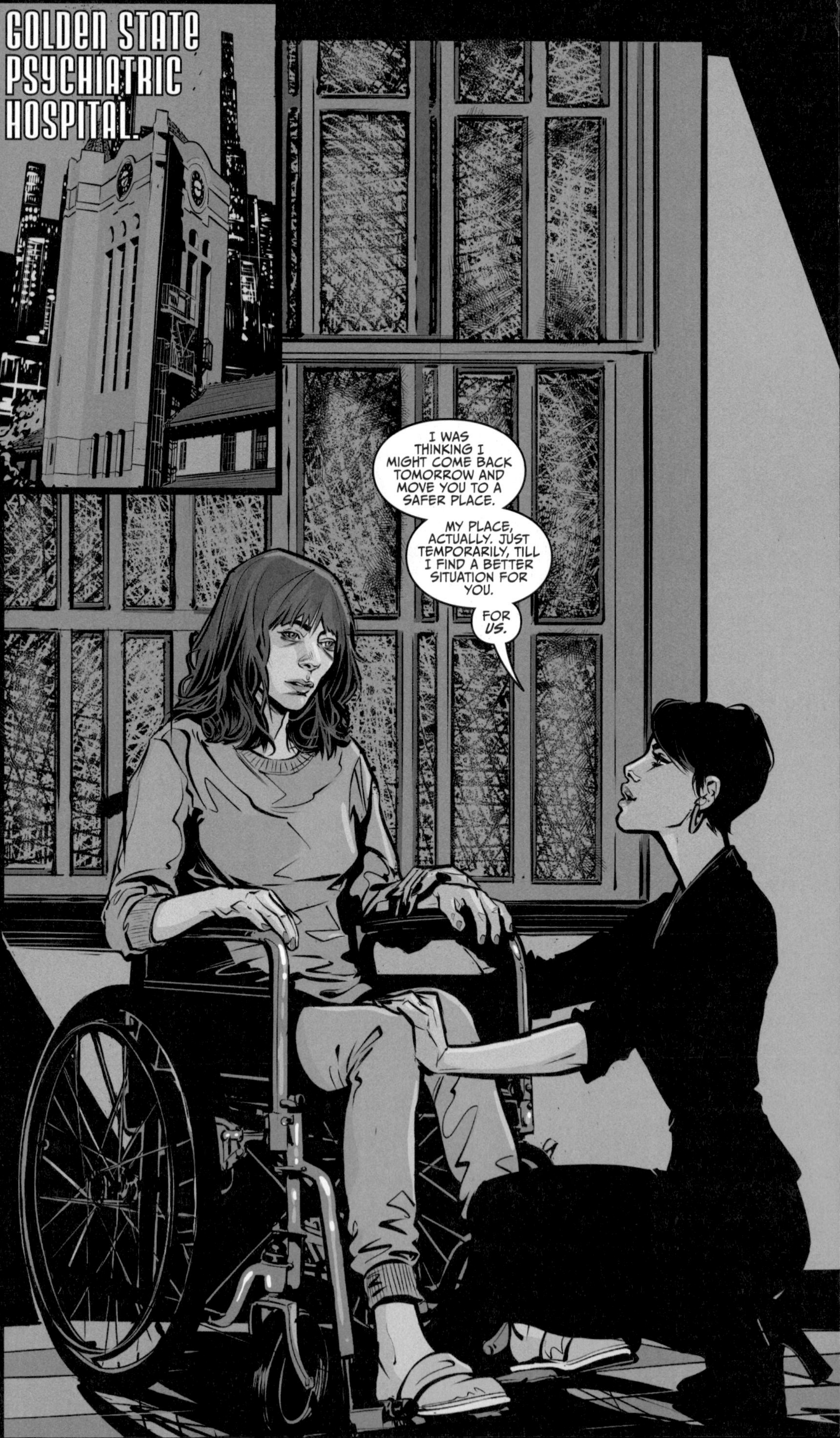

GOLDEN STATE PSYCHIATRIC HOSPITAL.
I WAS THINKING I MIGHT COME BACK TOMORROW AND MOVE YOU TO A SAFER PLACE.
MY PLACE, ACTUALLY. JUST TEMPORARILY, TILL I FIND A BETTER SITUATION FOR YOU.
FOR *US*.

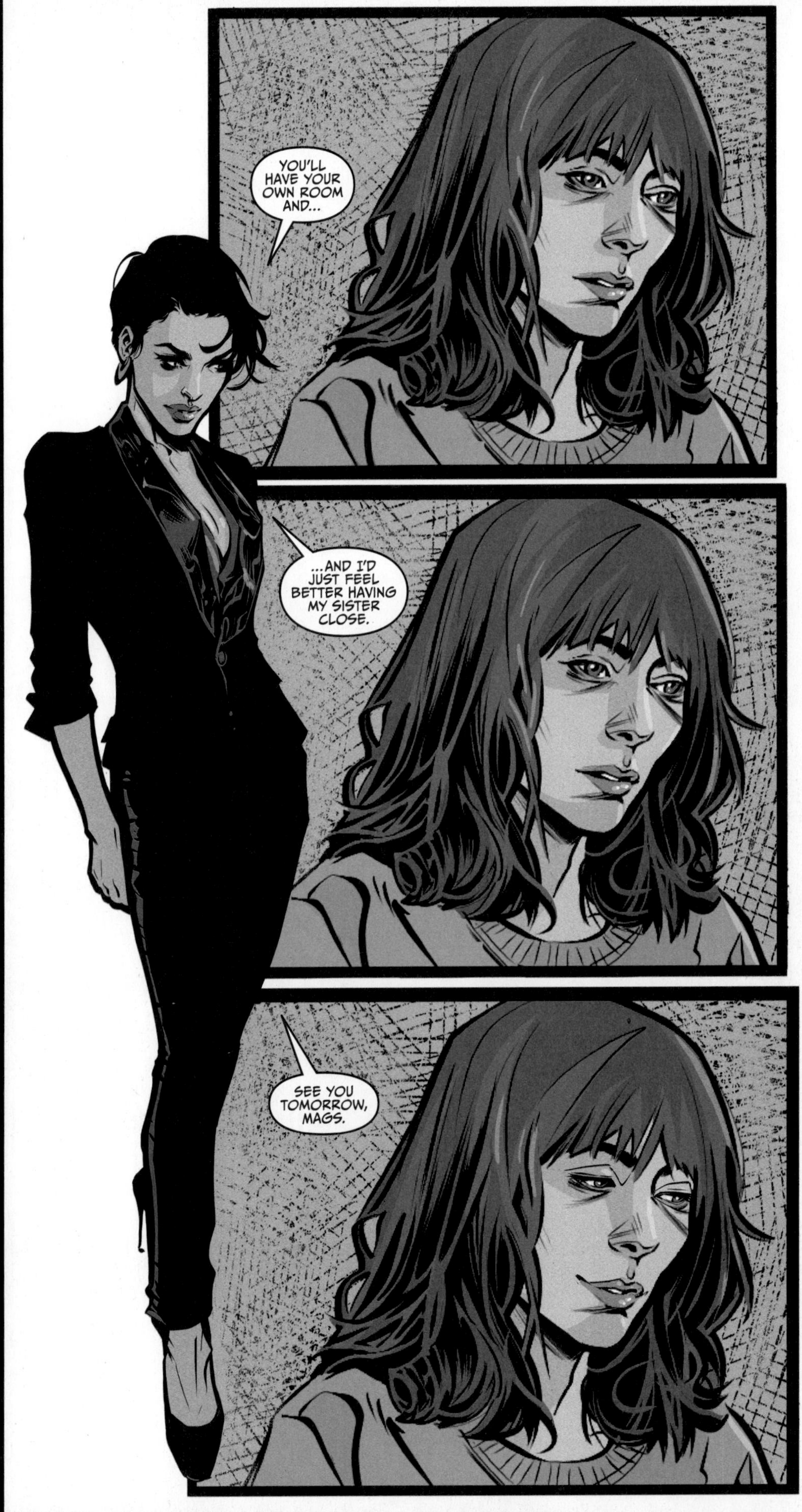

YOU'LL HAVE YOUR OWN ROOM AND...
...AND I'D JUST FEEL BETTER HAVING MY SISTER CLOSE.
SEE YOU TOMORROW, MAGS.

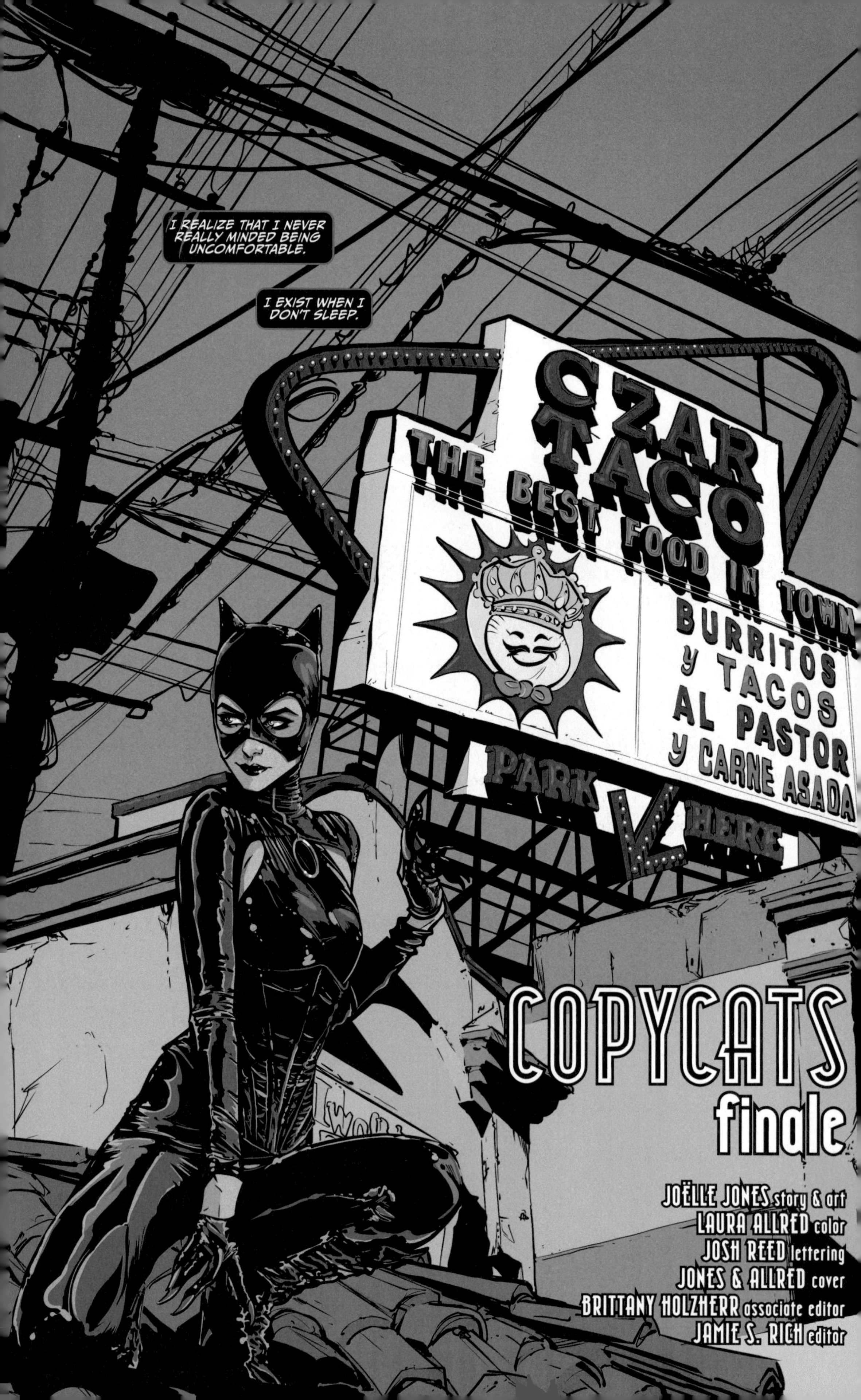
I REALIZE THAT I NEVER REALLY MINDED BEING UNCOMFORTABLE.
I EXIST WHEN I DON'T SLEEP.
CZAR TACO
THE BEST FOOD IN TOWN
BURRITOS y TACOS AL PASTOR y CARNE ASADA
PARK HERE
COPYCATS
finale
JOËLLE JONES story & art
LAURA ALLRED color
JOSH REED lettering
JONES & ALLRED cover
BRITTANY HOLZHERR associate editor
JAMIE S. RICH editor

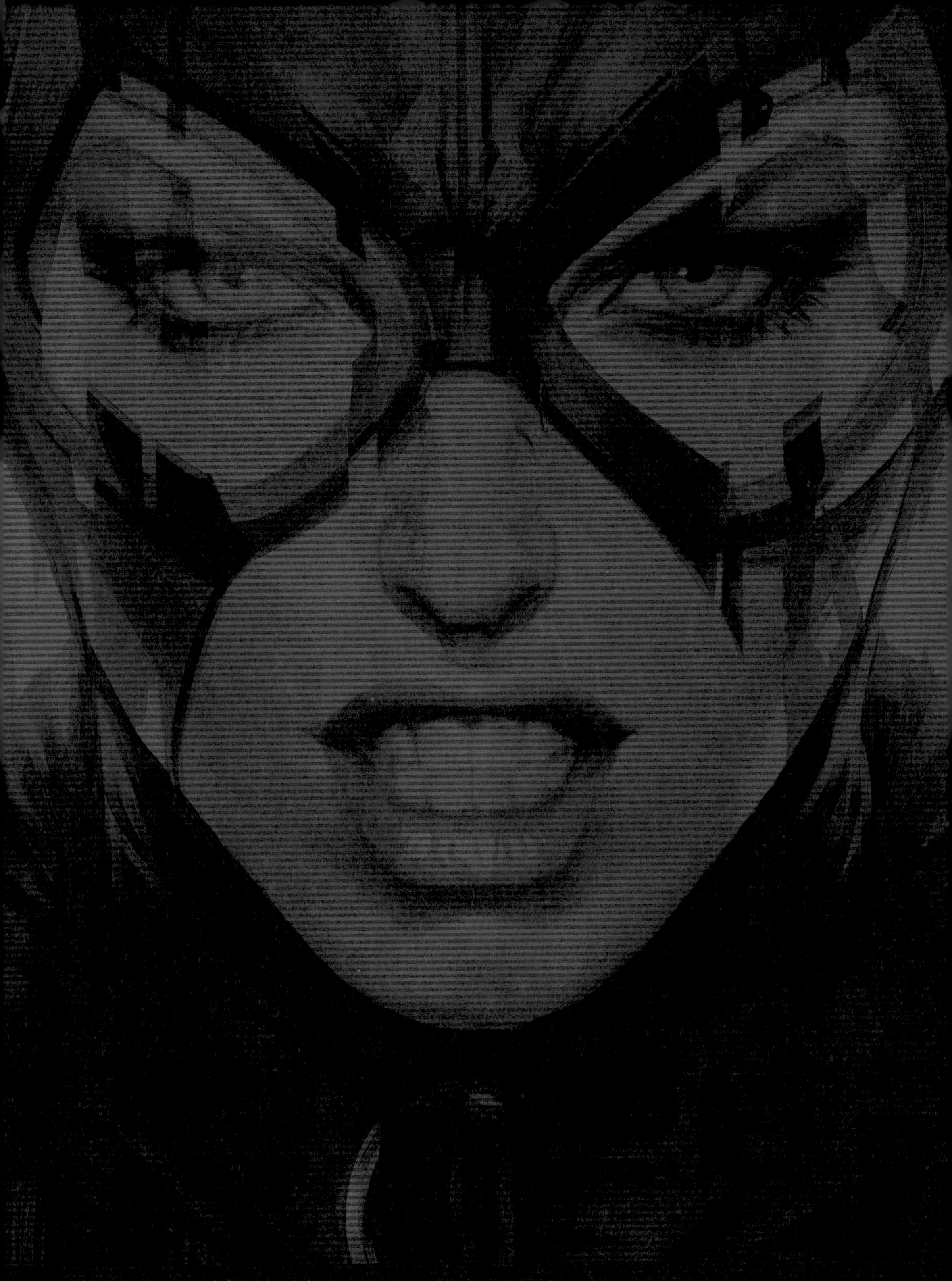

VARIANT COVER GALLERY

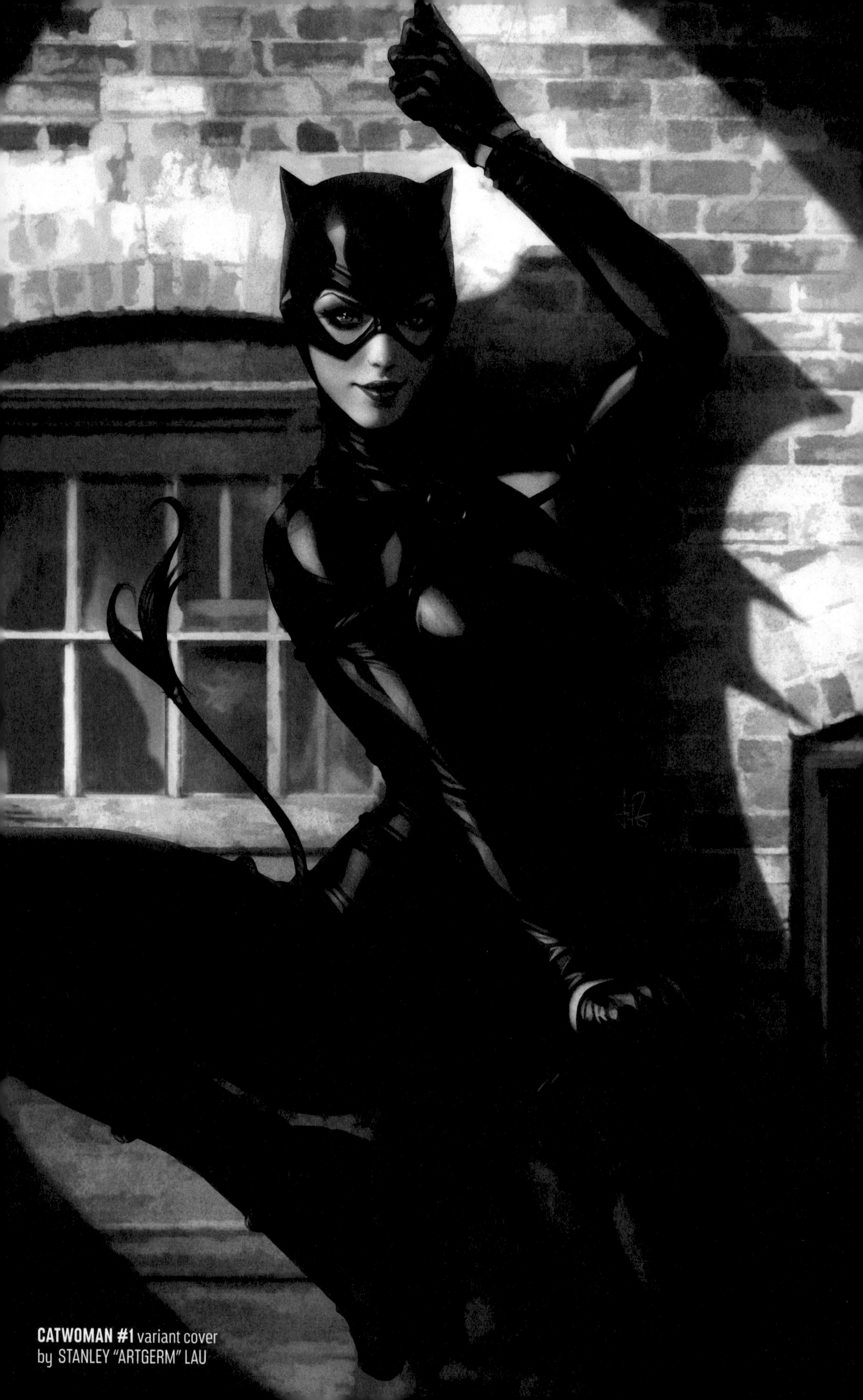

CATWOMAN #1 variant cover
by STANLEY "ARTGERM" LAU

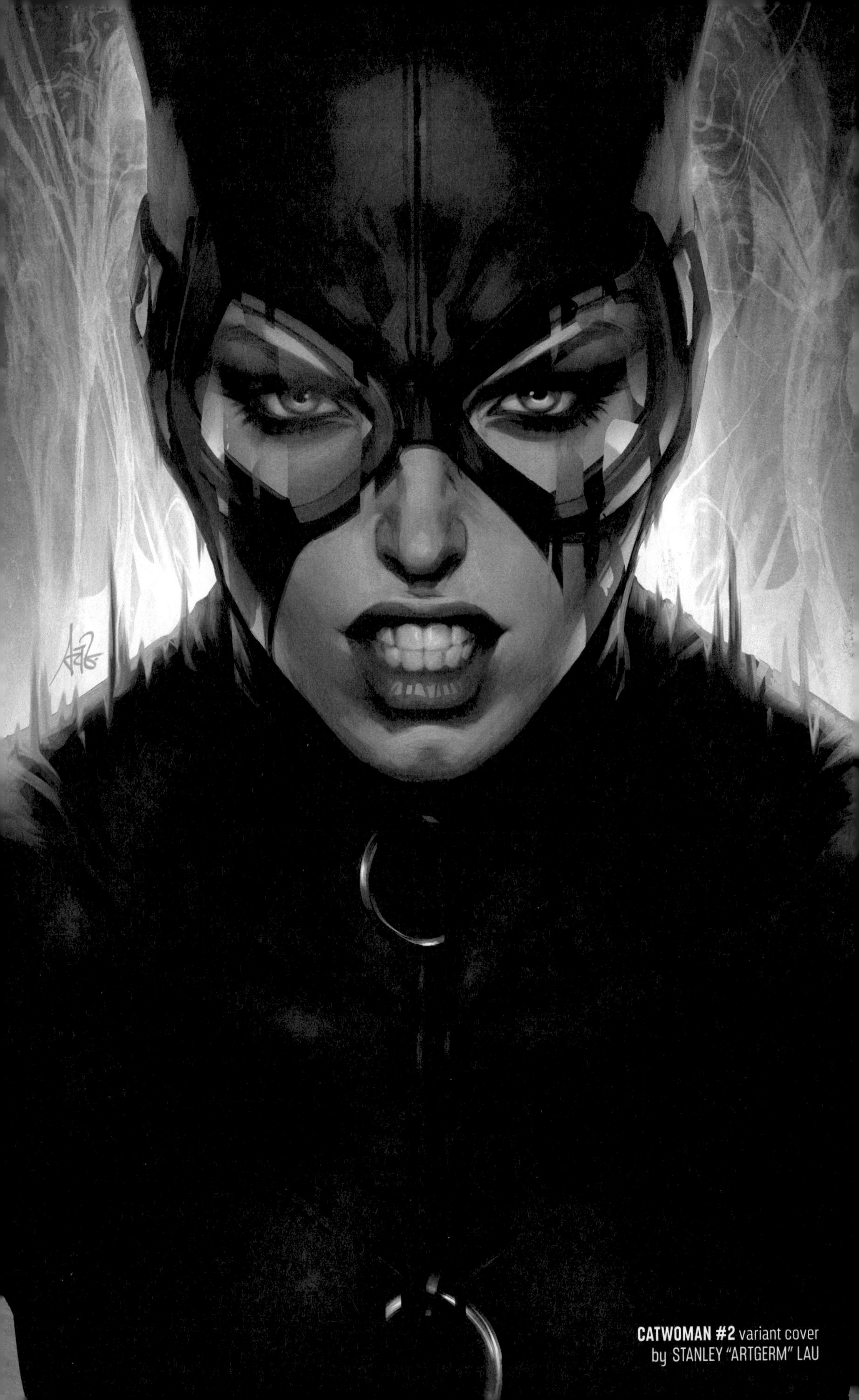

CATWOMAN #2 variant cover
by STANLEY "ARTGERM" LAU

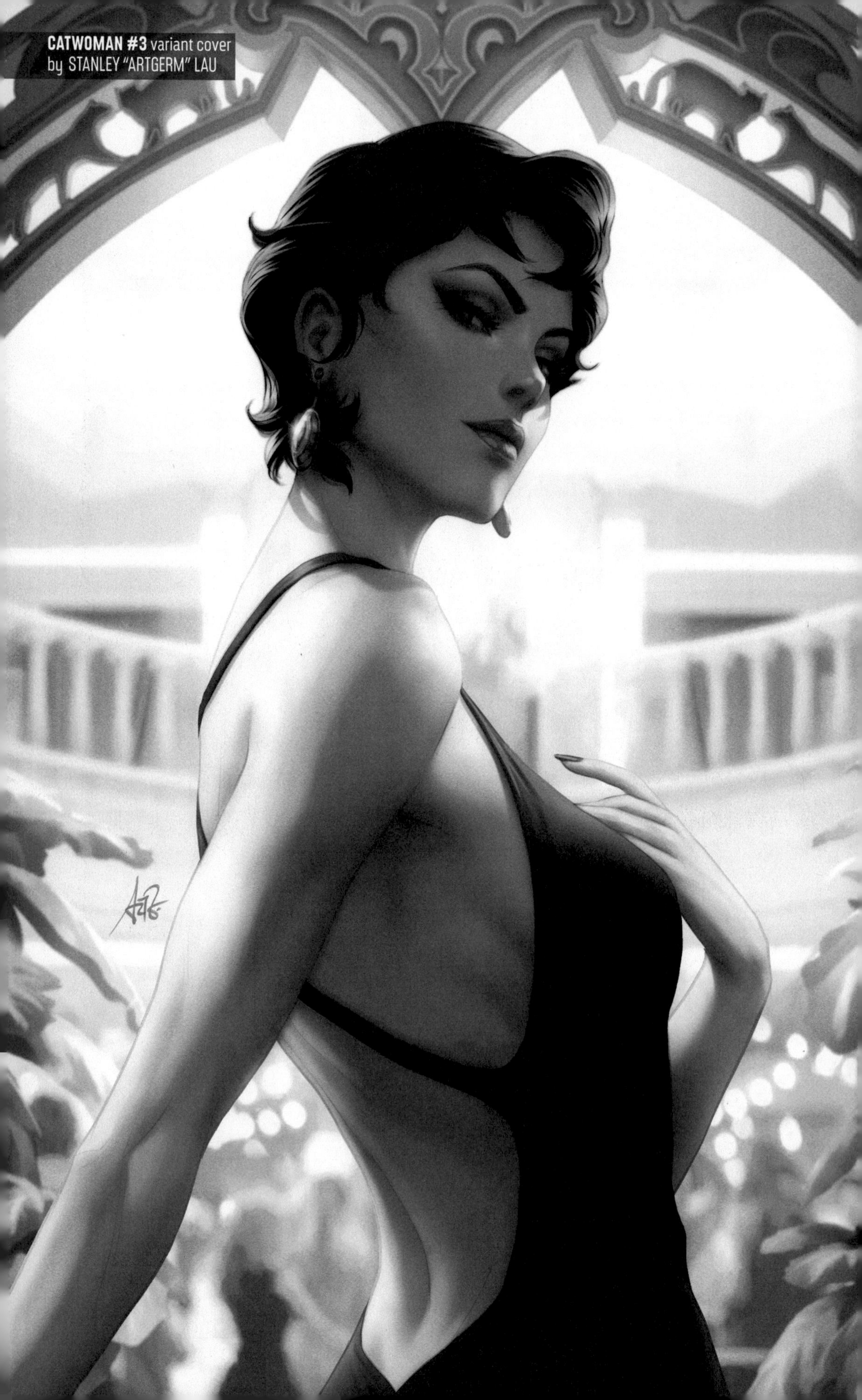

CATWOMAN #3 variant cover
by STANLEY "ARTGERM" LAU

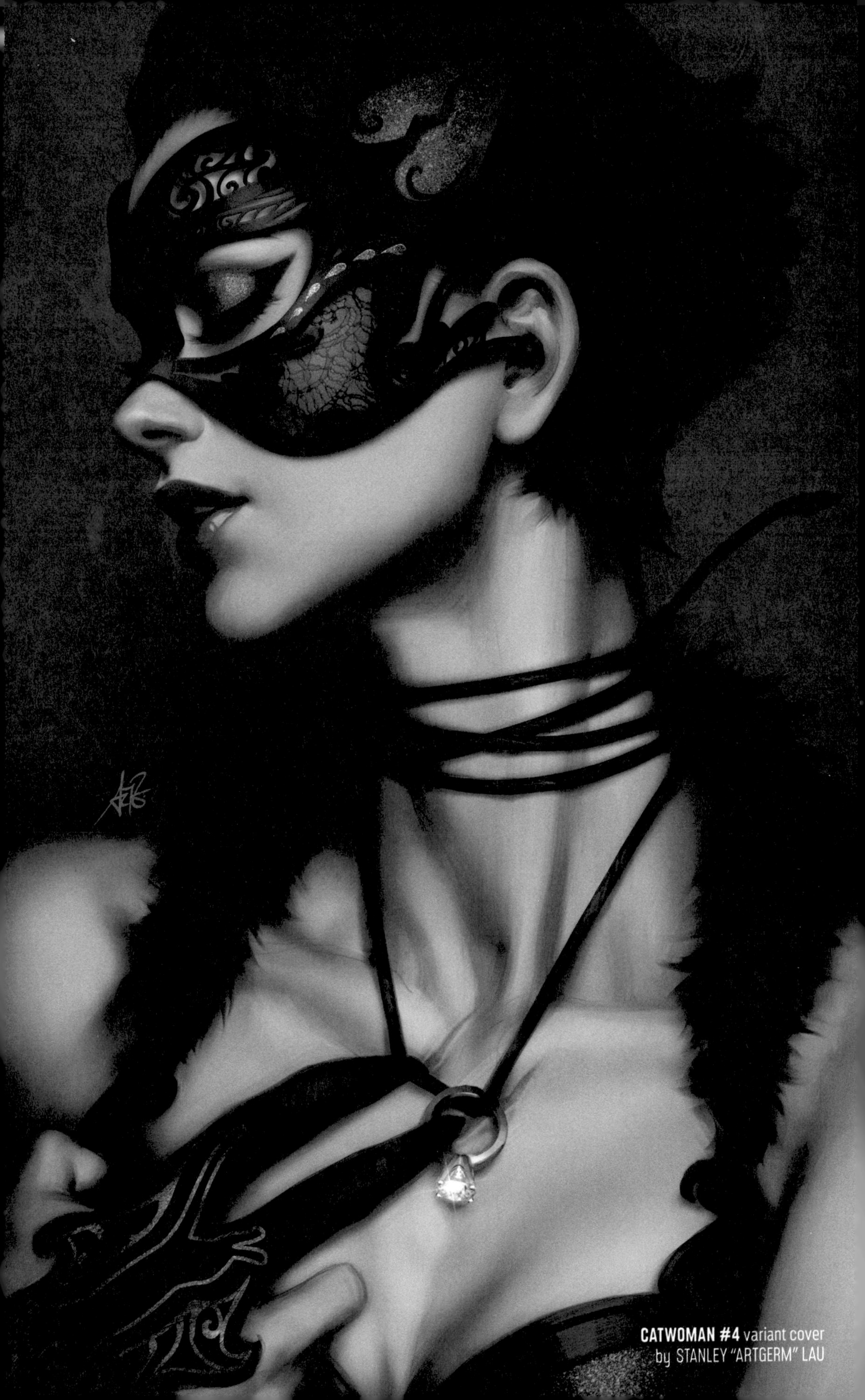

CATWOMAN #4 variant cover
by STANLEY "ARTGERM" LAU

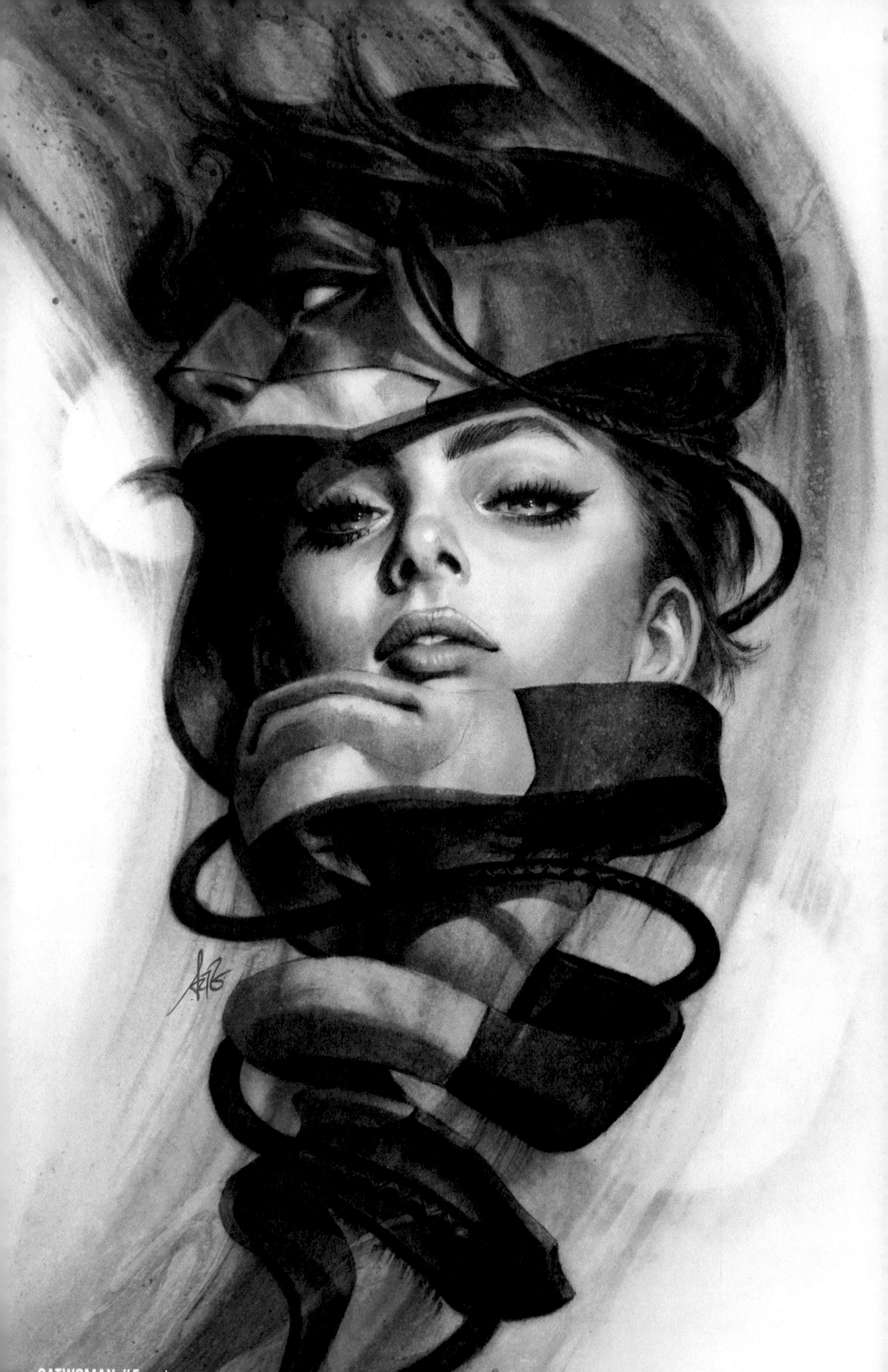

CATWOMAN #5 variant cover
by STANLEY "ARTGERM" LAU

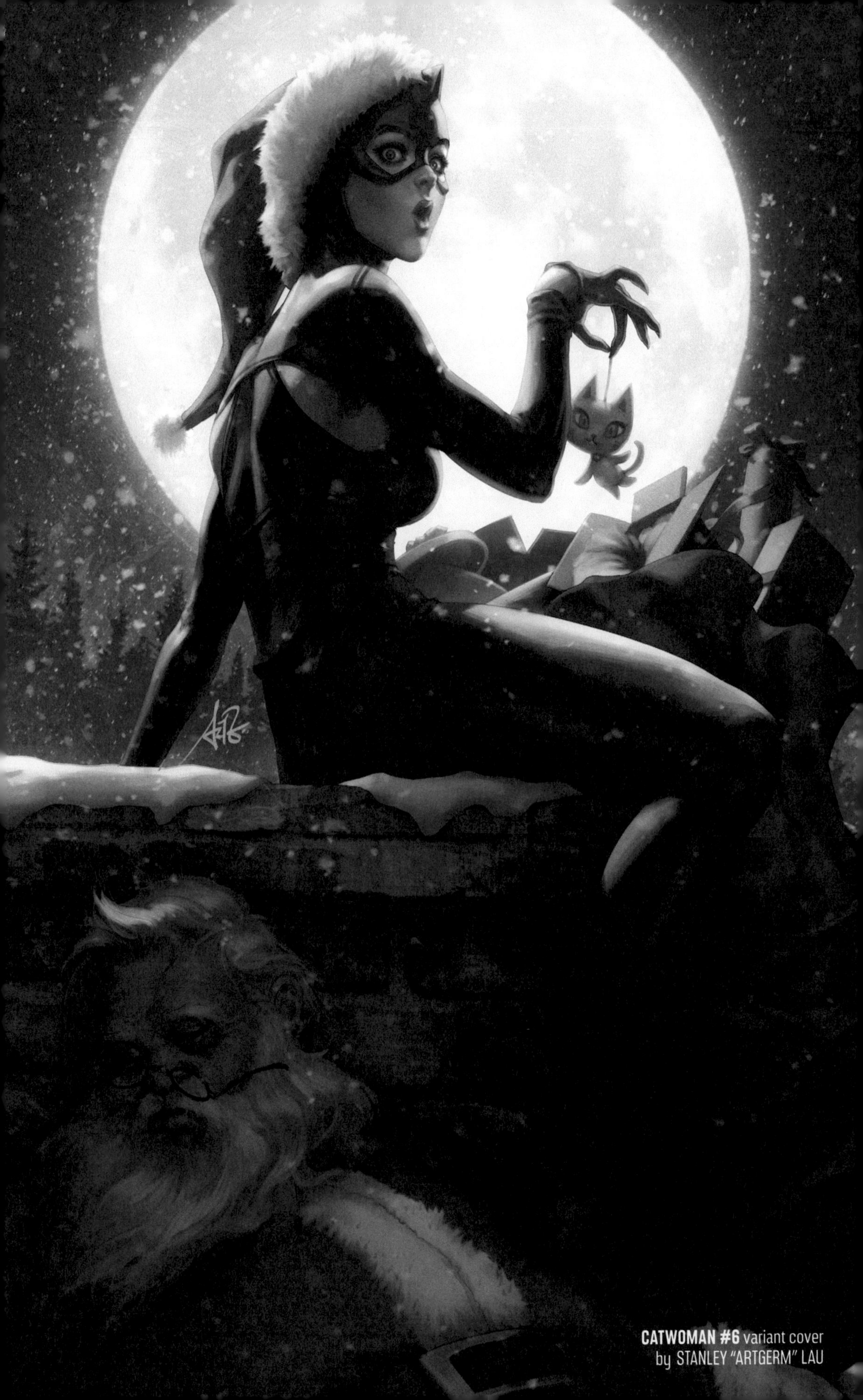

CATWOMAN #6 variant cover
by STANLEY "ARTGERM" LAU

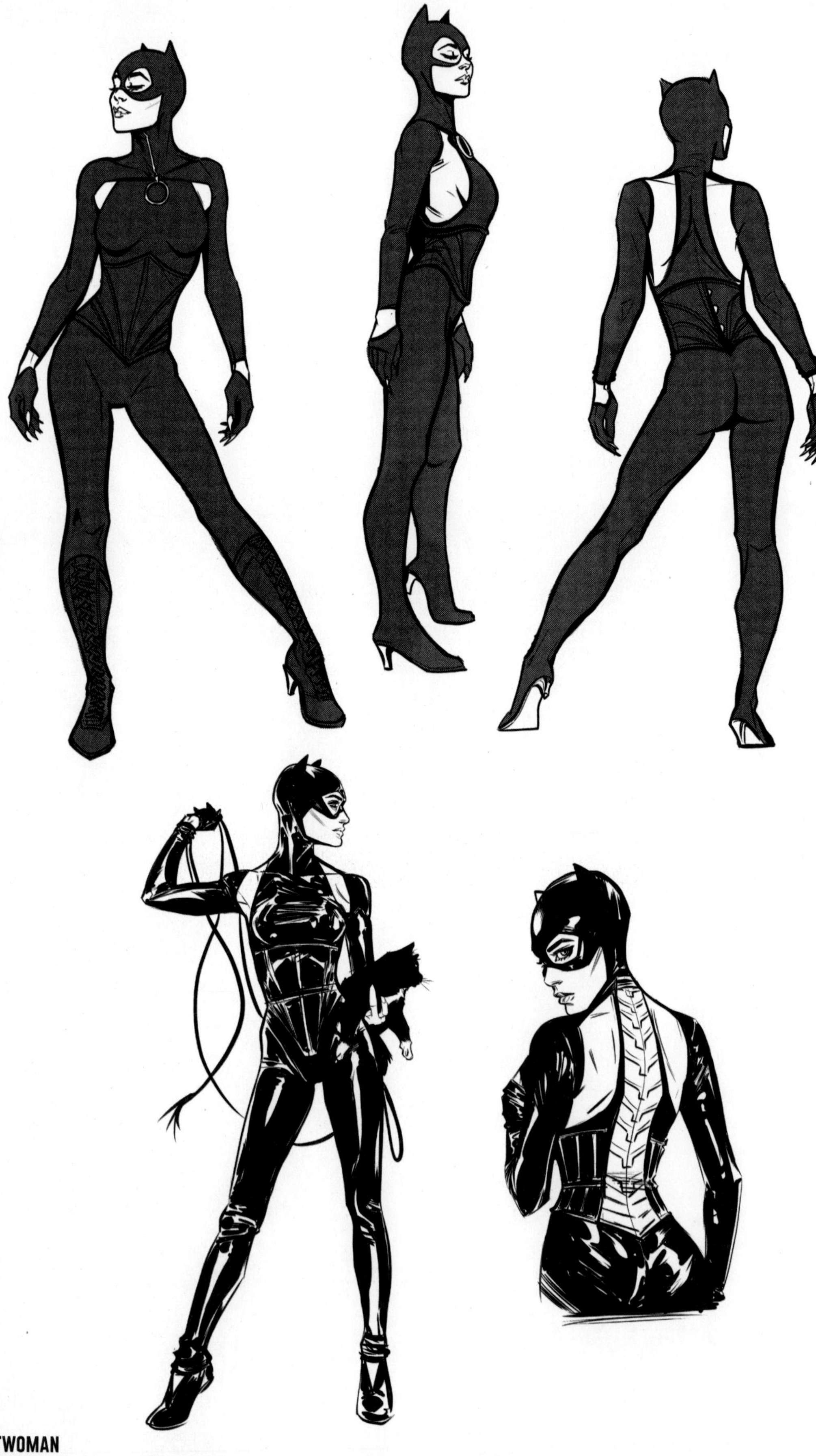

CATWOMAN
Character sketches by **JOËLLE JONES**

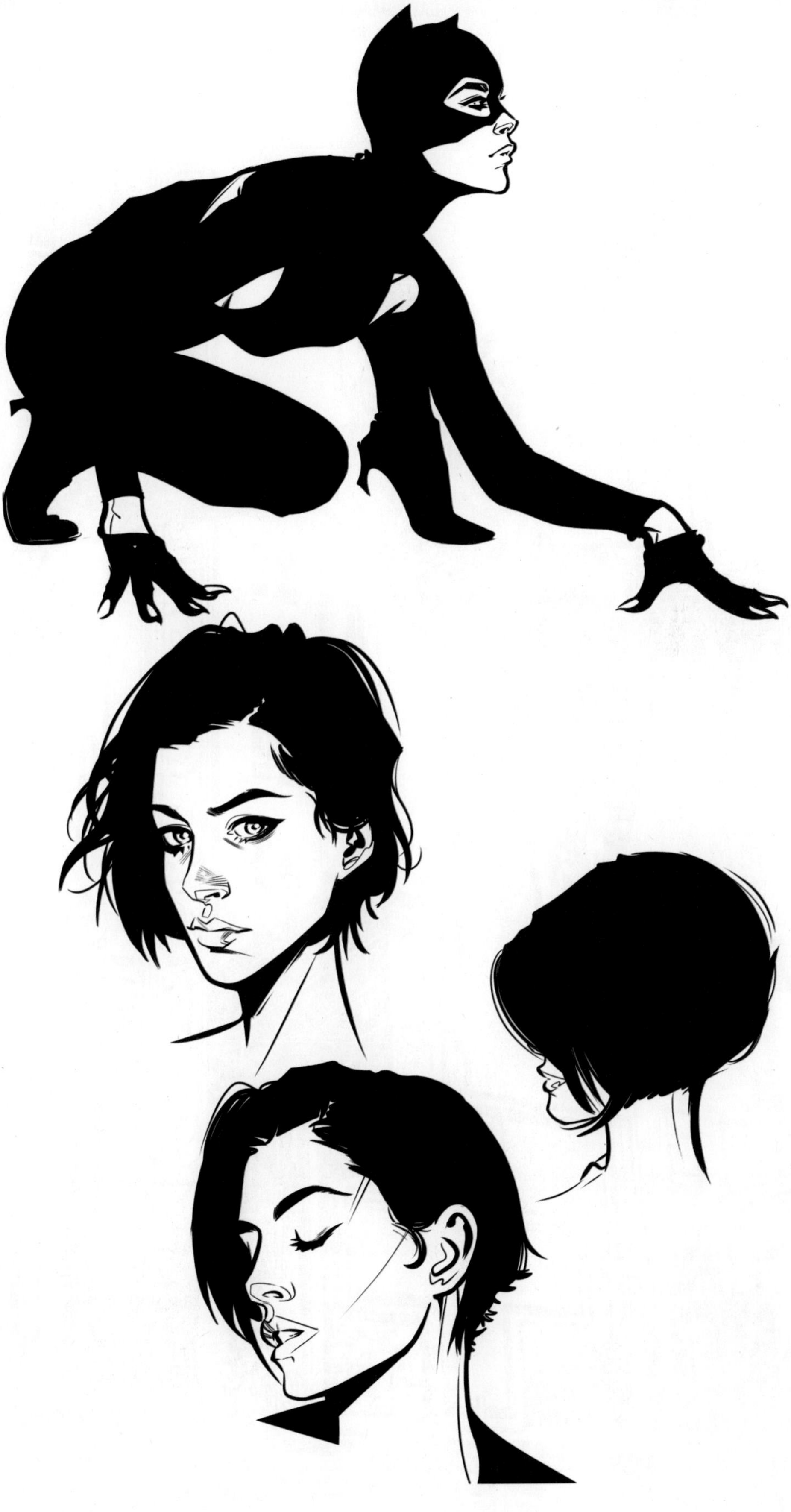

CATWOMAN #1
by **JOËLLE JONES**

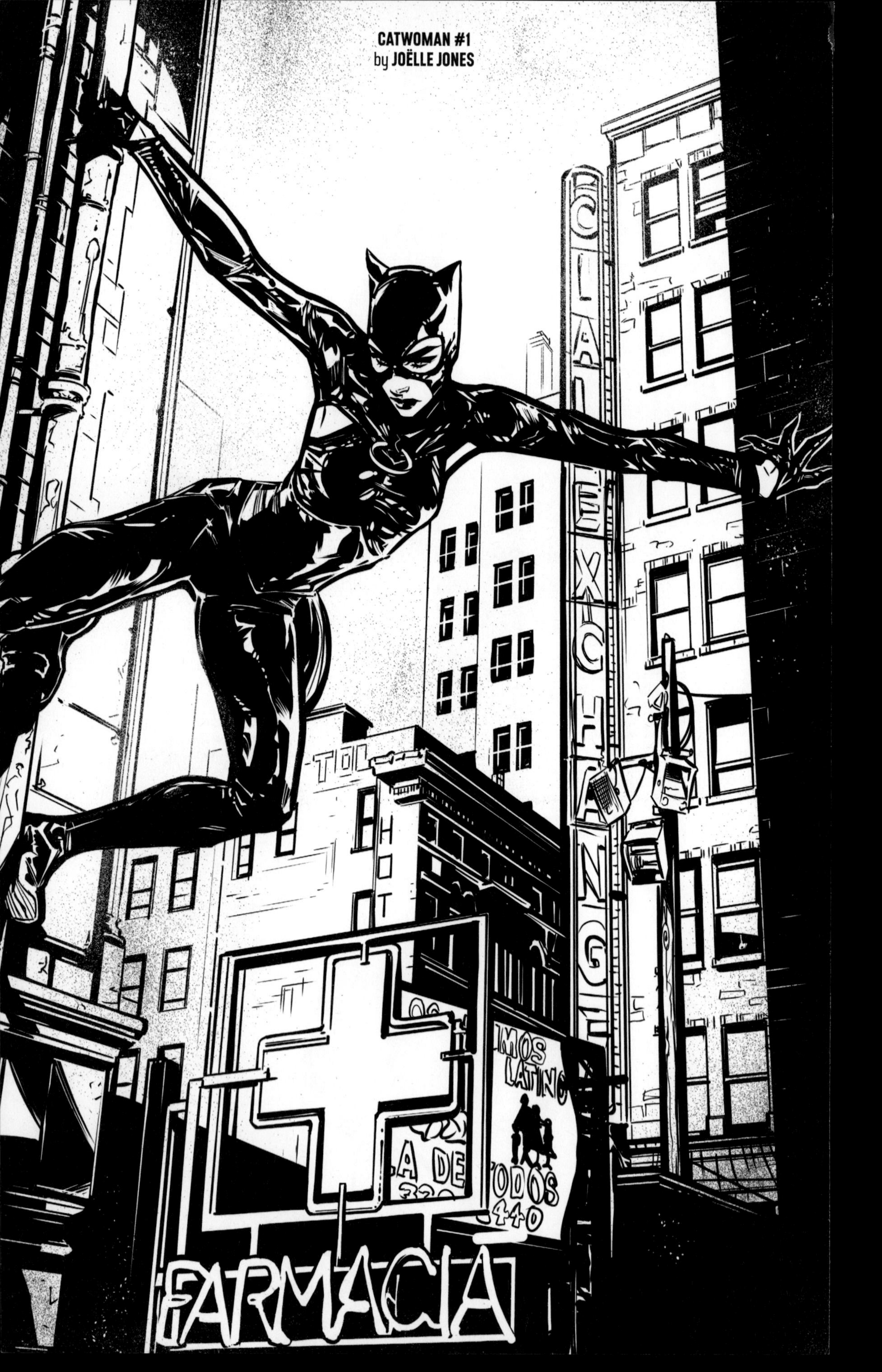
FARMACIA

CATWOMAN
Character sketches by **JOËLLE JONES**

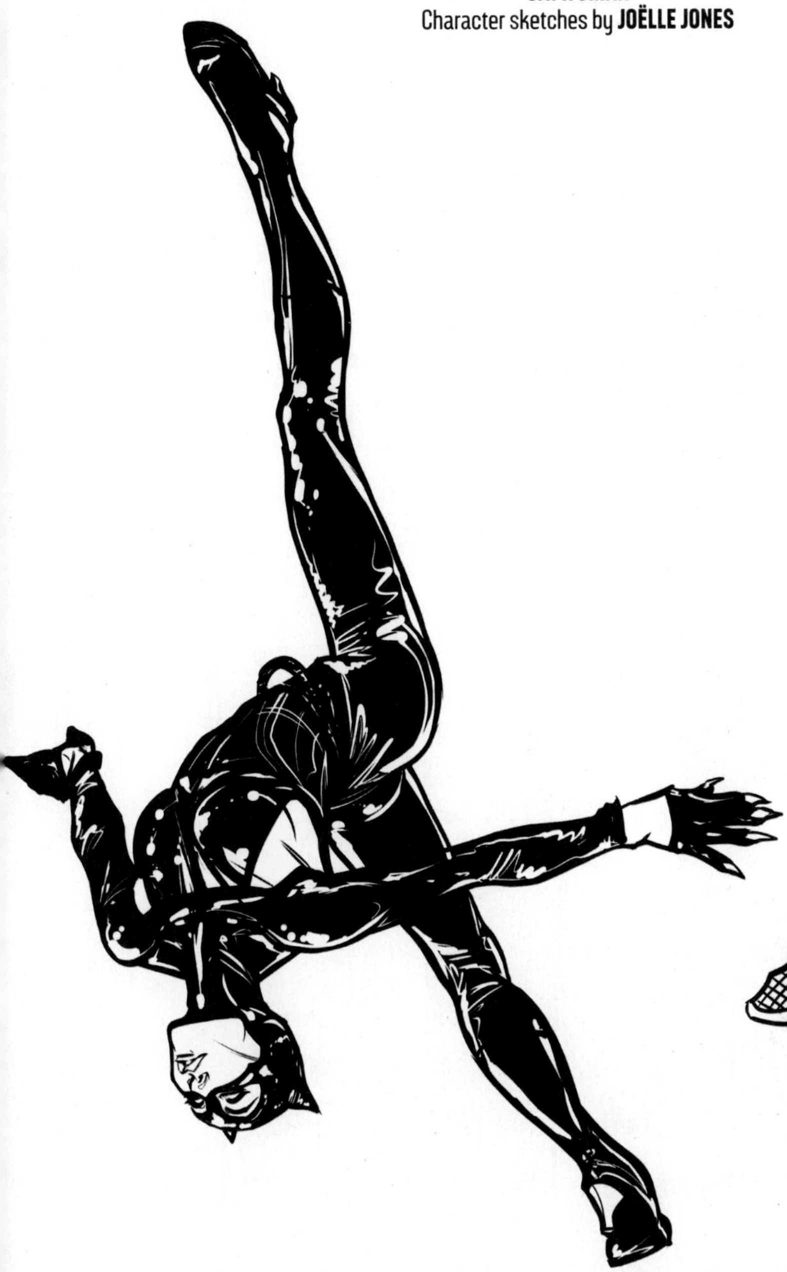

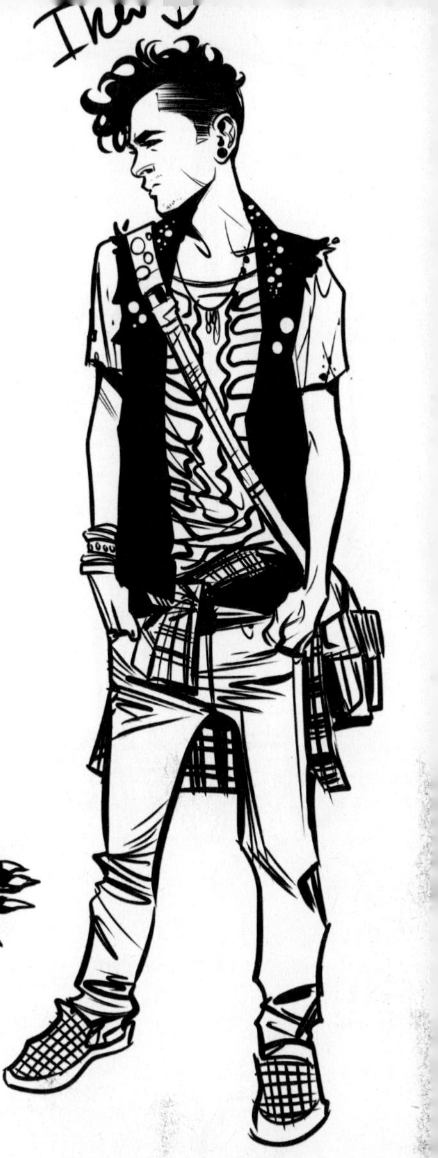

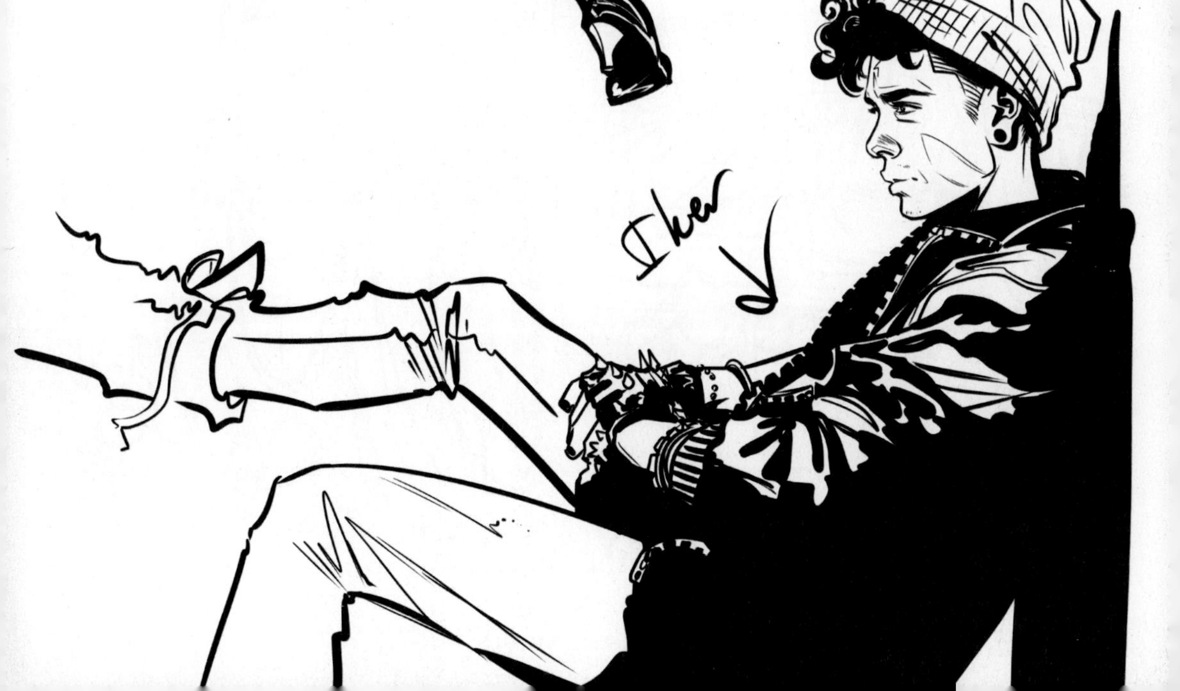
Iker

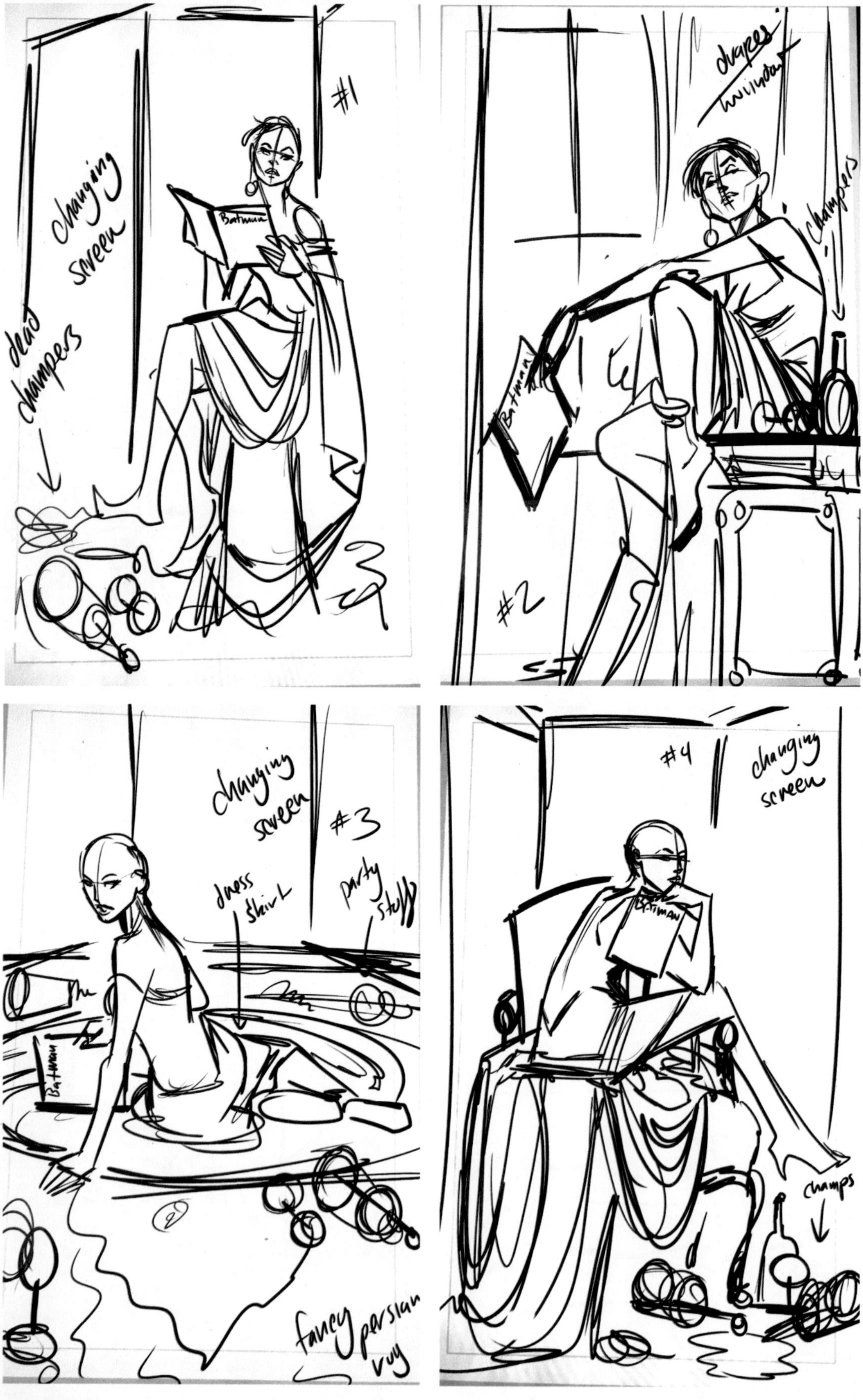
#1
changing screen
Batman
dead champers
drapes
window
champers
Batman
#2
changing screen
#3
dress skirt
party stuff
Batman
fancy persian rug
#4
changing screen
Batman
champs

CATWOMAN #1
Cover sketches by **JOËLLE JONES**

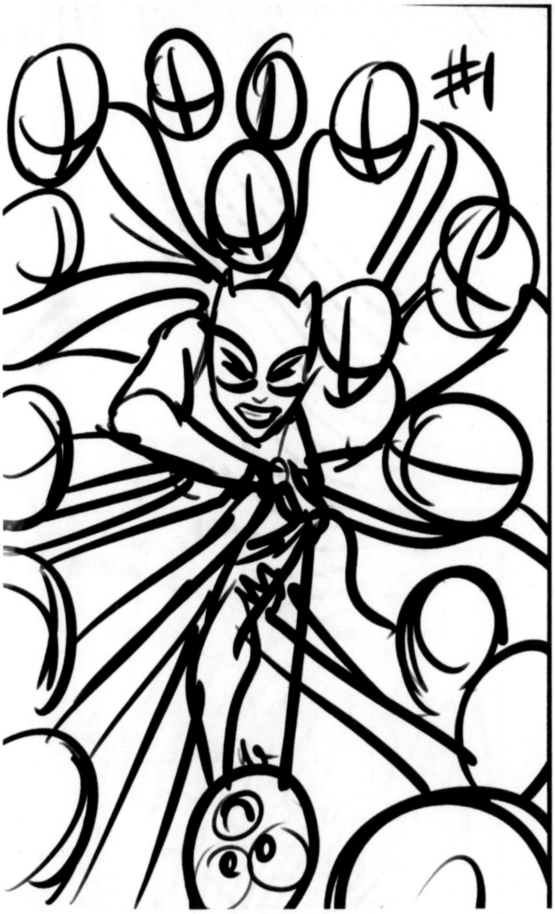
#1

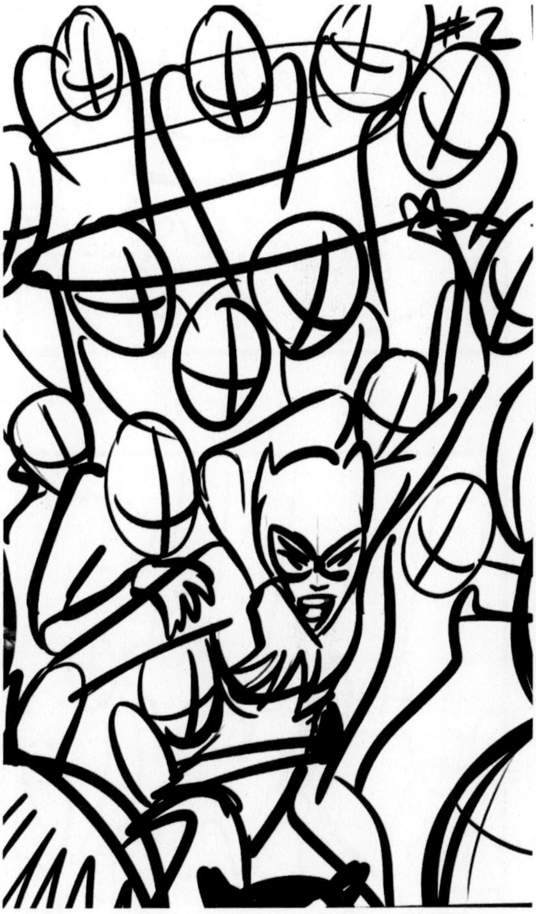
#2

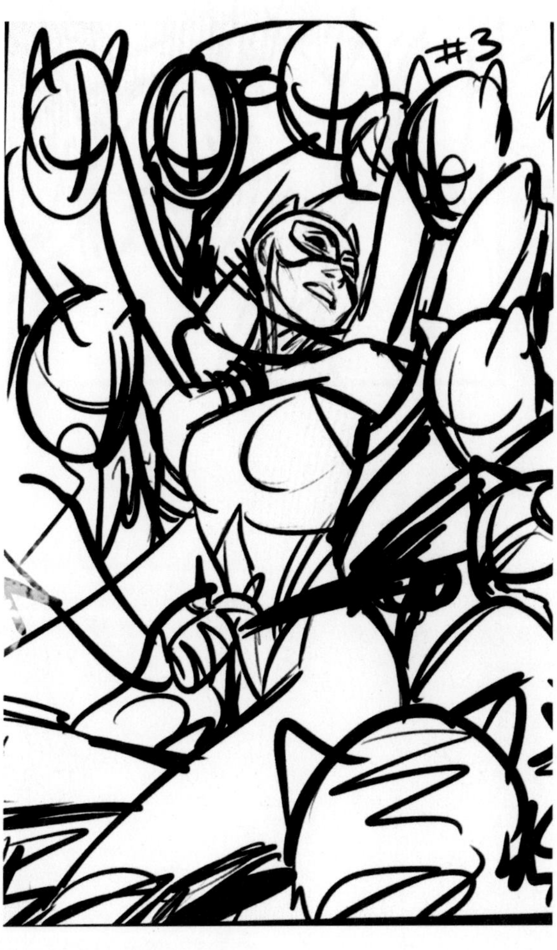
#3

CATWOMAN #2
Cover sketches by **JOËLLE JONES**

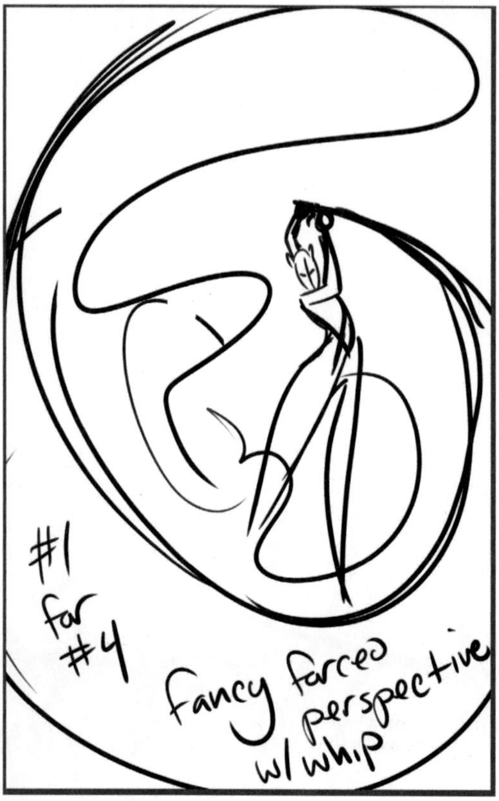
#1
for
#4
fancy forced perspective w/ whip

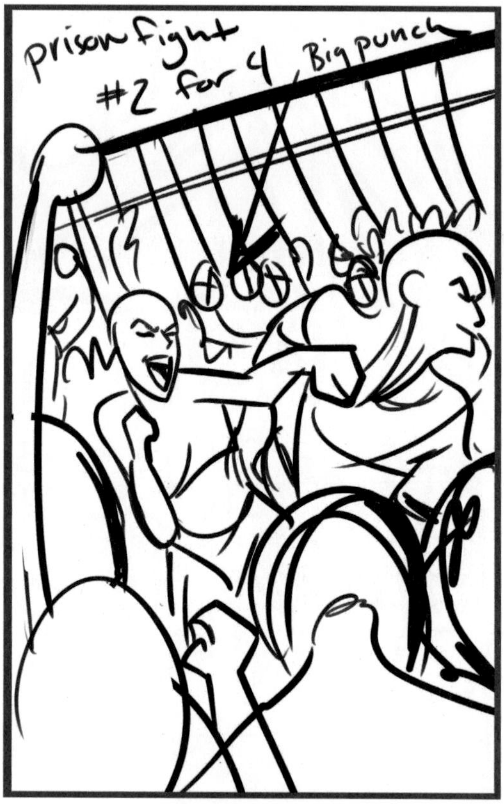
prison fight
#2 for 4
Big punch

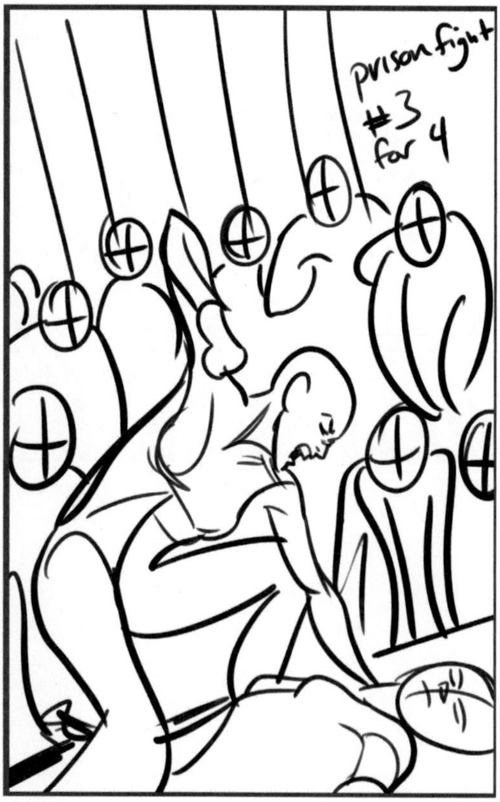
prison fight
#3
for 4

CATWOMAN #4
Cover sketches by **JOËLLE JONES**

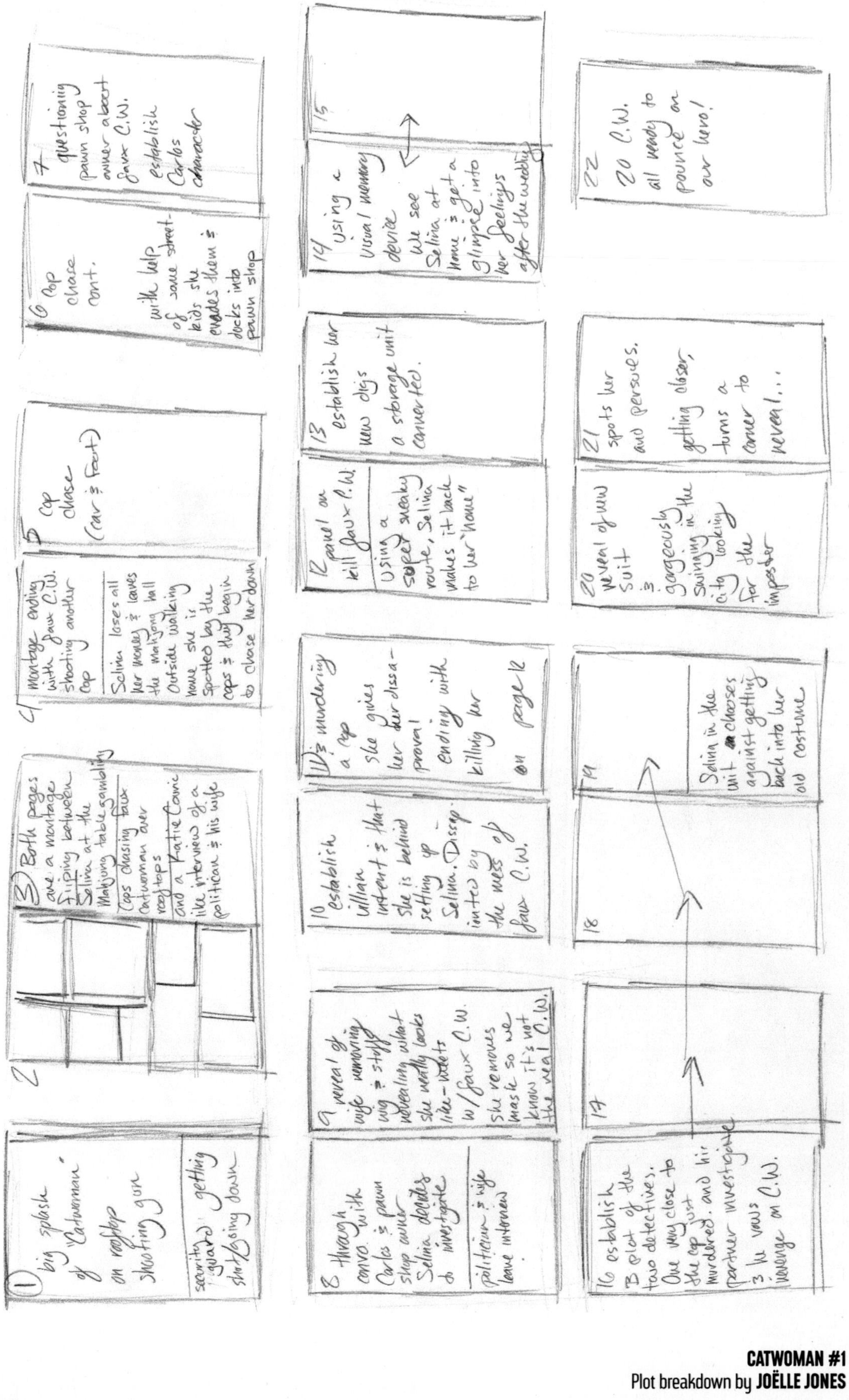
1 big splash of "Catwoman" on rooftop shooting gun
security guards getting shot/going down
2
3 Both pages are a montage flipping between Selina at the Mahjong table gambling
Cops chasing faux Catwoman over rooftops
and a Katie Couric like interview of a politician & his wife
4 montage ending with faux C.W. shooting another cop
Selina loses all her money & leaves the Mahjong hall Outside walking home she is spotted by the cops & they begin to chase her down
5 cop chase (car & foot)
6 cop chase cont. with help of some street kids she evades them & ducks into pawn shop
7 questioning pawn shop owner about faux C.W. establish Carlos character
8 through convo with Carlos & pawn shop owner Selina decides to investigate
politician & wife leave interview
9 reveal of wife removing wig & stuff revealing what she really looks like—watches w/ faux C.W. She removes mask so we know it's not the real C.W.
10 establish villian intent & that she is behind setting up Selina. Dissapointed by the mess of faux C.W.
11 & murdering a cop she gives her her dissaproval! ending with killing her on page 12
12 panel on kill faux C.W.
Using a secret sneaky route, Selina makes it back to her "home"
13 establish her new digs a storage unit converted.
14 using a visual memory device we see Selina at home & get a glimpse into her feelings after the wedding
15
16 establish B plot of the two detectives. One very close to the cop just murdered. and his partner investigate & he vows revenge on C.W.
17
18
19
Selina in the unit chooses against getting back into her old costume
20 reveal of new suit & gorgeously swinging in the city looking for the imposter
21 spots her and pursues. getting closer, turns a corner to reveal...
22 20 C.W. all ready to pounce on our hero!

CATWOMAN #1
Plot breakdown by **JOËLLE JONES**

"An incredible story."
—NERDIST

"A clean, simple gateway into the Batman franchise."
—IGN

"King sets a new stage and tone for Batman and Gotham."
—POPMATTERS

BATMAN
VOL. 1: I AM GOTHAM
TOM KING
DAVID FINCH

VOL.1 I AM GOTHAM
TOM KING • DAVID FINCH

BATMAN: VOL. 2
I AM SUICIDE

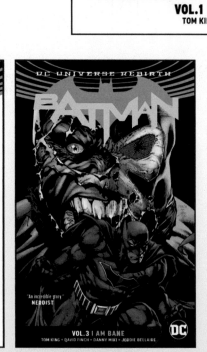

BATMAN: VOL. 3:
I AM BANE

READ THEM ALL!

BATMAN VOL. 4: THE WAR OF JOKES AND RIDDLES

BATMAN VOL. 5: RULES OF ENGAGEMENT

BATMAN VOL. 6: BRIDE OR BURGLAR?

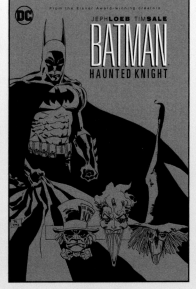

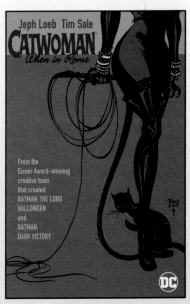

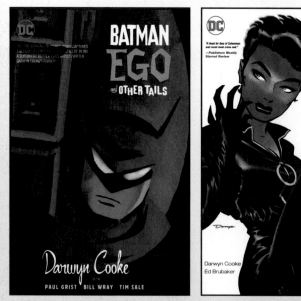